The Texture of Identity

The Fiction of MG Vassanji, Neil Bissoondath and Rohinton Mistry

Martin Genetsch

TSAR

Cover photos courtesy of www.free-pictures-photos.com

Library and Archives Canada Cataloguing in Publication

Genetsch, Martin

The texture of identity : the fiction of MG Vassanji, Neil Bissoondath, and Rohinton Mistry / Martin Genetsch.

Includes bibliographical references and index.
ISBN 978-1-894770-41-5

1. Vassanji, M.G.—Criticism and interpretation. 2. Bissoondath, Neil, 1955– —Criticism and interpretation. 3. Mistry, Rohinton, 1952– —Criticism and interpretation. 4. Identity (Philosophical concept) in literature. 5. Multiculturalism in literature. I. Title.

PS8089.5.S68G45 2007 C813'.5409353 C2007-904918-4

Printed in Canada by Coach House Printing

TSAR Publications
P. O. Box 6996, Station A
Toronto, Ontario M5W 1X7
Canada

www.tsarbooks.com

Contents

Introduction

Globalization and Multiculturalism

We are currently living in an age of globalization, the effects of which increasingly influence considerable parts of our life worlds. Globalization no longer simply describes international cashflows; the semantics of the term have broadened to include other dimensions, too. No longer does globalization refer to the sphere of economics but draws attention to the colonial/neocolonial underpinnings of the wealth of the Western world and the deprivation of the so-called developing countries, too. From its origins as a merely descriptive term, globalization has become a critical vocabulary demanding social justice and global responsibility from the countries of the Western world whose wealth depended and still depends on the exploitation of the resources of the southern hemisphere.

While the global village certainly disguises a global pillage, as Anthony Giddens has so succinctly put it,[1] globalization also forces us to rethink issues of culture and community. Interesting for our purposes here is not so much the McDonaldization of the world or the ubiquity of CNN and MTV but the increasingly multicultural character of Western societies.[2] In the wake of colonialism and neocolonialism large numbers of people all over the world have turned their backs on their home countries and migrated to flee either persecution or poverty.[3] The large-scale wanderings of people from Africa, the Caribbean and the Asian subcontinent into the Anglo-American diaspora have altered the composition of Western societies profoundly. The point here is that the changes which these immigrants to Britain, Canada or the United States have initiated have not only been sociological but also cultural. Inasmuch as both the Western host culture and the respective culture of the migrant are challenged and therefore raised to a new level of consciousness and awareness, the cultural implications of globalization demand a double perspective.

Multiculturalism has been proposed as the new paradigm said to recognize the effects of globalization by accounting for the cultural differences between migrant and host society. A multicultural perspective acknowledges that migration is a move with consequences for the host societies but also—often more drastically—for the individual migrant. Arguably the most pressing problem for those forsaking their homes for a new country is the construction of a new identity. In more accessible terms, the central concern for many who feel themselves uprooted is how to make life in the diaspora 'liveable.' My phrasing here is deliberately vague. 'Liveable' can refer to an attempt to reproduce the old country in the new, however, in some cases it might also imply that the country of origin is happily discarded in favour of the country of adoption. In general, the implications of what 'liveable' entails will be negotiated along a spectrum of possibilities ranging from assimilation in a new culture to the retention of the old, or, put differently, along a continuum from sameness to difference.

This study will probe the poles of the range of possible identity constructions in a functionalist analysis of contemporary English Canadian fiction. Although 'identity' will refer first of all to the protagonists of a corpus of texts, it will be eventually argued that the search for a personal/cultural identity enacted in immigrant fiction opens up perspectives for reconfiguring Canadian national/multicultural identity. While the aspect of 'construction' implies that a self-image does not rely on essentialist formulations but is in need of a difference against which it can be defined, 'functional' here means that the kinds of difference together with the purposes towards which difference is invoked will be analysed in particular. If it is understood that identities are constructed, i.e. in principle open to modification and change, advertising cultural difference need not be regarded as the overriding characteristic of immigrant fiction, as it is frequently assumed to be. To the extent that immigrant fiction is concerned with identity, the host culture does not necessarily constitute the difference necessary for the projection of the self-image in question. Multicultural fiction does not have to accept a cultural tradition or adopt it uncritically; it may well encompass stories in which protagonists feel burdened by a cultural tradition and modify or even discard it. MG Vassanji, Neil Bissoondath and Rohinton Mistry, the three writers with which my thesis will be concerned, are cases in point inasmuch as they reflect the complex implications and interrelations of the politics of difference and identity.

It is striking that immigrant writers such as MG Vassanji, Neil Bissoondath, Rohinton Mistry, and also Michael Ondaatje, Nino Ricci, and Joy Kogawa do not simply negotiate identities in a globalized world by exploring Canada and its multicultural society but also come to an understanding of themselves by directing their attention to their respective countries of origin and working through their past and histories.[4] It will be argued that while the work of Vassanji, Bissoondath, and Mistry is typical of immigrant fiction in that it is concerned with both Canada and the country of origin respectively, an adequate and comprehensive analysis of their works becomes only possible once they are treated as Canadian writers.[5] So far most critics of their novels and stories have refrained from doing precisely this, and it such a view that I would like to contest. Although I will not rely on representative sources of deconstructive criticism, my aim in this study is deconstructive as well as revisionist insofar as it implies a critique of the body of texts which are said to constitute Canadian literature. A brief survey over the scholarly debate about the canon of Canadian literature and the problems of its formation will prove useful in positioning immigrant fiction of the kind that Vassanji, Bissoondath, and Mistry produce and provide the critical vocabulary with which their narratives are approached in the analyses to follow.

The Question of the Canon

The point of departure for recent discussions about the canon of Canadian literature has been the double focus of much of the contemporary literature produced in Canada. Critics have made the same observation outlined in the previous section, namely that many writers in Canada write about their respective homes, i.e. their respective countries of origin outside of Canada. The confusion about how to conceptualize literature 'produced in' as opposed to 'set in' Canada has prompted a lot of scholarly work about the character of Canadian literature and identity. The question most often raised is: Are writers who live in Canada, who are naturalized Canadians even, but do not deal with Canada as a subject matter, to be qualified as Canadian writers?

A good starting point for the following brief survey of some of the core statements about the canon question is the poet and critic Frank Davey. In his 1993 monograph *Post-National Arguments* he demands that Canadian literature should be approached without taking recourse to the concept of the nation. The nation and nationalism are criticized by Davey as ideological formations that are too homogenising in their implications.[6] Strikingly enough, however, he refuses to engage in a discussion of writers who are concerned with the countries of their origins and narrate stories set outside the borders of the Canadian nation. While it would seem that it was precisely such writers whose works made Canada postnational and thus an entity less monolithic and more diversified, the fiction of writers such as Ricci, Vassanji and Mistry is relegated to a footnote. Frank Davey prefers to

> exclude from direct examination some recent novels of Canadian ethnic communities [. . .] such as Nino Ricci's *Lives of the Saints*, MG Vassanji's *The Gunny Sack*, and Rohinton Mistry's *Such a Long Journey*, novels which contain few if any significations of Canada or of Canadian polity.[7]

The corpus of texts that he has chosen for his study is restricted to "books that have been important to particular Canadian audiences and have offered some portrayal of Canada as a semiotic field."[8] While immigrant fiction set in a land other than Canada may have nothing to say about Canada directly, Davey acknowledges that such fiction may be important to a minority audience inside Canada which might profit from the construction of a collective community identity in works of fiction. The important point to emphasize in this context, however, is that in his opinion such fiction is not qualified to make interventions into Canada's 'semiotic field.' Taking into account that it is Frank Davey's aim in *Post-National Arguments* to make his readers aware of "the heterogeneity of the Canadian discursive field,"[9] neglecting authors writing about places other than Canada seems at best counterintuitive and at worst a methodological shortcoming.[10]

Challenging Davey's allegedly postnational argument, the critic Arun Mukherjee reminds us that the "exclusion [of immigrant literature about other countries] is highly ironic given the title of Davey's book which declares that Canadian literature needs to be studied beyond the confines of nationalism."[11] Mukherjee demands that underlying assumptions of what constitutes Canadian experience should be reconsidered. While in fact Davey's definition of Canadian literature still owes to a traditional understanding of Canadian identity connected to place, Mukherjee maintains that the contemporary Canadian experience is often an experience of a country other than Canada. For her a truly postnational approach transcends concepts not only of the nation but also of place. The absence of Canadian experience corresponds to a focus on memory work, which is an important aspect of the lives of minority communities and deserves, indeed demands, to be studied as Canadian experience, too.

Arguing along much the same lines, Ranu Samantrai suggests the inclusion of immigrant literature that is set elsewhere. Calling for a revision of the canon of Canadian literature, she maintains that it is necessary to critically rethink the basis of Canadian identity. Taking Rohinton Mistry as an example, Samantrai suggests that the inclusion of immigrant writers into the Canadian canon ceases to be problematic once the basis of Canadian identity is no longer sought in terms of ethnicity or multiculturalism but in one's identification with the polity:

> By displacing the racial and cultural norm for national identity, we can acknowledge Mistry as a Canadian, and not because he adds to Canada's diversity. If the nation is a political community and not a cultural, spiritual, or ethical entity, then citizenship is a political affiliation. Race, origins, ethico-cultural life-forms: none of these are appropriate criteria for measuring Canadianness. These are differences that, for judging qualifications to engage in the public life of the nation, do not obtain. Mistry

> belongs to the ongoing process that is at the very heart of the life of the nation: the making and remaking of the nation itself. He need not be given a hyphenated classification at all, because his work is Canadian literature today.[12]

While Samantrai arrives at a viable conclusion, she fails to base her claims on textual evidence. Her critical vocabulary, largely derived from political science, is not useful in the context of my study. To claim that a writer is Canadian because he is a naturalized Canadian while maintaining that he is a Canadian writer because his work is Canadian literature is tautological and therefore falls short of an acceptable model for our purposes.

Pursuing a similar vein, Ajay Heble also implicitly argues against the purism of Davey's point when he rejects his narrow frame of intelligibility in favour of a postnational and discursive approach:

> Indeed, the emergence in Canada of writers like Mistry, Joy Kogawa, Dionne Brand, and Tomson Highway indicates the necessity of moving beyond a nationalist critical methodology—where "the desire to come to terms with oneself in place and time and in relation to others" is, as David Tarras [in *A Passion For Identity: An Introduction to Canadian Studies*] suggests, "a national instinct" (10)——to a cross-cultural exploration of the discourse of hybridity as it is played out both within and beyond our national borders.[13]

The advantage of Heble's 'cross-cultural exploration' lies in the fact that it allows reading texts as Canadian that are not concerned with Canada on the surface. However, whether such an approach will always have to be synonymous with hybridity is contigent not only on the respective definition of hybridity, i.e. syncretistically or poststructuralist, but will also have to depend on the perspective from which a literary text is addressed.[14]

While Mukherjee, Samantrai and Heble agree that Canada's internal ethnic diversity as well as the diversity of its literature calls for critical interventions in order to arrive at a broader understanding, all three remain virtually silent on how exactly such a literature might be studied. Like Mukherjee, Samantrai, and Heble, Rosemary Sullivan's emphatic call for a more inclusive approach to Canadian literature is indicative of the appreciation of diversity, too. That she is also concerned with extending the definition of Canadian literature becomes evident when she admits that she is "bored with Canadian being a term of exclusion; I want a new inclusive version of Canadian literature."[15] Reading especially Frank Davey's early critical work against the grain, Sullivan postulates that Canadian literature can be divided into texts concerned with 'here,' i.e. Canada, and 'there,' i.e. the country of origin of the respective writer:

> The mental landscapes of the writers have two poles: *there* and *here*—but this is not a cheap polarity of eelgrass and snow, of a vapid idealized image of a past that is the focus only of nostalgia and a simplified alienating here. It is tougher than that. *There* and *here* are interlocked: the work is continually shaping and being shaped by the need to view *here* as possibility.[16]

Sullivan's argument does not only have the advantage of conceptualizing the different settings and focus of the works of many Canadian multicultural writers, she also demands that both sides be seen and discussed together. In my argument I will follow Sullivan in proposing a deixis of 'there' and 'here' in order to reflect the double encoding of Canadian immigrant literature.[17] While my study does not claim to be an exhaustive analysis of Canadian multicultural fiction, it attempts to exemplify the complexity and interrelatedness of 'there' and 'here' in a paradigmatic fashion. MG Vassanji, Neil Bissoondath, and Rohinton Mistry will be approached as Canadian writers who deal with Canada as well as with the countries of their origin: their narratives are concerned with 'here' and 'there.'

'Here' and 'There'

In the course of my argument the terms 'here' and 'there' do not merely refer to spatial configurations but acquire wider significance. Extrapolating from Sullivan's argument, it will be proposed that the treatment of 'here' is concerned with the immigrant's attitude towards Canadian multiculturalism, while 'there' corresponds to a working through past experiences in the country of origin. The approach towards 'here' and 'there' in Vassanji, Bissoondath, and Mistry is informed by an emphasis on cultural difference, the underlying assumption of multiculturalism as well as the central analytical category of postcolonialism. Behind the concern with difference is, of course, an interest in issues of identity. If it is agreed upon that identity should not be a matter of essentialism, then this must apply to difference as well. In this study it will be assumed that difference is a category which can be filled differently. As sociologists remind us, difference is no intrinsic quality or an objective factor in a social relationship but the definition of such a relationship. The decision to regard someone as different is always a positioning or an interpretation ("Zuschreibung").[18] In the functionalist reading that I am going to propose, difference, albeit in various forms and configurations, is the tertium comparationis between fictions that might otherwise be difficult to compare. A focus on difference links the work of the single writer whose work is partly set in Canada and partly elsewhere. I will argue that in their treatments of difference, Vassanji, Bissoondath, and Mistry come up with comparable identity constructions 'here' and 'there' respectively. These identity constructions should be considered, and appreciated, as a reflection of the pluralism that lies at the heart of Canadian multiculturalism, and therefore, as the following chapter will argue, at the centre of what it means to be Canadian.

With respect to 'here', I will examine Mistry, Bissoondath, and Vassanji as to how they view Canada and its attitude to and treatment of cultural diversity. At the centre of interest will be questions of race and ethnicity, difference and assimilation. I will examine how the Other, as represented in Vassanji, Bissoondath, and Mistry, fares in the face of institutionalized tolerance. Of particular importance will be the question of whether multiculturalism is experienced as liberation or whether it provokes racism in a more subtle form because it may in itself be informed by a racial bias. Among my chief interests is finding out if the paradigm of difference underlying multicultural models of society is experienced as a prerequisite for a dignified existence in the diaspora, or whether it is an assumption that prevents the immigrant from opting for other models of integration, such as, for example, assimilation or acculturation. Especially interesting in this context is the role that other categories of difference play. Is home as well as host culture experienced differently by the protagonists in Vassanji's, Bissoondath's, and Mistry's fictions once other categories of difference, such as age, social class etc., are introduced? Do second-generation immigrants experience Canadian multiculturalism as liberation from a colonialism which they themselves have not had to suffer under? How do members of former colonial elites such as Mistry's Parsis or Vassanji's Shamsis experience the racism of lower-class ghettoes?

At the heart of Vassanji's, Bissoondath's, and Mistry's narratives from 'there' are likewise issues of culture and identity. Operating with the vocabulary of postcolonialism, the question at the centre of interest will be the relevance of difference and to what extent the three authors subscribe to it. My working hypothesis is that Vassanji emulates cultural difference but eventually transforms it, while Bissoondath configures cultural difference in terms of group difference against which he posits the difference of the single individual begging to differ. Mistry, finally, reflects a certain awareness of cultural difference but offers vistas beyond postcoloniality by taking recourse to cultural exchange and also to humanist positions.

An exploration on the uses and abuses of difference as well as on the ways cultural difference figures and/or is overcome contributes towards a more comprehensive understanding of identity and the variety of ways in which it may be constructed. Vassanji, Bissoondath, and Mistry are comparable not only with respect to how they view Canadian culture but also with respect to how they corroborate their different understandings of identity. An analysis of difference 'here' and 'there' presupposes a definition of identity that transcends the borders of the nation and thus truly meets the demands of a postnational argument. Hence at the centre of what has famously been termed the Canadian 'passion for identity,' should no longer be questions exclusively concerned with 'here'[19] or interrogations solely preoccupied by the consequences of 'there.'[20] My assumption, which is also reflected in the structure of my argument, is that in an increasingly multicultural Canada 'there' informs 'here,' and vice versa. In short, 'here' and 'there' can and must be seen dialectically.

Difference and Identity in Multicultural and Postcolonial Discourse

A. Multiculturalism and Canada

Multiculturalism in Canada: A Brief Survey

Hugh MacLennan's famous novel *Two Solitudes* can serve as a reminder that Canadian multiculturalism is firmly rooted in English Canadian and French Canadian biculturalism. The dualism between the two so-called 'founding nations' harks back to the eighteenth century when, after the conquest of La Nouvelle France in 1760, the British refrained from interfering in the culture of the francophone population. In the Quebec Act of 1774 the British, contrary to their usual policy of assimilation, granted the French settlers the right to their own social order as well as the right to practise their faith and to speak their own language.[1] Thus were laid the foundations for Quebec to become not merely a separate culture but a 'distinct society,' which is, of course, a self-definition that continues to put Canada's national unity in question to this very day.

It becomes evident that while Quebec has successfully managed to construct an identity in the context of what is usually referred to as Quebec's 'Quiet Revolution,' English Canada, on the other hand, has faced severe problems in shaping a satisfactory self-image.[2] The reasons for success or failure in this case have to do with the particular definitions of difference on which identity always depends. Whereas what is today known as Quebec was clear about the difference against which it wanted to construct an identity, namely English Canada, the matter was more complex for the rest of Canada whose national identity, on the one hand, was dangerously close to that of its American neighbour and its English mother country and, on the other hand, was faced with many regional identities. Defining itself against the cultural difference of Quebec was problematic, moreover, because this would endanger the unity of Canada by undermining it from the inside. Needless to repeat that English Canada was and is interested to prevent precisely this from happening.

While the Ottawa-Quebec biculturalism has characterized the image Canada projected of itself for a long time, such a view is nothing short of a myth. As a matter of fact, Canada's colonial history and the theft of land based on the preconceived notion of a terra nullius, or an empty space,[3] excluded the Inuit and the Native Indians, both of which were never accorded the status of a founding nation or chartered group. Biculturalism, therefore, stood revealed as a simplification of a reality infinitely more complex. When the report of the Royal Commission on Bilingualism and Biculturalism was published in 1967, it became clear that Canada was not so much bicultural but multicultural also for other reasons. As a country with a long history of immigration, many people in Canada belonged to neither of the two so-called First Nations or were of French Canadian or English Canadian descent.[4] Canada was officially recognized to be multicultural in 1971 by Prime Minister Trudeau. Subsequent to the Official Languages Act of 1969, which made Canada an officially bilingual country, he argued that 'multiculturalism within a bilingual framework' constitutes the official state policy and marks the essence of Canadian identity. Though there were now two official languages, there was no official culture and no ethnic group would take precedence over any other.[5]

There can be no doubt that a description of Canada as consisting of a community of communities was and still is an accurate reflection of the country's historical as well as sociological situation.[6] However, from a different angle Canadian multicultural policy, officially declared and entrenched in the Charter of Rights and Freedoms of 1982 and the Canadian Multiculturalism Act of 1988, also was a deliberate attempt at forging a national identity. As Smaro Kamboureli explains, "the discourse of multiculturalism [. . .] serves as a culmination for the ideological construction of 'Canada.'"[7] When the Canadian government maintained that the variety of its cultures need not assimilate but, in turn, deserved to be encouraged, supported and funded by the state,[8] this move, or this "passage from assimilationism to normative pluralism in Canada,"[9] effectively cast Canada's neighbour America, which had long since favoured an alternative immigration policy, as different. If the American understanding of national identity was conveyed in terms of the melting pot, the central metaphor by way of which Canada's national character could be symbolized became the mosaic. Whereas American nation identity was homogeneous, Canada's identity, according to Trudeau, was grounded in the unity of its diversity, which was officially interpreted as resource rather than limitation. While it is understood that identity depends on difference, in Canada, if one follows Trudeau, national identity lay in the very difference of the nation's many cultures.[10] This conflation of identity and difference in the case of Canada led to a problematic construction, as will be seen below.

A reading informed by an awareness of the ideological underpinnings of culture and its manifestations cannot fail to register the wider significance of Trudeau's measure. Notwithstanding the accurate and perhaps well-meaning hopes that the government placed in multiculturalism, as a policy it was no doubt also directed against the secessionist tendencies of Quebec.[11] By inaugurating multiculturalism the federal government hoped to defuse Quebec's claims, or as a critic pointedly describes it: "The unassimilable 'others' who, in their distance from English Canada, need to be boxed into this catch-all phrase [i.e. multiculturalism] now become the moral cudgel with which to beat Quebec's separatist aspirations."[12] Not surprisingly, Quebec feared for its special status within the Canadian federation and intensified its endeavours to become independent. As a consequence, the gulf between the two so-called founding nations appears to be widening, and isolation rather than MacLennan's (i.e. Rilke's) caressing solitude characterises the relationship between English and Franco-Canada. It seems safe to suggest that at least with respect to the containment of Franco-Canadian separatism, multiculturalism in Canada must be regarded as a failure.[13] Whether in enshrining difference multiculturalism has managed to make a difference for other solitudes, to echo two well-known anthologies of Canadian multicultural fiction,[14] will be explored in greater detail by taking a closer look at the recent political and literary debates surrounding difference and identity in Canada.

Discourses of Difference and Sameness I: The Political Debate

In general, the uses and limitations of multiculturalism have been discussed controversially in terms of difference and sameness. There are two main types of argument, the one appreciating difference as liberation (and viewing sameness as oppression), while others maintain that multiculturalism prevents equality by inscribing difference. A representative of the former school of thinking is Charles Taylor who advocates that the recognition of difference is not only a moral but a vital human need in that it is tied up with the process of identity construction. Borrowing from symbolic interactionism as well as dialogism, he points out that

> in order to understand the close connection between identity and recognition, we have to take into account a crucial feature of the human condition that has been rendered almost invisible by the overwhelmingly monological bent of mainstream modern philosophy. This crucial feature of human life is its fundamentally *dialogical* character. We become full human agents, capable of understanding ourselves, and hence of defining our identity, through our acquisition of rich human languages of expression.[15]

As we all have the same claim to a 'good life,' we should respect that for some cultural autonomy may be a core requirement for precisely such a life. Thus for Taylor, in a move resembling the Kantian imperative, a politics of difference may help to foster equality.

Perhaps the chief representative of the opposite view, namely that a recognition of difference can be as oppressive as liberating, is Neil Bissoondath. Like Taylor's, Bissoondath's argument hinges on the importance of culture. However, while Charles Taylor's functionalist perspective emphasizes the stable, and therefore stabilizing, character of one's native culture, Bissoondath's normative definition stresses the dynamic nature of cultures in general. For him "no consequence of multiculturalism policy is as ironic—or as unintended—as what I would call the simplification of culture."[16] The fact that the migrant may not want to remain the Other but prefer to assimilate throws into question that a politics of difference is the kind of recognition that every immigrant deems indispensable for his well-being and expects from the host society. Whereas Charles Taylor warns against non- or misrecognition of one's cultural difference,[17] for Neil Bissoondath it is precisely multiculturalism's inscription of cultural difference that constitutes the chief misrecognition: "I am still being judged on the colour of my skin and not simply as a human being with strengths and weaknesses. I am still, even with my best of intentions, being viewed racially—and that is offensive to me."[18]

The range of positionings as exemplified by Taylor and Bissoondath illustrates how difference is controversially discussed in the context of the construction of national identity. At the heart of the recent citizenship debate within Canada is the issue of national unity and how difference fosters or impedes integration. This discussion has been characterized by the question of "how much difference can actually be accommodated within a federal system of centralized cultural and political authority."[19] While it is sometimes pointed out that multicultural unity in diversity is a problematic concept for the configuration of a national identity, such claims typically discuss multiculturalism with respect to its degree or discard it as a policy that should be given up in favour of assimilation, or a policy of 'e pluribus unum.' In trying to answer the question whether Canadian multiculturalism has integrative potential or not, I will outline some arguments on the state of Canadian society that may be seen as representative of the general debate since 1990.

Arguing from a sociological perspective, Lance W Roberts and Rodney A Clifton draw on social systems theory to explain multiculturalism in terms of the constraints of culture on the one hand and social structure on the other. Culture refers to "a shared set of symbols that identify what members of various ethnic groups believe" and social structure refers to the group's "collective patterns of conduct."[20] Roberts and Clifton identify four alternative stances in a multicultural situation and argue that, apart from assimilation, three distinct types of multiculturalism may be distinguished. Within so-called 'institutionalized multiculturalism' an ethnic group commands conformity in terms of thoughts and actions. An example is the case of the Hutterites. Within 'ritualistic multiculturalism' the ethnic group commands behavioural conformity but has difficulty in instilling its values and beliefs in its members: "An ethnic group whose members participate in religious ceremonies, or some political process unique to that group, without understanding the symbolic meaning of these activities would be an expression of this form of multiculturalism."[21] Finally, within 'symbolic multiculturalism' members of an ethnic group identify with the group's values but do not feel constrained in their actions by the group's patterns of behaviour. The policy implications for Canada as a multicultural state are predictable. While 'institutionalized multiculturalism' is problematic for financial but also for reasons of national unity, 'ritualistic' and 'symbolic' multiculturalisms will be encouraged by the government of a multicultural state like Canada. Interestingly enough, Roberts and Clifton maintain that "symbolic multiculturalism not only is what the federal government favours but, in many instances, is all that members of ethnic groups desire."[22] Giving 'ritualistic' and 'symbolic' multiculturalism in Canada a higher profile serves two ends. It endows the ethnic group with an anchorage in tradition, which, in turn, allows countering "meaninglessness, or 'alienation.'"[23] At the same time, such a moderate form of multiculturalism also allows us to imagine a national community.

Strongly disagreeing with such an argument, Neil Bissoondath doubts whether "cultural diversity can be preserved and enhanced when the ultimate goal is, and must be, immigrant integration."[24] Rather than fostering social cohesion, prototypical Canadian multiculturalism, which roughly corresponds to Roberts's and Clifton's 'ritualistic' multiculturalism in its emphasis on cultural difference, impedes the construction of a national identity. Bissoondath criticizes in particular the folklore celebration of cultural diversity, which, rather than being a solution to the dilemma of national Canadian unity, has made it more difficult to arrive at a consensus about common values, which he deems indispensable for integration. Multiculturalism Canadian style "leaves little room for the unity offered by shared experiences, ethics, values. [. . .] In eradicating the centre, in evoking uncertainty as to what and who is a Canadian, it has diminished all sense of Canadian values, of what is a Canadian."[25]

Celebrating cultural difference may be harmless according to Roberts and Clifton, but for Bissoondath however, it threatens a sense of national identity and unity both for those practising it and for the larger society that tolerates it in its libidinous desire for exoticism.[26] Neil Bissoondath emphasizes that the articulation of cultural difference in what he calls "exhibitionistic multiculturalism"[27] should not receive undue attention. The reason is that to him it is merely epiphenomenal, i.e. a second-order manifestation of an underlying sameness. Rather than advocating unity in diversity or deep diversity, Bissoondath argues in favour of a colour-blind sameness that renders difference in terms of race or ethnicity superficial: "Canadians, because they are of so many colours, are essentially colourless, in the best sense of the word."[28] Significantly, Bissoondath's universalist programme emphasizes that sameness is not only a matter of rights but also of obligations. And it is precisely with respect to the kinds of obligations that Canadian citizenship entails that he sees problems with the current configuration of Canadian identity in terms of multiculturalism:

> Citizenship, whether through birth or naturalization implies belonging. It implies a basic commitment of intellectual and emotional loyalty. It is a thing of value. And yet, in recent years, the diminishing value of Canadian citizenship—the creation of the hyphenated Canadian with divided loyalities [. . .] the idea that citizenship is a matter of rights and not of obligations—means that the opposite has also come to be true. Canadian citizenship is frequently seen not as a means of committing oneself to the country but simply as a way of abandoning it with an assurance of safety.[29]

Like Neil Bissoondath, John Harles is interested in how integration can be accomplished. He argues that in order to arrive at some form of national integration, it needs the identification of the members of the polity either with a culture or an ideology. However, Canada, due to the notorious English Canadian and French Canadian cleavage, lacks the former and, consequently, has been unable to formulate the latter. As a consequence, Trudeau's policy of multiculturalism, as an attempt at homogenising the heterogeneous, seems the only viable option in a country in which assimilation is ruled out as an "implausible integrative strategy [. . .] [, for] conceptually there is little to assimilate to."[30] Absent multiculturalism, what is left for Canadians to identify with are the

> essential propositions of liberal-democratic political practice—political authority based on the consent of the governed as effectuated through electoral representatives, equal policy rights, including the equal ability to influence political decision-making, toleration of dissent, freedom of expression, conscience and association.[31]

However, as Harles knows, values such as these are not enough to guarantee a distinct national identity for Canada, not least of all because they are not different enough.[32] Thus while the implementation of a multicultural policy is understandable, it cannot disguise its unsatisfactory character, for "in the interest of championing the politics of difference, multiculturalism actually denudes the public sphere that makes [. . .] [a] common life possible."[33] Culminating in an outright provocation, Harles arrives at the conclusion that Canada's search for a national identity will never be ended "as long as Canada includes Quebec."[34]

If Neil Bissoondath and John Harles see too much diversity and too little unity in Canada's multicultural policy, Eric Breton claims that multiculturalism demands too much unity while neglecting important cultural differences.[35] He corroborates his argument by pointing to the fact that Canadian multiculturalism is a policy that is centred on the individual and neglects the importance of community to the Québecois, the First Nations, and some immigrant groups.[36] Eric Breton thinks that

> since the policy of multiculturalism fails to acknowledge the centrality of community to members of Canada's minority nations' sense of who and what they are—and thus of their identity as 'Canadians'—it implicitly denies the legitimacy of their senses of 'Canadian-ess.'[37]

While multiculturalism as a policy has been instrumentalized to balance Quebec's separatist tendencies, Eric Breton demands that approaches to diversity should in themselves be diverse. Reminding us that "there are at least three distinct multicultural contexts in Canada: Aboriginal Peoples, Quebec and Anglophone Canada,"[38] he demands a recognition of different types of multiculturalism with different underlying assumptions.

Eric Breton's analysis is indebted to Will Kymlicka's seminal and by now almost classical discussion of multicultural citizenship in Canada.[39] According to Kymlicka, whose arguments, in turn, owe to the writings of Charles Taylor, multiculturalism as a term "can be confusing, precisely because it is ambigious between multinational and polyethnic."[40] In his terminology, multination states refer to polities which have incorporated "previously self-governing, territorially concentrated cultures"[41] who call for a special political status, i.e. wish to maintain a distinct status with respect to the majority culture. Within Canada, Quebec and the First Nations are examples for 'distinct societies' or, as Kymlicka calls them, "national minorities."[42] Polyethnicity, in turn, signifies a form of cultural diversity that is largely a result of immigration. According to Kymlicka, polyethnicity is characterized by immigrants who

> wish to integrate into the larger society, and to be accepted as full members of it. While they often seek greater recognition of their ethnic identity, their aim is not to become a separate and self-governing nation alongside the larger society, but to modify the institutions and laws of the

mainstream society to make them more accommodating of cultural difference.[43]

Polyethnicity within Canada refers to all immigrants to Canada who neither belong to one of the First Nations or to one of the two chartered groups. In his subsequent discussion of group rights that may result from various forms of cultural diversity or multiculturalism,[44] Kymlicka distinguishes three different types of rights: 'Self-government rights' devolve power to local bodies and thereby grant "political autonomy or territorial jurisdiction, so as to ensure the full and free development of [a] [. . .] culture,"[45] 'polyethnic rights,' i.e. group-specific measures, guarantee that ethnic groups may be able to maintain their cultural particularity, while, finally, 'special representation rights' challenge the underrepresentation of racial and ethnic minorities within a country's organs of political administration.[46] While polyethnic rights will never be dangerous to the cohesion of a polity because they presuppose a willingness to integrate, self-government rights pose a more severe problem to national unity: "Demands for self-government [. . .] reflect a desire to weaken the bonds with the larger political community, and indeed question its very authority and permanence."[47] As values are not a common point of reference in a multinational state, social cohesion has to be constructed in a different way. Referring to Charles Taylor's concept of 'deep diversity,' Kymlicka concludes that

> the members of a polyethnic and multination state must not only respect diversity, but also respect a diversity of approaches to diversity. [. . .] A society founded on 'deep diversity' is unlikely to stay together unless people value deep diversity itself, and want to live in a country with diverse forms of cultural and political membership.[48]

Richard Sigurdson likewise understands the citizenship debate in terms of divergent concepts of belonging. The 'liberal universalist notion of universalist citizenship' centres on the identification of the individual with a polity. Inequality is to be abolished, and inequality concerns also privileges based on ethnicity: "Rejected as illiberal and unfair is any type of preferential treatment based on one's racial identity or ethno-cultural heritage."[49] Within such a view, special representation rights as well as self-government rights are discouraged. On the other hand, there is a 'cultural pluralist notion of differentiated citizenship' based on a "politics of difference [which] would replace the liberal priority of the abstract individual with an emphasis on one's cultural or ethnic group, for it is the group which is the source of identity."[50] Sigurdson shows that, taken to their logical conclusion, both concepts are detrimental to national unity as the principal loyalities are in neither of the two cases with the Canadian polity. A third way between "excessive individualism and illiberal groupism"[51] seems elusive. If it can be found, then, according to Sigurdson, it lies in the identification of the members of the Canadian polity with their political institutions: "The ties that bind then, would have to be political-constitutional, not ethno-cultural."[52] Notwithstanding such an argument, the role of culture in determining Canadian identity continues to be hotly debated. As the following section shows, some of the core arguments in this context are put forward by writers and literary critics and can likewise be understood in terms of discourses of difference and sameness.

Discourses of Difference and Sameness II: The Literary Debate

While "the Canadian imagination was trapped by its colonial heritage until at least 1945,"[53] multiculturalism has fostered the production of a literature that is unique in its diversity of subject matters and different modes of articulation. An assessment of multiculturalism in literature would number among its chief benefits atmospherical, material and aesthetic factors. For one thing, the climate of tolerance stimulated by multiculturalism (as well as postmodernism) proved beneficial for the development of various literary voices. While these voices were often unique aesthetically,[54] multiculturalism also had an enormous psychological effect in that it enabled ethnic writers "to gain a more secure emotional base from which to reinterpret and reevaluate their past."[55] In the very terms relied on in the pages to follow, being 'here' has made working through 'there' possible.[56] Secondly, an official multicultural policy has fostered not only a general acceptance of immigrant literature[57] but also improved the means of publication and distribution of that sort of literature. As Janice Kulyk Keefer knows, in a pre-multicultural Canada

> no immigrant artist writing of a non-Anglo-Celtic country of origin [. . .] could hope to publish her work and have it received in any significant way. [. . .] [F]or immigrant experience to have taken persuasive hold of a country's imagination [. . .] something significant must have happened to create the agency presupposed by this "hold." This "significant something," I would argue, was the advent and development of [. . .] multiculturalism.[58]

In addition, the official support of multiculturalism as a policy has resulted in generous funding by the Canada Council[59] and by the Multiculturalism branch of the Secretary of State[60] so that authors who otherwise might not have been able to afford full-time writing suddenly were free to explore issues that preoccupied them.[61]

Multiculturalism has, first of all, been acclaimed because it stresses that tolerance and pluralism are 'values' in themselves.[62] The support of culturally different expressions manifest in multicultural literature is not only a moral obligation, however, but can be profitable for society at large. Behind this is a sociological argument which emphasizes that the foreign, far from being an encumbrance, can also be a resource. Literary multiculturalism may reflect an immigrant's or a community's right to determining his/her/its self-image, for example, by way of stories.

Secondly, multiculturalism can also be of use for a society in that it expands a polity's store of cultural knowledge and practices. Given man's relatively narrow horizon of experience, alterity, in principle, allows for a stock of alternative knowledge that a society may draw on and borrow from. Literature can take on an important function in that it may mediate between several culturally distinct traditions and offer insight into other cultures. In the context of such a functionalist argument, Fleras and Elliott rightfully stress that "it is the sharing and understanding between cultures that is crucial, not simply the promotion of diversity for its own sake."[63] Pursuing a similar vein, Enoch Padolsky points out that multicultural fiction illustrates and documents the dynamics of culture at work. For both writers and readers, such a literature may be said "to reflect or incorporate their acculturation options."[64]

Multiculturalism in literature is certainly fostering intercultural learning and paving the ground for intercultural understanding. However, it might also be critically asked whether multiculturalism has not lost whatever idealist overtones it once possessed when it was introduced in the early 1970s and become a commodity that is made to sell. Thus calling a writer 'ethnic' might be offensive to some because he/she may feel labelled in a way that is indistinguishable from a commodification strategy. While market pressures demand that the exoticism of the writer and his work is stressed, these writers may feel they are subtly marginalized once again, pointing out that ethnic is a byword usually reserved for writers belonging to a so-called visible minority. As Batts reminds us:

> To speak now of "ethnic" literatures, as though "Canadian" and "Quebec" writers possessed no ethnicity [. . .] makes even less sense, for this implies that these ethnic literatures are somehow not Canadian, when it is precisely the immigrant experience, the diversity of cultures, and the interrelationship between these cultures that make literature in Canada what it is.[65]

In that sense, invoking ethnicity for some reflects a desire for difference, i.e. for the Other, which might be said to have racist underpinnings. Michael Thorpe, for example, polemically contends that multiculturalism is "almost a euphemism: an earlier generation would have spoken of multi*racism* [sic]."[66] To address this racism, one could opt in favour of a more assimilationist policy, i.e. opt for more sameness, which might render the Canadian polity more resistant against racism as a whole (although this might in itself be debatable).[67] Secondly, it would also be possible to call for a modified form of multiculturalism, which would have to accept the history and continuing presence of racism in Canada and make an effort to challenge it.[68]

Far from conceiving of ethnicity in terms of a confining label, some writers, on the other hand, regard it as a liberating stance because of its potential to challenge a monologic tradition. Ethnicity for a poet like Fred Wah is a position from which the writer may attempt to come to terms with society as well as his own position within it. When he holds that "to write (or live) ethnically is also to write (or live) ethically, in pursuit of right values, right place, right home, right otherness,"[69] it becomes evident that ethnicity, and hence a space of difference, is of moral relevance. Multicultural pluralism provides him with a space from which a "poetics of difference"[70] becomes possible, and Wah elaborates on such a poetics in the following way:

> The site of this poetics for me, and many other multi-racial and multicultural writers, is the hyphen, that marked (or unmarked) space that both binds and divides. This heno-poetic (Grk heno, one) punct, this flag of the many in the one, yet "less than one and double" [. . .], is the operable tool that both compounds difference and underlines sameness. Though the hyphen is in the middle, it is not in the centre. It is a property marker, a boundary post, a borderland, a bastard, a railroad, a last spike, a stain, a cypher, a rope, a knot, a chain (link), a foreign word, a warning sign, a head tax, a bridge, a no-man's land, a nomadic, floating magic carpet, now you see it now you don't. The hyphen is the hybrid's dish, the mestiza's whole wheat tortillas [. . .], the Metis' apple (red on the outside, white on the inside), the happa's egg (white out, yellow in), the mulatto's café au lait.[71]

In allowing for hyphenation, Canada for Wah offers a hybrid space in which a writer may refuse to be either same or Other. Rather than referring to a syncretistic concept, hybridity for Wah figures as the in-between, as theorized by Bhabha, as well as the dialogic principle, as outlined by Bakhtin. Both are stances that allow the individual to appreciate what is best in multiculturalism and at the same time do not preclude addressing its shortcomings.

If it was argued initially that multiculturalism is a phenomenon of globalization, the critical vocabulary used in multicultural discourse, as, for example, exemplified by Fred Wah, is indebted to the ground-breaking work of postcolonial criticism. While migration and multiculturalism are in themselves reactions to the end of colonialism, multiculturalism, of course, also operates with the terms and concepts of postcolonialism such as ethnicity or hybridity, which will be discussed in the following. It will not only be argued that postcolonialism shares with multiculturalism an emphasis on difference as central analytical category but also that postcolonialism, like multiculturalism, may be conceived as a positioning that is the result of a struggle between discourses of sameness and difference.

B. Postcolonial Theory

Colonialism and Postcolonialism I: The Postcolonial Project and the Postcolonial Problematic

For social scientists, 'postcolonial' as a term supersedes the older designation 'third-world,'[1] while students of literature increasingly employ it to refer to the body of texts that have previously been called Commonwealth Literature or New Literatures in English. While the practice of naming indicates a shift of emphasis, attempts to define the postcolonial have been notoriously difficult. Within the field there continue to operate very different notions of what postcolonial should signify, depending on how one reads the 'post' in postcolonial.[2] In this study, a broad definition has been opted for. Thus, following the authors of a standard introduction, postcolonialism, a variant of which is multiculturalism, can be described as an attempt (scholarly and otherwise) to come to terms with the disrupting experiences of colonialism.[3]

Together with economic exploitation and the destruction of traditional societies, arguably one of the severest consequences of colonialism was the denigration of indigenous identities by colonial discourse.[4] According to Leela Gandhi, "colonialism [. . .] marks the historical process whereby the 'West' attempts systematically to cancel or negate the cultural difference and value of the 'non-West.'"[5] With the advent of postcolonialism, those formerly oppressed have tried to recover a sense of their respective histories, languages and traditions. In order to achieve this aim, the crippling images imposed on indigenous people by the colonizers had to be destroyed first. The core concern of the postcolonial project was to challenge the crippling Self-Other configuration in which the colonial subject was always represented as Other. In this sense, the 'post' in postcolonial becomes significant as a "space-clearing gesture,"[6] which can deconstruct the logic of the Manichean divide underlying colonialism.[7] While colonial discourse denied precolonial cultures morality, integrity etc. and refused to acknowledge that their difference called for a different mode of perception, i.e. a perception that granted an indigenous culture a dignity of its own, postcolonialism demanded that the difference of the culture it was concerned with be recognised. The reasons are grounded in the firm belief that "'difference,' which in colonialist discourse connotes a remove from normative European practice, and hence functions as a marker of subordination, is for postcolonial analysis the correspondent marker of identity."[8]

However, particularly in its initial phase,[9] postcolonialism's honourable agenda was not free from methodological shortcomings. In particular, the postcolonial project of giving voice to those previously marginalized frequently relied on structural principles similar to those colonial discourse operated with. As can be illustrated by the example of essentialism, i.e. "the assumption that groups, categories or classes of objects have one or several defining features exclusive to all members of that category,"[10] the patterns and assumptions to be deconstructed were often categories underlying the argument of the critique itself. While colonial discourse was informed by an essentialist bias in stressing the superiority of one race and one nation over the other, postcolonial counter-discourse often displayed the same essentialist ideas in trying to achieve a new sense of identity and dignity—only this time for the former colonized subject. Arguments which claimed that "in different periods the employment of essentialist ideas may be a necessary part of the process by which the colonized achieve a renewed sense of the value and dignity of their pre-colonial cultures"[11] have been called (and, to a certain extent, exculpated as) strategically essentialist by one of the leading critics within the field.[12]

Uneasy parallels between colonial and postcolonial discourse notwithstanding, postcolonialism has often successfully dismantled the master discourse of colonialism. If colonialism operated on race as a category of difference, contemporary postcolonial theory has abandoned race in favour of ethnicity, for example. Ethnicity accounts for "human variation in terms of culture, tradition, language, social patterns and ancestry, rather than the discredited generalizations of race with its assumptions of a humanity divided into fixed, genetically determined biological types."[13] Influenced by the work of Stuart Hall, Werner Sollors and others, ethnicity has been reclaimed as a marker of difference that relies on categories which are applied as much by the group that regards itself as belonging to a shared ethnicity as by the society at large. As it is a category that is not imposed from without, a great advantage of ethnicity is that it allows for "an identity that cannot be denied, rejected or taken away by others."[14] Whereas membership to an essentialist category such as race consigned one to a particular group, ethnicity stresses that belonging to a collective relies on affiliation, or the will to belong. Furthermore, because it is "relative to time and place,"[15] ethnicity is also a category of difference more flexible than race in that it allows for a dynamics. In other words, the subject is not only free in deciding to which ethnicity, or ethnicities, he/she belongs, the very nature of ethnicity allows both for changes of what constitutes a particular ethnicity and for the subject switching from one ethnicity to another. At any rate—and this will be important for my argument—the new understanding of ethnicity precludes locating any subject, be it white or black, outside of ethnicity.

Although postcolonialism cannot but criticize the crippling implications of a racialist understanding of indigenous cultures, abandoning ethnicity in favour of race runs counter at least to an (strategically) essentialist understanding of postcolonial thinking outlined above. From thinking in terms of such a definition of ethnicity (rather than race) it logically follows that the inversion of Manichean divides can never occupy the position of a condition sine qua non for postcolonial identity formation. If postcolonialism is all about challenging Manichean divisions, then ethnicity, as defined above, is quintessentially postcolonial. While ethnicity complicates the politics of difference considerably, such a complication is a gain rather than a loss, as Manichean divisions are suddenly undercut by potentially infinite possibilities of affiliations and identifications. A postcolonialism informed by an awareness of the character of difference as a positioning can, and indeed must, account for a variety of identity constructions, a point which is hard to accept for an oppositional postcolonial theory eager to retain an implacable enmity between former colonizer and colonized.[16] Such an activist stance has difficulties with the flexibility inherent in the concept of ethnicity because generalizations become more difficult and indeed immoral, provocative as it may sound. To the same extent that the concept of ethnicity empowers the subject, postcolonial claims in the name of a collective or ideology are, if not totally ruled out, open to criticism and modification. Succinctly put, ethnicity calls for a rethinking of postcolonialism and demands that an essentialist, activist postcolonialism is replaced by a broader, more inclusive understanding of the term. It is towards such an understanding that the analyses put forward in the subsequent chapters want to contribute.

While taking into consideration that a return to a merely temporal understanding of postcolonialism would be reductive, postcolonialism, rather than being understood as a solution to the problems posed by colonialism, should in itself be conceived as a problem, or rather, as Stephen Slemon has called it, a "problematic."[17] At least within the realm of identity-constructions, postcolonial literature and theory have come up with such a multitude of reactions to colonialism that one should be wary of subsuming them under a hegemonic reading. Such a hegemonic reading could, for example, take on the form of a claim for essentialism and the recovery of a culture's difference; such a hegemonic reading could also be the contention that the inscription of a different culture must be valued positively for a literature to be postcolonial. In the analyses to follow, it will be maintained that postcolonial literature offers a space in which different readings of another culture's difference are possible without the work of fiction ceasing to be postcolonial. Difference, as a necessary prerequisite for the construction of an identity, will be taken as a category which may be filled differently. As identity is "not an essence but a positioning,"[18] we have to ask critically who the Other is against which an identity outlines itself and how this Otherness, i.e. difference, is evaluated. In this thesis a wide understanding of what postcolonial literature can signify with respect to the politics of identity has been consciously opted for in order to account for a variety of positionings with respect to difference: Advocating difference (cf. Vassanji) as well as deconstructing (cf. Bissoondath) and transcending it (cf. Mistry) are all equally legitimate solutions to the problematic of postcolonial identity construction.

Colonialism and Postcolonialism II: Discourses of Difference and Sameness

Prescribing the rules according to which certain issues are talked about, a discourse, as defined by Michel Foucault, is a way of knowing as well as a means of exerting power.[19] The notion of a discourse has been influential in theorising colonialism because it draws attention to the underlying politics of exclusion that both colonialism and postcolonialism rely on in their construction of Otherness. In much the same way as colonialism employed discourses of sameness and difference to install inequalities, postcolonial literature draws on both discourses in order to come up with a solution to the problem of self-fashioning after colonialism. I would like to suggest that the very ambivalences of the discursive construction of Otherness with respect to difference and sameness are productive insofar as they hint at alternative approaches towards the pressing issue of identity formation in postcolonial times. In the following paragraphs the relevance of discourses of difference and sameness will be discussed and exemplified briefly with respect to colonialism and postcolonialism.

The way different cultures were talked about within colonial discourse relied on concepts of race, age and sex/gender difference. A few examples may illustrate the pattern of the arguments. Thus the association of blacks with (medieaval) notions of evil and bestiality, and the accompanying rendering of whites as innocent and pure, helped to justify the "impetus to trade, plunder and conquer"[20] new lands. Similarly, the culturally foreign was imagined as female or as a child because both sexuality and age could be measured against a male, adult standard. With respect to the covert purpose of colonialism as exploitation, the use of gender and age difference helped to set up and perpetuate a hierarchy that allowed the centre to corroborate his position of superiority.[21] The insufficiency of the Other-as-child called for the instruction, tutelage and care of the colonizer (as adult), an example of which was, of course, the relationship between Canada and the British Empire.[22] The expected obedience of the Other-as-woman allowed the colonizer to rule supreme by way of analogy to patriarchal discourses circulating in Europe at that time.

If civilizing the native and educating him/her was the overt purpose of colonialism, colonialism's moral legitimization was often questioned by the contradictions within colonial discourse itself. While it is crucial to realize that colonialism's "fascination with difference competed with a reliance on sameness and familiarity,"[23] it is equally important to stress that the border between the known and the unknown as well as between the homely and the uncanny was porous. The Other, rather paradoxically, was represented in ways that could suggest difference as well as sameness, depending on who did the defining and for what purposes. In what follows, some of the contradictions produced by colonial discourse's practices of Othering shall be sketched briefly for each of the categories of difference discussed above.

For a long time the West believed that the fact that some people were born with a darker skin than others referred to polygenesis, or the fact that mankind did not develop from one progenitor. According to this mythological interpretation the black race was fathered by Ham, who was ridden with sin, and therefore black, because he saw his father Noah naked. This specifically Christian explanation of racial difference, however, clashed with the also paradigmatically Christian idea that all men were created equal. Thus, if Christian doctrine were taken seriously, Otherness could never amount to more than superficial differences in outward appearance, and this would have rendered the colonialist enterprise immoral rather than inevitable. In addition to that, if Christian belief entailed the promise to wash all men free from sin, the bringing of Christianity to the colonies would necessarily lead to a washing white and hence to a levelling of the very difference constructed to justify exploitation and oppression. Such a possibility raised the uncomfortable idea that all racial difference was eventually unstable, an idea that did not only question the colonial venture but the identity of the colonizers as such.[24]

With respect to age difference, suffice it to say that the colonial authorities had an interest in discursively establishing the fact that age as a category of difference remained relevant in the perception of Otherness. In an absurd and grotesque fashion, colonial regimes depended on the eternal childlike nature of the Other in order to justify their rule as well as their system of exploitation. As growing up and maturation would inevitably entail a cutting loose of the Others from the parental home of the colonizers, the colonizers were unwilling to admit that the Other would grow up. To admit the obvious, i.e. a growing up, raised the danger of a questioning of the very dependence on the colonizer (as parent) that the metropolis advocated in order to veil its real, i.e. material, interest. Moreover, the universal, because biological, dimension of age as a category was downplayed in favour of a difference that had to be enshrined in order to guarantee the colonizer a relatively stable self-image.

Likewise, sex/gender within colonial discourse is a contested field charged with mutually exclusive representations. Drawing attention to the fact that the colonial enterprise is as much characterized by desire as it is by fear, Ania Loomba reminds us that "if colonial power is repeatedly expressed as a white man's possession of black women and men, colonial fears centre around the rape of white women by black men."[25] In the wake of the British Mutiny, for instance, the usual gender stereotypes were inverted so that the Other-as-female suddenly became a rapist intent on ravishing white women, discursively projected as precious, innocent and vulnerable at the same time.[26] The threat to the female, which hitherto had characterized the (male) native in representations, became metonymic of the colonizer's fear of racial pollution and impurity and thus of a transgression of difference. As Loomba explains, "the fear of cultural and racial pollution prompts the most hysterical dogmas about racial difference and sexual behaviours because it suggests the instability of 'race' as a category."[27] As mutually exclusive configurations of sex/gender difference were employed to corroborate and protect racial difference, possibilities to challenge racial difference and with it the foundation of colonial discourse presented themselves to postcolonial critics. In other words, because the representations of Otherness were contradictory in that they oscillated between fear and desire, postcolonial critics perceived a chance of destabilizing the truth value of colonialism's crippling system of representation, a point on which more will be said below.

Once attention is shifted from colonial to postcolonial discourse, parallels and overlaps with larger discourses of sameness and difference become evident, too. The fact that there are not only points of divergence but also of convergence renders impossible an understanding of postcolonialism as a project that only relies on difference in its answer to the problem of identity. Rather, postcolonialism is an "umbrella term"[28] under which discourses of sameness, e.g. Marxism or liberation theology, and discourse of difference, e.g. poststructuralism/postmodernism, have come up with a variety of solutions to what has been called the postcolonial problematic. In their variety the following three distinct readings of difference reflect in an exemplary fashion the diversity of stances with respect to difference within postcolonial studies today.

In the late 1980s and early 1990s postcolonial studies saw a fierce debate in the course of which the relationship between poststructuralism/postmodernism and postcolonialism was discussed. Materially, postmodernism had a beneficial effect on postcolonialism by helping it gain acceptance as well as posts within the Western academia.[29] Methodologically, postcolonialism profited from the poststructuralist/postmodern impetus to deconstruct all metanarratives.[30] Particularly in its foregounding of difference, poststructuralist/postmodern positions dovetailed with postcolonialism. Recognising that colonialism meant "that the natives accept a version of the colonizers' entire system of values, attitudes, morality,"[31] poststructuralism/postmodernism helped postcolonialism to put colonialism's crippling and traumatizing ideologies into perspective.

Poststructuralism/postmodernism and postcolonialism were both opposed to a discourse that posits a universalist human nature in an attempt at oppressing those who diverge from the norm of the metropolis.[32] Both poststructuralism/postmodernism and postcolonialism were sceptical of humanism because

> the humanist valorisation of man is almost always accompanied by a barely discernible corollary which suggests that some human beings are more human than others—either on account of their access to superior learning, or on account of their cognitive faculties. [. . .] The underside of Western humanism produces the dictum that since some human beings are more human than others, they are more substantially the measure of all things.[33]

Disclosing the ideological nature of humanism as a specifically Western epistemology, and thus as a colonialism in disguise, poststructuralist/postmodern critics stressed the irreducibility of difference as an ontological given and an ethical objective of the postcolonial project. This was an argument that, in the context of a European crisis of authority, contributed to a "qualification of monocultural thinking."[34] As Helen Tiffin points out, "the dis/mantling, de/mystification and unmasking of European authority [. . .] has been an essential political and cultural strategy towards decolonisation and the retrieval of or creation of an independent identity."[35] Implying that homogeneity translates as hegemony, poststructuralist/postmodern critics celebrated pluralism and heterogeneity as the only morally acceptable positions.[36] This celebration, however, was not a celebration for the sake of celebrating the deviant; it rather had profound political implications, at least for postcolonialism. For while poststructuralism/postmodernism can be helpful for postcolonialism in some respects, two problems remain. First of all, granted that colonialism is really over, a problem exists with respect to the constructive aspect of poststructuralism's/postmodernism's/postcolonialism's deconstruction of the old. While postcolonialism operates with a political agenda, postmodernism lacks an explicit political commitment.[37] Secondly, and closely connected with the first point, the relationship between poststructuralism/ postmodernism and postcolonialism is ambivalent inasmuch as the postcolonial project does not only question the authority of colonial discourse but is also interested in giving those who have previously been marginalized a voice. If poststructuralism/ postmodernism can help with the former, its attitude towards the latter is rather more complicated. Emphasizing the nature of representation as inevitably bound up with ideological formations, postcolonial critics with a postmodern/poststructuralist background often draw attention to the fact that making the Other speak may be an impossible endeavour.[38] For some critics the Other can never be authentically represented but only translated.[39] This may be problematic for an activist stance but allows a more creative representation of Otherness for a literary postcolonialism.

If one follows another school of thinking within postcolonial studies, the emphasis on the irreducible difference of the Other that postcolonialism is concerned with may disguise more than it discloses. Rather than highlighting the ontological difference between colonizer and colonized, Marxists contend that the West and the rest are anything but ontologically different. Materialist criticism, like liberation theology, stresses sameness rather than difference with respect to the nature of colonialism as well as with respect to its end.[40] More precisely, inasmuch as there was mention of difference, this difference was located on a different level: as postcoloniality was understood as part of capitalism, it was not so much an issue of race or ethnicity but of social class. The focus on class had consequences for the use of the term postcolonialism as well as for postcolonial studies in general. First of all, insofar as exploitation did not end with the formal end of colonial rule, the very term postcolonialism was of little analytical value and was, by and large, rejected by these critics. With respect to literary studies, it was pointed out that "what used to be known as 'Third World literature' gets rechristened as 'postcolonial literature' when the governing theoretical framework shifts from Third World nationalism to postmodernism."[41] Behind this scathing indictment was a distinction between an ideal of 'postcolonial' criticism and the way it was practised by those holding positions within the Western academia. The latter were regarded as 'bourgeois subjects' who were complicit with postmodernism as 'the cultural logic of late capitalism.'[42] If Marxists acknowledged a close relationship between the postcolonial and the postmodern, they condemned it as 'false consciousness.' An ideal postcolonial criticism, i.e. a third world criticism, they said, would distance itself from poststructuralism/postmodernism because its activist stance was irreconcilable with nonmaterialist thinking. While poststructuralist/postmodern critics envisaged the remedy for the postcolonial condition in the recognition of difference, Marxists saw the solution to the postcolonial predicament in combat and overthrow. Identifying the poststructuralist/postmodern with the postcolonial was problematic to a Marxist critic because in its lack of a theory of agency poststructuralism/postmodernism helped to obfuscate the very issue at stake in postcolonialism, namely oppression and exploitation. Far from being illuminating, poststructuralism/postmodernism is considered part of the problem for a Marxist and not part of the solution.[43]

In between a politics of radical difference and a yearning for sameness, postcolonial studies increasingly opted for a third way which challenged the fatality of a Manichean logic while retaining a concern for cultural difference as barrier against conceptual hegemonization.[44] Postcolonialism precludes a return to cultural origins, and as the indigenous cultural tradition that colonialism destroyed systematically cannot be recovered, nativist or essentialist attempts at reconstructing that tradition are flawed and thus bound to fail. Colonialism is an aspect of a culture's history that cannot be denied and must be taken into account. While cultural difference continues to be a vital aspect of postcolonial identity construction, it is no longer located in a reverse Manichean divide but in hybridity.[45] Originally, hybridity is a term derived from biology describing the process and product of cross-fertilization. The observation that offsprings of parents belonging to two different species were often infertile—the mule being a case in point—was borrowed by colonial discourse in order to warn against the degeneration that was said to be the result of a mixing of races.[46] However, while hybridity was negatively connotated within colonial discourse, postcolonial studies have reclaimed the term and understand it in a markedly different way.

Hybridity is a heterogeneous concept. In its syncretistic sense, it foregrounds a mixing of diverse cultural influences to a more or less homogeneous new whole. Recent arguments have stressed the dynamics of hybridity as process and thus as infinitely creative. Within such a view, hybridity connotes not so much a fusion of cultures than an opportunity for an individual to draw on the best of a multitude of worlds and thus to escape conceptual restrictions. Discarding the myth of authenticity and purity, culture is not only seen as mutable and inherently diverse but also viewed positively as horizon rather than limitation.[47] In this respect, hybridity has affinities with the diaspora as the space in which hybridity is acted out. In a way similar to hybridity, diaspora is also reclaimed by postcolonial critics. As Stuart Hall astutely points out:

> Diaspora does not refer us to those scattered tribes whose identity can only be secured in relation to some sacred homeland to which they must at all costs return, even if it means pushing other people into the sea. This is the old, the imperializing, the hegemonising, form of 'ethnicity'. [. . .] The diaspora experience as I intend it here is defined, not by essence or purity, but by the recognition of a necessary heterogeneity and diversity, by a conception of 'identity' which lives with and through, not despite, difference; by *hybridity*. Diaspora identities are those which are constantly producing and reproducing themselves anew, through transformation and difference.[48]

The critic whose writings present the most marked as well as most influential departure from a syncretistic and creolizing understanding of hybridity is Homi K Bhabha.[49] Bhabha's work can be read as taking issue with *Orientalism* "because it fails to accommodate the possibility of difference within Oriental discourse."[50] Drawing on Lacanian psychoanalysis, Bakhtinian dialogics and

Derrida's notion of différance, hybridity for Homi Bhabha defies fixed identities which are ordered by binarist categories. Apart from stressing the cultural resourcefulness of hybrid formations, Bhabha foregounds hybridity's potential for resistance. Hybridity is a stance that, far from lacking power, allows for waywardness and cunning to subvert a colonial authority that in a colonial situation needs to cooperate with the Other it marginalizes discursively. Bhabha has shown that colonial discourse can never suppress the Other totally because it consistently fails to reproduce itself in a colonial moment.[51] In such a situation

> the word of divine authority is deeply flawed by the assertion of the indigenous sign, and in the very practice of domination the language of the master becomes hybrid—neither the one thing nor the other. The incalculable colonized subject—half acquiescent, half oppositional, always untrustworthy —produces an unresolvable problem of cultural difference for the very address of colonial authority.[52]

Hybridity undermines the monolithic character of colonial discourse and turns it into a form of heteroglossia. Hybridity can become a source of resistance because in its ambivalence it precludes to draw clear-cut positions between colonizer and colonized. Seeing traces of what is familiar in the Other as well as seeing traces of Otherness in oneself upsets a dichotomous imagination that relies on difference in order to come up with political stability as well as a stable new self-image. While this makes it more difficult for the colonizer to consolidate his identity in the colonies, it opens up possibilities for the Other. By destroying any Manichean divide or, more precisely, by showing that a Manichean divide has always been a colonial fantasy rather than colonial reality, Bhabha draws attention to the fact that seeing in the Other as much sameness as difference opens up possibilities for nonessentialist identity formation.[53]

Supplementing Difference
MG Vassanji

MG Vassanji[1] was born in Nairobi, Kenya, in 1950, brought up in Dar es Salaam, Tanzania, and went to the United States in 1970 to study physics at MIT (SB, 1974). In 1978 he received a PhD in nuclear physics from the University of Pennsylvania and went to Canada. There he became affiliated with Atomic Energy of Canada (1978–80) and with the University of Toronto, where he worked as a research associate and lecturer in physics from 1980 to 1989 and published widely. In 1982 he founded and edited the *Toronto South Asian Review* (*TSAR*), which became the *Toronto Review of Contemporary Writing Abroad* in 1993. His interest in fiction is a long-standing one, and on looking back it seems like a logical consequence for him to have become a full-time writer in 1989. This was also the year his first novel *The Gunny Sack* was published to instant critical acclaim and initiated the long list of books that were successful with the critics. In 1990 *The Gunny Sack* won the Commonwealth Writers Prize for best book in the Africa region. In 1994 MG Vassanji won the Bressani Prize as well as the prestigious Giller Prize for *The Book of Secrets*. Likewise in 1994 he received the Harbourfront Prize in recognition of his achievement as a writer. The same year he was also chosen as one of twelve Canadians on *Maclean's* Honour Roll. In 2003 he won the Giller Prize once again, this time for *The In-Between World of Vikram Lall* (2003). To date Vassanji has published six novels, *The Gunny Sack* (1989), *No New Land* (1991), *The Book of Secrets* (1994), *Amriika* (1999), *The In-Between World of Vikram Lall* (2003), and *The Assassin's Song* (2007), which was a finalist for both the Giller Prize and the Governor General's Award. He has also published two collections of short stories, *Uhuru Street* (1992) and *When She Was Queen* (2005), as well as edited a collection of essays, *A Meeting of Streams: South Asian Canadian Literature* (1985). Vassanji lives in Toronto.

A. 'Here': The Promise of Hybridity. *No New Land* (1991)

At the centre of Vassanji's fiction is the Indian Shamsi community, his fictional rendering of the Gujarati Khojas, traditionally a syncretistic sect combining elements of Shia Islam and Hindu Vaishnavism, and identifying themselves as Ismailis in modern times.[1] Starting out as shopkeepers and businessmen settling on the coast of British and German East Africa, like most other Indians they had supported British Colonial rule. As the narrator of *No New Land* has it,

> the idea of empire was relinquished slowly in the Asian communities. [. . .] The Asians had spawned at least two knights of the empire in their slums, they had had Princess Elizabeth in their midst, greeted Princess Margaret with a tumultuous welcome. They spoke proudly of Churchill and Mountbatten, fondly of Victoria. What schoolboy or girl had not heard over the radio the reassuring chimes of Big Ben before falling asleep, or the terrified voice of Dicken's Pip, the triumphant voice of Portia, the Queen's birthday message.[2]

In postcolonial times, the position of the Indian communities in East Africa became difficult, with policies of Africanization and economic restriction, and the socialism of Nyerere's Tanzania, which was accompanied by the nationalization of rental properties. There was also the outright expulsion of Asians from Uganda by Idi Amin. Many of Tanzania's and Kenya's Asians emigrated overseas.

By narrating the story of the Shamsi community, Vassanji gives voice to a Canadian immigrant experience that hitherto has not found its way into literature and public awareness. *No New Land* illustrates the community's fate in Toronto where Nurdin Lalani emigrates with his family. The protagonist, an average man, is regarded by his father as a useless "good-for-nothing" (19), an underachiever: "One brother making millions in the diamond business, the other making his—so Nurdin had heard—in the black market. Always he, Nurdin, the middle one, neither here nor there" (169). While he is a failure in Africa, Nurdin Lalani is also in an uneasy position in the Canadian diaspora, and *No New Land* can be said to detail "the ironies, the pathos and the hardships of having to live between two worlds, neither of which provides the harmony of a life that the mind imagines and craves for."[3]

No New Land has as its central theme the tension "between assimilation and acculturation to mainstream Canadian culture, versus maintaining some kind of racial or cultural integrity brought over from the old land."[4] Canada is a land of opportunities but at the same time it becomes the space of cultural dislocation. Already at an early stage the novel alludes to the troublesome complexity the Canadian experience is fraught with. Thus the snow that Nurdin and his family encounter on entering Canada becomes metonymic of Otherness:

> Snow had fallen, a blistering wind blew squalls on the road and, as they stepped outside the airport building, it made sails of their ill-fitting second hand clothes, which had seen better days on the backs of colonial bwanas and memsahibs on chilly African evenings. "So this is snow," Zera remarked. It had been cleared into unimpressive mounds and at their feet was a fine powder blown about by reckless gusts. Toes freezing, faces partly paralysed, eyes tearing, they stood outside, shoulders hunched. The two children were moaning and shivering, weeping, hiding behind adult coats, creating fresh pockets and exposing fresher areas of anatomy for the wind to snatch at. (35)

Symbolically, snow foreshadows the emotional coldness of the metropolis rather than the potential of the unknown in realizing ambitions and dreams. Later on, the whiteness of the snow is juxtaposed with the whiteness of the immigration official's colour of skin: "Finally someone welcoming you, a white man welcoming you. Finally a place to lay down your head" (34). While the hostility of the weather anticipates that Canada is a country causing alienation and isolation for Nurdin and his family, the warm reception by a white man immediately triggers colonial fantasies and desires inherent in the psychological dispositions of the members of a colonial elite decolonized against its will. Taken together, the symbolic undercurrent suggests that Canada takes on the paradoxical quality of a dream and a nightmare at the same time. The Canadian diaspora is invested with desire and hope but—with few exceptions—delivers only disappointments and disillusionment. While Canada holds in store many frustrations, Canada can also be said to offer possibilities to the immigrant. However, as will be seen shortly, Nurdin Lalani fails to seize them,[5] which constitutes a major irony in a novel chiefly written in the ironic mode.

A House for Mr Lalani: Accommodation and Adaptation

MG Vassanji's novel conveys the immigrant experience in terms of cultural retention on the one hand and systemic marginalization on the other. After their arrival in Canada, Nurdin and his family have trouble finding accommodation. Eventually they move to Don Mills where various members of the community who have migrated to Canada before now live under appalling circumstances, cherishing the "illusion of 'home' and shelter from an alien society."[6] While Nurdin and his family continue to live in the same way culturally and socially, they overlook the fact that their social networks are confined to an enclave. As Neil Bissondath points out,

> Vassanji's description of this community of exiles—so tight, so self-contained, so alienated from the mainstream—is that of an almost classic ghetto. It is not an extreme of multiculturalism but its ideal: a way of life transported whole, a little outpost of exoticism preserved and protected.[7]

Cultural practices are not translated but simply transplanted to a new cultural context. A case in point is the A-T Shop of Dar which finds its emulation in the community's meeting place in Don Mills (28,71). Nurdin's failures in the new land frequently draw him towards the familiar, i.e. the cultural security that the Canadian simulation of the A-T Shop guarantees.

It is crucial to realize that the novel suggests that Nurdin's mimicry is not merely inauthentic but also inadequate in a new land. This has to do with the assumption of culture Nurdin operates on. The familiarity of Don Mills and the retention of indigenous culture accompanied by it may be comfortable; however, in the context of the novel it is also dangerous because the familiarity offered prevents the immigrant from making an effort to engage with (perhaps even to adapt to) the foreign environment. An understanding of culture as essence is thereby implicitly refuted. Acceptance and mutual understanding among the members of the Shamsi community inside the block of apartments in Don Mills must not supersede the culture outside. Significantly, the agent of the cultural exchange called for here is the individual, and what the text draws our attention to is that the immigrant's participation is an integral part for the utopian potential of Canada, its potential to truly become a new land, to be realized.

It is noteworthy that in the novel the security granted by the culture taken over from East Africa is restricted to a house, a traditional symbol at least in the Western literary tradition of shelter as well as of psycho-social sanity and hygiene. While, psychologically speaking, clearly demarcated fixed abode can serve vital human needs such as, for example, a reduction of complexity, within the perspective of the text the image of the house also indicates a limitation. The danger here is of Don Mills becoming a system of its own, and a system without permeable boundaries at that. If culture is a negotiation, then the Shamsis living in Don Mills fail to recognize the importance of cultural exchange, and thereby run the danger of replicating the purist stance towards culture that characterized the community's attitude in East Africa (71–2). Vassanji implies that in Canada both the culture brought over (and cherished inside) and the culture encountered (and neglected outside) are, in theory, at the immigrant's disposal. However, opting for one, while at the same time discarding the other is revealed to be at worst fatal and at best erroneous. The question as to which side to privilege becomes a pressing one for Nurdin and other members of the South Asian communities of Toronto. It thus seems safe to suggest that at the heart of *No New Land* is the interrogation of how much retention is necessary and unproblematic and how much adaptation is called for and essential in a multicultural context.

While the issue of accommodation has so far been interpreted as a critique of cultural retention on an individual level, Vassanji's novel allows for an alternative reading that sees the reasons for Nurdin's eventual failure to adapt less in individual shortcomings than in structural limitations of the society the protagonist has migrated to. The ghetto of Don Mills can be seen as an aspect of the underside of a Canadian multiculturalism which cannot prevent cultural difference from taking on the aspect of social injustice. The novel would then illustrate that Canada's multicultural policy of cultural unity in cultural diversity may also disguise social gulfs. What is demonstrated in *No New Land* is how social class transforms the ideal of the cultural mosaic into a socio-economic vertical mosaic.[8]

As the next sections will argue, *No New Land* demands a balanced interpretation. The novel enacts the tension between structural/social and individual shortcomings in the multilateral process of adaptation without resolving them. Nurdin and his family do not want to face the new, i.e. Canadian reality, head on. In that they are to be criticized. However, *No New Land* also testifies to the new land's systemic flaws, something which calls for a more complex reading of the migrant experience in Canada. In order to determine the factors that thwart Nurdin's migrant experience, one must take into account that individual and structural shortcomings are equally responsible for his failure. In *No New Land* no reading prevails over the other, both interpretations are true to a certain extent. In fact, the inscription of ambivalence is Vassanji's major artistic achievement in his second novel, as an analysis of the category of race as a marker of difference will illustrate.

A Fearful Symmetry: Racism and Racialism

Nurdin's individual flaw and the structural problems of Canadian multiculturalism overlap in that both rely on race as conceptual tool. There are two instances of racism in *No New Land*. The first concerns Esmail who initially is discriminated against and eventually beaten up in a Toronto subway station (95–8). His fate attracts the attention of the media, and the nobody Esmail becomes a celebrity, a somebody. Cynically enough, not until he is victimized does he receive the recognition of his Canadian host society. Due to the racism of an allegedly nonracist Canada, Esmail begins to paint indigenous masks and thereby makes ethnic difference his one and only artistic theme. Racial violence triggers a return to indigenous art as a means of coping with aggressive Othering. Speaking about the inspiration for Esmail's coming out as an artist, Jamal and Nanji comment: "'Dar didn't do it—Canada did.' 'By breaking his legs, you mean'" (164).

By being violently discriminated against, the hitherto apolitical Esmail is politicized and leaves Canada for the country of his birth, Tanzania, while continuing to paint. His return to his origins is not only an aesthetic endeavour, it also has an additional dimension in that it brings about a valorization of (his) community as well as a valorization by his community, the Shamsis. Not only has his art benefitted from his return home, Esmail's apocalyptic self-expression is apparently better understood by the members of the community he belongs to than by a Canada that rejects his works as aesthetically inferior. When connected to their socio-cultural context, the masks he paints acquire additional layers of meaning insofar as they have a particular cultural/ritual function within Tanzanian society. The fact that Esmail's art has not been understood by Canada reflects not only how impoverished his art has seemed to a first world audience but also how rootless he himself is in North America. In this context, his new role as an artist preoccupied with a community's culture and collective memory also has a therapeutic function.

If Esmail ends his dislocation and disorientation by giving up his struggle to make Canada home, it must not be concluded that his story is that of a failure. For one thing, Esmail becomes a positive foil for the equally traumatized protagonist Nurdin Lalani because he manages to cure himself while Nurdin's trauma will only be therapied with external help. A second, perhaps more important reason that should prevent us from regarding Esmail as a failure is money. While his story, due to the structural shortcomings of a Canadian multicultural policy, is that of a thwarted adaptation, Esmail succeeds economically. Ironically enough, as a human being, Esmail is rejected in Canada because of his ethnic difference; as an artist working in and about Africa he is eventually embraced by an international postcolonial art history establishment eagerly responding to the ethnic difference reflected in his works: "Students—American students, nice pretty girls—go and study this art" (163). While Canadian culture has failed him by aggressively harping on his alleged essential difference, racism proves a blessing in disguise at least moneywise. Involuntarily, Esmail is made to discover the cultural capital inherent in the very difference constructed to marginalize him.

While Canada has operated on the Judeo-Christian understanding of Esmail as the archetypal outcast, Esmail's country of origins celebrates him and thereby faintly echoes (albeit for different reasons) the worshipping of his ancient namesake within an Islamic tradition.[9] The allusiveness of his name makes evident that Esmail's fate is encoded in two different ways which, in turn, correlate to two different cultural frames of reference. Inherent in his name is the promise of a double vision guaranteed by a diaspora experience, but the point is that this is something that the novel denies Esmail. Admittedly, his fate, unlike that of Nurdin, does not end in an impasse in-between cultures;

however, his experience of cultural diversity does not result in a hybrid existence either. Esmail's return to East Africa as well as his traditionalist understanding of art may signal a new belonging beyond dichotomies and ambivalence, but within the perspective of the novel the new awareness of difference underlying Esmail's success is not unproblematic either. Esmail's choice is the underside of an aggressive politics of Othering that has become a beacon in its critique of multiculturalism. Ethnic difference, enacted merely in the realm of art, can be read as a strategy of survival which, in spite of its inarticulateness, speaks eloquently about a Canadian society in which the possibility of transculturalism is aggressively ousted.

While Esmail's fate provides the dramatic climax of the plot, Vassanji also narrates the fates of those who experience racism on a lesser, i.e. less violent, scale. A case in point is Nurdin Lalani desperately seeking employment. In spite of being sufficiently qualified (as a seller of shoes), he is offered only menial jobs, in which, ironically enough, he as an Other is discriminated against by other immigrants, this time of East European as well as of Asian descent (86–7). Strikingly, Toronto's multicultural reality does not foster solidarity among those on the margin of society but presents itself as competition instead. Given the racial discrimination experienced in multicultural East Africa, Canada cannot appear as a new land. In addition to blatant prejudice, Nurdin also encounters a more subtle form of racism inherent in Canadian society. The absurdity of Nurdin's humiliating quest for a job is epitomized in the employers' recurring demand for "Canadian experience" (48). For Nurdin this is a catch-22 situation, and Vassanji goes to great lengths in order to outline the absurdity of his protagonist's endeavour to obtain something that is the prerequisite of itself: Canadian experience becomes a "trump they always call, against which you have no answer" (44). Nurdin's search for a job becomes a low-key quest that turns in on itself and becomes circular. And it is precisely the circular trajectory of his endeavours that causes Nurdin's despair. Cynically speaking, Canadian experience takes on a new quality; it does not translate as work experience in a new cultural surrounding but as constant exposure to racial discrimination. This is a feature of Canadian society that makes integration a feat particularly hard to accomplish. Nurdin's failure to find an occupation that is not beneath contempt forces him into a vicious circle: Being without a job erodes his personal identity as breadwinner and head of the family; the fact that his wife does find a job erodes his personal identity as husband and father. Thus the new land alienates him from those that have hitherto provided an antidote against alienation, i.e. the members of his family:

> Out of this world Nurdin would wander in search of a job and return dejected, plunged into deeper despair. Sometimes he took daily jobs,

> invariably menial, loading and unloading with fellow Dar immigrants, and would come home and lie and say 'filing', until that became a joke. Everyone knew what 'filing' meant. Sometimes he simply refused to go out to these humiliations, watching game shows and talk shows at home, and joining the 'A-T' crowd of idle men who met for chitchat and tea downstairs in the lobby in emulation of Dar's famous A-T Shop. On his idle day, in the afternoons he would clean up at home, sweeping away evidence of any degeneracy, giving the television time enough to cool. You could be sure that Fatima on one pretext or another, or when you were not looking, would detect any telltale residual warmth on its body. And when she did—did the girl show contempt already at this stage. (65f.)

No New Land illustrates that what to the racist looks like culturally ingrained laziness is in fact socially instilled depression. Rejection causes dejection, marginalization leaves self-consciousness where integration should foster self-confidence. Taken together the disappointments and humiliations that Nurdin experiences bring about an unwillingness to adapt culturally. He must remain an alien because he is profoundly alienated by a new land that does not embrace the Other because it feels braced by the Other.

A further indicator that Nurdin's Otherness is in fact socially produced is the second climax of the novel. In the novel's central episode Nurdin is accused of having raped a woman whom he encounters on his way home from work:[10]

> As he approached the small lobby facing the two elevators, he saw in front of him a girl in blue jeans sitting on the floor, leaning against the side wall. Her legs were drawn up in front of her, her hands hung limp on the raised knees, and her head was lowered. Obviously she had been crying, the blonde hair was dishevelled, the face—what he could see of it—was puffy and red.
>
> Instinctively he hurried towards her, parking the trolley on the way. "Madam—Miss—is anything wrong? Can I be of any help?"
>
> There was no response. He looked up again, turned round, there was no one coming. He tried again. "Miss, shall I call a doctor?"
>
> He was almost squatting beside her now, his hand was on her shoulder. He realized he had never been so close to a white woman before. And he realized he had become aware of her femaleness. He caught, quite strongly, the whiff of creamy makeup. Her blouse was white, embroidered at the neck. A button was open and he could see the curve of a breast. The skin there was pale, almost white, and dull. He was waiting for her to respond to his offer of help. (178)

It becomes evident that Nurdin is still regarded as an Other; the fact that the Portuguese Canadian girl attempts to sue him for attempted rape is indicative of Nurdin's vulnerable status as a visible minority. Not only does Nurdin (as seen above) fail to accommodate to Canada, Canada also fails to accommodate Nurdin. For Canada, Nurdin is merely a threat and thus a burden at this point. Thus Canada, despite its multicultural policy, fails to realize that Nurdin's difference is also a cultural resource. For a land that prides itself on its multicultural ethos this is a remarkable failure.

Nurdin's skin colour becomes the target of lower-class racism propelled by frustration and greed. Not only is the girl's attempt at blackmail deliberately racist, but the reactions of Nurdin's colleagues are characterized by instantly establishing a connection between sexual desire and racial difference that is nothing short of racist, too:

> "I'm not going to serve this rapist!" she [i.e. Nurdin's colleague] said, running away.
>
> "I thought in this country a man was innocent until proved guilty," said Romesh, to no one in particular.
>
> "Where he comes from, both his hands would be chopped off, announced Mrs Broadbent. "Yes, and—"
>
> "And his marbles, too," added Romesh. (180)

The rape Nurdin is associated with is allusive in that it reflects fantasies of infiltration and disintegration circulating within colonial discourse. In that sexual difference functions not only as equivalent for the cultural Other but also as a sign of the essence of one's own culture, Vassanji's text suggests that colonial discourse continues into postcolonial times. Mrs Broadbent articulates a moral panic that establishes a connection between visible difference and Orientalism.[11] Nurdin's racial and religious difference becomes suspect because it is assumed that the Other, i.e. in this context the African-Indian and Muslim, is lewd at heart and, in addition to that, cannot contain his lewdness. Ironically, in her claim for punishment Mrs Broadbent is convinced of understanding the Other on his own terms. She suggests that Canada is just in that it prevents the criminal from having to suffer traditional punishments. However, what she really does is 'understand' Nurdin along lines dictated by colonial/racial discourse. The punishment that Nurdin would allegedly have to suffer "where he comes from" is informed by the antimodernist prejudice of the West about Islam. Not only is chopping off hands not the punishment that the Koran prescribes for rape, but it is something that has not been practised as punishment for thieves for a long time.[12] Thus in a perfidious, albeit unconscious, move Mrs Broadbent's claim displays Canadian racism and not

Canadian justice to the unjust and thus contains rather than embraces Otherness. Her blaming Nurdin is not only inadequate; in revealing her racist assumptions it also says more about her than about Nurdin. The same holds true for the police, who questions Nurdin and suspects him of being responsible for a variety of other crimes, too (181). The fact that Nurdin is almost brought to court reflects a multiculturalism underpinned by prejudices and a desire for segregation. A society capable of invoking the law to act out hidden fears of the Other is anything but tolerant and plural. By virtue of the variety of pressures and prejudices that the Other is exposed to, multiculturalism rears its ugly head. It takes on an aggressive form and faces the Other as "multivulturalism" (111). Metaphorically, Nurdin falls indeed prey to a multicultural reality that is nothing short of voracious. One could also say: Canadian multiculturalism feeds on the notion of the immigrant as Other and thereby of necessity fosters racism instead of actively opposing it.

Vassanji's novel endows Nurdin's story with an ironic twist. While Nurdin's offer for assistance is characterized by genuine empathy, the event is suffused with ambivalence. For his initial impulse to help the apparently injured girl is complemented by a fatal, i.e. sexual, attraction. Ironically, Nurdin's desire is in itself racialist. It is not or not merely the attractiveness of the girl that fascinates Nurdin; the novel leaves no doubt that for Nurdin her attractiveness is connected to the colour of her skin. The adjectives "white" or "pale" surface several times in Vassanji's description of the encounter and testify to Nurdin's hidden fantasies barely checked by a superego that is under constant strain in face of an alien Canadian culture. The nexus between sexual tension and colour of skin is reminiscent of an event in his father's life that involved a similar encounter with a German woman in Tanzania:

> One day a young fräulein stopping over at the mission came into the shop to look for gifts for her servants in the European settlement of Wilhelmstal up north, whence she came. She carried a parasol and had the most delicate features. As she stepped in from the glare of sunlight outside, it took a while for her presence to materialize in the relative darkness inside the shop, where Haji Lalani sat with his servant. The girl was accompanied by one of the fathers, who stopped at the doorway to chat, and a servant girl who carried her shopping. As the fräulein raised her arm to point to a string of beads hanging from a nail, Haji found himself staring at her—she was flushed with the heat, her face lightly perspiring, and her armpit a delicate wet patch—and he felt the faint stirrings of a desire inside him. They did not go very far, in fact he would have quashed these forbidden thoughts there and then had not his face been brought alive by a stinging slap from the girl's hand. (14)

Nurdin is clearly unaware of this episode and its implication for himself as someone who has not managed to sever his ties to his father and is thus perpetually and self-consciously ridden by guilt. The irony inherent in the novel's structure suggests that the sins of the father come to haunt the son regardless of time and place. Nurdin and Haji are fascinated by white in a way paradigmatically outlined by Fanon in *Black Skin, White Masks*. In his psychoanalytical/postcolonial analysis of the relationship between colonizer and colonized, Fanon, who implicitly calls for conceiving the colonial encounter also in terms of sexual difference, writes about the relationship between the black man and the white woman: "I [i.e. the black man] marry white culture, white beauty, white whiteness. When my restless hands caress those white breasts, they grasp white civilization and dignity and make them mine."[13] For Fanon the black man's desire is the result of an inferiority complex. Thus desire is symptomatic and compensatory at the same time. Racial difference becomes sexually attractive precisely because it becomes metonymic of a perceived cultural superiority that the Other wants to partake of. For Fanon the nexus between race and skin colour is a structural problem, and Haji's and Nurdin's desire would thus be representative of any colonial encounter between black and white in general. By connecting cultural difference with sexual difference Nurdin Lalani displays a yearning for another culture that is clearly neurotic. So far *No New Land* pursues a Fanonian reading. However, the novel adds a personal dimension by shifting the focus away from the systemic shortcomings of a racist society towards individual flaws, i.e. in this case towards Nurdin's traumatic relationship to his father. Nurdin's identification with his father and his father's view of the world impedes his identification with Canadian culture.

Summing up, Vassanji shows that neither Nurdin nor his environment is free from an understanding of Otherness informed by race as a category of difference. While the society is to blame in that it does not pay attention to the individual but to his/her colour of skin, Nurdin himself is also partly responsible for his situation in that he operates on inadequate and unacceptable cultural assumptions. While Canada is racist, i.e. does not even refrain from a violent assertion of racial difference, Nurdin is at least racialist, i.e. he thinks in terms of race even if he does not act aggressively because of race. However, in the final analysis, not even the fact that Nurdin's racialism remains unconscious while Canadian multicultural society acts out its racist prejudices can alter the pervasiveness of ambivalence tied up with the immigrant experience in *No New Land*. On the contrary, the ambivalence constituted by the ubiquity of race as a concept instrumental in ordering the world enhances the irony of Vassanji's novel. For Nurdin and Canada to draw on race as conceptual tool closes the gap between Self and Other precisely where one would not have wished for it. In other words, race becomes the axis of a symmetry that is fearful because it reflects the worst of both worlds. It is a symmetry that in its fearfulness no one in *No New Land* dares to frame. Unless racism and racialism are contained, Vassanji seems to suggest, Otherness will not be (truly) embraced.

Look Back in Guilt: Sexuality and Spirituality

Although Nurdin's fascination with the Portuguese woman is racialist rather than libidinous, there is abundant evidence that he is a man harbouring repressed erotic desires. Nurdin's eroded identity as a man almost makes him succumb to the temptation of an affair with a woman he knows from his time in Dar. Ironically, his flaw as a character, i.e. lust, does not seem to be a problem in a liberal Canada. As a matter of fact, the one relationship with a woman that makes him happy, because it is fulfilling, is with Sushila, a Hindu outcast girl he knows from Dar, and not with his wife Zera. His only attempt to break out of his miserable Canadian existence takes the value system of the liberal Western world for granted but is enacted as nostalgia for the unrealized possibilities of the past,—except that they had never been possibilities in the first place, for to marry an untouchable would have been out of the question for a member of Haji Lalani's family. Ironically enough, what would thus not have been possible in Dar, i.e. to marry an outcast girl, is bound to fail in Canada, too, albeit for different reasons: while it fails in Dar because of social barriers, it fails in Canada precisely because of the absence of any comparable social constraints. At the heart of this paradox is the fact that Nurdin in trying to make a Western/Canadian experience, i.e. an affair, happen on Shamsi terms is haunted by guilt: "With someone like her you could do anything, not be afraid to go anywhere. He realized the illegitimacy of the thought, the hidden desire it contained" (173). Nurdin is plagued by guilt in the course of his affair with Sushila because he still operates on the value system he was brought up on. As the author of *No New Land* himself has it, "he [Nurdin] wants to reach out, but his past doesn't let him go."[14] Anthropologically speaking, Nurdin's native culture as a set of rules for finding his way around in his home society considerably complicates orientation when taken over into another society. Moreover, not only does it practically preclude orientation, it will of necessity cause disorientation as well. This disorientation results from conflicting impulses which prevent Nurdin from fully belonging to the past and the 'there' as well as to the present and the 'here.' Nurdin's position is that of a displaced subject that is unable to define his position in relation to place and time. He is operating outside clearly defined categories of spatial and temporal deixis because in his affiliations he is awkwardly and uncomfortably partaking of two mutually exclusive space and time schemes in which a Canadian here and now clash with a mythical Tanzanian there and then.

In exploring what makes for a home, it becomes evident that alienation from the sphere of religion is a prominent feature of the Lalanis' diaspora experience. For Nurdin and his wife, Canada is not only a segregated country but also a secular one. Both of them are conscious of their actions in an alien environment that is experienced as potentially threatening. Because religion used to be a core aspect of the Lalanis' subject status, Canada by way of its secular nature constitutes a danger to Nurdin's and Zera's identity. Interestingly enough, however, both react differently to the threat Canada constitutes. While Zera becomes increasingly inward looking and compensates a secular universe by piety and obedience to the community's spiritual leader, ironically called Missionary (138), Nurdin becomes paranoid. He suspects sin everywhere but, in marked contrast to his wife, does not react by taking recourse to metaphysics as an antidote against temptation. Rather his attitude towards Canada is ambivalent in that he is also fascinated by what he fears. Cases in point are food (pork) and drink (alcohol) but also, as outlined above, sexual licentiousness. All three are traditionally forbidden to Nurdin by his religious socialization; all three of them, however, become temptations in the context of Canadian culture. By eroding the religious foundation of Nurdin's culture, his own moral standards do not simply become questionable; Nurdin's Canada experience is characterized by considerable disenchantment because any morality is eventually felt to be arbitrary by the protagonist. Put differently, the fascination with promiscuity instils in Nurdin the unsettling postmodern idea that every value system is relative: "It was enough to destabilize you forever, question all the inhibitions and prohibitions of childhood and youth—do this, don't do that: who had thought them up?" (145)

Vassanji finds an apt image for Nurdin's spiritual estrangement from his faith. On a symbolic level, the tower of the mosque is replaced for Nurdin by Toronto's CN Tower, with 533 metres the highest free-standing structure in the world. However, instead of offering spiritual guidance, the tower becomes a symbol of secularization as well as capitalist alienation. The mosque as the place where Allah is worshipped is replaced by a radio and TV communications tower with a restaurant on top. Thus the sacred is replaced by the profane. Moreover, in contrast to the tower of a mosque, the CN Tower remains mute and merely sends light beeps that remain a mystery to Nurdin. Hence what is worshipped in Canada presupposes a sign system different from the one Nurdin is able to decode. Cultural Otherness presents itself as an instance of unreadability. Unreadability, however, constitutes an aspect of spirituality that Nurdin is not familiar with.

At the same time, the CN Tower, which on a clear day allows seeing for almost 200 kilometres while on hazy day does not offer a view at all, stands for hope and yearning.[15] By way of intertextual reference to *The Great Gatsby*,[16] the tower's lights resemble for Nurdin what the green lights of West Egg are for Jay Gatsby. According to the novel's narrator,

> Gatsby believed in the green light, the orgastic future that year by year recedes before us. It eluded us then, but that's no matter—tomorrow we will run faster, stretch out our arms further . . . And one fine morning—So we beat on, boats against the current, borne back ceaselessly into the past.[17]

As the green light signals, hope is not immediately present but spatially and temporarily removed. Nurdin and Gatsby, both worshippers in a secular universe, yearn for a different time and place, and thus cherish illusions. The past that haunts them both as well as the dreams that both hunt render Gatsby's and Lalani's endeavours problematic. While Nurdin eventually realizes that what he is worshipping is a chimera, Gatsby does not stop believing in the power of the past to exert its influence on the future. That is why Nurdin's story ends on a positive key, whereas the story of Gatsby ends tragically. While Nurdin is an antihero, which thus precludes identification at least to a certain extent, Gatsby's potential for the reader's identification lies in his unfaltering belief in his ideals, however questionable they may be.

Vassanji suggests reading his postcolonial novel as a coming-of-age story, or a postcolonial bildungsroman. For Nurdin the sinfulness of the Western world is a cause of guilt. The authority that he fears is not, however, a transcendent God but his own father. While Nanji is "alone, adrift and floating" (99) because he has had too little of his parents, Nurdin is adrift and floating because he has had too much of them. His initial failure to establish himself in the new world thus appears as a failure to sever his attachments to the old country. In Neil Bissoondath's words:

> Bitter-sweet descriptions of Dar es Salaam offer a nostalgic vision of the past and make the present even darker than it really is, emphasizing the central point that there are, as the title states, no new lands, only new circumstances.[18]

It is only after Missionary, the novel's "deus ex machina,"[19] has managed to exorcise Nurdin's trauma by way of a role play that he can hope for a new life in a new land (196). Although in a sense he has merely replaced one father figure for another, the mock trial presided over by Missionary wearing his father's fez has led to a demystification of the past that is crucial for a regeneration of the present and a brighter view of the future: "In one stroke that photograph on the wall had lost all potency, its once accusing eyes were now blank, its expression dumb. Suddenly they were here, in the modern world, laughing at the past" (197). The exorcism of his father has brought about a shedding of old cultural conventions that is responsible for the optimistic outlook with which the novel ends.[20] The parameters of the old are finally open to modification:

> Before, the past tried to fix you from a distance, and you looked away; but Missionary had brought it across the chasm, vivid, devoid of mystery. Now it was all over you. And with this past before you, all around you, you take on the future more evenly matched. (207)

It is not so much cultural amnesia that is regarded as the key to successful adaptation but a putting of the old into perspective. Vassanji's revisionism suggests that Canada is not only no new land because of racial discrimination (which the Asians of East Africa have been exposed to ever since they settled in Tanzania, Kenya, and elsewhere); it essentially resembles the old land because of the rigidity of Nurdin's psychological disposition. From that perspective, the success of the immigrant in Canada depends not on Canada's multicultural policy alone; arguably, the decisive factors are less external circumstances than the conditions of the immigrant's psyche instead. Once the father, allegorically representing the past, is challenged, *No New Land* can become a successful coming-of-age story for the son.

The (Ab-)Uses of Difference: Age and Marginality

It has been argued that overcoming the law of the father is of key importance for the immigrant's successful adaptation to a new environment. In this context is crucial to perceive that MG Vassanji connects immigration and generation, thereby pointing towards a difference often overlooked in a post-colonial context. *No New Land* suggests that adaptation has less to do with social standing or race—it underlines the importance of age as marker of difference.[21]

Generally speaking, it is the young in Vassanji's novel that by shrugging off "the restraints of ethnicity"[22] manage to forge out a living for themselves in the diaspora far easier than Nurdin and Zera. While Fatima's and Hanif's parents are stuck in Don Mills, their children will head for a university education. They socialize without visible problems and learn to speak the host language without any noticeable accent. Vassanji seems to be of the opinion that immigration is a step which does not automatically lead to adaptation. As the narrator has it: "We are but creatures of our origins, and however stalwartly we march forward, paving new roads, seeking new worlds, the ghosts from our pasts stand not far behind and are not easily shaken off" (9). Adaptation is a time-consuming process for people like Nurdin and may not be accomplished at all. While Nurdin has to struggle, those young enough to identify naturally will manage to adapt more smoothly and will make the system accommodate them more readily.[23]

It would be a gross distortion of the facts to claim that adaptation for the young in *No New Land* is to be had without paying a price.[24] Adaptation is a process in the course of which, for example, family structures will be affected because the speed and ease of integration is markedly different for the old and the young. Not only does Nurdin have to experience how his daughter seeks and finds a new role model in the widely travelled intellectual Nanji, a lecturer at the University of Toronto, he also has to stomach that his children turn from the community they have been brought up in/by:

> For the crime of being her father when he wasn't anything like what she had in mind. She was ashamed of this little Paki-shitty-stan of Don Mills, as she called it. She didn't belong here, she would pull herself out of this condition: everything about her attitude suggested that. She would rise to where they had neither the courage nor the ability to reach. Where had she picked up this abrasiveness, this shrillness, this hatred of her origins? (167)

For Fatima as a representative of the second generation, the emigration/immigration experience is no longer centrally concerned with nostalgia, guilt, disorientation and memory work. It is the offsprings of the first generation, in other words the young, who manage to conform to Bissoondath's demand that immigration is about renewal.[25] Fatima's loyalties are no longer with the Shamsis, she affiliates with Canada, which can therefore become a new land for her. Fatima Lalani stands for "the distancing of the next generation."[26] The progress made by her generation is that ironically enough she can sever the ties from her father in a way that her father had never managed to do with his father.

The price to be paid in the course of adaptation and assimilation also has repercussions on a different level, that of ethics. When we take a look at the strategies by way of which Fatima Lalani constructs an identity by defining as different what used to be same, the problematic aspects of her Othering becomes evident. That Fatima does not only turn from but even against the Shamsis becomes explicit when she draws on racist prejudice circulating in Canada in order to underline her difference from the community. Ironically and sadly, the strategies employed by her to signal her difference from the Shamsis are virtually identical to those used by the racists beating up Esmail, which raises the question as to how we are to judge her behaviour. Clearly Fatima is not a racist in the sense that she systematically employs stereotypes on an Us-Them logic in order to marginalize one group at the cost of another. Drawing on Gayatri Spivak's influential terminology, Fatima's use of race can be called strategic racism. Strategic racism in Fatima's case would count as the personal attempt to liberate herself from what she perceives as the constraints of the Shamsi community.[27] Nevertheless, while her use of strategic racism forms an insular instance rather than part of a more systematic abuse, her behaviour remains morally inacceptable, and she cannot be exculpated on the basis of what she pursues.

By presenting us with Fatima's turn against her community, which is motivated by her feeling that it is no longer *her* community, Vassanji demonstrates that the diaspora debases the importance of collectives. Implicitly, this is also a refusal of (Canadian) multiculturalism as a policy that assumes that the notion of community is indispensable and of prime importance. Canada for Fatima is not a country where identity hinges upon belonging to a community and a tradition. As a matter of fact, identity is conceived in a radically different way by Fatima Lalani. For her identity is dynamic. It is not filiation that determines identity; identity is a matter of construction that defies stasis.[28] Put differently, identity relies on affiliations rather than a stable and unchanging tradition. Not surprisingly, this is a point on which the generations in Vassanji's novel differ. One could say: Canada is a postmodern country where pluralism is saluted by the young as liberation and opportunity while it is lamented as alienation and disenchantment by the old.

While anthropologically the parameters of orientation provided by culture are still flexible or fluid enough in the young to change with a change of surroundings, the old in *No New Land* can only compensate by a conscious effort. Interestingly enough, there is only one other group of people that make it in Canada apart from the young generation. It is those who have already occupied marginal positions in the homeland that are at an advantage in the diaspora. Outsiders like Jamal or Sushila are the new marginal men, i.e. those flexible enough to be open to and eager on innovation. In the context of the novel, the marginal men/women are those who have less trouble in rejecting the culture they have been brought up on. Thus Sushila has been able to escape the limitations of caste which have been particularly restricting for her as an untouchable. For her Canada equals freedom from community and gender constraints (154). Life in Canada enables Sushila to pursue her dreams of acquiring a higher education. In that respect, she emphasizes not so much the tolerance (or intolerance) of Canadian multiculturalism but stresses the freedom of opportunities traditionally associated with the myth of America as a country in which everyone regardless of (racial, social, gender) difference can make it.

For Jamal, a way in the new world is synonymous with a career as a lawyer. Jamal can prevent the new land from becoming the old because he radically privileges the new over the old. He is unscrupulous insofar as he opportunistically pays attention to the conventions of the old society only when it is to his advantage. While Jamal cannot risk offending the community's spiritual leader, his affiliation is only temporary and thus strategic (189). The same holds true for his marriage. At the same time that he rejects the old, he pragmatically accepts the new, i.e. his marriage to a Canadian girl, as part and parcel of his will to success and social rise:

> First he married a "good" girl: respectable and educated, practical and with both feet planted on the ground as only a Dar girl could be, with whom he could talk—as he told Nanji—as only with a Dar girl. But she was English. Young and average-looking, tending to plumpness (114).

His marriage is "a rite of passage" (114) into mediocrity that is an initiation into respectability at the same time. Loyalty to the community appears as an old state of mind/living that is shed. Ironically, Jamal's wife changes her name from Nancy to Nasim (160), thereby implicitly countering his Westernization by Indianization on her part. Both Jamal and Nancy, however, subscribe to notions of identity as change and negotiation and refute claims to cultural essentialism as the basis for identity.

Jamal can keep his distance to the Shamsis because success in Canada depends less on belonging to a community than on individual achievements. The tragic fate of Jamal's father who has been ostracised by the community because in his scientific publications he did not pay attention to the constraints of the community has been insightful to Jamal (72–3). Like Fatima, he turns against his community deliberately, and, significantly enough, the leitmotif of racial prejudice against the Shamsis in calling them Pakis is also reflected in his discourse. Referring to the Shamsis cooking in Don Mills he says: "These Pakis! Cooking twenty-four hours a day!" (71) Instances of community construction like remembering, story telling and keeping alive indigenous traditions are counterproductive for Jamal. However, that too little indigenous culture can be as dangerous to questions of identity is something that does not occur to him, which renders his story profoundly ambivalent.

Conclusion: Difference and Cultural Exchange

No New Land seems equivocal in its evaluation of cultural difference. Some of the novel's characters, such as Fatima, Hanif, Susheila and Jamal, view assimilation as entirely positive. Moreover, some, e.g. Nanji and Sushila, manage to assimilate without giving offence to others, i.e. without treading on the culture and community they were born into. That not all of those who adapt to a new land easily are lifted onto a higher ontological level is demonstrated by Jamal who prefers to be forgetful of the past in order to effect a smoother adaptation. If there is a conflict in *No New Land* as to whether assimilation or cultural retention should be opted for by the migrant in a diaspora situation, then the novel opts for hybridity as a third way. The evidence here is the novel's protagonist. While the Canadian host society conceptualizes cultural difference as a threat to a woman's virginity, Nurdin's sexually charged perception of others is reductive and thus inadequate, too. Vassanji projects identity as a process in the course of which a desire for Otherness, conveyed in terms of sex/gender difference, has to be abandoned. As Victor Ramraj asserts, "Vassanji sanctions efforts at assimilation and syncretism on the part of the diasporic community."[29] In that sense, the novel is not the gloomy and depressing text signalled by the title. In fact, Nurdin undergoes a development from a person traumatized by his personal history to a person who sees the necessity of intercultural exchange. Maintaining a fine balance between remembering and forgetting, Nurdin at the end of the novel is free to follow Vassanji's advice of as to how to deal with displacement productively: "You acknowledge the past and you move forward."[30] After Missonary has paved the way for a more adequate attitude towards the Canadian host culture, Nurdin is free to face Canada as a new land. That hybridity is only a promise and not a reality yet is not least of all the fault of a Canadian multicultural society that has so far failed to address the problem of racism and thus impedes the immigrant's identification with its culture. However, in the final analysis, recognising the difficulties of identity construction in the Canadian diaspora does not question the fundamental value of hybridity and cultural exchange that the novel subscribes to.

B. 'There': Transforming Difference. *The Book of Secrets* (1994)

The Book of Secrets likewise emphasizes cultural exchange and hybridity; in its view on the nature of cultural difference and identity construction it is similar to *No New Land*. *The Book of Secrets* is a novel of the in-between that explores the border between the self and the Other, between giving voice and remaining silent, between the centre and the periphery as well as between the pure and the hybrid. Vassanji's text is located at the intersection between story and history, between the fictional and the factual as well as between realism and the representational character of all art. *The Book of Secrets* is a postcolonial as well as a postmodern novel,[1] albeit in a distinct form deserving and demanding careful scrutiny. I will argue that while postmodern discourse is utilized to corroborate a postcolonial concern with difference, difference is eventually transformed by way of storytelling.

Postmodernism I: Historiography, Imagination and Representation

Pius Fernandes, the protagonist of *The Book of Secrets*, is a former schoolteacher who has worked for several decades at a community school in the former German colony and British protectorate of Tanzania. In 1988 Pius accidentally gets hold of the diary of Alfred Corbin, a British colonial officer who has served many years in various East African colonies. Immediately before the outbreak of World War I he is District Administrator in Kikono and Moshi. Corbin's diary interests and inspires Pius personally as well as professionally. He sets out to write a scholarly history of Tanzania from the end of the German colonial rule to the end of the 1980s.

The diary introduces Pius and Vassanji's readers to the local Indian, African, and Arab communities. It also familiarises us with the central characters Mariamu and Pipa. Reading the novel, it is striking that while Pipa is given abundant scope, Vassanji denies Mariamu an independent voice. At the same time, there is no denying the fact that she is at the centre of the fictional universe Vassanji creates. In fact, she becomes an obsession for Pius's/Vassanji's main character Pipa as well as for Pius himself. The secret that the title of Vassanji's novel alludes to refers to a gap in Mariamu's biography. Apparently, Mariamu on being married to Pius is no longer a virgin. When she conceives, the question arises as to who is the father of her child. The text, however, resists a definitive answer to that question, just as it refuses to shed light on the circumstances of Mariamu's death. In the course of the novel, Pius becomes involved in the history he is about to write. We learn that he has fallen in love with Rita who at that time is married to Mariamu's son Ali. Moreover, Pius finds out that he is linked to his historiographical project through an English friend and fellow teacher, Robert Gregory, who is friendly with Corbin and his wife.

Pius's historiographical project originates with the diary of Alfred Corbin. The fact that the starting point for Pius's history is a diary is significant. First of all, a diary is a discontinuous genre that does not need markers of cohesion or plotting of any kind and can display considerable temporal gaps. A diary is not only a form of describing events, it also is a highly selective and eclectic text which credits only those events with the status of memorable facts that its writer deems worth recording. The function of a diary is to record and order events, and thus to discipline reality for an individual. Insofar as the unity of the diary is provided by the unity of the writing subject, it could be argued that a diary lends itself to psychohistory more readily than to the writing of public history: a diary is an exploration of a person's character rather than a reliable access to the past.

It should not be overlooked that while the genre of the diary as such is always discontinuous, discontinuity in the case of Corbin's diary figures in other respects also. The diary comes upon Pius as a fragment. Entire pages are missing, while others are barely legible. He makes attempts at reconstructing the accounts in Corbin's diary by inserting sections between two separate entries and speculating on the possible meaning of corrupt or elliptic syntactic structures. An extract from *The Book of Secrets* can serve to illustrate this:

> And this was what appeared to the new ADC as he approached the town: fleeting glimpses caught between bush and tree and anthill—a figure draped in white, dashing from left to right, cutting across his path in the distance. It could have been a man in kanzu but for the black hair flying, the lithe movement, the nimble step . . . then a red head-cover over the hair to complete the female figure. So amazed was he by the sight that he had stopped to watch. She disappeared behind an incline, where he was told lay the settlement . . .
>
> 25 March
>
> . . . a mound really, of red earth, covered sparsely with the predominant vegetation of the area, namely thorn. Soon after that apparition disappeared, into one side of it, as it were, there emerged from the other side and directly in front of us a party lead by a white man in sun helmet [. . .].[2]

Pius, faced with a fragmented entry, narrates at length what could have happened before Corbin has a fleeting glimpse of the veiled woman. In order to establish cohesion, the process of reading the diary becomes inseparable from commenting on it. Thus subsequent diary entries require Pius to infer a possible or probable connection. Corbin's entry from 3 March 1913 mentions the Mombasa club, while the entry from the previous day ends with Corbin's arrival in Kenya (14–6). The nexus between both events has to be filled in order to enable a coherent story, and it is only Pius's imagination that can interpolate the gaps within Corbin's discourse. The need to imagine what could have happened becomes even more pressing when entries are separated by a considerable time span. This is illustrated by the entries of 4 March 1913 and 17 March 1913, which in their cryptic nature demand editorial intervention (16–22). In the first entry, Corbin writes about a tour around Mombasa, while in the latter we learn that he is already posted to the small town of Kikono. Pius guesses that in the meantime Corbin must have met Maynard. While his textual intervention provides this necessary bit of information, it should not be overlooked that it does provide it in a specific form: Pius presents a scenic version of Corbin's encounter with Maynard and offers their conversation in direct speech. In rendering a scenic presentation of their meeting, the time of the action and the time of the narration become identical, the ultimate effect of which is the creation of suspense.

For Pius the writing of history is concomitant with embedding Corbin's diary. Not only does he fill gaps matter-of-factly, he makes use of the means of storytelling in order to order Corbin's diary, too. Pius is a scholar who becomes a narrator. Put differently, he is an editor who cannot elide that he is also an author, i.e. a storyteller. Reconstructing the history of an East African country entails constructing a possible but of necessity fictitious context for the fragmented diary of a colonial officer. Historical sources demand to be engaged with in a subjective way so that fact and fiction blend and become inextricably intertwined. This is of course problematic to the traditional historian's mind, for incorporating constructions into a reconstruction logically turns the reconstruction into a construction, too. Such kind of textual practice constitutes a provocation to history as a discipline, as historiographical scholarship becomes an act of poetic imagination. Literature and historiography are related enterprises because both rely on related metaphors and tropes and make use of similar emplotment strategies. History, strictly speaking, ceases to be an expository form of writing because on a deep structure historiographical discourse can no longer be distinguished from narrative discourse. That this nexus is crucial for an adequate understanding of *The Book of Secrets* is not least of all underlined by the fact that Pius Fernandes is a teacher of both history and literature.[3]

The close relationship between literature and historiography has another important implication. While both operate with comparable patterns of narrativization, both also share the same bias. As textual sources which are composed by a subject both fictional and historiographical sources are representations, i.e. semiotic practices that make the world understandable and allow access to it. The diary in *The Book of Secrets* epitomises the notion that any textual representation of reality is always already partial and never total. The insight that any mimetic rendering of reality is a futile endeavour dawns on Pius only at the end of the novel (331–2), but the reader will have realized earlier that Corbin has by no means captured historical facts. *The Book of Secrets* questions the very notions of historical objectivity, fact and truth. By inscribing a multitude of versions of events, the novel makes it evident that Corbin's account is not the only valid one. From the point of view of the Shamsi community, Corbin has, for example, distorted the exorcising of Mariamu by describing it as an instant of "ill treatment at the hands of her family" (324), while Pius's representation throughout the novel allows for the possibility of the supernatural. The question of what really happened remains not merely undecided but, in fact, undecidable, as any account of the event is always already inflected by a particular subject position. Alfred Corbin's position as a diary writer, for example, is informed by his status as colonizer, as upper or middle-class British subject, as male, as private and public man. Striving for accuracy in representing his of necessity partial account will not only remain in vain but also become dangerous. After all, Pius's history might reinscribe Corbin's distortions of a historical reality, the character of which must be dubious if instrumentalized for any totalizing metanarrative. Historiography, as it appears in *The Book of Secrets* cannot pertain to objectivity or a transcendent truth any longer. As will be seen in the next section, this also applies to all textual manifestations in the novel.

Postmodernism II: Textuality, Epistemology and Truth

The fact that Pius begins his historiographical project with Corbin's thoughts and thereby attributes documentary status to a diary not only mirrors modern historiography's emphasis on social and psychological history, it is also informed by New Historicism's notion of the ubiquity of discourse.[4] Discourse is conceived as a web of multiple strands which is to be disentagled by the cultural critic. According to this school of thought, studying culture means to grapple with a multitude of texts from various genres, all of which are believed to be informed by and to contribute to the same respective discursive formation. In practice, this allows the historiographer to start research practically anywhere. Whether s/he consults novels, pamphlets, contemporary histories, letters, or diaries does not matter, The discourse to be studied can be approached through a multitude of texts, all of which are thought to be related in a universe consisting of texts and intertextual connections.[5] *The Book of Secrets* is a novel that self-consciously engages with a variety of textual sources. Preparing his history, Pius does not only read Corbin's diary and letters but also his memoirs and the manuals instructing British colonial officers in the 1910s. Through his friend and former pupil, the historian Sona, he also follows up on the scholarly literature on Tanzania's colonial period as well as drawing on Robert Gregory's poems about Dar es Salaam and the country of his adoption. The fiction of HR Haggard is familiar to Pius from his training as a teacher, and *Romeo and Juliet* becomes the foil for the fate of Patani and Parviz as well as for the relationship between Ali and Rita.

Frequently, the sources of these texts and their genres are self-consciously alluded to in Vassanji's novel. Thus Corbin's letters are mirrored by Pius's letters to Sona, Corbin's memoirs are reflected by Pius's notes, and Gregory's poems from and about exile are counterbalanced by Vassanji's fictional rendering of his native country. Most strikingly, ambiguity is introduced by Pius's diary echoing that of Alfred Corbin. Corbin's diary may be the book of secrets alluded to in the title, but the fact that Pius finally abandons his project because he cannot elucidate the secret at the heart of Corbin's diary turns his own notes and research into a book of secrets, too. Emphasizing the essential incompleteness of every textual manifestation, Pius eventually regards his scribblings as a "new book of secrets" (331) for anybody reading them henceforth. As the only person who definitely reads Pius's notes is the reader, Pius reading Corbin's notes also foreshadow us going over Pius's notes.[6]

In working through Pius's reconstruction of Corbin's construction, any claim to truth, i.e. the resolution of secrets, is refuted by the play of intertextuality.

The notion of independent evidence is deconstructed by the complex structure of mise-en-abîme,[7] of diary pointing to diary presupposing diary. This does not only permanently unsettle and decentre notions of authorship and originality, another fundamental insight of Vassanji's text is that the secrets at the heart of the diaries and the novel are essentially unsolvable. Sona calls it "an inconclusive battle" (330). While the project of traditional historiography relies on textual sources which are endowed with truth value by the scholar, Vassanji grants his narrator the deconstructive insight that all forms of textuality are unreliable and truth is infinitely deferred.[8] His research is "a book as incomplete as the old one was, incomplete as any book must be. A book of half lives, partial truths, conjectures, and perhaps even some mistakes" (331–2). Texts will come down to us interpolated by generations, and they will of necessity be grounded in ideological formations. In a textual universe, i.e. in a world conceived of as a sign system, unknowability takes on the form of unreadability. What cannot be read in Vassanji's book, *The Book of Secrets*, is Mariamu's story which could be said to constitute an "Unbestimmtheitsstelle,"[9] allowing for different possibilities of reading as the process of filling in gaps. The practice of reading is no longer a decoding of essentialist (because unquestioned) truths, reading has become a performative act which allows for many equally acceptable claims to truth.

Vassanji's novel is obsessed with secrets and gaps. As an analytical novel, *The Book of Secrets* displays elements of the classical detective story.[10] 'Classic' detective fiction (as opposed to the hard-boiled school of Hammett, Chandler, and Woolrich) relies on mysteries and secrets to propel the plot. In Doyle's and Sayers's novels, for instance, the end of the plot is, roughly speaking, also the resolution of the secret.[11] In contrast to that, postmodern texts such as Auster's *City of Glass*, Eco's *The Name of the Rose* or Pynchon's *The Crying of Lot 49* resist this nexus. Here the exhaustion of the plot does not bring about the resolution of the secret. Frequently, the secrets are not resolved and retain their status as secrets, clues are deceptive, and leads turn out to be red herrings. Postmodern fiction mimics the pattern of detective fiction in that the disclosure of secrets remains inconclusive and leads into an aporia. The only exploration worthwhile seems to be the exploration of self, and even this endeavour does not seem to always guarantee success.

In postmodern fiction the analytic structure of the traditional detective novel roughly takes on the ancient form of the quest, albeit in a very different form. In medieaval verse narrative the quest involves a journey which is embarked upon in the context of a specific setting. The setting out of a hero takes place in the context of a court culture informed by the values of chivalry, honour and deference. The hero's journey is motivated by an outward stimulus, e.g. adventures and romances, however, in the course of the journey, the original purpose turns in on itself and the ultimate goal becomes a longing for the grace of a metaphysical presence, i.e. a Christian God. Postmodern novels, such as Pynchon's *The Crying of Lot 49*, parody the journey motif in that adventure and love as motives for the journey are replaced by the execution of a will. Thus the redistribution of wealth in a capitalist context deflates the high ideals of a premodern society. Moreover, Oedipa Maas, recalling her Greek namesake, is engaged in a search that finally turns into a search of her self. In marked contrast to medieaval narratives, the search for both inward and outward goals is not deemed essentialist but revealed to be libidinous instead. Oedipa's longing for coherence and meaning and her desire for closure provoke questions which must remain unanswered in a postmodern, postreligious, posthistorical universe. Instead of a transcendent signifier addressing the subject in need, Oedipa is faced with a metaphysical void symbolized by an open end and the secrets of Pierce Inverarity's will. *The Crying of Lot 49* defies any claims to truth as well as any pleasure of reading for a plot. While Vassanji's novel is not as radical in parodying traditional literary motifs as early postmodern fiction,[12] the longing of hobby historian Pius for historical truth is a search which resembles that of the detective and is equally informed by desire. As Pius himself admits, both are inextricably connected:

> But the story doesn't end here, of course. Questions remain. Like a snoop I must follow the threads, expose them in all their connections and possibilities, weave them together. What else is a historian but a snoop? But no, the urge is stronger. Like a bloodhound I will follow the trail the diary leaves. Much of it is bloody; it's blood that endures. (91)

Pius's will to knowledge is a lustful activity promising the satisfaction of cohesion and coherence in a world characterized by Habermas's shibboleth of the "neue Unübersichtlichkeit" and the stalemate of Gehlen's posthistoire.[13] However, Pius's will to knowledge is also a will to power, for knowing the past implies having mastery over it. This notwithstanding, Vassanji problematizes Pius's archaeology of knowledge by showing how the intention of truthfully recounting the past can turn into a fetish. Like other postmodern novels, *The Book of Secrets* takes issue with the notion of truth as such and debunks its epistemological value. By recourse to Pius's development as a character throughout the book, Vassanji's novel enlightens us about the delusionary character of so-called truths. Displaying an awareness of the lesson of post-structuralism/postmodernism, Pius at the end of the novel realizes that truth always escapes an analytical grid. He gives up on his historiography of the past by admitting to its opacity.

The Book of Secrets is not only a detective novel by way of its form or merely a postmodern parody of the quest in its narrator's futile desire for meaning and closure. Vassanji's text is also a spy novel, which teems with agents and double agents. During the time of World War I, Maynard spies for the British, while Hamisi, and afterwards Juma, are undercover agents for the Germans. The pedlar Abdalla carries information for both sides, the albino Fumfratti is a double agent spying for British and German intelligence, too. All of the central characters of Pius's representation of East Africa in the 1910s are engaged in creating, selling and delivering information, or in buying, probing and discarding it. Everyone is involved in the production and dissemination of knowledge, and the confusion this entails for characters and readers is deliberate. Neither the former nor the latter can distinguish between information and disinformation, or can tell apart the important from the unimportant. The spy motif continues Pius's historiographical obsession with truth. For it is truth, albeit not historical truth which all are after, and it is stories that all come up with:

> Encrusted in foul dirt, and hiding the secrets of an enemy army, these bits of information would be sniffed at by Maynard, the Fisi—what an apt name, because the hyena is also an indiscriminate scavenger—who would piece together a truth, a story, the secrets of the enemy. (154)

Obviously, Pius's scholarly research and the spying and prying differ in that spying does not give pleasure to the carriers of information, such as Pipa, who is forcefully recruited by both sides. Unlike a more famous Indian character in British literature, spying for Pipa is not "the Great Game" which may entail dangers but also offers an opportunity to prove oneself as a man (as well as an Englishman). Pipa does not have the resources to live with ambivalence; Kim, however, masters dangerous situations playfully. Due to his hybrid nature, Kim can enjoy masquerade, role-playing and the switching of identities. By virtue of his socialization (but also through his genetic disposition) he is ideally suited for a position of the 'same-but-not-quite' (Bhabha). While Pipa and the Shamsis are in-between against their will, Kim becomes a go-between. The difference is crucial. If Kim is a loner who can affiliate with opposite sides strategically, Pipa is attached to his community whose occupation as shopkeepers means that they are in need of a fixed abode and the continuing support of the colonial administration. While Kim's dislocated existence makes him the ideal spy, Pipa's insecure position makes him inflexible. Drawn into both the British and Germans' radical wills to truth, spying becomes dangerous for Pipa and the community he has married into. In *The Book of Secrets* it is only Maynard who profits from working for intelligence (118).

Summing up, the futility of the desire of historian-detective Pius and that of spies like Maynard to probe into secrets and to disclose truths has philosophical repercussions. In the context of postmodernism's questioning of epistemologies, truth as such has become a problematic concept. Totalizing claims as to the truth value of unifying master narratives are discredited, and objectivity is no longer a given. Instead, the petit recits, the local and private histories are moved to the centre of critical attention, and those marginalized and discriminated against are endowed with a voice. Histories are no longer regarded as flawed only because they are inflected by a particular gender position, or discredited because they focus on a small ethnic community. Instead, representations of the hitherto neglected Other are celebrated. An attempt is made to see the Other in his/her own right and no longer instrumentalize him/her for the construction of a monolithic metropolitan, patriarchal, capitalist identity. This essentially postmodern enterprise of rehabilitating difference accepts the dilemma of representation, i.e. the impossibility of ever capturing the 'real thing' in any kind of sign system.

As the following section sets out to show, although Pius abandons his historiographical project, the possibility of writing histories is not ruled out as such. In the absence of historical truth, there is a choice between withdrawing to a fatalist position informed by the futility of any representational endeavour and looking for other forms of constructing meaning.

Postmodernism III: Silence, Story, History

The Book of Secrets offers two alternatives of constructing meaning. The first one consists in forgetting, the second one in remembering; the latter position is associated with Pius, the former with Rita. Intruding into other lives, disclosing their private character and arbitrarily connecting them so as to arrive at an allegedly truthful story is presumptuous to Rita. She holds that to claim that it is possible to explain other people's lives is hubris, especially if one does not understand one's own. Insinuating that Pius is latently homosexual, Rita confronts Pius with a blank spot in his own biography. Her point is that not everything can/must be known about one's own life as well as about the lives of others. Rita advises Pius against prying into the lives of others and illustrates her point metaphorically: Rita accuses Pius's project of shallowness and, by implication, of speculation, when she maintains that his "history is surface" (297). The questionable epistemological value of Pius's history is underlined by the orientational metaphor of TRUTH IS DEPTH.[14] Because an essentialist, i.e. a solid and reliable account of past events is precluded by the very nature of representation, representations as such have become dubious. Thus far from celebrating postmodern (sur)fiction,[15] Rita's function is to criticize the methodological shortcomings of Pius's historiographical project. While Pius's access to the past is likened to vision, the semiotic value of the picture he is constructing of the past is limited according to Rita because the parts that the picture is made up of are in themselves pictures which are in themselves pictures again and so forth. As "each dot is infinity" (297), truth is never arrived at but deferred in an infinite regress. Drawing on chaos theory, Rita suggests that there is too much complexity in real life to be ever captured in representations. The logical conclusion for her is to dispense with representations altogether.

Pius's position fundamentally differs from that of Rita. While the difference of the Other is not necessarily an obstacle impossible to overcome for Pius, for Rita it most certainly is. While Pius comes to believe in the truth of the poetic imagination, Rita condemns the imagination as speculation and as unethical because it intrudes into other people's privacy and has the potential to harm. While Pius narrates a story, Rita argues in favour of forgetting. Rita is influenced by Pipa whose attitude towards the diary changes from worship to burial, from voice to silence. For Rita, the project of giving voice is immoral and should be abandoned in favour of an ethics of silence which figures as an explicit rejection of storytelling: "Let it lie, this past. The diary and the stories that surround it are mine now, to bury" (298). While Pius believes that the past should be represented (even if it cannot be fully known), Rita draws a diametrically opposed conclusion: "Of course the past matters, that is why we have to bury it sometimes. We have to forget to be able to start again" (298). Whereas Pius assumes that his archaeology of knowledge is beneficial, Rita rejects the historiographical practice of uncovering/discovering and demands that the past be laid to rest. By way of metaphorical consistency it is indicated that for her the past should be removed as far as possible from the here and now (BURIAL IS FORGETTING, FORGETTING AND BURIAL ARE DEEP, DEEP IS REMOVED). To Rita's mind, it is more important for those about to forge for themselves a new life to look towards the future and not into the past. Metaphorically, the new is approached from the outside, while the old should not be pried into.

Within the perspective of the novel, Pius's position prevails over Rita's. The past according to Pius should be represented because it can offer meaning: "And so I would construct a history, a living tapestry to join the past to the present, to defy the blistering shimmering dusty bustle of city life outside which makes transients of us all" (8). The wish to oppose transience is a wish for transcendence; it reflects the desire to order the events in such a way as to shape possibilities of identification. History is to provide an anchoring in tradition and togetherness deemed indispensable in fighting alienation and isolation. In his opinion that an awareness of the past is crucial for coping with the present and the future, Pius is seconded by Sona, who testifies that he "has always railed—given the opportunity—against the lack of a sense of history in us" (92), but also, for example, by Corbin who in the 1960s writes a memoir about his time in East Africa (327).

While a majority of characters stress the necessity of representing the past, an interesting point in Vassanji's novel is how exactly the past should be remembered. At the end of *The Book of Secrets* Pius's position is characterized by the insight into the limitations of his historiographical project. Making a case for a history of respect and dignity, he says:

> What better homage to the past than to acknowledge it thus, rescue it and recreate it, without presumption of judgment, and as honestly, though perhaps as incompletely as we know ourselves, as part of the life of which we all are a part? (332)

As incompleteness and subjectivity inevitably shape representations, a possible solution lies, in a kind of account which makes use of the means of fiction. Apart from the insight into the epistemological doubts of research and writing that Vassanji reflects, the novel advocates the transformation of post-modern doubts and dilemmas in the process of narrativization. Furthermore, paying homage to the past rather than fixing it dogmatically implies that the writing subject accepts the subjectivity of his story. If there is a 'truth' to be had from a history, it will be a subjective truth, a truth that depends on the writer's abilities, needs and perspective. Thirdly, paying homage to the past adequately also implies the idea of a history as an open text. In other words, although Pius initially has a personal reason for writing his history, any historiographical work according to the novel's perspective should be democratic in that it allows for various readings and interpretations. While it has been pointed out in the previous section that the writer of a diary establishes an idiosyncratic order, this holds also true for the respective reader. For Pius and his reconstruction of Corbin's diary the unity of the writing subject is eventually replaced by the unity of the reading subject. It goes without saying that the account of this reading will, like all other so-called objective accounts, be a fiction. But the point is that it is a more legitimate one because it does not deny its fictional character. Moreover, because it is open to multiple interpretations, it subscribes to a pluralist attitude and thereby resists incorporation into a hegemonial master discourse. Fourthly, historiography as homage to the past should not merely be democratic in that it allows for subjective readings. It also should be democratic in that it includes as many voices as possible. The pluralist vision of *The Book of Secrets* emphasizes the importance of including voices that have not been represented previously. Giving voice to those hitherto marginalized has particular relevance to the postcolonial implications of the novel, and it is towards these that I will turn in the following.

Stories, Magic, and the Body, or: Postcolonialism?

The Book of Secrets is a polyphonic novel offering a variety of stories, e.g. Corbin's, Rita's, Pius's, Rita's and Ali's. While Vassanji's novel presents us with a plurality of voices because it has internalized an important lesson of postmodernism, i.e. that only a pluralist vision can approximate to something like a 'true' representation, it is worth bearing in mind that the abundance of voices presented in the novel are overtly or covertly constructed by Pius Fernandes. Pius's textual intervention is comparatively slight with Rita's tale, while his editorial intrusion into the stories of the other characters is greatest with that of Alfred Corbin. As will be seen, this is by no means a coincidence.

As a formally colonized subject, Pius Fernandes reads a colonizer's text against the grain. By filling in the gaps of the Englishman's diary Pius dismantles colonial discourse from within. He undoes Corbin's discourse by interpreting gaps as contradictions and decentring the text as the product of a unified subject. Pius engages in a powerful textual practice when he strategically appropriates the colonizer's voice. By way of destroying the authenticity of Corbin's textual manifestation, he does to the colonizer what has been done to many a colonized people before: A silencing of (indigenous) voice and thus a marginalization of (native) culture. In this way, Pius's engagement with Corbin is also a settlement of accounts that asserts a new cultural dominance and self-confidence for postcolonial Tanzania as a nation. The book of secrets is a poetic revenge directed against those responsible for political injustice.[16] However, this is not the end of the story. For whereas Pius metonymically deconstructs colonialism by debunking one of its core tools, i.e. the book,[17] his destruction of the surface structure of Corbin's diary results in the construction of a new text, a new story. This is of considerable importance for an evaluation of the novel as a whole.

The relationship between Pius and Corbin is complex. *The Book of Secrets* does not only point towards the difference of the Other and the epistemological troubles involved in engaging with him/her. It also suggests parallels between the colonizer and the colonized, which become evident once the narrative surface of the novel is taken into consideration:

> He knew it to be four o'clock when the rich and rising cry of the brave muezzin rallied against the thick darkness. Such a desolate cry of the human soul in the vast universe. Was there an answer, a response? And then the Shamsis preparing for their mosque. They were a hardy lot, who could match the early Christians in their zealousness. (52)

Pius's representation blurs the boundary between the comment of an omniscient narrator and free indirect speech.[18] While the missing copula (second and fourth sentence), the interjectional character (second sentence), the parallelism (third sentence) and the conjunction with "and" (fourth sentence) suggest a shift from an omniscient narrator (first sentence) to a personal one, any clear distinction between passages of omniscient and personal narration is impossible. Both cannot be separated because the only criterion for determining either mode of narration is the use of the third person participle. While this might constitute analytical problems, the momentum of undecidability is, however, of considerable attraction for literary discourse because it creates narrative irony and ambivalence, and it is precisely such an ambiguity that lies at the heart of *The Book of Secrets*. By employing free indirect speech, Vassanji suggests that Pius is not only commenting on Corbin's diary; he is also placing himself in Corbin's mind and presents us with his thoughts. In other words, in the passage quoted above, Pius's imagination signals that he, at least partly, identifies with Alfred Corbin. This is not surprising at all, when linked to the relevant socio-cultural context of East African societies at that time. As a Christian and as an educated man Pius in East Africa may quite possibly feel closer to the British than to the Africans. Both Pius and Corbin share an outsider status, which also links them to the isolated Shamsi community. As Simatei explains:

> Vassanji [. . .] is not interested in constructing a discourse overtly oppositional to the colonial one. This certainly has something to do with the position occupied by the East African Asians in the racially layered colonial system where they were more part of the colonising structure than a colonized people.[19]

The hybrid character of Vassanji's novel as a colonial as well as a postcolonial text is not only an attempt at understanding the latter out of the conditions of the former without, however, taking on the form of a postcolonial reckoning with the British past; it also is indicative of a paradox of postmodernism, i.e. the double encoding of cultural manifestations as both subversive of and complicit with what they criticize.[20] Pius does not display an activist stance towards a former oppressor, a position usually associated with postcolonialism; while he deconstructs notions of authenticity and authorship, there can be no denying the fact that his engagement with a colonizer's diary is no deconstruction of empire.[21] Rather, the stance Pius adopts towards a colonizer is ambivalent. His attitude towards Corbin and Britain is characterized by identification and distance at the same time, thereby displaying a complexity of feelings which is troublesome for an activist polemic or ideological attack against a former colonizer.[22] Taking Pius Fernandes's development as a character as a point of departure, he might be said to mature from postcolonialism to postmodernism. In this context it is only fitting that Pius, at the end of the novel, should no longer be driven by the wish to track down agency, a step regarded as crucial by many a postcolonial novel concerned with working through the past in an attempt at nation building. Abandoning the desire to remember who did what to whom is not only not postcolonial, it is informed by postmodernism and its distrust of traditional modes of producing 'knowledge' instead.

Notwithstanding the points raised above, however, *The Book of Secrets* does reflect significant parts of what we can associate with the postcolonial agenda. It is noteworthy that Pius's deconstruction of textuality still comes up with (the construction of) a text that allows to identify concerns which are generally linked to the postcolonial project. For MG Vassanji and other writers from the former Commonwealth storytelling and orality are particularly important for the postcolonial project: "Not only must he [the postcolonial author] recreate, he must *tell* [sic]."[23] In accordance with the role Vassanji assigns to the postcolonial writer, Pius also becomes "a preserver of the collective tradition, a folk historian and myth maker."[24] A case in point are riddles.

Riddles can be conceived as a form of oral literature projecting indigenous African culture(s). Riddles are culture-specific short tales providing entertainment and insight. Besides a didactic dimension, they display a distinct community element in that they require the participation of an audience with which to interact. Their oral character makes them flexible and mutable as well as fleeting (58). In order to save them from oblivion, they must be inscribed into a textual manifestation, which may be the postcolonial novel. What is not understood because it is alien to a culture, e.g. the Great War, is made accessible by way of narrative (109–10). Riddles thus inscribe an indigenous and therefore alternative epistemology and become metonymic of cultural difference. They offer a way for a culture to assert itself in an oppressive colonial situation. Interestingly, riddles by way of their Otherness also contribute to the central concern of the novel with secrets. Riddles share an important property with secrets in that both rely on something which is not known but is subject to a desire to know on the part of those faced with either of the two. In contrast to secrets, riddles are posed and suggestions as to their possible solution meet with an answer by the person posing the riddle. While secrets are characterized by the wish to retain information by the parties involved, storytellers posing riddles usually only defer the solution in order to create suspense. Attempts at disclosing secrets as well as the posing of riddles are stories. The latter, however, are stories informed by a sense of community, which is crucial to many a postcolonial attempt at recovering lost origins.

Riddles are not the only genre by way of which Vassanji inscribes indigenous culture, *The Book of Secrets* also foregrounds proverbs and myths as ways of making sense of the world. The outbreak of World War I, for example, is not only talked about in terms of riddles in order to underline the cryptic quality of warfare on that scale, the uneasy position of the indigenous African and Indian cultures, among them the Shamsis, is also epitomized by the metaphorical speech of proverbs: "How do the little people fare in a war between big powers? In answer, the Swahili proverb says, "When two elephants fight, it is the grass that suffers" (149). Pius's representation of indigenous African and Indian reality accounts for the mythopoeic quality of alternative ways of structuring reality. Mythopoeic means that the stories told tend "to create or recreate certain narratives which human beings take to be crucial to their understanding of the world."[25] An example of how the Shamsis talk about German-British hostility can serve to illustrate this:

> The German man-of-war Königsberg prowled the ocean from Lamu to Kilwa with its fearsome guns, appearing like a spectre in the mist and destroying British warships. The terrible German demoness Bibi Malkia went around with a troop of her own, appearing from behind hills and trees to wreak havoc on British forces, leaving hacked, mangled bodies behind, especially of the white settler troops. (150)

Indigenous riddles, proverbs, and other stories in *The Book of Secrets* explain the world in a way which is alien to a European or American readership. The terror of warfare is understood in the terms which are at the disposal of the indigenous culture, in this case the world of spirits and demons. Needless to say that the indigenous belief in an animistic universe is radically different from Western approaches towards the world; in an act of subversion, Vassanji's novel inscribes different cultural practices in order to counter the rationalist rationale of colonial discourse. Other voices, which are also voices of Otherness, undermine the hegemonic discourse and preclude an unproblematical reading of the world.

Similar to the abundance of foreign words and indigenous terms which the text is replete with, magic in *The Book of Secrets* becomes an indicator of cultural difference. Comparable to foreign words that are indicators of resistant and wayward Otherness in that they cannot be translated adequately, magic in Vassanji's novel points to a cultural resource which cannot be mastered by colonial discourse.[26] When Corbin complains that "administration's all right [. . .] but how the devil do you deal with another culture's ghosts?" (72), he reflects the complexity of other/Other epistemologies the colonizer is faced with and confused by. The diachronic perspective of the text reveals that he has not managed to deal with them effectively at all. Corbin's rationalistic administration and the traces British colonialism have vanished and not left a mark on Tanzanian society, while the power of magic has prevailed and continues to exert a strong influence on people. A case in point is Feroz, for whom the supernatural is unfalteringly strong and continues to be a vital and envigorating aspect of indigenous East African culture (95). A case in point is also Pius's textual intervention in Corbin's diary detailing a passage about the Englishman's recovery from a serious fever. Corbin's assessment of his own illness is characterized by Western rationalism. After he has come down with blackwater fever, the mukhi and an exorcist compete with a local doctor and Mrs Bailey for Corbin's recovery. For Corbin himself the exorcist has had no share in his cure: "I did not believe in his powers, of course" (82). For Pius, however, the maalim is the one who really saves Corbin. The exorcist prays over the brandy, while Mrs Bailey is absent and mimics praying over the water during the time she is present in the room. Mrs Bailey, who does not trust the maalim, throws away the water, while Corbin drinks "the brandy, with its promise of recovery" (83). Pius's representation of the event strategically mentions the maalim's trick at the end, thereby relying on discourse's end weight principle in order to insinuate the reality of magic in Corbin's life. Corbin's recovery can inscribe magic as trait of indigenous culture in such a powerful way because Corbin does indeed survive the fever, which, given the seriousness of his illness, is something so unlikely that it borders on the supernatural. Moreover, Pius underscores the truth value of Alfred Corbin's magic recovery/recovery by magic by suggesting that he has independent evidence. Countering the novel's poststructuralist doubts about the reliability of textuality, it is the body that becomes proof of the existence of magic.

The body as a register of experience constitutes an alternative way of knowing that runs counter to the Enlightenment tradition so influential in the Western world. The physicality of the body as sensor indicates immediacy and thus suggests evidence beyond rationalist categories. In the example above, it is only Pius's representation of Corbin's recovery which suggests the success of the maalim's cure. Playing off Clifford Geertz's notion of culture as text/textum,[27] Vassanji's also reveals the pitfalls of the interpretative turn in cultural anthropology. Cultural anthropology's paradigm of the readability of cultural manifestations as basis for an understanding of the Other is reflected critically in *The Books of Secrets*. As the body of the Other is a sign which can be read in more ways than one, the body becomes as much a source of understanding as of misunderstanding, hence even a 'thick description' might misfire. The body of Mariamu, for example, both ethnic and sexual Other for Pius, escapes definite interpretations: Who has murdered her? Who has raped her? Has she really lost her virginity prior to marriage (after all there is a trickle of blood)? Is blood an indicator of the proper consumption of a marriage? (121) If she had an affair, did she have it with Corbin or with someone else? Did Mariamu become pregnant from Corbin and would thus have born Ali as the representative of a new, hybrid generation?[28] Is Aku's allegedly lighter skin colour a reliable indicator for an affair of his mother with a European? All of these questions are raised because the body constitutes a sign that demands a reading. However, as any answer is of necessity speculative, only approximations to the 'truth' can ever exist. Harking back to an earlier argument, one could also say that in its resistance to definite readings the body is a secret (rather than a riddle).

The supernatural is not only instrumentalized against the former British colonizers. Pius imagines Mariamu as a spirit communicating with Pipa after she has died. Whether Mariamu really exists as a spirit demands less critical attention than the fact that even as a spirit Mariamu refuses to yield her secret to Pipa, who asks her the (to him) all-important question "to which she would give no answer" (212). The supernatural in *The Book of Secrets* does not simply signal cultural Otherness, it also suggests that intercultural understanding might be impossible because understanding the Other is put into question in general. In that sense, magic functions as a reminder of the epistemological differences between different cultures. The impossibility of ever knowing the Other serves a postcolonial aim insofar as it strengthens another culture's resilience against acts of appropriation. A radically postmodern epistemological critique is thus applied to postcolonial usage.[29]

There is no denying that *The Book of Secrets* explores the intricacies of knowing. If it has been implied above that the body provides epistemological certainty to the person experiencing with his/her own body, this assumption requires qualification now. While Mariamu's body constitutes an instance of the unreadability of the Other for Pipa, the novel also raises the question whether the body truly enables a knowledge of the self. As Rita suggests at the end of the novel, Pius does not know himself and thus should not presume to know others/Others. Neglecting to take issue with the dialectic that Rita advocates for an epistemology of the Other, *The Book of Secrets* suggests that she is not completely mistaken in her judgement of Pius. The quality of the relationship between Pius and Gregory cannot be specified by Pius Fernandes when he remembers an evening at his friend's house:

> Of that moment I remember a feeling of dislocation, a sense of empathy; a feeling of being utterly alone, with another human being in my arms. The sound of waves in the distance. An occasional car on the road outside.
>
> It was the next morning when I left; he was still in bed; fast asleep. (310)

While Pius remembers that both have "reconciled and touched" (311), he is not sure what to make of it, i.e. how to interpret the signs registered on his body: "Was it because I was afraid of what more there was, or could have been? I honestly don't know" (311). Vassanji's scepticism and distrust of conventional methods of 'knowing' is so pervasive that even the certainty granted by the body is questioned. In Pius's case the body only registers Gregory's touch, but he does not clarify his feeling for him. At this point, even the body cannot fill in all the gaps. A Freudian reading would have no trouble in identifying Corbin's behaviour as an instance of repression. In other words, while the body signals Pius that he finds Gregory attractive, the super ego exerts its influence on Pius's faculty of reason so that morals and conventions (which Gregory does not have to pay attention to in the colonies) preclude giving in to the inclinations of the body. It is striking that the most important part of the account of his night with Gregory is missing, something which is indicated typographically by the text's paragraphing. Pius fades out the experience of the body and subconsciously veils the 'truth' about his sexual orientation to others but also, and this is crucial, to himself. Thus it is fitting that he should describe his relationship to Gregory as "a long friendship that I could never quite explain" (233). While for the most part *The Book of Secrets* subscribes to the importance of the body as counterdiscursive device in the context of a postcolonial writing back, ironically, in Pius's case it is mind over matter once again.

The analysis has thus come full circle. Starting out with Pius's textual practice in his attempt at reconstructing Corbin's diary, the analysis has returned to the narrator of Vassanji's novel. His gender orientation allows the conclusion that his well-meaning interpolation of Corbin's diary cannot be exclusively explained by the affiliation of a colonial with a British colonial administrator. Neither his national identification as well as his sexual inclination are reflected upon. Possibly, Pius's political project of writing a postcolonial history is undermined by an identification which is of an entirely private nature. This, of course, would question a reading of Vassanji's novel as postcolonial in the conventional sense. Whether it is appropriate to do so will form the focus of the following section.

Histories, Communities, and the Diaspora, or: Postcolonialism

The poststructuralist doubts expressed at the beginning and end of *The Book of Secrets* affect the reading of the main part of the book, i.e. Pius's attempt at narrating Tanzania's history from the beginning of the Great War to the end of the 1980s. While it is true that the middle part of the novel does not display authorial interruptions and self-conscious reflections metafictionally laying bare the novel's structure as well as the process of its construction, the frame of *The Book of Secrets* does not allow the reader to forget the premises of Pius's historiographical endeavour. After the authenticity and reliability of all textual manifestations have been undermined beyond recuperation, Pius's version of Tanzania's colonial and postcolonial history cannot aspire to universal truth any longer but is characterized by the particularity of any writing subject. This is underlined by the fact that Pius is confronted with the intrusion of his biography into the history of Tanzania, which he set out to research conscientiously and objectively:

> There are many paths to choose from. And no one path is quite like any other, none of them will return to quite where it began. The path one takes is surely in large measure pure accident; but in equal measure, it must be determined by predisposition. And so I know, am forewarned. Ultimately the story is the teller's, it's mine. (92)

Reflecting the postmodern truism that the private and the political are interchangeable, the national history he is about to write infringes on his personal history. The narrating subject becomes himself narrated and the novel describes a circular trajectory. What began with Corbin's diary, ended with Corbin's and Gregory's letters, both of which are text types characterized by their personal and intimate nature. Thus what started out as biography/autobiography and continued as public history eventually ends up as autobiography again. Ironically enough, the middle part of the novel narrating Tanzania's history is a story without references, while the private stories of those marginally involved in its shaping are exceptionally well documented, even if the documentary status of these sources is in itself questionable.

Whereas the exploration of the diary has confronted Pius with epistemological uncertainty, the middle sections of the novel are narrated in a markedly different way. One should emphasize that they are narrated, which means that having accepted the impossibility of historical truth, the only way of establishing coherence and, by extension, meaning, is for Pius to rely on the means of storytelling. If *The Book of Secrets* can be called a postcolonial novel despite the poststructuralist scepticism it displays, then this is due to the fact that at this stage of the novel self-conscious postmodern narration gives way to a more 'realist' mode of narration, without, however, subscribing to the assumptions of totality, mimesis and truth traditionally bound up with the concept.[30]

The action of the novel oscillates between British East and German East Africa, thereby indicating that postcolonial Tanzanian identity is grounded in a double colonization.[31] This double colonization, or, if one were to put it more positively, Tanzania's cultural as well as multicultural history, is presented by Vassanji in a way that displays affinity to the national allegory, which Jameson regards as the predominant mode of postcolonial narration.[32] Although not subscribing to that form of (postcolonial) writing to such a degree as Rushdie's *Midnight's Children* for example, *The Book of Secrets* certainly does provide instances that are characteristic of allegorical representation. A case in point is Pipa and Mariamu's marriage. Both do not come from pure, respectively respectable, family background, Mariamu's mother is a Shamsi, Rashid, her stepfather, is not (50). Pipa is also a child whose father has disappeared; the shame of a child without a father is added to by a mother who is a prostitute (127–9). Moreover, Pipa comes from German East, while Mariamu from British East Africa; their union is an allegory of the hybrid nature of the postcolonial nation-state.[33] It is tempting to read Pipa's death allegorically also. He dies at the very same day that the socialist government of Tanzania nationalizes its (rental) properties and thus robs the Asian communities of their income. Deprived of the foundation of his living, Pipa, the representative of the Shamsi community, dies (312). At the same time, his death is indicative of the fact that the modus vivendi of the various communities in multicultural East Africa has become obsolete.

Although *The Book of Secrets* is topical in that it alludes to German rule in Tanzania from 1890 until 1918 as well as to its status as a mandate under British administration from the 1920s onwards, Vassanji's novel is not a historical novel in the strict sense of Lukács's definition.[34] It does not make use of characters as background material to demonstrate the dynamics of history, rather it employs selected events of Tanzania's and Kenya's history since World War I as backdrop to foreground the biographies of two characters, Pius Fernandes and Nurmohamed Pipa, neither of whom meets the demands of Lukacs's ideal hero: Socially, neither is of middle standing and neither is sufficiently removed from the time of the action to grant a neutral and objective access to the past. In this context, it is noteworthy in particular that the narrated time catches up with the narrator. As pointed out before, objectivity is not what Vassanji has in mind at all. This can be concluded from the mode of narration that the plot is presented from. To employ Stanzel's influential distinction, the narrator Pius involuntarily becomes a reflector.[35] Needless to say, the latter does not lend itself to an impartial analysis of history, i.e. as an example to demonstrate its character. Vassanji is not interested in giving us a panorama of Kenyan or Tanzanian society. Unlike Scott in *Waverley*, for example, the scope of *The Book of Secrets* is deliberately limited. Both Pipa and Pius occupy somewhat uncomfortable and insecure positions on the fringe of the society they live in. Pius's position as an Indian living in the African diaspora ethnically inflects his perception of Tanzania. It could be said that he approaches the representation of the country of his affiliation from a marginal perspective. As a Goan, Pius comes to the former German now British colony of Tanzania from a small Portuguese colony in India. He does not belong to one of the Indian communities who have settled in East Africa, and there can be no doubt that he is to some extent an outsider.

The Book of Secrets is not interested in telling an authoritative, official, grand narrative of the nation but, in a way not untypical of postcolonial narratives, presents national history as community history. For example, the issue of boundaries is illuminated on less from a national perspective than from the point of view of the Shamsi community,[36] which is separated by the border between Kenya and Tanzania (150–1). What historically appears as the hybrid character of national identity, takes on the form of division and displacement, when looked at from the angle of a particular community.

The Shamsis are Vassanji's fictional rendering of the Ismailis, a Khoja Muslim community which had migrated to East Africa from the Northwest of India in the nineteenth century.[37] The Khoja Ismailis are a Shiite community that converted from Hinduism.[38] Vassanji does not portray the Ismaili community directly but clearly has them in mind when recreating the Indian experience in the African diaspora.[39] He engages in a narrative form of community construction while paying attention to postmodern doubts at the same time. That means that in accordance with *The Book of Secrets*' grounding in postmodern thought, Vassanji does not make a claim to 'truth' in writing the Other. On the contrary, his ethnography does not deny the limits of representations and its inherent epistemological intricacies but explores the possibility of approximations to 'truth' by offering a portrait which is almost the same but not quite.

The Shamsis, as they appear in *The Book of Secrets*, are a tightly knit community with its own channels of communication (158). The close ties between its members are indicative of strong bonds of solidarity, which have also characterized the brotherhood of the Khoja Ismailis historically.[40] The Shamsis help and assist each other with material support or with finding suitable marital partners. An example is Pipa who is married to Mariamu. The Shamsis adapt easily and welcome outsiders. The friendliness of the Shamsis as well as their inside knowledge of the country and the lingua franca Swahili make them valuable for the British. By supporting the colonizers in many ways, the Ismailis and other Indian communities settling in East Africa are accorded privileged status by the British. They eventually acquire the status of a colonial middlemen because "they had learned the colonial game well" (267). In the context of the colonial system of Indirect Rule, which for pragmatic more than ideological reasons attempts to leave indigenous power structures intact, the Indians prove indispensable as cultural translators.[41] The Asians may not be important politically, but they are of considerable importance for the economic structure of the region.[42] In the East African countries of Kenya, Uganda and Tanzania they are an economic power to be reckoned with and thus acquire considerable political influence:

> Powerless though the individual Indian is beside a European, as a community they have a voice that is heard [. . .] more than three-quarters of the country's business passes through their hands, in towns just as small as this one. And no less a personage then Mr Churchill has supported their cause publicly. (49)

One of the things Vassanji achieves by giving the Khoja Ismailis a voice is to disclose the economic underpinnings of British colonial discourse. The Ismailis and other Asian communities in the coastal region of East Africa were not only tolerated by the British; the British needed them desperately. Churchill, himself undersecretary for the colonies at an early stage of his career, was wiser than East African rulers to come. How much damage to the colonial economy could be caused by antagonising the Indians of East Africa became evident in the early 1970s when Uganda's Idi Amin provoked a severe economic depression by nationalizing rental properties and thus letting racism and greed prevail over tolerance and economic/political farsightedness.

In demonstrating the importance of Asian cooperation with the British colonial administration, Vassanji underlines the potential powerfulness of indigenous resistance. While the English naturalist Henry Johnson requires a cook and porter, the Shamsi sect sends Jamal Dewji to spy on the colonizer: "In his country he may be king [. . .] but here I trust nobody" (26). Another case in point is Fumfratti who is to lead Corbin's expedition (but turns out to be a German agent). Similarly, the Unsworths give testimony to the importance of native assistance in coping with the colonial reality: "That's Omar Khan," said Anne. "He's from South Africa and absolutely indispensable in this town" (62). The conclusion to be drawn from the evidence the text provides is clear: Any Manichean division between colonizer and colonized becomes a projection of wishes which is ultimately refuted by the complexity of everyday colonial reality. Colonial discourse's underlying desire for purity and for separation along borders is contradicted by *The Book of Secrets*' emphasis on cross-cultural empathy (Corbin and the mukhi), cross-cultural marriage (Pipa and Mariamu, Jamal and Khanoum, Parviz and Patani), cross-cultural breeding (Corbin and Mariamu) and homoeroticism across cultural and racial divides (Pius and Gregory). Corbin may go local besides sleeping with Mariamu (59–60), Maynard goes native and becomes a savage, Gregory affiliates with the postcolonial nation-state, Pipa becomes a Shamsi, Pius identifies with Corbin whose story he narrates and with Gregory, whom he latently loves—all these instances serve to show that Vassanji's novel deconstructs the very notion of borders and/or compartmentalizations. While it sets out to show that the colonial reality was never clear-cut, *The Book of Secrets* advocates border crossings and hybridity as a strategy for coping with the postcolonial predicament.

Pius narrates how the Asians in East Africa have always been in an insecure position. Needed by the Germans, they have always had to struggle for formal rights and recognition nevertheless. Despite their riches, they remain mere colonial subjects regardless of what they achieve:

> However rich an Asian merchant, to the Germans he was a native because he could not observe German civil law. This greatly offended Asians among whom colour racialism was deeply engrained. Their chief political aim throughout German times was to secure a higher legal status than Arabs and Africans.[43]

Under the British the Asians are treated with more respect and become British subjects, although they still occupy a somewhat awkward position. However, from insecure and uncomfortable the fate of the Asians in East Africa deteriorates to untenable in 1972. With the advent of the nationalization of properties in the context of Tanzania's socialist phase, many members of the Shamsi community migrate once more. The refusal to exchange elitism for socialist mediocrity forces the community to migrate into the US or Canadian diaspora.

The notion of the diaspora is a recent term in postcolonial studies. While colonialism has suppressed the assertion of indigenous identities, postcoloniality has not automatically led to the reclamation of that identity. Recent postcolonial literature and theory has advocated the futility of nostalgically looking towards origins and roots. The postcolonial condition is said to be inevitably characterized by hybridity, thereby denying that there is an unbroken native tradition and a pure cultural essence to lay claim to. For some postcolonial critics, diaspora has become a concept which describes nonessentialist identities, i.e. identities which, for example, do not depend on history, tradition and place. The global migrations taking place with the advent of postcoloniality make issues of diaspora, place and identity particularly pressing questions.[44]

Not least of all because of the attention paid to the issues of migration and identity can *The Book of Secrets* be labelled postcolonial.[45] Every major character in *The Book of Secrets* migrates at least once. While Corbin, Maynard, and Mariamu are displaced, the three most interesting instances of deterritorialization in Vassanji's novel are Pipa, Pius, and Gregory. Pipa, born in Moshi, moves between Moshi, Tanga, Dar es Salaam and Kikono. He migrates to escape shame, to marry, to escape German and British agents, to forget Mariamu, and, finally, he also migrates for economic reasons. Pipa is not only a restless character but also a homeless one. Interestingly, home does not translate as place for Pipa but figures as a location that becomes home only by virtue of his recognition by the society he lives in: "His given name was Nurmohamed—Pipa was the nickname given to the family by the neighbourhood, and it had stuck. It made him feel a lack: of respectability, of a place that was truly home" (127). Pipa longs for status and respectability in his hometown Moshi, something that he has not been born with. His doubtful origins are psychologically crippling: The fact that his father leaves his family behind is experienced as a "hidden deformity" (127). Because he is "simply an Indian" (127), i.e. an Indian without a community and with a mother who is a prostitute, economic rise and status do not come easy within the conventions of the society Pipa is born into. His allegedly inferior social background is responsible for the fact that ingrained in his personality is an inferiority complex which becomes manifest as "guilt at his inadequacy" (129). Pipa's rise in the world is not conceivable without the support and protection of the Shamsi community. The new respectability the Shamsis endow him with allows him to rise economically and to acquire social status:

> Whether he was of the Shamsi community or not, Pipa could not say with certainty. Like many others before him, he accepted the Shamsis and the rewards that followed: a job and a place to stay; eminent men to vouch for him; and, if he wanted, a bride. So he could become the camel who at last stopped his endless journey and found a home. (133)

Eventually, it is status and not a place which approximates home for Pipa. He attempts to go back to Moshi several times but has to find out that "leaving home had been easy, not so the return"[46] (134). Pius's wanderings, ending in Dar es Salaam and not in Moshi, illustrate that the recuperation of home as essence is a futile endeavour. Home, as a matter of fact, has become a psychological category.

Vassanji's narrator is confronted with the diaspora, too. Although Pius Fernandes is a man with a university education, this does not protect him from racism. Paradoxically, he is to train colonial subjects but is himself trained on the premises of colonial discourse: "The African servant, like the Indian, we learned, did not have a sense of 'mine' and 'yours'" (238). His training, informed by colonial discourse, has consequences when Pius and his fellow teachers leave India in the early 1950s with hopes for freedom and modernity. Pius's colonial education has crippled him psychologically insofar as ingrained in his personality is a hatred of his own culture: [47]

> We were sailing to freedom: freedom from an old country with ancient ways, from the tentacles of clinging families with numerous wants and myriad conventions; freedom even from ourselves grounded in those ancient ways. (239)

If a colonial inferiority complex prompts Ali and Rita to exchange East Africa for an allegedly more sophisticated London (252), Pius moves because of the political instability and economic crisis in his homeland. Like Pipa, whose name he echoes phonologically, he is disoriented and has lost his sense of belonging. Like Pipa, moreover, he is also surrounded by cultural difference translating as discrimination. As a colonial subject he migrates to a place where he cannot hope for an adequate recognition of his subject status. From the position of one formally colonized he moves to that of an in-between in Tanzania. However, unlike Pipa his marginal status allows him to understand those who are in a comparable situation. Thus the shared experience of displacement links Pius and the British, despite the fact that their very different experience of colonialism should alienate them from each other. Although essentially on opposite sides of the divide, Pius, Corbin and Gregory are in the same situation in East Africa. For each of the three a change of place raises questions of identity. This is what induces Pius to feel empathy for Corbin. Moreover, that might possibly be what attracts him to Gregory, one of the most interesting characters in the novel.

By giving up his British passport at the time when Tanzania becomes independent in 1961, Gregory, like Pipa, subscribes to the notion that home is a place of affiliation rather than of origin: "'I've lived here most of my life, now,' he said. 'This is home'" (305). While this is a crucial step for a postcolonial subject like Pipa because it transcends a way of thinking that sees place as an essence impossible to recover, Vassanji, strikingly enough, credits a colonizer, and not a (post)colonial subject, with such an insight. One reason for privileging Gregory in that way might be that he deviates from the usual characteristics of a member of the British Empire, such as rigid discipline and a stiff upper lip. Rather his queerness makes him receptive to other kinds of Otherness, or, put differently, his homosexuality likens him to the ethnic Other. It is no wonder then that Gregory has gone local. He has identified with Dar es Salaam, literally 'haven of peace,' to such an extent that the colony has become a haven for him. It is on the margins of empire that Gregory has found a space of rest from migration and displacement as well as from discrimination and prejudice.

Furthermore, Dar es Salaam, culturally different from England as well as internally diversified, has also become a source of artistic inspiration to Gregory as the gendered Other. His poetry collection 'Havin' a Piece' does not merely echo the English translation of Dar es Salaam ('Haven of Peace'), and employs phonologically almost homophonous sounds in order to testify to the influence of the foreign city on Gregory's imagination. The title of his collection also suggests that Gregory encourages his reader to immerse into the culture of the Other by way of art. Reading his poems becomes a way of partaking of his perspective on Otherness (317). Where the body fails, Vassanji seems to suggest, art can be of epistemological value. Poetry becomes a means of bridging cultural gaps, a way of transcending cultural boundaries. After the dangers and pitfalls of cultural translation, i.e. the implications of appropriation, have been disclosed by Vassanji's fiction, the title of Gregory's fiction reminds us of the benefits of translating culture. After the postmodern lesson of *The Book of Secrets*, it goes without saying that, while offering a piece of the Other, the process of translation also includes the translator. 'Havin' a Piece' not only portrays/interprets another culture, it also projects the identity of its writer, i.e. Gregory. In this way, the book of poems reflects the private nature of Gregory's book of secrets as represented in Vassanji's *The Book of Secrets*.

Conclusion: Postmodernism, Postcolonialism and Transformation

In a seminal essay John Clement Ball observes a division of the novel into a metafictional and a realist/historicist part and identifies both with the postmodern and the postcolonial respectively.[48] In the course of his argument, however, he neglects postmodern passages while simultaneously stressing those parts of the text allegedly offering a more mimetic rendering of the historical facts.[49] In contrast to such a reading, I have argued that it is not acceptable to highlight the postcolonial aspects at the cost of downplaying the postmodern ones.[50] When Ball assigns the poststructuralist considerations of the first part of the novel the status of a topos without repercussion in the main body of the book,[51] i.e. without relevance to the postcolonial aspects of the text, he fails to take account of the novel's complexity. Even if it is granted that Pius history is indeed topical and narrated in a way more straightforward than the account of Pius's engagement with Corbin's diary, it should not be forgotten that the main body of *The Book of Secrets* is still a construction and not the history of Tanzania. An adequate response to Vassanji's novel cannot fail to take notice of the fact that the novel is not a document but an artefact. What's more, not only does the novel demand to be read as something that is 'made,' *The Book of Secrets* also metafictionally includes the process of writing in the course of its story. In other words, the narrative frequently foregrounds its narration.

While Ball acknowledges that Vassanji offers two ways of working with texts, he overlooks that both are of equal importance to the novel as a whole. Rather than playing off one discourse against the other, Vassanji's novel must be understood in the context of both postmodernism and postcolonialism. The key to an adequate understanding of *The Book of Secrets* is to realize that firmly anchored at the centre of Vassanji's narration is the insight into the importance of difference, which is the analytical paradigm that both postmodernism and postcolonialism partake of. Both postmodernism and postcolonialism assume that difference is not only (i) an ontological but also (ii) an epistemological category.

(i) The postmodern emphasis on pluralism, originating from the insight into the ubiquity of difference, finds its application in postcolonialism with its stress on the counterdiscursive. The postmodern ideas of tolerance and respect are reflected in a modified form in postcolonialism and its assertion of the subject's cultural/ethnic difference. Ontologically, the postmodern insight into the constructedness of the subject can, however, be problematic for postcolonial studies. While postmodernism denies any ontological essence, postcolonialism frequently relies on a strategic essentialism that posits the former Other as the new self/subject. The rejection of any subject position, which postmodernism celebrates as a liberation, is liberating for postcolonialism only conditionally, i.e. only if the deconstruction of the subject concerns the former oppressor. The own subject position cannot be given up, otherwise colonialism's denigration of (native) voice would simply be continued, albeit by different means. Thus it seems safe to suggest that an activist postcolonial narrative can hardly be a full-fledged postmodern text. *The Book of Secrets* is postmodern in that Pius is not only critical of colonialism but also complicit with what he criticizes. His identification with Corbin precludes any reading of *The Book of Secrets* as activist. Moreover, in Pius Vassanji embodies postmodernism's lack of a theory of agency, which is a central concern for old-school postcolonialism.

(ii) Postmodern about *The Books of Secrets* is also its distrust of epistemologies. Vassanji is concerned with how to understand ethnicity, i.e. "human variation in terms of culture, tradition, language, social patterns and ancestry."[52] While Vassanji suggests that to know an Other might eventually be a futile endeavour, epistemological difficulties are enforced in *The Book of Secrets* insofar as they include the subject, too.[53] Thus postcolonialism employs the postmodern attention paid to the different ways of knowing in other cultures as instances of resistance. Again, such a form of resistance is not unproblematic. By deconstructing their crippling image in the eyes of the Western world, many postcolonial writers have overlooked that operating with a postmodern epistemological critique ultimately makes any epistemology questionable.

What about *The Book of Secrets* then in the context of an analysis of discourses of difference?—MG Vassanji seems to argue a case in favour of a postcolonial literature that has vistas to offer for the future as well as something to say about the past. Its deconstructive impetus has to be complemented by a constructive element; in other words, deconstruction must be understood as de-construction. In order to arrive at some form of cultural assertiveness, Vassanji's postcolonial literature, while implementing a critique of the colonial past, transforms its epistemological doubts. The impossibility of knowing, which, on a narratological level, rejects mimesis, draws on constructions, i.e. the means of poiesis, to make possible a more constructive treatment of past and present. From a postcolonial vantage point this means that the deconstruction of any history will have to be supplemented by the construction of stories. A radical critique of the old is insufficient; what is called for is also a new story, and the way out of the epistemological and ontological dilemmata lies in subscribing to the power of the imagination. Although the Other cannot be known objectively, attempts can and must be made to know him subjectively. Ethnography, women's history, the history of the body, the writing of the nation, magic—all may and have to be narrativised. It is in-between the affirmation of storytelling and poststructuralist doubts that *The Book of Secrets* oscillates between revealing and re-veiling.[54]

Although in general all difference (in *The Book of Secrets*) is irreducible, *The Book of Secrets* manages to narrate the irreducibility of difference and thus transforms it into something that can be understood. What can be known about object and subject is that not much can be known about them, if 'knowledge' translates as essentialist truths. Debunking the myth of essentialist truth/knowledge, stories constitute a way of bridging the gulf of difference in Vassanji's novel without closing it. On a narratological level Vassanji thus argues a point he also arrived at in *No New Land*. Succinctly put, this point concerns the possibility as well as necessity of hybridity and cultural exchange. It will be seen in the next chapter that Vassanji's positive outlook on multiculturalism has not remained uncontested within Canada. Among the most prominent writers to have opted for a more critical approach is Neil Bissoondath, whose central works will be discussed in the following.

Deconstructing Difference
Neil Bissoondath

Neil Devindra Bissoondath[1] was born in Arima, Trinidad, on 19 April 1955 to Crisen Bissoondath, a merchant, and Sati Naipaul, sister to Shiva and VS Naipaul. Exposed to Western influences from an early age onwards, Neil Bissondath attended a Presbyterian primary school, founded by Canadian missionaries, and a Catholic high school in Port of Spain. When he was seven years old, Trinidad became independent. The departure of the British in 1962 brought about army rebellions, violence and riots. As a member of a comparatively wealthy, although politically underrepresented minority within Trinidadian multicultural society, Neil Bissoondath did not experience Independence as an improvement of his opportunities. Thus after he had graduated from high school in the early 1970s, he decided to move to Toronto to attend university. From 1973–77 he studied French at York University, completing a BA four years later. From 1977–85 Neil Bissoondath taught English and French as a second language in Toronto, while devoting his spare time to writing. His first collection of stories was completed in 1982 and published in 1985 as *Digging Up the Mountains*. Three years later Knopf launched his first novel *A Casual Brutality*. Another volume of short stories, *On the Eve of Uncertain Tomorrows* (1990), as well as three novels have appeared ever since, *The Innocence of Age* (1992), *The Worlds Within Her* (1999), which was short-listed for the Booker Prize, and *Doing the Heart Good* (2002). Neil Bissoondath also is the author of *Selling Illusions: The Cult of Multiculturalism in Canada* (1994), a best-selling essay on Canadian multicultural policy already referred to in greater detail above. At the moment, Neil Bissoondath lives in Quebec City. He is married to lawyer Anne Marcoux, a former ESL student of his, and has one daughter. He teaches literature and creative writing (in French) at Laval University.

A. 'Here': Multiculturalism and its Discontents. *The Innocence of Age* (1992)

Bissoondath's second novel *The Innocence of Age* is concerned with multiculturalism and its problems. Interestingly enough, the novel, although written by an immigrant, is narrated by a member of the dominant ethnicity. The fact that Bissoondath writes about multiculturalism from such a position can be understood as a reflection of his insight into the possibility, perhaps necessity, of switching ethnicities in a diaspora situation. Considering himself a Canadian rather than an immigrant, Bissoondath refuses to let his writing be restricted by stereotypes.

The Sounds of Silence: The House as an Allegory of Multiculturalism

The Innocence of Age talks about multiculturalism in an allegorical way by taking recourse to the motif of the house. Houses and metaphors of housing abound in Neil Bissoondath's second novel and become instrumental in making a point about the way people live together in a multicultural society. In an interview, Neil Bissoondath admits that writing about multiculturalism resembles

> writing about a beautiful mansion, a glittering place—a place of music and joy, and people in the living room sipping champagne. That's all very wonderful, but what interests me as a novelist is the foundation of the house, what's happening down there. And if there are termites eating at it, that attracts me.[1]

Bissoondath's imagery here suggests that what he is interested in is what keeps a multicultural society together and what drives it apart. As such, he is concerned with the centripetal as well as centrifugal forces at work in Canadian society.

The central importance of the house as a metaphor is already illustrated by the occupation of one of its protagonists, Daniel Taggart, who works for Mr Simmons, a real-estate agent in Toronto. In the course of the narrative, Daniel is to refurbish a flat for Mr Simmons but the task of renovating the house according to his employer's wishes turns out to be difficult. Daniel lacks the inspiration to meet Mr Simmons's demands because the parts of the house refuse to become a good gestalt in his mind:

> Danny sat in the darkness and listened to the silence. [. . .] The house was still resisting him, defeating his efforts to draw it fully into his imagination, the vision he had pieced together sitting incoherent in his mind, like

> pieces of different jigsaw puzzles forced together [. . .] The work shouldn't have been so demanding. All the elements had been handed to him. He had only to arrange them in the desired order to achieve the desired effect. But something mischievous—he couldn't tell what—was playing with him, displacing one piece when he was occupied with another.[2]

Underlying Daniel's reflections is the nexus between the foundations of the house and the foundation of multiculturalism. More precisely, the difficulty of renovating Simmons's house also indicates that Canada's multicultural policy is in need of rethinking and reform. The troubles Daniel has with refurbishing the flat are not only conceptualized by a visual metaphor but also by referring to Daniel's sense of hearing. The house resists Daniel not only in terms of its gestalt but also by virtue of its persistent silence. If it is understood that the house symbolizes the Canadian polity, the silence pervading the house hints at an unnatural atmosphere under its roof. In particular, the silence of the house is closely connected to the silence of its (illegal) tenant Sita, a nineteen-year-old girl from the Caribbean who is sexually exploited by Simmons. It is her presence that makes the house 'unheimlich', i.e. both unhomely and uncanny. The consequence is that on overhearing how Sita is being raped by Simmons, Daniel feels "as if the house itself were smothering him" (235).

Within the perspective of the novel, the silence Sita involuntarily imposes on the house is less indicative of her cultural marginalization than of her marginalization as an individual. This point is crucial for an understanding of the text in terms of its treatment of cultural difference. Failing to perceive her essential humanity, Simmons treats her as an Other who can be exploited sexually as well as financially. It is not that her essential cultural difference were not recognized in the context of the text's allegorical representation of Canadian society; on the contrary, Sita experiences too much of a recognition of difference and that in a problematic form. *The Innocence of Age*, rather cynically, presents the acknowledgment of difference as an Othering that has fatal consequences for the subject.

To the same extent that Sita is reduced to her commodity value and disregarded as a full-fledged human being, Daniel's refurbishment of the house, which hints at a reform of Canadian multiculturalism, is doomed to fail. Put differently, a failure to accommodate Sita reflects a failure to accommodate the immigrant in his/her sameness rather than in his/her difference. The house, and, by extension, Canadian society cannot be invested with inspiration and spirit until the Other is integrated, or rather until race and gender as categories of difference cease to be the all-informing matrix underlying Canadian multiculturalism. If Sita's uncanniness makes itself felt as "the demons of Mr Simmons's house" (237), then the only possibility of exorcising these ghosts lies in a politics of articulation that allows Sita to speak. However, in contrast to a specifically postcolonial concern, giving voice is not part of an endeavour to recover an indigenous identity here. The inhumanity of Simmons consists not so much in his failure to acknowledge Sita's cultural identity but in his callous and cruel treatment of her as a human being. And it is as a human being rather than as a subject determined by racial/ethnic and sex/gender difference that Sita wants to be heard.

The Heart of the Matter: The Family as a Deconstructive Device

The Innocence of Age alludes to Edith Wharton's famous novel *The Age of Innocence.* By way of changing the intertext's title, the novel indicates a switch from issues of social class to age as a marker of difference. Bissoondath offers a glimpse into family structures and the difficulties of maintaining family ties[3] caused by the clash of generations within two families respectively.[4] The family in *The Innocence of Age* is a narrative device employed to write against an obsession with racial difference. The novel may be read as a polemic against multiculturalism in that it replaces the displacement felt by the immigrant cut off from his community, history and tradition with the alienation of a family, i.e. of a father from his son and vice versa. In other words, Bissoondath subverts the genre of migrant writing by transposing the migrant's obsession with space onto the generation gap between Pasco and his son so that travels in space figure as travels in time. The result is that Bissoondath "universalize[s] the experience of migration."[5] By having father and son inhabit two different worlds, live in different emotional environments, and speak two different languages,[6] Bissoondath ethnifies members of the dominant group in Toronto society and demystifies the irritation and alienation experienced by the immigrant. Within his universalist stance both become part of the human condition.[7] Furthermore, by enacting a rapprochement between father and son, Bissoondath also implicitly makes a point about the possibility of bridging cultural differences, to the extent that they become irrelevant.

There can be no doubt that father and son have quite different personalities. In accordance with his pragmatist outlook on life, problems for the ambitious Daniel, in contrast to his father, appear as opportunities rather than obstacles. What presents itself as innovation for Daniel, is in fact an invasion for Pasco; Daniel embraces the new, his father retains the old. If Pasco's son merely has his career in mind, Pasco displays altruism when he serves prostitutes and the homeless meals for free. Moreover, while Daniel calculates the real-estate value of his father's house, the house also has a sentimental value for his father, for it is his wife Edna's spirit that Pasco finds access to only in the house that both had inhabited once. Daniel even counts the costs of a one-night stand, and he, in contrast to his father, is unable to form a lasting relationship because he is unable to love. Daniel's materialism and his calculating manner contrast negatively with Pasco's idealism, and whereas Daniel's social contacts remain superficial, Pasco's social life is characterized by genuine affection. That father and son are alienated from each other, is also underscored by the use of names. When Pasco calls his son "Danny," he fails to notice that his son prefers to be addressed as "Daniel" (10).[8] Thus while Daniel fails to perceive the importance of Pasco's meetings with his friends, Pasco fails to make an effort at learning what sort of a person his son really is. At this stage in the novel their respective views of each other are incompatible and that this is a cause for strife and quarrel between them.

Daniel does not only work at refurbishing Mr Simmons's flat, he is also keen on renovating his father's house. Significantly enough, the one job proves as tough as the other, which is underlined by the fact that both tasks involve the troublesome overcoming of a silence. If Simmons's house remains silent for Daniel because Sita's presence has not been accounted for, his father's house is silent for his father because he has not come to terms with the death of his wife Edna (69). From the perspective of the novel, both father and son are to be criticized for not challenging the silence lying at the heart of their problems. Pasco's extended period of mourning becomes problematic because it prevents him from getting on with his life, which, in turn, affects the relationship to his son. Likewise, Daniel is seen in a negative light in that he identifies too readily with the values of Simmons, which are nothing short of inhumane.

Daniel's situation is elaborated by way of intertextual reference. *The Innocence of Age* insinuates that Danny resembles the biblical Daniel, who is cast into the lion's den for misplacing his faith and worshipping the wrong deity. Thus implicitly Daniel Taggart's job at Simmons's company is viewed as a punishment for praying to Mammon. Daniel Taggart is trapped by a capitalist and egotist world view is represented by Mr Simmons, whose first name is Leon, i.e. literally, the lion. His danger and greed is also underlined by his reputation as a "money-making machine" (57). While Pasco and his friends display empathy and warmth towards others, Simmons is associated with a machine or with barren nature:

> Viv has pointed out to Danny that the dais on which the statue stood—large and round, the sides tiled, the plywood surface swathed in green carpeting—had once been a fountain. Sal, prattling on one day, told him that Mr Simmons had intended it to be a wishing well, figuring that over time the value of the coins tossed in would not only pay for the work and materials but provide a continuing profit, too. However, the pennies had clogged the pipes so frequently, and the plumber's bills had grown so astronomical, that Mr Simmons had ordered it sealed up. (83)

As the dried-up fountain in the lobby of his office building illustrates,

Simmons's world is doomed. That Daniel Taggart's life world falls short of the positively valued organic quality of his father's attitude towards life is corroborated by the withered and stunted orange tree he has been given by Simmons (40). The aridness of a plant becomes indicative here of the emotional distance and coldness concomitant with Daniel's capitalist, Social Darwinist vision of life: "If you don't become a lion . . . you'll become his food" (169).

While Simmons's end constitutes a kind of poetic justice, Daniel at the end of the novel changes and distances himself from the values of his boss. In particular, Sita's story has concrete effects on Daniel's relationship to Pasco. In an epiphany triggered by her rape, Daniel begins to understand his father. When Daniel has to overhear what Simmons does to Sita, the words that he has addressed to his father in a conversation about their respective views of the world surface once again, this time, however, with a difference in that they reveal that his cynicism has given way to pity and remorse: "*Everything's a product, Dad. Everything can be bought or sold. Even people.* The words materialized by themselves in Danny's mind, rising without warning" (237). Questioning both Simmons's as well as Daniel's association of love with sex and of sex with race (Simmons) or money (Daniel), the novel makes Daniel experience to which ends his philosophy can be applied. Thus after Sita's revenge on Simmons, Daniel decides to help her return to her Caribbean home. His change as a person is signalled by the fact that at the end of the novel he helps the homeless in much the same way as his father does. One of the punch lines of *The Innocence of Age* is that the text no longer distinguishes between homelessness in a social and homelessness in a cultural/ethnic sense of the word. Daniel, at the end of the novel, has learnt to look at people as full-fledged human beings, which is also the process of learning that Bissoondath wants to initiate in his readers. In that sense, his prose may be called didactic.

The Ace of Race: Multiculturalism and Racism as Strategy

The novel reenacts Pasco's problems with his son in those that Montgomery has with his daughter Nutmeg. But while the generational conflict between Pasco and Daniel ends happily, the very same conflict ends tragically in the case of Montgomery and Nutmeg. By showing that generation conflicts are not peculiar to a particular ethnicity, Bissoondath deconstructs race as the sole explanation of human behaviour. Despite Montgomery's hope that Nutmeg "can't be so different from her family" (15), his daughter proves him wrong. Changing her name from Nutmeg, the family's term of endearment, to Spice, she underlines that as a personality she consciously decides to defy her family. Structurally, Nutmeg is a foil for Sita. While Sita may be forced to prostitute herself, Montgomery's daughter runs away and becomes a prostitute of her own accord. If Nutmeg's age strongly suggests that her decision is to be understood as the rebellion of a teenager, it is significant that within the novel the structural constraints influencing her are not social. Whatever determines her course of action, it is not racism.

In his treatment of multiculturalism, Bissoondath shows that often social relations in a multicultural situation cannot be adequately described by race as a conceptual tool, and that conflicts between different ethnicities cannot always be described exhaustively by racism. Implicit here is a trenchant critique of multiculturalism as a view of society that reduces the complexity of life to matters of ethnicity. By keeping constant the same phenomenon for two ethnicities, *The Innocence of Age* defies (racial) difference as conceptual frame for understanding human behaviour. According to Bissoondath, individual complexity should replace the simplifying label of ethnic difference: "Pasco had to admit to himself that, with some shame, he hadn't been able to look past the colour of the forest to see the individuality of the tree" (13). A superficial view of a human being as belonging to an ethnic group prevents an active engagement with the individual under the label of a group. Moreover, it may lead to social tensions because if (racial) difference remains the sole basis of social discrimination, a society becomes prone to the invocation of racism, rather than to racism proper.[9]

Although society in *The Innocence of Age* is accused of being racist for killing Montgomery, one must not overlook that in a way it is Montgomery himself who has failed and not the society that has failed him. This is a departure from the more ambivalent treatment of the immigrant predicament in Vassanji's *No New Land*. Montgomery dies in the course of an act of self-defence by Kurt, a young and overly nervous police officer who, ironically enough, in an earlier episode of the novel actively fought racial violence.[10] The point of this episode is that not every quarrel between people of different skin colour can be explained by a racial logic. This is also made explicit by Montgomery's son.[11] The one person who might have a reason for bearing a grudge articulates a moderate view:

> These people, they won't leave us alone. They see a racist under every bed. One of 'em even told my sister that having white skin automatically means you're racist. Guilty until proven innocent. Well, just saying that is racist, if you ask me. They say they're on our side, but there's only one side as far as I can see, and that's their side. If they didn't have us, I don't know what they'd do. They'd be nobodies. Well, I want no part of it. I have a life to live. (306)

Racism occupies a prominent position in the works of Neil Bissoondath, but, as the passage quoted above demonstrates, his position is provocative.

Montgomery's son becomes Bissoondath's mouthpiece in demanding that racism is a term that should be used sparingly. It is too often invoked in order to compensate for a weak subject position which itself relies on a problematic notion of (racial) difference for the construction of an identity. Neil Bissoondath has elaborated on this point elsewhere, too, as a look at his frequently anthologized short story "Dancing" shows, which will conclude this chapter.

By Way of Conclusion: Strategic Racism and Multiculturalism in "Dancing" (1986)[12]

> In the West Indies, long and boisterous parties, on the whole, inconvenience no one. They are held at houses, both inside and outside. Neighbours tend to be invited; children sleep where they fall. Food and drink are in plentiful supply, music is loud and lively, meant not as background filler but as foreground incentive to dance. There is nothing sedate about the archetypal West Indian party. So central is "a good time" to the West Indian sense of self that someone—not a West Indian—once wryly commented that she had the impression that parties, and not calypso and reggae, were the great West Indian contribution to world culture. Booming music, the yelp and rumble of excited voices, the tramp of dancing feet are accepted as an integral part of the region's cultural life. Transfer this to, say, Toronto or Vancouver—not a house surrounded by an extensive yard but to an apartment hemmed in by other apartments. Transfer the music, the dancing, the shouting—everything but the fact that the neighbours, unknown and uncommunicative, are unlikely to be invited. It takes little imagination to appreciate the tensions that may, and do, arise.[13]

"Dancing" features a black servant woman migrating from Trinidad to Toronto, where she experiences racism as the underside of "ethnic separatism."[14] However, provocatively enough, it is not the dominant Canadian ethnicity that is racist in "Dancing" but the Caribbean immigrants. If *The Innocence of Age* holds that racism is often an inadequate, simplistic way of describing conflicts, "Dancing" deconstructs racism by showing that it is not exclusively relied upon by the dominant ethnicity. As Bissoondath has it, "this is a story that says: not only whites are racist. The fact is that non-whites can also be racist."[15]

While *The Innocence of Age* charts how people unconsciously draw on racism in order to explain social conflicts between two different ethnicities, in "Dancing" racism is consciously opted for by the Caribbean immigrants.[16] Thus whereas racism in *The Innocence of Age* is a matter of understanding social interaction too simplistically, "Dancing" primarily projects racism as a moral problem characterising the immigrant's attitude towards the Canadian host society. Racism in "Dancing" figures as a subtle strategy on which the immigrant community relies in order to manipulate the dominant social paradigm, i.e. multiculturalism. More precisely, racism can be used to exploit a social policy in which tolerance towards other ethnicities is institutionalized and in which any violation of this policy can be made to pay. While racism on the part of the ethnic majority is nonexistent in "Dancing," those allegedly marginalized in the Western metropolis discover the financial potential of "the constant assertion of cultural difference."[17]

Whereas there are obvious differences between racism as depicted in "Dancing" and in *The Innocence of Age*, there are striking similarities once it comes to the analysis of its root causes. Both "Dancing" and *The Innocence of Age* reflect a view of Canadian multiculturalism as a policy that in its liberalism and tolerance fosters rather than impedes racism. As Syl, an immigrant character of "Dancing" reveals in a conversation with the protagonist Sheila: "We have every right to be here [i.e. in Canada]. They [i.e. the Canadians] owe us. And we [i.e. the Caribbean immigrant community] going to collect, you hear me?"[18] If *The Innocence of Age* criticizes the almost universal applicability of racism as a label for any disagreement or conflict involving different ethnicities, "Dancing" reveals that those Trinidadians who claim to be discriminated against may also display the very racialist thinking they accuse the ethnic mainstream of. Not surpringly, Bissoondath criticizes such functionalizations of difference as cynical.

Almost all of Bissoondath's narratives argue a case against the constraints of community which prevent the individual from exerting his free will. An essential part of one's free will is of course the right to change, i.e. to leave behind a culture that subjectively is not deemed worth clinging to. This is an issue in "Dancing," as a story that is also centrally concerned with cultural expressions of the Caribbean immigrant community. As it turns out, for Sheila calypso, limbo, and reggae do not have an inherent value; as a matter of fact, the story's protagonist regards the songs played by the Caribbean community as "old and stale."[19] According to her, carrying the old culture over into the new country merely distorts the essence of that culture. Thus "the central paradox of 'Dancing' is that the Trinidadians' efforts to make Canada 'just like Trinidad' [. . .] falsify the culture they seek to preserve."[20] For example, dancing in "Dancing" is not viewed as an assertion of Caribbean cultural specificity; decontextualized from its Caribbean enviroment it becomes a farce. Forced to dance by the expatriate Trinidadians in an attempt at claiming her for a dubious community identity, Sheila's dancing in "Dancing" is not characterized by the release and ecstasy that the Carribean culture is said to provide for the other immigrants. Metaphorically speaking, Sheila's dance becomes indicative of the vertigo of a ghetto mentality both inhumane and oppressive in its denial of individuality. Sheila does not feel like dancing once her fellow immigrants from Trinidad have displayed precisely the kind of cultural chauvinism that she initially wanted to escape by leaving the Caribbean. However, as the following extract illustrates, she is not given a choice:

> Then Syl grab me and shout, "Somebody put on the music. Turn it up loud-loud. For everybody to hear! This whole damn building! Come, girl, dance. Dance like you never dance before."
>
> And I dance.
>
> I dance an dance an dance.
>
> I dance like I never dance before. (209)

Tragically enough, it is in Canada that Sheila, by way of an involuntary and, in fact, violent initiation into a community no longer her own, becomes, or rather is made, West Indian.[21] The means employed to this end consists in a ritual that for Sheila is separated from its relevant time and place and therefore has lost all of its significance as a meaningful cultural practice. While Canadian for Bissoondath translates as the chance of redefining oneself, Sheila, like so many other protagonists of Bissoondath's novels, is made to succumb to the constraints of the old community and its culture. For Sheila, Caribbean culture as practiced by the community in Toronto does not preserve tradition but ossifies it. Measured against her search for a new identity, Caribbean dance in Canada, as it is portrayed in "Dancing," is nothing short of a danse macabre, a dance of death.

B. 'There' I: An Area of Darkness. *A Casual Brutality* (1988)

Neil Bissoondath's first novel is set on the fictive Caribbean island of Casaquemada. Partly for materialist and partly for idealist reasons, the protagonist's Raj Ramsingh returns to the island of his birth and experiences again the culture he has been brought up on. One could also say, he is faced to force the culture from which he has sought to distance himself. Raj's unease on Casaquemada proves to be prophetic, for his stay in the Caribbean ends in a catastrophe culminating in the violent deaths of his wife and his son. Throughout the novel, the representation of the island is deeply disturbing. Its portrayal is one of "decay and disintegration, and the recurrent images in the novel are those of brutality, insensitivity, forlorness and annihilation."[1] Raj's portrayal of his Caribbean origins provides an insight into Neil Bissoondath's evaluation of difference and sameness. As will be outlined below, Bissoondath's treatment of ethnicity and community difference renders *A Casual Brutality* a controversial text that has much in common with *The*

Innocence of Age.

By narrating the story from the perspective of a character that is in the process of switching a Casaquemadan ethnicity for a Canadian one, Bissoondath makes a point about the arbitrariness, and indeed arrogance, of an obsession with community difference. In an attempt to invest his characters with complexity, Neil Bissoondath finds he must also write back to the former colonized rather than to the former colonizers solely. In writing against the counterdiscursive characteristic of much of postcolonial fiction, Bisoondath displays "a very different agenda from that of Caribbean writers who consciously participate in a postcolonial 'writing back' to the centres of colonial power."[2] What nevertheless qualifies him as a postcolonial writer is his attempt to come to terms with the disrupting experiences of colonialism and its aftermath. While his narratives are set against political and historical events, it is really the characters and the way they cope that Bissoondath is interested in.[3] As a critic has it:

> Among South Asian Canadian writers from the Caribbean, Bissoondath may be regarded as the most perceptive and skilled commentator on characteristic themes of disorder and persecution leading to flight or displacement, and ultimately to uncertainty or inner disorder.[4]

In what follows, Raj's view of Caribbean nature will be examined as an example of his alienation from his country of origins first. His view of nature, which indirectly reflects his cultural assumptions, finds its objectification in an analysis of the political situation, which will be analysed subsequently. For Bissoondath and his alter ego Raj Ramsingh Caribbean/Casaquemadan society becomes guilty of imposing a collective identity on the individual. It excludes diverging opinions or individual transgressions discursively or punishes them by inflicting violence. In the context of the novel it does not seem exaggerated to claim that community constraints and violence reflect the underside of a culture best avoided.

The Rejection of the Other: Culture and the Culture of Nature

In *A Casual Brutality* nature is viewed as a chaotic force in need of containment. Containment, however, presupposes a will to order and as such a human endeavour. A case in point for such an endeavour can consist in the building of houses, which become representative of culture. Casaquemada's nature is an untamed nature which imposes itself on man's habitation against his will. Thus Wayne's house, "mysterious in the grip of vegetation [. . .] [,] seemed forever on the verge of vanishing into an embrace of leaves and branches."[5] Nature claims the essence of human culture by destroying its signs. On

Casaquemada, literally the island of the 'burnt house' ('casa quemada'), culture becomes delicate insofar as it is exposed to the threat of a destructive nature.

The containment of nature can also consist in gardening, which has for Raj an element "of holding off jungle, of beating back an insistent interloper" (64). However, generally speaking, gardens on Casaquemada are in a pitiable state:

> My grandfather's garden, the little plot of land in which he had laboured so long and so intensely, showed no signs of ever having been cultivated. Its weeds were thick, its flowers clustered with an almost deliberate disorder. Banana trees reached their long, floppy leaves into the lower branches of a centrally placed pomme-cythere tree, which, tall, dense and spreading, effectively blocked out the sun while, behind it, in the greater gloom, the narrow stalks of papaya trees merged hazily into each other. Under my shoes, the ground was soft and damp, springy with dead vegetation. (115–6)

As Penny van Toorn explains, "the garden of Raj's grandfather, once an epitome of controlled cultivation, erupts into a wild profusion of anarchic growth."[6] While Wayne could make an attempt to impede nature's growth, he is forced to use his cutlasses to defend the lives of Raj and his family when a state of emergency is declared.[7] At this point it becomes obvious that it is no longer a value-free struggle against the realm of the organic that Bissoondath presents us with. Rather the novel suggests that both culture and nature are endowed with political overtones that are worth exploring in greater detail.

Emblematic of the process of taming nature is also the construction of roads. It is a "narrow asphalt road that seemed [. . .] the only line of defence from the forest that sat, dense and sullen, on the other side" (62). In this context, a road can symbolize man's will to explore and probe the unknown, of which the forest is emblematic.[8] A road is part of an infrastructure that attempts to shape the amorphous; as such it is a cultural manifestation demonstrating man's inventiveness in making nature subject to his needs. The asphalt road Raj has in mind becomes symbolic of human civilization. One could also say, it becomes metonymic of man's achievement in paving the way for culture.[9]

The road is viewed as a (cultural) means taken against the dangers of nature represented by the forest. The forest is not merely a realistic description of a Caribbean topography; psychoanalytically, a forest symbolizes the unconscious,[10] which, for Freud, is the locus of the suppressed. Man's superego is said to defy morally ambivalent, and hence culturally unacceptable, desires and to relegate them to the sphere of the unconscious. One could say that Freudian psychology conceives of the suppressed as a residual of the natural. As a realm where existential dangers lurk, the forest is dangerous and a site of the uncanny.

In general, the novel suggests that culture's power to contain the chaos of nature is limited. Whereas culture is perceived to be stable, nature is felt to be dangerously dynamic. Casaquemadan nature is not characterized by variety, it is characterized by its growth. In other words, Caribbean nature in Raj's eyes is forever growing but never changing, a fact that obsesses Raj because it has significance for his analysis of the stasis and inertia of the political situation on Casaquemada at large. Raj's country of adoption, Canada, contrasts favourably with Casaquemada in terms of nature:

> Beside it, in black ink and in the neatest hand I could muster, I wrote "Toronto" and the date, hoping, by capturing a splinter of the beauty, to preserve strokes of the excitement I felt at what was happening around me: at the rapid interplay of cloud, at the freshening of the air, the rusting of the trees, the brittle crinkling of dried leaves underfoot on the sidewalk. At this display of a nature that was not static, of a nature that was spectacle in its inconstancy. (164)

Both Canadian nature and nature on Casaquemada are dynamic. But whereas Canada's is simply an organic nature, Casaquemadan nature is demonic. Raj's view of the landscape equates excessive growth with the female and sexualizes what he fears.[11] In much the same way as Casaquemadan nature can never be cultivated, Raj resists Casaquemadan culture as a place to which he cannot become naturalized in its profusion and voluptuousness.[12]

To argue that nature and culture are pitted against each other is not to say that Raj's perception of nature is not profoundly cultural, too. Of necessity, the way he describes nature is also based on a construction that is informed by cultural assumptions. However, in his case they are no longer the assumptions operating unconsciously in the mind of a Casaquemadan gone Canadian. The naturalized Canadian Raj experiences the clash between two cultures, a Canadian and a Casaquemadan one. As he is increasingly operating on the cultural premises of the Western world, Caribbean nature constitutes at best a sort of interference and at worst an impediment. Whereas culture to him translates as civilization and refinement, (Caribbean) nature becomes a force beyond control, which, by way of its chaos, defies the Enlightenment basis on which Western culture is founded, subjectivity: "It was the kind of vegetation, deceptive in its beauty, that could swallow you whole, a vision of green annihilation into which a man could, unnoticed, disappear without a trace" (141). Leaving a trace is, of course, a quintessentially human desire informed by the wish to make life meaningful, and it is culture that can address this need. Succumbing to a nature that erases the traces of cultural artefacts is the ultimate chaos conceivable in this context. Nature becomes an element that threatens to uproot man's order on Casaquemada as well as the order of man in general. On an island where the signs of material culture (e.g. a house) merit no investment because they are likely to be destroyed anyway, "escape [. . .] becomes the only rational option."[13] As such, "the name Casaquemada vindicates Raj's abandonment of the island: anyone who fails to leave a burning house is obviously out of his or her own mind."[14] Bissoondath departs from postcolonial activism, but not necessarily from postcolonialism as such, in that he has his protagonist leave his place of birth and shed his Caribbean ethnicity. Bissoondath's novel is concerned with a reckoning with postcoloniality and not with the uncritical affirmation of ethnic difference sometimes proclaimed by it. The implications of this reckoning become more pronounced when exploring in greater deatil the political dimensions of the novel.

A Postcolonial Reckoning: Politics and the Body Politic

Nature in *A Casual Brutality* is a fraught concept. While the previous section set out to show how nature symbolized Raj's uneasiness with Casaquemadan culture, nature also becomes a repository of images that alludes to Casaquemada's political situation. Three cases in point are particularly insightful in the context of a discussion of the political implications of the novel.

That Casaquemada is an island deprived of hope[15] is conveyed by reference to stars and star-gazing. While these are traditional symbols of transcendence and hope as well as the longing for it, in *A Casual Brutality* hope is ruled out for Raj and his family, as the following piece of dialogue corroborates: "'Look,' I said, 'how much more clearly you can see the stars here.' 'Yes,' she replied. 'But that only means that the night is darker'" (345). Asha corroborates that the future for Raj, Jan and Rohan is bleak. When, in an instance of foreboding she warns Raj of lightning (189), she intuitively feels that nature is not merely indifferent to their fate but is out to harm them. It is important to realize that whereas both the lack of stars and the threat of lightning on the Caribbean island of Casaquemada are endowed with significance for the individual, both ultimately also pertain to the public sphere, for it is the latter that brings about the former: life on Casaquemada is depressing and ridden with lethal dangers because the political situation is too instable to provide its population with hope and security. It thus seems adequate to describe the plot of the novel metaphorically in the following way: Jan's and Rohan's deaths are caused by (the darkness of) a postcolonialism that is anything but a light at the end of the tunnel (of colonialism). Raj, Kayso and Jan are to be blamed insofar as they have not avoided this darkness in the first place: "You tell me, Raj. What the hell *are* [sic] you doing here? Why the hell did you come back? Didn't anyone ever tell you the new motto of the place—If you're out, stay out; if you're in, get out?" (209) Tragically, Raj's disposition prevents him from reading the signals of warning. He is not sensitive enough to follow the subtle clues that his environment has provided for an accurate evaluation of the situation. Eventually, it needs Grappler's political analyses and the immediate experience of the revolt for Raj to fully comprehend the atavistic nature of Casaquemada's culture.

The sinister character of Casaquemadan culture is underscored by an intertextual reference that has hitherto not been commented on exhaustively.[16] When Raj reviews the catastrophe that claims his wife and son and ponders that "this is how the world shatters, with a peep at the soul" (367), he alludes to TS Eliot's famous poem "The Hollow Men" in order to refer to Casaquemada's political as well as existential crisis.[17] On a par with the hollowness and shallowness that a postreligious modernity brings for Eliot, Bissoondath detects cultural and moral degeneration as well as a lack of authenticity within Casaquemadan postcolonial society. Modernity and postcoloniality overlap in that they are conceptualized as wastelands by Eliot and Bissoondath respectively. Furthermore, both the hollow men of modernity and the hollow men produced by the postcolonial experience on Casaquemada have in common that they do not expect a grand finale at the end of the world. Although both Eliot and Bissoondath's Raj imagine it as anticlimactic, the world, according to Eliot, ends "not with a bang but a whimper,"[18] whereas Bissoondath grants Raj at least an (admittedly) limited epiphany, i.e. a "peep at the soul," at the very moment that his private world shatters. While the end of the hollow men in Eliot's poem is not apocalyptic in the Biblical sense because it does not provide the hope (of resurrection) that world downfall also entails, Bissoondath envisages a source of hope for Raj in the possibility of a new beginning, although such a new beginning is not to be envisaged on Casaquemada. As Casaquemada is seen as a place that drains the subject of substance, hope for Raj can only lie in migration. In order to survive, but also to preserve its essence as a human being, he has to shed his old ethnicity and escape. He "flees a Caribbean world of nothingness, fear, and insecurity."[19] At the end of the novel Raj reasons: "I go like my forebears, to the future, to the challenge that lies elsewhere of turning nothing into something, far from the casual brutality of collapse, far from the ruins of failure, across thousands of miles of ocean" (378). Displaying traits of the postcolonial migrant as theorized by Bhabha and others, Raj leaves with a positive outlook which even the possibility of not finding a permanent home cannot alter.[20]

A closer look at Raj's epiphany into his life and the true nature of Casaquemada reveals that his insight is conveyed by way of a description of nature, too. "As darkness closed over me, inky and inexorable, I thought: I have spent my life polishing shadows. It was the only truth, in that moment of extinction that occurred to me" (370). Nature becomes indicative of the epistemological agenda also at stake in Bissoondath's novel. While the colour of the sky in Toronto is described as "a fine, high, glazed blue, pure and insubstantial, with the clarity of crystal" (154), Casaquemada's nature is chimerical. While Canada is a place where lucidity of thought is possible, even if it involves a certain element of "chilliness and dispassion,"[21] the Caribbean appears as a place that is deceptive. At the end of the novel, Raj realizes:

> Not only to have trusted as reality the distracting sideshow of sunlight dancing on primary colours but to have coddled it, fostered it, to have wanted it to be the reality; to have listened without challenge to all those could-have-beens and should-have-beens, all those sorrowed expressions of hope lost and possibility shattered: it was life swimming in delusion, life shimmering in fantasy, life in which the slope was flat and the swamp solid. (372)

In marked opposition to Canada, the Caribbean is a place where illusions acquire the status of facts and certainties become ambiguous. What is disturbing is that for Bissoondath the Caribbean is a simulacrum precisely because the (postcolonial) subject constructs the object reality according to his needs and desires. The arbitrariness of perception is so pervasive on Casaquemada that reality becomes unreliable. The effects of a perversion of reality are disorientation, confusion and instability, which can be felt on many levels. It becomes an issue with respect to the private sphere, in which Lenny, for example, betrays Raj's family and becomes responsible for Jan's and Rohan's death (362). Furthermore, it holds true for the economic sphere, an example of which is the brief oil boom that the island has enjoyed in the recent past:

> The oil money, so easily acquired, flowing to the island not from effort but as a consequence of distant events, had given Casaquemada cosmopolitan tastes. We came to prefer the frozen to the fresh, paper to peel. Crystal was imported from Italy, glassware from Germany, leather goods from Brazil. The roads became clogged with Fords and Chryslers, Mercedes Benzes and Rolls-Royces, Toyotas and Hondas, Suzukis and Hiaces. Fortunes soared. Women flew to Miami for day-long shopping trips. Champagne was bought not by the bottle but by the case. (75)

The oil boom erases the traits of local culture. Globalization makes culture on Casaquemada inauthentic and sterile. It becomes secondhand and thus second-rate, to borrow from Naipaul's diagnosis of Caribbean culture in *The Mimic Men*. Most importantly, however, Casaquemada is chimerical in terms of its political situation at large (359). This is underlined by the sudden outbreak of an Emergency, which brings along anarchy, violence and destruction.[22] Chimerical here means that Casaquemada is not merely deceptive but willingly so. As Grappler pinpoints, Casaquemada does not merely forget to question itself but consciously refuses to do so. The difference is of importance, for Casaquemada's conscious self-deception is not merely irresponsible, it also is deeply immoral.[23] The most striking example of this kind of policy is the way in which the murder of Kayso is received by Casaquemadans: "Truth was completely irrelevant. The man was dead, and the manner of his death had importance now only in its entertainment value" (344).

Drawing on an ancient concept, Bissoondath employs the symbol of air in order to make a point about society and politics. The quality of the air becomes symbolic of the political atmosphere on Casaquemada and in Canada respectively. Casaquemada's air is mostly stale contrasted with Toronto's fresh breeze (164, 314). Whereas the former is confining, the latter signals freedom. In particular, Canada guarantees freedom to the individual, a notion informed by a liberal-humanist line of thought. Metaphorically, while Canada lets the individual breathe, Casaquemada's repressive atmosphere is asphyxiating. Even the most fundamental rights, i.e. human rights, are not recognised, as the example of Kayso demonstrates.

Kayso's return to Casaquemada is informed by a sense of obligation to the country of his origins (156). The responsibility for his community is inflected by the liberal education he received in Canada as a lawyer. However, fighting for equal justice and pleading human rights in a court is a moralistic stance he is not gratified for on Casaquemada. On the contrary. Grappler, commenting on his death, holds that

> [o]n the island of Casaquemada, life was worth less than a house or a car; it could not be bartered for anything; it could not be graced with monetary value. It was, I thought, the final blow of colonial heritage: life as financial transaction. It was why Kayso, speaking of human rights, of life as having an intrinsic value of its own by the mere fact of its existence, was seen at best as odd, at worst as a publicity seeker. It was why, too, in the end, a man such as he had to be ridiculed, his legacy vilified. He had come demanding competence and honesty and effort in an island that no longer, if it ever had, cared about such things. He had challenged too many deeply held prejudices. He had challenged a rape of the land colonial in its actions and attitudes. He had, in the end, challenged history, and in this he could not be the winner. (345)

Kayso becomes a casualty of his own illusions about Casaquemada. His vision of reform is thwarted by a Caribbean not interested in betterment. Human rights and Casaquemada clash as two different worlds; Kayso's humanism is hopelessly at odds with Casaquemada's greed and corruption. Most importantly, however, it is at odds with Casaquemada's tribalism. For, ironically, it is precisely the sense of obligation Madera demands from Raj that is behind the murder of Kayso. Kayso's underestimation of such an obligation is tragic, and Madera's harping on community ties appears cynical.

On a metaphorical level, *A Casual Brutality* alludes to the political, social and cultural crisis on Casaquemada in terms of illness and disease. Drawing on the metaphor of society as body, Bissoondath describes Caribbean society in terms of an organism suffering from an illness that is nearly fatal: "All ideas of selflessness and service took a plane out of Casaquemada years ago. It's one of our diseases" (219). The advanced state of national degeneration calls for a cure; as the name of the city of Salmonella indicates, the body politic in Bissoondath's novel is sick and in need of treatment. Because the society at large suffers from structural problems, the individual living in that society becomes prone to illnesses, too. That place and atmosphere seem especially detrimental to mental health is underlined by Surein, who suffers from paranoia, and Jan and Raj, who both develop claustrophobia. Surein's paranoia exemplifies a problematic identity construction. He "needed something to fear, he needed someone to hate, and it was only through these passions, their stir and their consequence, that he could fashion an image of an unassailable self" (88). Surein is too weak a personality to dispense with a prejudiced view of an Other; he needs an enemy against whom he can construct an acceptable self-image. In this sense, Othering becomes a compensation for the shortcomings of his personality. Claustrophobia is another telling symptom of the disease of the body politic. It becomes indicative of the personal arrest the individual has to face on Casaquemada: "Small places, places of limited scope, of brutal past, hesitant present and uncertain future, offer but scanty possibility, offer at best a life proscribed" (142,143). In addition to that, claustrophobia also refers to the absence of rest in a country that demands constant vigilance and wariness: "She [Jan] looked out again at the passing fences, the near lawns, the shuttered houses, and her chest rose and fell as she fought the touch of claustrophobia she had acquired not long after our arrival in Casaquemada" (81,173). The thought of a society that comes to haunt the individual with its problems (cf. paranoia) proves as disturbing as the thought of a society that offers no space to withdraw to (cf. claustrophobia). In each case, the individual displays a compulsory neurosis, which manifests itself in an obsession with control: "Where did it come from, and why, this sense of life as running water, turbulent, and beyond control?" (325) Whereas Surein develops an affinity to weapons, Raj begins to survey his property and hires Wayne as a bodyguard.

It is no coincidence that Bissoondath's character is a doctor of medicine. He reflects on difficult cases, and he is especially interested in the contribution of the patient in the healing process: "The positive patient puts up a better fight than the patient who, deprived of hope, cannot rally his resources" (19).

Eventually, Bissoondath endows the art of healing with a metaphorical significance. What is really at stake in Bissondath's novel are not illnesses of the body but of the body political. The political situation of Casaquemada is deemed to be critical, and a doctor's powers of healing illnesses are said to be limited. While Raj suggests that there remains only one chance of cure, i.e. letting the illness run its course and trust the body politic to heal itself, Grappler's diagnosis suggests a therapy more radical. To his mind, Casaquemada is rotten, corrupt and self-deceptive. It is a nation that is not multicultural at heart but merely celebrates the "carnival of intolerance" (201). The lack of tolerance is accompanied by a lack of commitment to the nation (210), i.e. Casaquemadans, in Grappler's eyes, are unwilling to bring sacrifices for their country. At the same time, intellectuals are engaged in "a politics of blame" that is backwards and unproductive in its victimization (202). Furthermore, Grappler accuses Casaquemadans of immaturity; the island's "failed experiment in nationhood" (203) is due to a political irresponsibility that marks Casaquemadans as children in need of (colonial) guidance (203). In his eyes, Casaquemadans avoid hard work (206) and have not learned to accept criticism (203). As postcolonial Casaquemada is dismissive of his (neo-) liberal credo emphasizing solidarity and core values, Grappler's cynical assessment of a patient disregarding his advice demands "to cut out the cancer" (211). Less metaphorically, Grappler cynically suggests that the impending coup and the possibility of a military dictatorship are not only what Casaquemada deserves but also what it is in need of: "And if we're *payols*, with *payol* problems, then maybe we need *payol* [sic] solutions" (211). Grappler argues that postcolonial Casaquemadan identity merely mimics colonial mentality. For Grappler, Independence has come to signify "the right to do nothing" (138) as well as "the right to loot ourselves" (199). As the following section will show, the independence of the nation will often be buttressed by the discourse of community and community difference, which in its deterministic logic proves fatal to the independence of the individual.

Claiming the Individual: Community and Community Constraints

Neil Bissoondath is concerned as well with the power that the notion of community can exert on the individual. In *A Casual Brutality* the impact of community on questions of difference and sameness is examined in greater detail with respect to society and race, and the family.

Raj's encounter with the past also entails an encounter with a former schoolmate of his. Doug Madera, in contrast to the protagonist of Bissoondath's first novel, has not left Casaquemada for a career elsewhere. The constellation Raj-Madera is not only indicative of two different ways in the world but is of crucial importance for an adequate understanding of

Bissoondath's text, too, because the central conflict between Raj (as the protagonist) and Madera (as the antagonist) reflects the central issue of the novel.

Casaquemada is a society that is portrayed as racialist and racist. Caribbeans of African American, East Indian and European descent coexist in a way that is representative of the social situation in the Caribbean at large. The "theorem of race" (88) informs the segregationist character of society. Metaphorically, Casa-quemada signals that the architecture of a multicultural society has been set on fire. One of those responsible for burning down the house, i.e. for the failure of multiculturalism on Casaquemada, is Surein, who wants "to do something to keep the niggers out" (81). Another case in point is Madera who does not merely believe in the ubiquity of racial difference on Casaquemada but also underlines its usefulness as a structuring device. Put differently, for Madera racial difference is a crucial factor in determining one's cultural identity. Raj, on the other hand, cannot deny the humanist ideals underlying his professional training as a doctor. Just as medicine's view on man acknowledges no essential difference between different races and ethnicities, Raj denies any allegiance to a collective. His wish to save lives sharply contrasts with that of Madera, who used to torture pupils as a teenager and since that time has become involved in organized killings. For Raj the plot of the novel becomes an exercise in knowing himself. Madera's flaws are unalterable because he does not perceive them as faults as such. Whereas Raj undergoes a development as a character, Madera remains tied to an irrational and fanatic logic of violence. The trajectory of the novel allows for the conclusion that this is so for the simple reason that violence to him appears a good and necessary thing and is not recognized as unethical. While Raj's mistakes have repercussions on his family that have been unpredictable, Madera consciously harms other people. His aggression against others is justified in the name of a community ideology profoundly at odds with Raj's humanism.

Interestingly enough, both Raj and Madera have essentialist ideas about the relationship between the individual and the community. Succinctly put, for Madera there is a close connection between the individual and the community into which he was born. For Doug Madera the human being is not an individual qua essence but merely comes into existence as a member of a collective. In more accessible terms, for him group identity overrides personal identity. For Raj, this is an argument that is unacceptable. Just as for him growing up together does not mechanically make Madera and him friends, so does their common place of birth not automatically lead to the same community allegiance. In effect, Raj's rejection of racial allegiance results in a reshuffling of Self-Other dichotomies. In his radical denigration of the individual in the name of an essentialist idea of community belonging, Madera becomes an Other for Raj. His denial of the individual runs counter to Raj's notion of a human essence overriding community identity as well as difference between communities. Despite the fact that Madera feels suppressed and victimized by colonialism, postcolonialism and neocolonialism, there can be no doubt that in Raj's eyes he becomes a new suppressor resembling the old in the use of his means. Bissoondath's first novel thus narrates the story of an Othering, the quality of which is a bone of contention with the critics.[24]

As was argued with Vassanji's *The Book of Secrets*, closely connected to the idea of belonging in *A Casual Brutality* are the reasons for belonging. To think about these reasons is crucial in this context because belonging, at least for Raj, is dynamic. Ethnicity is a matter of affiliation and does not constitute an irreducible ontological divide. According to Raj it is possible to switch ethnicities; according to Madera it may be possible but not acceptable. To switch ethnicities qualifies as a betrayal of the community one was born into and consequently deserves ostracizing, which is envisaged as the greatest calamity conceivable. The difference inherent in the different forms of belonging is an ethical difference once again. For Raj, shifting affiliations is not immoral because one commits oneself to one's self and not to a collective. While betrayal is also what Raj theorises, it is a betrayal of the individual and not of a community that he thinks of (90). Raj's attitude is that of a liberal humanism, whereas Doug Madera's ideal is communitarian, or rather totalitarian, i.e. a commitment to the spirit of the community and the welfare of the collective. In this context, the individual is irrelevant. It is important not to overlook that both Raj and Madera represent idealist positions. However, the means employed to implement their respective idealism vary greatly. Raj's liberalism may appear unethical to Madera—but Raj does not harm others. At the same time, Madera's commitment may be idealist (262)—but the means he relies on to realize it are unacceptable within the perspective of the novel. For Madera's vision infringes on others and claims lives, Espinet being a case in point. In marked opposition, Raj's position proves the morally more acceptable alternative.

Madera's as well as Surein's assessments of Raj testify to the fact that on Casaquemada any deviation from a cultural norm is interpreted as betrayal (257, 87), and hence, at least implicitly, as a crime. Deviation becomes a violation of order also in the context of the family as the second major instance where a community lays claim to the individual: "Family. A big word in a small place, a word that went beyond mere legality, mere blood relationship, to a kind of claiming, a cocoon that comforted and confined at the same time" (196). While the family also seems to provide for, it is the demands it makes on the individual that are emphasized in the text. Comfort and constraints prevent the invidual from finding his/her own way or prevent him/her from pursuing a way of his/her own. Once Raj has realized the problematic nature of the family collective, its depiction becomes increasingly demonic: "The hole was beginning to gape, and in the widening aperture the viper couched in the heart of comfort was coming clear" (214).

A Casual Brutality contains several instances in which the detriments of the institution of the family are fully disclosed. Family in Bissoondath's novel is characterized by dishonesty; it demands "the affectation of affection" (79). Raj's family does not even refrain from economic blackmail in order to foster loyalty and faithfulness to its norms: "*Give me a kiss or I not leaving you anything when I die* [sic]" (111). The family is a collective that imposes its cultural assumptions and traditions on the individual. This includes the new role Jan is expected to play as the daughter-in-law (129). However, it also entails a rejection of individuals of different social standing and race. Not only does Raj's grandmother complain about his dark colour of skin (40), she also insists on Raj maintaining his distance to their black servant Wayne (66) and feels uncomfortable when he plays with the black Presbyterian girl Angela (69). Ironically, it is only through disobeying his grandmother's family ideology and by approaching Wayne without prejudice that Raj at least temporarily succeeds in protecting his family. Another case in point underlining the danger the family is capable of exerting is Surein, whose unannounced visits to Raj and Jan underscore the cultural relativity of privacy:

> It was to Jan an intrusion, this privacy that held always a public element, while to the Casaquemadans, to my family and friends, it was a right they could not imagine being denied. Jan at first made no secret of her feelings, accepting with equanimity the inevitable unpopularity that her frankness attracted. Mine, with the possible exception of Grappler, was not a family that appreciated honesty; it was one that demanded games. (78)

Due to a diffuse obligation felt towards his family, Raj at first does not dare to intervene in the curtailment of his privacy (90). He has not sufficiently matured yet in order to resist the claim to a collective identity he does not really wish to identify with. What Surein takes for granted on the basis of a sameness perceived to be essential and inalienable becomes a cause of complaint for Raj only in the course of the novel. What is a social cohesive on Casaquemada becomes an instance of disruption and alienation for the protagonist of *A Casual Brutality*. Raj learns that, in the realm of ethnicity, difference and sameness are matters of conscious choice. Even family ties do not have to be binding if the individual refuses to be bound by them. Sameness, or difference for that matter, are not inherent in the social micro-/macro-structure of the fictional universe of Bissoondath's first novel. That the antagonists in *A Casual Brutality* claim they are is something Bissoondath's first novel shares with most of the narratives he has published so far.

Raj's family operates on a myth of racial purity. Raj defies his grandmother and her fear of miscegenation by marrying a white woman (123). The trajectory of Jan's and Raj's unhappy marriage seems to support Grandma's segregationist credo, but their marital crisis is no veiled criticism directed against racial intermarriage. The novel leaves no doubt that Raj's and Jan's marital problems have nothing to do with the different racial background that both come from. Bissoondath's novel argues that just as marriages do not function of their own accord because of the racial identity of the partners, so marriages do not automatically fail when member of different races marry. On an abstract plane, race ceases to be of relevance as a problem as well as a solution, what counts is the individual not the community. Jan and Raj face an unhappy marriage because they refuse to recognize the lack of communication that characterises their relationship. As Raj has it on looking back: "So that Jan and I moved forward, more by event and the passage of time than by decision and the exercise of choice, less in a life together than in lives parallel" (318; cf. also 47). As individuals they are responsible for their problems, just as only they as individuals could have solved them.

An analogous case can be constructed for Raj and his grandmother's longtime servant Wayne. While the example of Raj and Jan shows how individual difference can be more of a barrier than racial/community difference, Raj and Wayne demonstrate how empathy between members of different races can elide the difference of community. The fact that Wayne helps Raj defend his property at the dawn of the coup seems to be indicative of an interracial understanding between East Indians and African Americans.[25] However, while this is a reading that is not necessarily false, it does not go far enough in its implications. For Wayne makes it clear that it is out of a personal obligation to Raj that he helps him and his family (310). His help is not primarily a solidarity transcending racial divides but to be understood in the context of a give-and-take between two individuals who accidentally were born with different colours of skin. Thus, rather than being a relationship transcending racism, theirs is a relationship that transcends race as a category. The concerted efforts of Wayne and Raj to hold back brutality and violence is less illuminating as an instance of two representatives of different communities working together than as an understanding between individuals who feel that they represent more than their respective community membership. In its complexity, the individual resists any definition based on race alone.

Society's insistence on the communitarian is the other side of its disdain for the individual. On Casaquemada, individuality is marked as deviance from a way of life constructed as the norm. This norm is connected to the notion of community membership and the cultural practices prescribed by it. Those who deviate from the norm are discursively marginalized as eccentrics and, subsequently, excluded as madmen (177). A case in point in the novel is reading, which for Casaquemadans is said to be the ultimate in eccentricity: "In

Casaquemada reading was considered at best antisocial" (107). In this context, the death of Raj's mother, a woman who loves to read (41), may have been an accident, but it is certainly no coincidence. Reading is an indicator of culture in *A Casual Brutality*, just as the lack of a desire to read signifies the opposite. Moreover, by virtue of its cultural implications, reading becomes a form of travelling. If it is argued by Raj that the only hope for the postcolonial Casaquemadan subject is migration, one can also escape by way of one's imagination (107, 108).

Semantically, eccentricity signifies being outside of a centre. In the context of the novel, this centre has been reclaimed for a postcolonial Casaquemadan identity in a problematic way. The notion of a monolithic identity entails that those who refuse to be encompassed by the collective ideology of postcoloniality cease to be postcolonial in the eyes of those who regard themselves as prototypically postcolonial or politically correct.[26] Under Casaquemada's "ethnic eyes" (230) a policy of inclusion/exclusion is institutionalized that becomes manifest in "racial camaraderie" (153). Not only does Bissoondath make a point here about the continuing influence of binarisms, he also draws attention to the flawed logic of a school of postcolonial thinking which claims difference in the realm of ethnicity but demands sameness on an individual level. Neil Bissoondath shows that ethnic difference is a strategy which installs difference between communities while constructing sameness within a community. Bissoondath emphasizes that the "racial brotherhood" (192) springing from such a politics is operating on racialist assumptions. It is "a form of racism, not one that rejected but one that claimed" (162). While sameness is argued to be an essential by postcolonial Casaquemadans who harp on "the brotherhood of skin and race" (230), Bissoondath questions precisely such an assumption by pointing to its constructedness. For him it is not an essential but a discursive formation constructed in order to reduce a complexity that is uncomfortable. The invocation of community is for Bissoondath a simplification of a reality that is too complex to be understood in other than individual parameters. Thus it is no surprise that the protagonist of his first novel eventually finds himself "coveting the lack of community" (163) in Canada:

> I had not come to Toronto to find Casaquemada, or to play the role of ethnic, deracinated and costumed, drawing around himself the defensive postures of the land left behind. And this display of the rakish, this attempt at Third World exoticism, seemed to me a trap, a way of sealing the personality, of rendering it harmless to all but the individual. (221)

A yearning for community and the communitarian is revealed as a compensation for an inadequacy, be it the drill sergeant, who joins the army, or Madera, who joins the police, or Nadan, who joins a monastery, or the members of a family, who live by the law of the family. Because man is a reality too complex in its individuality, Casaquemadan (but also parts of Canadian) society relies on the collective. As was argued in greater detail above, it is not only colonial discourse but also multiculturalism that Bissoondath understands as attempt at subjecting the individual by emphasizing the collective.

The Enforcement of Community: Violence and Violation

Like Vassanji, Bissoondath in *A Casual Brutality* is concerned with two kinds of difference. However, not only are the types of difference Bissoondath plays off against each other structurally different, his underlying concern is also diametrically opposed to that of Vassanji. As a matter of fact, Bissoondath deconstructs collective differences while arguing a case in favour of the difference between individuals.[27] A good example for this is the cricket game that Surein and Raj discuss. While Surein deplores that the West Indian team does not have enough Indian players to make it West Indian, Raj maintains that the team may have been selected on the basis of the class of the individual player and not according to community/racial criteria (88). Multiculturalism in Casaquemada (and Canada) is a policy informed by the importance of community, while it neglects the role of the individual. On Casaquemada, individual differences are not tolerated but fought. The battle against idiosyncrasies relies on two strategies, discursive marginalizing and physical repression. In other words, the fight against the individual is concomitant with a violation of rights and the violence used to enforce it.

Violence and violation figure as theme, symptom and leitmotif in *A Casual Brutality*. They feature in Raj's Caribbean experience as well as in the course of his stay in Canada. Surein's threat of using violence against Raj (85) is mirrored by Andy's aggression against Raj in Canada (169f.). Surein's disrespect of Jan's need for privacy is reflected by Joey and Andy's intrusion into Raj's apartment in Canada (225f.). Although violence and violation are of a lesser quality in Bissoondath's representation of North America, the cooccurrence of the casual (associated with calm and peace) with brutality (associated with destruction and aggression), prove no less disturbing 'here' than 'there.' Both violation and violence appear as transgressions to the humanist Raj. What appears as transgression to Raj and Jan is in fact culturally acceptable to Casaquemadan society; what is impolite to Jan is polite to Surein; what might appear an instance of deviation is, in fact, the norm in a Caribbean society that Raj is gradually alienated from. Once the cultural gap between the Caribbean and Canada is realized/felt by the central characters of the novel, Jan cannot help but feel "fucking helpless in this place" (140), while Raj deplores the lack of control by imagining a time when "everything had at least seemed manageable" (33).

The ubiquity of violence in Neil Bissoondath's first novel is already indicated by the title. *A Casual Brutality* "augurs the bleakness of life in the postcolonial Caribbean"[28] by literally teeming with casualities of casual brutalities. The earliest instance of a pairing of the harmlessness and cold-bloodedness of 'casual' with the violence and aggression of 'brutality' is the threat advocated by Espinet: "But, of course, that was what had been intended: a veiled promise of violence delivered with carefully weighed calculation, an offering softly spoken of a casual brutality" (23). The pervasiveness of casual brutalities in the text indicates that Espinet's case is endowed with a significance that transcends the individual. In a society where hope is replaced by illusions, the seemingly oxymoronic becomes paradoxical, i.e. eventually explicable despite its seemingly contradictory character. For what appears unnatural—the connection between casual and brutal—is, in fact, naturalized as a different norm within which violence, and, by extension, the inhumane, become cultural.

Bissoondath posits an essential humanity that the Caribbean fails to live up to. For Kayso and for Raj, violence is the absolute Other of a liberal/humanist frame of reference. By virtue of their secondary socialization in Canadian academia as medical doctor (Raj) and lawyer (Kayso) both partake of a discourse that emphasizes anthropological constants. While Raj is aware that the human body suffers from the same illnesses regardless of ethnic difference,[29] Kayso believes in the same rights for anyone regardless of different ethnic affiliations. For both, violence and culture exclude each other. Raj's and Kayso's definition of culture is not only informed by cultural anthropology, which poses a set of rules providing orientation in a given surrounding, but also by a humanist tradition that stresses the moral implications of a normative concept of culture, i.e. civilization and refinement. In the postcolonial Caribbean such a normative notion of culture seems not to be binding, instead "arson and assassination become norms."[30] As culture on Casaquemada is chiefly understood as a cognitive matrix, violence and vengeance are not inherently inacceptable. For migrants to the Caribbean such as Raj, Jan and Kayso, on the other hand, violence becomes the locus where two definitions of culture clash. It is for this that both Kayso's as well as Raj's encounter with the island of their birth must end tragic. Jan, Kayso and Raj become protagonists in an archaic story. While their hamartia consists in a willingness to be claimed by a tradition they are alien to or alienated from, it takes the climactic scene of Jan's and Rohan's murder to bring about a peripetia. Raj recognises that the return to the Caribbean has been a fatal mistake. His anagnorisis makes an escape from the Caribbean inevitable and a return unlikely.

Violence is tragic in that Raj's wife and child die, but it is useful in helping Raj come to terms with his own position in the world. The unnaturalness of casual brutalities makes the Caribbean culture Raj has been brought up on strange to him. Raj's Caribbean identity is foregrounded by Bissoondath and thus made strange and self-conscious. In the context of the novel, this is a first step in freeing himself from his Caribbean ethnicity that is increasingly felt to be a burden by Bissoondath's protagonist. The function of casual brutalities lies in objectifying Raj's conflict between Canadian and Caribbean culture. Violence must thus be understood in the context of a personal crisis, the implications of which are by definition ambivalent. Violence orders the chaos of Raj's identity and reduces the complexity of his situation by re/drawing a boundary between Self and Other.[31] Journeying to the island of his birth takes on the quality of a journey into the heart of darkness. The positive effect of that journey is that it triggers off a process of learning that is valuable as well as irreversible. In experiencing the dark side of Casaquemada as the violence of the Other (as well as the Other as violence), any allegiance to origins will finally be shed for good. Raj will not return to Casaquemada, the place of scorched earth and the burnt house, the place where multiculturalism proves to be searing, i.e. hurtful but also cauterizing and thus purifying. As Raj experiences the hurt and healing involved in any purification, so does Casaquemada at large. The impending coup appears as a punishment for the sins of the recent past in that it claims casualties. The end of the novel thus confirms Raj's private reflections on a public level. The illness of the island's society must run its course with the ritualistic quality of a morality play and the fatality of a Greek tragedy.

In terms of genre, *A Casual Brutality* comes across as a nonlinear, discontinuous bildungsroman oscillating between two layers of time.[32] The water crossing involved in Raj's trip from Canada to the Caribbean signals an initiation. In his journey from innocence to experience, the lesson to be learned concerns the deixis of time and place. Raj has to recognize that the past and the Caribbean as his place of origin can be crippling and that any kind of nostalgia (cf. Kayso) or exoticism (cf. Jan) is misplaced. Only after Raj has realized that community, family and roots arrest the development of the individual, does he reach a higher ontological level. A similar case can be made for Casaquemadan society at large. Multiculturalism on Casaquemada suffers from racial as well as class tension, and Bissoondath's implies that this state of affairs is dangerous, as social/racial antagonisms can give way to political instability. As clinging to one's people impedes overcoming division and strife in a society characterized by prejudice and segregation, Bissoondath suggests that multiculturalism can be remedied by fostering individualism. As the relationship between Wayne and Raj exemplifies, dialogue and interaction, communication and consensus on a one-to-one basis can save the project of multiculturalism, which is essential for the running of Caribbean (as well as Canadian) society at large.

C. 'There' II: Hurt and Healing. *The Worlds Within Her* (1999)

Playing off two narratives against each other, *The Worlds Within Her*, in contrast to *A Casual Brutality*, is a polyphonic text. Shakti is an elderly woman born in the Caribbean but living in Canada at the time she tells the story of her life to a comatose friend, Mrs Livingston. The centre of consciousness in the remainder of the text is Yasmin, Shakti's daughter, who journeys to her native country in order to fulfil her mother's last wish. Shakti, who has died by the time the second part of the novel sets in, wants her ashes to return to the Caribbean island she was born on. While Shakti merely recounts experiences from 'here,' Yasmin, out of a sense of personal obligation, travels 'there.' The novel relegates the deixis of place to a deixis of time, for in journeying to the Caribbean Yasmin also pays homage to the past. However, as the ensuing analysis will attempt to show, her journey should be understood not so much as a pilgrimage than as a kind of exorcism.[1]

Both protagonists of *The Worlds Within Her* are survivors. Shakti has endured ostracism by her mother-in-law, betrayal by her husband and marginalization in the diaspora. Whereas she is victimized by both private and political circumstances, Yasmin's concern is of an entirely personal nature. While she is trying to come to terms with the death of her daughter Ariana, who died in a traffic accident, her identity and the roots and traditions of her parents are in need of clarification, too. In Yasmin, Neil Bissoondath presents us with an identity construction in progress. The development she undergoes as a character in the course of the novel ironically mirrors that of her mother in that it is also connected to a crisis of ethnicity. The relationship to her Caribbean family contributes to the consolidation of her self-image, albeit ex negativo. Rather than presenting a point of identification, the Caribbean becomes the difference against which a diaspora identity can be outlined. Thus, paradoxically enough, Yasmin's crisis, which will be at the centre of this chapter, is triggered off as well as resolved by an encounter with ethnic difference.

As a matter of fact, *The Worlds Within Her* inscribes difference on several levels. It reveals a concern with class difference (Amie and Myra as opposed to Ram's family), age difference (Yasmin as opposed to Shakti), racial difference (Ram's and Ash's political ideas) and sex/gender difference (male vs. female characters, Cyril vs. Penny). While superficially racial difference seems to figure prominently in *The Worlds Within Her*, Bissoondath's narrative also might be read as a feminist novel concerned with postcolonial issues.[2] One could say that Bissoondath combines an orthodox feminism with an unorthodox postcolonialism. While adopting a feminist agenda, Bissoondath's postcolonialism is not solely directed against the former colonizers. In fact, Neil Bissoondath plays off both discourses of difference against each other in order to install a notion of difference that is more traditional, namely individualism.

Bissoondath, in an instance of deconstruction, posits individual difference as an Archimedean point from which to criticize collective difference. The individual becomes the anchor of a new, neohumanist metanarrative that is at odds with mainstream postmodernism as well as mainstream postcolonialism, both of which are celebrated in *The Book of Secrets*. As the following sections will examine in greater detail, Bissoondath, as a confirmed universalist,[3] cannot but be suspicious of an orthodox understanding of postcolonialism.

Difference Unbound, or the Ostentation of Community I: Postcolonial Politics and the Nation

That the setting of *The Worlds Within Her* lacks any historical specificity beyond the fact that it has been an English colony is not necessarily an artistic flaw. By virtue of the very vagueness of its portrayal Bissoondath insinuates, first of all, that the here and now should be emphasized over a diachronic perspective, and, secondly, that the political circumstances on a variety of Caribbean islands can be generalized. The island in *The Worlds Within Her*, like that of *A Casual Brutality*, becomes representative of the Caribbean condition at large, problematic as that may be. On the other hand, it could also be argued that the setting remains deliberately vague because Bissoondath is not interested in the Caribbean as such. His text might be taken as a parable of the relativity of ethnic difference and its relevance to individual identity constructions. Such an approach does not rule out the possibility of context, analysis and diagnosis, but it shifts the focus of analysis. In other words, in Bissoondath's revisionism the downplaying of indigenous history, colonialism, and, to a certain extent, sociology, is concomitant with the highlighting of the individual. The former are only of interest insofar as they elucidate the condition of the latter. Bissoondath proceeds dialectically in deriving his appreciation of the individual from the arguments of postcolonial essentialists, of which Vernon Ram Ramessar in *The Worlds Within Her* is a prime example.

Shakti's husband and Yasmin's father Ram is a politician whose ambition is to lead the people of an anonymous Caribbean island into what appears as a bright post-Independence future. Ram's commitment to the island of his birth is characterized by a radical political activism that the novel portrays as morally ambivalent. Although his commitment is by no means unidealistic, it is depicted as problematic. Ram's political involvement seems misplaced because it neglects his wife and family in favour of the welfare of the nation: "So you see what I mean about being exotic, my dear. It means you are never at the centre of things, and the centre was where my husband always wanted to be. He used everything, even our wedding, to get there" (34). Not the unselfishness of his activism is emphasized but his egocentrism. "I knew my husband to be in some ways a monster" (163), says Shakti when Ram, having barely escaped death by assassination, does not worry about her but of the fate of his political programme first.

Ram's neglect of Shakti is a consequence of his political work which is understood in terms of a relationship competing with his marriage. The nation is anthropomorphized by Shakti and imagined as a woman whom Ram has an affair with. His political commitment is endowed with sexual overtones and understood as illicit because Ram's catering for the collective is a betrayal of the personal obligations to his wife:

> And I thought that his dreams, which went well beyond the possibilities we had been brought up to expect, could accommodate the big We and the little we. What I didn't realize was that the big We would prove to be a demanding mistress. She fed his appetite and in so doing made it larger. (241)

Ram's behaviour displays characteristics of addiction and monomania. He is a slave to what he perceives as his mission. For Shakti, Ram is not simply having an affair; he is having an affair with an overly demanding mistress, the dubiousness of which insinuates that she is also a prostitute. The female allegory of the nation prostitutes herself by selling the 'big We,' which, in the context of the novel, translates as the addictive drug of tribalism and the confining constraints of community. Capitalizing on the collective, Ram abandons individual concerns in an egoism disguised as unselfishness and altruism. For him the larger entity of 'his people' overrides the individual needs of his wife and his children. Not only does the collective absorb the needs of the individual, it also satisfies selfish desires. Employing sexual metaphors, Bissoondath's protagonist compares Ram's political activism to onanism: "Gesticulations of caution and exhortation, the pumping fists of the passion that is, let me be blunt, a kind of masturbation" (243). Ram is not even conducting a 'proper' illicit affair with (the female allegory of) his people. He is not interacting with a partner but merely satisfies his own ego by eroticising the political as well as politicising the erotic.

Ram's position as a politician is obsessed with the idea of a postcolonial reckoning with the former oppressors. Obsessed with the history of colonialism and its treatment of humans as Others, Ram intends to instrumentalize the past for a politics of blame. He argues in the name of 'the people,' thus advocating himself as the spokesperson of a collective. In general, Ram's politics is nothing short of simplistic, for clustering individuals to a collective violates reality by abstracting from it. He employs a theory of agency that eventually turns out to be more crippling than liberating, for it categorically rules out blaming members of the postcolonial collective for faults of their own, which might well have contributed to the social and political crisis of the

Caribbean. A liberal vision of postcolonial politics would advocate an unprejudiced view towards those inside and outside of any kinds of community, and it is such a view that Bissoondath offers. Bissoondath's individualism is more complex and thus more ethical than Ram's community spirit because it does not spare postcolonial subjects the (necessary) recognition of faults of their own in governing the postcolonial nation-state. Bissoondath writes against the blind spot of postcolonial politicians like Ram who argue in favour of an undifferentiated politics of victimization and thereby exempt the postcolonial subject from being prosecuted for his/her perpetration on the basis of a misunderstood political correctness. Such an exemption can neither be a true salvaging from colonialism nor a protection from neocolonialism. Within the perspective of the novel it merely is an exercise in self-delusion that eventually proves a Phyrric victory for postcolonialism with its promise of a new dawn. If "*dawn follows midnight* [sic]" (163), Ram remains ignorant that postcoloniality might have to wrestle with a moral darkness of its own.

In an ironic inversion of colonial discourse, the political dawn Ram imagines for the young nation is symbolized by a torch (163). While the torch may have significance as a specifically Hindu symbol, it involuntarily ironises Ram who believes that unless he carries the light, i.e. leads the way politically but also culturally, the postcolonial future will be bleak. The darkness he fears for in a postcolonial future without him is complemented by a missionary spirit similar to imperial discourse's torch symbolism. While the implications of Ram's imagery are no less emblematic of arrogance than those of colonialism/imperialism, Bissoondath blames him for the fact that he makes himself the mouthpiece of 'his people,' whereas a closer look reveals that Ram's political ideas, like those of the former colonizers, are particularistic and by no means beneficial to everyone. There can be no denying the fact, for example, that Ram is a racist and intends to carry his prejudices into society at large. As a descendant of Indian indentured servants, he primarily caters to the demands of the powerful East Indian lobby of the island. By highlighting his ancestry, Ram ostentatiously emphasizes his difference from both the former British colonizers and the descendants of former slaves.

Ram's egoism/sexism as well as his racism are side effects of his political commitment for 'his' nation. Such an 'imagined community'[4] can be particularly troublesome because of the casualties it produces. One victim of Ram's morally ambivalent lobbying is his sister Penny who, like Shakti, suffers from/for his political commitment. Penny sacrifices her love to the black Zebulon Crooks for her brother's segregationist vision of Caribbean society (336–7). By allowing those who claim to represent a larger collective to dominate her life, Penny becomes a victim of an ideology that deserves criticism in the context of Bissoondath's individualist vision of life. Ram's postcolonial commitment does not merely resemble colonialism/imperialism in that he is imbued with a missionary spirit; not unlike colonial discourse he also excludes the Other. That Ram's political vision continues the racial segregation of colonial times is not only a failure to take into account Caribbean societies' multicultural composition but a crude way of dealing with that reality also. Similar to the discourse of colonialism, Ram's postcolonial politics is an oversimplification in its emphasis on the collective over the individual. Pretending to carry the light of progress for all postcolonial subjects is not an Enlightenment vision in Ram's case. The light of Enlightenment he has in mind may result in freedom for some but, as the repression of others/Others such as Zebulon Crooks and the treatment of women characters prove, within his imagined postcolonial community some are more equal than others.

It should not be forgotten that because the novel's space of enunciation is a female one, Ram is never allowed to articulate his own version of events. It is not Ram who is given voice but Shakti who speaks. Her account deconstructs the political by emphasizing the private repercussions of events. Moreover, she deconstructs the collective by referring to the casualities of community and by pinpointing the individual needs of its characters. *The Worlds Within Her* does not show politics in the making but undoes politics by telling it to pieces. By way of narrating Caribbean politics from the point of view of a woman, Bissoondath, in fact, subtly translates postcolonialism. Mediating Ram's political ideas by interpolating and inflecting them from a female space of articulation establishes a powerful counter-discourse to a discourse aimed at countering colonialism. By pitting both against each other, Bissoondath reflects the exclusionist effects of postcolonial (Caribbean) discourse.

The shaping of a postcolonial national identity seems in need of Others against which to outline a new self-image. Furthermore, the novel could be said to suggest that the more Others are invoked to shape the Self, the more the Self remains in need of Others in order to reassure itself about its identity. If this is agreed upon, then *The Worlds Within Her* can be said to detail a severe crisis of national identity. This crisis is reflected in Ram's argument in favour of community, which takes issue with three Others, thereby multiplying difference in order to construct a more solid, yet dubious spirit of sameness. The Others postcolonial discourse, as depicted in Bissoondath's novel, tries to write against/exclude are the metropolitan centre, racial minorities, and women. In other words, the discourses of difference that his novel orchestrates pertain to race/ethnicity, sex/gender and age.

Difference Unbound, or the Ostentation of Community II: Race and the Family

Bissoondath's novel reflects a concern with those marginalized by discourses of difference and with those who engage in a practice of Othering. As indicated above, there are three different kinds of collectives that preoccupy Bissoondath in *The Worlds Within Her*, the nation, race, and the family.

While Ram's political and national arguments have been discussed in the previous chapter, it is the young Ash who in *The Worlds Within Her* claims to be representative of a larger racial collective. This collective defines itself, i.e. its self-image, by drawing on history and ancestral tradition. Hindu fundamentalism in *The Worlds Within Her* advocates an unbroken tradition with an Indian 'homeland' from where many of today's Caribbeans of East Indian descent had come in search of work.[5] Ash and his fellow fundamentalists read the Hindu scriptures anachronistically, i.e. according to their whims, thereby misunderstanding a postmodern epistemological critique in order to come up with a story of origins (369).[6] Ash evidently overlooks the constructivist character of his credo, which becomes the more ironic because it is employed to construct a story that becomes the reference point for dubious constructions of identity. From the outside, the notion of origins and the history of Hinduism as an uninterrupted history do not appear as disinterested scholarly findings but as a partial (and dubious) reading elevated to the status of fact. However, what is labelled 'fact' by some characters cannot disguise its mythic character in the context of the novel's perspective at large.

While it becomes obvious that Hindu fundamentalism circulates myths, the novel reminds us that these myths are also instrumentalized for a certain purpose. Ash's 'facts' become ideological in two distinct ways. First of all, the idea of an ancient, highly developed Hindu civilization is designed to demonstrate the cultural superiority of India over the Caribbean. However, this in turn diminishes the commitment Ash is willing to make for the Caribbean as his actual place of abode. He refuses to actively engage actively with the Caribbean multicultural and social reality precisely because he does not regard it as his home, the very notion of which is fiercely contested in the text. For Ash, home is an essentialist reality; it is a fixed and stable entity and not a matter of affection. Home might only be said to be where the heart is for him because his heart has not stopped being with and beating for a mythic India that does not exist anymore, or never existed at all. Thus Ash's homeland/heartland is truly a no-man's-land. India is no concrete place but becomes a space of projections and chauvinist fantasies. Secondly, Hindu fundamentalist history, by virtue of its manipulative potential, infringes on the sovereignty of the individual and his/her free will to determine whether or not to belong. As Ash has it:

> "All that humiliatin' history. We have to get rid of it, you know. We still in chains—His fingers jab at his chest—even if we ain't know it. Even if we think we made it big somehow. Here"—his gaze sharpens at her—"or in other people land." (236)

Ash wants to claim Yasmin for his view of history as a story of racial oppression. In that respect, he resembles Ram, who argues an analogous case for the collective of the nation. Ash's (as well as Ram's) story is a metanarrative in its allegedly all-informative character. However, Yasmin refuses to have her life included in an undiscriminating history of colonization. History for her translates as lived experience and individual remembrance rather than community tradition and collective memory. While Ash prefers the mystique of traditionalism with its myths of purity and authenticity to the reality of firsthand knowledge (273), history for Yasmin is only valuable as petit récit. Radical revisionist postcolonial history according to her (and, by extension, to Bissoondath) can be dangerous because insisting on victimization as well as ceaselessly asserting the allegedly irreducible essence of (community) difference is paralysing. It arrests personal growth and thus fosters cultural inertia and sterility. Moreover, in demanding sacrifices from the individual in the name of a larger collective, it sacrifices the individual.

Not only with respect to the construction of a homeland is essentialism an important marker of identification for Ash and the fundamentalist organization he is a member of. In the context of a historical continuum between then and now, Ash not only implies that cultural authenticity is to be cherished, he also claims that racial purity is a reality and of intrinsic value. While Hinduism is less than a religion for Shakti, Hinduism is more than a religious faith for Ash; it becomes a spiritual privilege to which one is entitled solely by birth. Not merely is Hinduism said to have a characteristic core essence, if one follows Ash, members of other ethnicities will never be able to completely understand its nature. According to the fundamentalist, the epistemological gap between object (Hinduism) and (uninitiated) subject is too wide to bridge. Indirectly, coming to terms with Otherness is discredited as futile. The ideology of Hindu fundamentalism insinuates that belonging is a question of blood, and difference is a logical outcome of belonging. This means that an individual, according to Ash, can only belong to one community. This is not only an idea refuted by recent research into the nature of ethnicities and subcultures but also by Bissoondath's fictional explorations. In Yasmin, for example, Neil Bissoondath showcases that identity is not monolithic. The notion of worlds in *The Worlds Within Her* signals that the individual may be part of many ethnicities that can overlap or be orbits hermetically separated from each other. Yasmin's development as a character is indicative of man's ability to integrate many influences. Where Yasmin acknowledges complexity, Ash is unable to come to terms with a multiplicity of life worlds. Ash's credo is a reduction of the complexity of life, which is tempting but eventually immoral because it is false in its distortion of reality. In an attempt to take issue with any simplistic vision of life, Neil Bissoondath stresses the importance of the individual in a postcolonial context obsessed with the fetish of community.

The freedom of the subject, i.e. his/her judgement and free will, is irreconcilable with an essentialist notion of home and belonging advocated by Ash. Culture, according to Bissoondath, cannot be conceived of as static or monolithic. As the examples of Shakti and Yasmin illustrate, Ash's purist, traditionalist, essentialist view of life is flawed and profoundly mistaken.

The 'brotherhood of race' is not the only collective that infringes on the individuality of the subject in *The Worlds Within Her*. Another group in the novel that demands allegiance by virtue of belonging is the family. As previously pointed out, Penny submits to the rigorous discipline of the family and abandons love for dubious bonds of blood. Shakti, too, has to suffer from family ties that unfortunately are made to bind. As punishment for her solidarity with a female servant, who is not able to cope with the amount of work she is in charge of, Shakti's mother-in-law publicly ostracizes her for interfering with the power imbalances within the family. As the family hierarchy forbids a member of the family to assist a servant in his/her duties, Shakti's humanist concern for Myra is severely punished; in order to wean her from her humanist concerns, she is burdened with doing the washing for Cyril's wife Celia. Thereby Ram's mother deliberately destroys the friendship between the two outsiders in the family, Celia, British by birth (and Caribbean by affiliation), and Shakti, Caribbean by birth (and British by affiliation). Shakti comments upon the mutual recognition which had characterized their first meeting in the following way: "We shook hands when my husband introduced us, and she held my hand a touch longer than she'd held the others, as if taking a little refuge. I felt then that she recognized me—a sister-in-law married into the family—as a fellow alien . . ." (49; cf. also 58). Humiliating Shakti by forcing her to do the laundry for Celia and embarrassing Celia by forcing her to have her laundry done by Shakti is perfidious. For those who fully belong by birth (Shakti) as well as for those who will never fully belong qua marriage (Celia), the family becomes a collective that demands submission and subjects the subject's longing for individuality. The hierarchy of the family does not tolerate deviance and its effects are generally devastating. While Penny betrays herself and Zebulon by uncritically perpetuating the tradition of the family and the lies of its collective mystique, Celia commits suicide and thereby also succumbs to the constraints of the family. On the other hand, those who survive migrate, or rather only those who migrate survive. While Shakti emigrates for England and Canada, Amie is left with the escapism of an inner emigration.

The family in *The Worlds Within Her* is depicted as a community that relies on an essentialist concept of belonging. For Penny, her brothers, and her mother, family membership is determined by blood. Not surprisingly, employing genetics as the decisive marker of constructing difference is a notion which is criticized by Bissoondath. The absurdity of a belonging solely dependent on kinship is underlined by the fact that Yasmin's real mother is the servant girl Amie. The hermetic character of the two stories that Shakti and Yasmin tell/experience, prevent Yasmin and Shakti's relations from ever fully recognising the character of their family and what 'family' as a concept may encompass. In the eyes of her Caribbean relations, Yasmin fully belongs by blood, whereas Shakti and the reader know that this is only partly true. Whether Yasmin, as the illegitimate child of Ram and the servant Amie, would qualify as a family member seems doubtful. However, for Yasmin her alleged identity (of whose true nature she is not informed in the course of the novel's plot) transpires as a productive misunderstanding. In the course of the novel she gains an insight into the accidental nature of family membership and learns that relationships are not inherently cordial but are invested with intimacy instead. Social relationships are no less incidental and constructed than casual ones. Who is a 'mother' is not determined by who one was born to but depends on who has cared for one at an early stage of one's life. When Shakti says that Yasmin "is my daughter—but she is not my child" (383), what could have become a tragedy proves to be a blessing in disguise for Yasmin.

To conclude, Bissoondath argues in favour of affiliation, which allows the individual to position himself more freely in relation to a group. While he is opposed to the passive inclusion and exclusion of the subject in the name of essentialist community ties, he promotes the individual's freedom to include as well as to exclude himself according to his own choice. It is precisely the conflicting impulses between the ostentation of community difference and the individual's right to manifold and shifting affiliations that *The Worlds Within Her* enacts against the background of postcoloniality as well as postcolonialism.

Undoing Difference: Race, Age, and Sex/Gender

While *The Book of Secrets* invokes one discourse of difference (i.e. postmodernism) in order to corroborate and stabilize another (i.e. postcolonialism), *The Worlds Within Her* employs a multitude of differences towards a deconstructive aim. Bissoondath's second but last novel discusses three markers of difference, racial/ethnic difference, sex/gender difference and age difference.

The Worlds Within Her subverts the nexus between racial and sexual difference that colonial discourse made use of. The West's 'legitimation' to colonize the New World was discursively constructed by recourse to natural law, according to which the male was considered superior to the female by virtue of a gendered culture-nature dichotomy: While culture was identified with the male, the female was considered a part of nature. As the indigenous people of colonies like America or the Caribbean were thought to be in a state of nature, and thus were gendered as feminine, subjugation could be veiled as cultivation, i.e. civilization. This is also the reason why colonial encounters were often represented as encounters between man and woman, why discovery was imagined as uncovering, and why exploration was frequently depicted as penetration. In *The Worlds Within Her* Bissoondath travesties this trope of colonial discourse by establishing an analogy between England and the Caribbean on the one hand and Ram and Shakti on the other. Suggesting that Ram patronizes his wife as the 'mother' country patronizes her 'child-like' colonies, Bissoondath transposes colonization onto a personal level in order to deconstruct it. The fact that Ram treats his wife as a Western man could have treated his; the fact that he does not accept Shakti as a full-fledged human being; the fact that his attitude prevents him from acknowledging her as an individual—all of this serves Bissoondath to make a point about the prominence of inequality and oppression outside of colonial discourse proper. If colonialism relied on gender in order to understand cultural difference and to justify oppression, Bissoondath severs this epistemological nexus by demonstrating that in a colonial/postcolonial context the oppression of a sexual Other can operate beyond issues of cultural difference. This in itself would be banal were it not situated in a postcolonial context resonant with the challenging of colonial discourse's denigration of cultural difference. What used to have epistemological value as one thread of a discourse designed to make colonization understandable/representable to the West is destroyed by Bissoondath in a way that superficially appears to be typical of postcolonial fiction with its emphasis on the counter-discursive. However, within the perspective of the novel, postcolonialism appears as a discourse which displays uneasy parallels to colonialism in its exclusionist practice of Others. The insight that not everyone is freed from every kind of oppression demystifies a visionary notion of postcoloniality as a new era in which, in Ram's words, freedom from oppression will be realized for all.

Only if the relationship between man and wife is understood to be colonialist in nature can *The Worlds Within Her* be interpreted as concerned with issues of decolonization. If decolonization is taken to imply a psychological dimension also, the exploration of colonialism in *The Worlds Within Her* is neither restricted to gender issues nor to issues of cultural difference solely. That Bissoondath is convinced of the necessity of 'decolonising the mind'[7] in more ways than one becomes evident once it is understood that Ram's and Shakti's relationship is imagined in terms of a third category of difference, age. The novel alludes to colonial discourse's analogy between the metropolis and the colonies as children: "We loved it—and we hated it, because that very majesty was what kept us, in their eyes and ours, childlike. England would always take care of us—but it would also always tells us what to do" (175). Discursively, the 'mother' country's right to rule the Other was also morally corroborated by emphasizing the duty and obligation of ruling the Other-as-child. In general, 'understanding' the Other as child allowed to 'know' him/her in familiar terms. Absurdly enough, the colonies were usually not imagined as capable to grow up, and the epistemological nexus between age and the culturally foreign proved resistant. The consequence was that the Other was locked in a position that was not merely inferior but permanently inferior, too. While colonial discourse employed both gender and age difference to underline that the alien does not match the known as well as to justify a discourse of exploitation and oppression, Bissoondath is once again more interested in the instances of colonization taking place within a private sphere. There can be no doubt that Ram treats Shakti in much the same way as England has treated the Caribbean, i.e. not merely as a woman but also as a child. But eventually Bissoondath's critique of such an inscription of eternal insufficiency cannot be understood in terms of postcolonialism's (strategic) affirmation of racial/ethnic essence.

Rather than drawing on sex/gender in order to understand race/ethnicity, as colonial discourse used to do, Bissoondath conceptualizes sex/gender against the backdrop of the postcolonial and multicultural Caribbean world. *The Worlds Within Her* can be read as a feminist text playing off the arguments of Ash and Ram against those of the female characters. In Bissoondath's fictional universe, women come to terms with cultural complexity better than the male characters.[8] Thus Celia was born English but becomes Caribbean, while Shakti was born Caribbean but becomes Canadian (because she is not allowed to become English). Yasmin, on the other hand, has become Canadian and does not want to become again what she was born, i.e. Caribbean. By virtue of their inner resources for coping with diversity and relativity, women are more mature and responsible than men. In general, women are better equipped to face the archetypal condition of life, which, in Bissoondath's eyes, is change.

While women in Bissoondath's novel are associated with the fluidity of culture and the flexibility of belonging, it is mainly men, such as Ram and Ash, who represent problematic opinions about race, culture and community membership. Interestingly, there seem to be two exceptions. On the one hand there is Penny who maintains that you can never belong to a community if you are not born into it. Like Ash and Ram, belonging for her is a question of birth. For her brother, on the other hand, the matter is different. In fact, it is diametrically opposed, for, in contrast to Ash, Cyril believes that nothing is less important than race (106). In contrast to Ram, Penny and Ash, Cyril holds that the only prerequisite to belonging is the will to belong. Belonging thus ceases to be a question of blood and becomes a matter of affiliation and identification. The examples of Penny and Cyril do not invalidate the argument but, in fact, corroborate it. Penny and Cyril only seemingly deviate from this pattern because their sex is mistaken for their gender, and it is their gender that is important here. In the context of the novel, the sensitive Cyril is more 'feminine' than the dominant Penny whose gender is male. As a matter of fact,

Penny does perceive Cyril's difference but mistakes it for mere effeminateness when she ridicules him for urinating like a woman. While openly advocating essentialist positions, Penny involuntarily and ironically subscribes to nonessentialist gender positions.

If the racial Other has been locked in a discursive prison that draws on essentialist notions of sex difference, the deconstruction of sexual difference in favour of gender difference also argues a case against essentialist racial difference and underscores the character of difference as a construction. The hermetic separation of (life) worlds is thus collapsed in the area of sexual/gender as well as in the realm of racial difference. The insight into the constructivist nature of both patriarchal and colonial discourses precludes the discursive instalment of any power hierarchy between whoever is Self and whoever is Other on the basis of inherent differences. While there can be no doubt that differences are a reality, the point for Neil Bissoondath is that only few differences are inherent. In his fictional cosmos, the essentialist underpinnings of community differences are deconstructed in order to pave the ground for an apotheosis of difference-as-idiosyncrasy. This clash of different understandings of difference finds its application in the context of migration and diaspora in particular.

The Nature of Culture: Migration, Diaspora, and Change

The Worlds Within Her is concerned with postcolonial political activism, as represented by Ram, only insofar as it deconstructs it in favour of an alternative approach. While the novel may fail short of being postcolonial in this respect, *The Worlds Within Her* is interested in those aspects of postcolonialism which concern individual identity constructions after colonialism. Of significance in this context are migration and diaspora experiences.

In Bissoondath's text it is specifically women who migrate, or temporarily return from their country of adoption in order to visit the country of their birth. Cases in point are Shakti and Yasmin. Shakti leaves the periphery of a Caribbean ridden by racism and sexism for England. At first, she enjoys England because life in the diaspora as the wife of a political refugee is not confining but liberating to her. If it does not provide total freedom from the restrictions imposed on Shakti by her husband, it nevertheless allows her to escape the regime of her mother-in law as well as the dominant morality of Caribbean society. England makes self-fashioning possible and as such initially allows Shakti to counter the arrest of personal growth that the institutions of family and community threaten her with. The fact that Shakti does not feel she belongs by virtue of an essence is a calamity only to the essentialist, and it is precisely such an essentialist position that Shakti implicitly counters in her account:

> Perhaps it was my displeasure at being forced to leave a land to which I was finding myself more and more attached—precisely, I think because of its strangeness, because of my lack of natural attachment to it. Nothing was expected of me, you see, and so I could make it all up as I went along. I suppose it was inevitable, wasn't it—that I would fall in love with a land that gave me such freedom. (218)

While the name 'Shakti' alludes to powerfulness, sources of energy and divine procreative potentials within a Hindu tradition,[9] in the context of the novel Shakti draws on a strength other than a religiously inspired one. She manages to survive by virtue of her individuality. While Shakti's biography underscores contemporary theories of diaspora experience which downplay its limiting and psychologically crippling implications in favour of new horizons and perspectives, it should not be overlooked that within Bissoondath's individualist vision alienation rather than alterity is the problem for her. The point is that Shakti takes issue less with the strangeness of England than with Ram's estrangement from her. In England, Shakti feels a foreigner in the relationship to her husband, the fact that she was born in a culturally alien environment never is an issue of sorrow or nostalgia. That it is in a diaspora situation that Bissoondath has his protagonist modify her self-image is postcolonial; that Shakti downrightly switches ethnicities is a provocation to postcolonialism, which, however, is in accord with Bissoondath deconstruction of racial/ethnic difference elsewhere.

Whereas the Caribbean poses a threat to Shakti with its political instability and the community constraints of the family, England seems to provide freedom. For Shakti, the lack of history and tradition of the Caribbean is compensated by the rich culture of the metropolis. Moreover, the encounter with a different culture entails for Shakti a change of paradigms of what culture means in general. Her switch from one culture to another is concomitant with a switch from one definition of culture to another. More precisely, the very moment Shakti feels more British than Caribbean, a (psychological) notion of culture as cognitive matrix providing orientation gives way to a (normative) concept of culture as refinement, and culture as civilization.[10] Provocatively enough, Shakti moves from a value-free understanding of culture to a value-laden definition. At the same time, however, the novel emphasizes the dynamic and flexible nature of culture, in the realm of which "-phobe" and "-phile" are revealed to be ultimately matters of conscious choice and deliberate affiliation (76).

However, Shakti's experience of England, while initially promising, quickly becomes disappointing. Due to her Caribbean national/racial community membership, Shakti is not allowed to live her British ethnicity in Britain and is exiled on the basis of a perceived similarity with others/Others. While she is not forbidden to stay on account of her individual personality, the English, ironically enough reject her for precisely the same reason she herself rejected the Caribbean in favour of Britain before. Even more ironic is that Shakti is not only anglophile where Ram was anglophobe; as a matter of fact, her love of English culture is also arguably more British than that of the British themselves. In the eyes of the British, however, her Caribbean origins outweigh her identification with the metropolis because belonging is wrongly assumed to rely on blood. Thus Britain may eventually be seen to operate on essentialist ideas of identity in much the same way as the postcolonial world, i.e. in a strategic way. Postcolonial Britain as well as the postcolonial Caribbean rely on essentialism as a means of exclusion; both make use of Self-Other divisions in order to structure their world, i.e. to police the boundaries of their identity. Binarist thinking still abounds in an attempt at holding complexity at bay. Ultimately, it is irrelevant that Ram relies on essentialist notions of community belonging that are diametrically opposed to the ones of Britain, for excluding the possibility of affiliating with an ethnicity remains immoral for Bissoondath. *The Worlds Within Her* (and *A Casual Brutality*) details how the individual, whose worth Bissoondath holds supreme, is overridden by various discourses intent on heightening the importance of a particular community. Postcolonialism (in its essentialist form) may be the most prominent of these discourses, although it is by no means the only one.

In the final analysis it is Canada that grants both Shakti and Yasmin a greater degree of individuality than either Britain or the Caribbean. In marked opposition to the uneasy parallels between England and the Caribbean, the Canadian diaspora is welcomed as a blank slate onto which immigrants truly can inscribe themselves. It is a country where the individual can find a space within which he/she can reinvent himself beyond the racist essentialism, of which neither the Caribbean nor England are free. In this respect Canada becomes a utopia because it allows

> being true to the central philosophy [. . .]: that individuals should have the freedom—from the culture and circumstances into which they are born—to shape themselves in the image and likeness of their choice.[11]

While the novel shows that individuals, especially women, have often had merely subaltern status in colonial as well as postcolonial times, be it because they do not fully belong (Celia) or are subject to rigorous family discipline (Shakti), Canada offers a space from which the subaltern can speak. At the same time, it also allows those who are displaced and deterritorialized to make a new start and find equal opportunities irrespective of their respective genders. In contrast to Vassanji's balanced analysis, Bissoondath views the

Canadian diaspora in entirely positive terms. Canada provides a valve and an escape as well as a possibility to grow by facing the foreign, which becomes metonymic of change. Implicitly, change is not associated with discontinuity and disruption but valued as creative and regenerating. Canada is a space in which the claim of the collective is disclosed as an impediment to the dynamics of culture. One could also say that culture and identity in Canada reject the usefulness of rigid boundaries and replace them by thresholds, which signify permeability.

Apart from Shakti, Yasmin profits from migration insofar as it teaches her relativity and helps to clarify issues she is preoccupied with. Before the journey to the Caribbean can contribute to the consolidation of her identity, Yasmin is confused and puzzled first. Yasmin does not feel comfortable in the Caribbean, however, in contrast to Shakti, she is not an alien as a consequence of alienation, or a stranger due to estrangement:

> And yet the feeling persists: that she is among strangers with whom conversation does not come easily; with whom, in the uneasy game of picking from the storehouse of memory, the rules are not defined, the traps not marked. She feels herself defenceless before words whose weight she cannot gauge. (98)

Despite allegedly belonging by blood, the novel makes it abundantly clear that Yasmin does not share an ethnicity with Cyril, Penny and Ash. The disorientation she experiences in the Caribbean is due to the lack of attachment to people and place, and no essentialist concept of identity can alter this fact: "There is to her no point in comparing the thickness of blood and water: with time, with distance, with no network of shared experience, blood might as well be water" (45). The cognitive matrix of Caribbean culture remains alien to Yasmin; in her Caribbean 'home' she remains a stranger in a strange land. While Yasmin travels from her country of adoption to her country of origins, it is in her Caribbean 'home' that she feels displaced. In an ironic reversal of what is a widespread motif in postcolonial literature, the diaspora in Bissoondath's novel becomes a relative concept contingent on the definition of what constitutes home. For Yasmin her journey to the Caribbean becomes a diaspora experience because Canada has become her home. In making an essentialist notion of home strange, Bissoondath paves the way for perceiving the diaspora in less essentialist ways, too. Put differently, what is familiar and what is foreign only depend upon each other and not upon a shared tradition.

In this context, it is illuminating that Yasmin Summerhayes keeps thinking about the myth of Icarus, thereby alluding to her journey intertextually.[12] There are two distinct parallels between Bissoondath's novel and the story of Icarus. For one thing, both are stories of a parent-child relationship. Moreover, and more interesting for our purposes, the myth of Icarus also is the story of an escape. While Dedalus and Icarus leave behind the labyrinth of Minos of Crete, Shakti and Yasmin escape from the psychologically alienating and crippling maze of the Caribbean. In the Greek myth as well as in the Canadian novel, escape and travelling are not without risks. Icarus dies because he disregards his father's advice; he overreaches himself and thus succumbs to his own hubris rather than to external circumstances. For Yasmin the matter is different: "She thinks of Icarus, condemned for the arrogance of overweening ambition when his only fault had been inadequate preparation" (9–10). The myth of Icarus is not so much an allegory of migration for Yasmin than an account of a personal fate. Of course, the question remains, for reader as well as for Yasmin herself, why she associates the myth at all. Only at the end of the novel does it become evident to the reader as well as to the protagonist of Bissoondath's novel that the story of Icarus first fascinated her in a children's book. While the book becomes indicative of a process of socialization Yasmin has undergone, the story of Icarus does not become a master text for her life suggesting that migration of necessity fails. *The Worlds Within Her*, while subscribing to the influence of the past, intertextually corroborates that its influence is not to be conceived of as determinist. As the novel succinctly puts it, Yasmin acknowledges a past she is influenced by but she refutes any suggestions that this past dooms her to a bleak future. Yasmin may be influenced by many worlds, but she is not the product of them.

For the novel as a whole the myth of Icarus also reminds us that in *The Worlds Within Her* journeying is a strategy of healing, the usefulness of which is only recognized by women. While Canada/the Canadian diaspora constitutes a resource rather than an encumbrance for Yasmin and Shakti, it signifies something fundamentally different for the male figures. For Ash, for example, the notion of diaspora is a source of strength only because it unites those who (allegedly) suffer from displacement. From the perspective of the novel, however, Ash's understanding of diaspora is an alibi to reenact the drama of victimization and practice the politics of blame. In its sterility Ash's treatment of the past also is an unproductive and barren way of dealing with the future. Diaspora thus figures as a possibility of easy identification with what is allegedly known and not as an opportunity to interact with the potentials of the unknown. From the perspective of *The Worlds Within Her* migration can heal because alterity is not a threat but a challenge that helps its protagonists to grow as persons. Otherness is perceived to be vital to culture rather than lethal to it. The diaspora is not a combat zone but a "contact zone," i.e. a "social space [sic] where disparate cultures meet, clash, and grapple with each other."[13]

The 'contact zone' of the diaspora becomes an area of transculturalism and intercultural understanding, an example of which is food and eating. For

Cyril, food becomes indicative of the dynamic nature of culture:

> "This food we eating," Cyril says, "is not really Indian food. Is *West-Indian* [sic] Indian food. So far from India, the people couldn' always get the same spice, they had to make do. Is history, is change, this food." (106)

Significantly enough, it is the sensitive, 'feminine' Cyril who points a way out of the stereotypical notion of diaspora advanced by Ash by arguing that the new is a challenge that demands an active engagement. Food becomes emblematic of the creative potential of the new and his improvised cuisine envisages migrant man as the agent of culture rather than its object. West Indian food does not mimic Indian cuisine but draws on Caribbean cooking to become something entirely original. What people like Ash and Ram deplore is thus revealed to be a blessing in disguise in the context of the novel's perspective, which Cyril voices here. The diaspora experience does not have to be barren and sterile, it can be productive indeed. While it may well be a space where the set of unconsciously operating rules informing an ethnicity are suddenly made conscious, such self-consciousness does not have to be calamitous, as the example of Cyril suggests. Depending on the individual's creativity and resources, the initial distance from both the old and the new can eventually turn out to be fruitful because in a diasporic context the individual may emphasize the loss of the old as much as the potential of the new. Like Shakti who refuses to celebrate Christmas the English way (341–2), Cyril reflects the embrace of transculturalism as a creative way of dealing with the diaspora. His nonessentialist understanding of culture embraces the fluid and dynamic nature of culture, of which migration becomes emblematic, too.

The Healing Power of the Self: Stories, Journeys, Memory, and Narrative Structure

If *The Worlds Within Her* outlines the problems of the postcolonial predicament for the individual, it also envisages remedies to come to terms with them. The protagonists of the novel learn how to counter marginalization and grief so that *The Worlds Within Her* ends on a much more positive key than *A Casual Brutality*. Neil Bissoondath's last novel but one negotiates the possibilities of healing the hurts of community constraints by taking into account the necessity for remembering and the bliss of amnesia.

One of the strategies the protagonists of Bissoondath's text employ is storytelling. Particularly interesting in Shakti's case is the question as to the text type or genre of her account. She narrates a story the character of which bears traces of a confession as well as a testimonio. Although it may be understandable that Shakti has something to confess, given the lie she has lived with respect to the identity of Yasmin's (biological) mother, the postcolonial context suggests parallels between her account and the testimonio.[14] However, if Shakti's oral account lacks the religious implication of a confession, it also discards the political overtones of the testimonio. In other words, her story is neither informed by a wish for expiation nor an urge to accuse perpetrators in the public sphere. If it displays properties of a confession, there is only a woman lying in a coma to listen and to absolve her. If it resembles a testimonio, it lacks the legal implications of a testimony in a court trial, which would of course be of particular use for an activist postcolonialism intent on tracking down ageny and colonial injustice. If Shakti's account is almost a confession as well as testimonio, the question remains as to the specific character of her story. A way out of this impasse might be to focus on the fact that Bissoondath polemicizes against postcolonial issues and strategies by investing Shakti's account with private importance solely. In other words, the relationship of her tale to the genres according to which it is modelled is ironic rather than serious. Neil Bissoondath parodies the genre of the testimonio by presenting Shakti's account as a (spiritual) biography, i.e. as a text type that focuses on the individual solely, and that in a much more radical way than would fit the moulds of either confession or testimonio. That Shakti tells her own story is significant as an attempt at ordering her life, and the coherence of her self-narration is mainly informed by a therapeutic drive. Narrating her own story, i.e. purging her biography of selected events while highlighting others at the same time, is a means of rendering her life meaningful. And meaning in life is what Shakti desires most in old age.

While Shakti narrates, Yasmin travels. If Shakti's account terminates with her death, Yasmin's journey initiates a new start for her in life, which is already anticipated by the archetypical symbol of the water-crossing that her trip to the Caribbean involved. As the burial of the past overlaps with an archaeology of the self, her journey to the Caribbean becomes a journey into her own personality which, in turn, provides inspiration for the larger journey of life. For Yasmin the circularity of her depression, manifest in a compulsory disorder that involves going over the death of her daughter Ariana, is resolved by the linearity of a journey into a different world, which becomes a prerequisite for making possible the journey (of life) into the future. Less metaphorically, it is a journey into the past that brings about clarification and provides momentum for the future, whereas hitherto only stasis has characterized the present. In that sense, Yasmin's journey is no less therapeutic than Shakti's story. Although she does not realize it at the outset of her journey, Yasmin will find new meaning in her life subsequent to the encounter with her roots. The progress of a journey (cf. Yasmin) resembles the progress of telling a story (cf. Shakti) in its imposition of order. And it is order that Yasmin desires most at this point in her life.

It is a commonplace that migration raises memories. If Yasmin's burial of her mother's ashes can be interpreted as a burial of her past, Shakti lays to rest the past as a source of unrest endangering the quiet and satisfied mind she yearns for. Both Yasmin's and Shakti's urge to see the past rest in peace hinges on the willingness to dissect it into pieces, a point underlined by the fragmented structure of the novel. In order to bury the past, a full excavation of it is necessary. Memory work proves elemental in evoking the past and coming to terms with its traumatic effects on Shakti and Yasmin. Memory as the common feature of both Shakti's and Yasmin's strategies of healing fulfills an important function in what amounts to an exorcism of the demons of the past. Remembering also implies forgetting, and a quintessential part of Yasmin's and Shakti's exorcism is the attempt to leave the past behind. Eventually the rituals of narrating and travelling prove successful and both Yasmin and Shakti acknowledge the past by facing it. In fact, both evoke the past only to be better equipped to discard it in the interest of shaping a future. That is the reason why Yasmin's journey and Shakti's tale are not only unique but single affairs. Both can/will not have to be undertaken and recounted again.

Shakti comments on her daughter's journey without knowing about it. From a different time and different place she advises Yasmin to see the journey as self-help. It is a fine irony of the novel that this is an insight that Shakti has internalized, while Yasmin has yet to become aware of it. In that sense, Yasmin travels not merely into her past but also in Shakti's direction, i.e. towards her position as the wiser one. It is the novel's structure that is particularly illuminating in this context. Both Shakti's and Yasmin's accounts are fractured, and the pieces of their stories are played off against each other. Chronology as well as linearity are disrupted, the purposes of which are diverse. On the one hand, the structure of the novel could be said to reflect the inner life of its protagonists. The fracturedness of the narration would then mirror the fragility and fragmentariness of life as a whole. In contrast to typically postmodern fiction, however, the notion of a decentred universe is less a cause for rejoicing than a cause of complaint that triggers off an urge for order. Yasmin's journey is aimed at finding herself; it is aimed at ordering her story, too. On the other hand, the structure of the novel might be interpreted as drawing to the reader's attention parallels and differences between the young and the old woman. Shakti's self-conscious oral tale is told on looking back while Yasmin as the centre of consciousness registers events more immediately. The fact that Yasmin is experiencing the very chaos of the Caribbean that Shakti tries to order retrospectively is an instance of structural irony. Also ironic within what looks like an exploration of the nature of representation is that an overeager concern with the past is deemed useless. Immediate access to the past can never be gained, and striving for truth is disclosed as an ultimately futile obsession. Truth is an abstraction that is found/lost in the interstices of potentially infinite versions that clash.[15] However, what seems an exercise in postmodern polyphony and epistemological critique is not a license to enact the ambivalence of différance poetically. Unlike Rita in Vassanji's *The Book of Secrets*, Bissoondath insinuates that epistemological uncertainty corresponds to an undead past that demands to be exorcised and buried.[16] While Vassanji's character accepts silence, Bissoondath's authorial voice at the very beginning of the novel maintains, and in fact complains, that "some silences vibrate with a voiceless chaos, felt but unheard" (3). As silence can have a paralysing and crippling effect, what is called for in *The Worlds Within Her* is an acknowledgement of the past so that it does not have a determining one on the individual in his/her personal growth any longer.

Conclusion: Difference, Complexity, and Essentialism

Neil Bissoondath evokes colonial discourse and its tropes not merely in order to invert them but to destroy them. He is critical of dichotomous approaches towards understanding social and psychological phenomena. Self-other divisions are not merely identified as a construction, they are also disclosed as a discursive practice more crippling than comforting. Bissoondath regards binarisms as a reduction of a reality that is too complex to be captured in simplistic terms. The very irresponsibility of binarist thinking makes him equally critical of colonial as well as activist postcolonial discourse. He suggests a third way beyond the confines of either racial discrimination or post-Independence strategic counter-discourse by opting for an appreciation of complexity, the locus of which is the single individual.[17]

Both *The Worlds Within Her* and *A Casual Brutality* constitute attempts at countering postcolonial counter-discourse. The novels set 'there' overlap with *The Innocence of Age* and "Dancing" in enacting the struggle between an emphasis on community and collective difference on the one hand and individualism and individual difference on the other.[18] As the former is perceived to be reductive of complexity, Neil Bissoondath's writings emphatically intervene in favour of the latter.[19] Bissoondath, who admits to "fear the automatic assumption of racial allegiance,"[20] points out that those stressing the 'racial brotherhood,' albeit in a move of strategic essentialism, must realize that the underpinnings of their claim are profoundly racialist. As harping on community ties and tradition is an oversimplification of a reality infinitely more complex, Bissoondath's narratives are directed against colonial/postcolonial activism as well as against a superficial multiculturalism. For Bissoondath any form of Othering, whether it be well-meaning or deliberately denigrating, is a discursive strategy that is immoral, and thus unacceptable, in its distortion of a reality infinitely more complex.

Perhaps the reduction of complexity, or stereotyping, is part of the human condition, i.e. is a necessary 'evil' for man to survive. But if simplifying the world and dispensing with any endeavour to engage with its complexity is precisely the function stereotypes fulfill, not all characters in Bissoondath's fiction rely on stereotypes to the same extent. With the possible exception of Jan in *A Casual Brutality*, women in Bissoondath's fictional universe are less dependent on stereotypes than men. Women, or men like Cyril, whose gender defies a clichéd masculinity, seem to be better equipped to come to terms with (cultural) complexity than Raj, Ram or Ash. The women in *The Worlds Within Her* display an ability to live and actively practice transculturalism.

Bissoondath repeatedly makes women the protagonists of his stories and novels. In the context of a gender as well as a racial dimension Bissoondath rejects the political implications that his ventriloquizing of Others has been charged with. Any accusation on the grounds of appropriating voices is regarded by Bissoondath as unfounded.[21] For him such a claim reflects the assertion of community exclusivity that denies the individual the freedom to affiliate his/her own free will with an ethnicity of his/her choice. Neil Bissoondath makes the point that if an appropriation of voice were by definition unethical, then those marching against apartheid were not making a stand against racism but would in fact support the very ideology that they are attacking.[22] It is the artistic treatment of a subject and not the subject of art as such that can render a text problematic. To realize the former opens up the opportunity of a critique beyond the ideological shackles of political correctness; to argue the opposite is nothing short of advocating censorship.

Bissoondath's challenging of absolute and irreducible difference is articulated as a critique of essentials that works towards an undoing of stereotypes. If Vassanji maintains that the recognition of community difference is a gain resulting from the concerted political efforts and common intellectual insights of both postmodern and postcolonial discourse, Bissoondath's radical individualism contends that (collective) difference is of limited value as an analytical tool in colonial and postcolonial discourse as well as in the context of sexual politics precisely because it is so ubiquitous as to lose its explanatory value. He departs from Vassanji in denying that community difference is complementary with individual complexity; the former should be subordinated to the latter, not vice versa. Neil Bissoondath subscribes to the irreducibility of ontological but not to the irreducibility of epistemological difference. Although his understanding of culture as transculturalism allows for a change of ethnicity and thus also for a change of identity, it is change that Bissoondath posits as archetypically human. Ontologically irreducible for him is the individual's ability to change, which must not be curtailed by denying the individual the right to change.

Difference in Neil Bissoondath's texts is deconstructed from a position that lies between essentialism and nonessentialism. The latter maintains that there is neither an absolute identity nor difference between people from various cultures because there is no static identity that can be fixed. Because identity is always already in flux, the logical foundation for an irreducible ethnic difference is lacking. Identity is revealed to be a matter of affiliation and allegiance rather than of skin colour, history and tradition. That means that the subject takes an active part in the process of identity formation. At the same time, identity for Bissoondath is not a product of external factors because he has not abandoned the category of the subject in favour of subjectivities. The individual is not subject to shaping forces such as, for example, language; rather there is a core essence of what man is constituted by, and this anthropological constant is grounded in a liberal-humanist frame or reference. Bissoondath believes that for human beings there is the potential of drawing on a common essence that makes intercultural hermeneutics possible but may also render it obsolete.

For Neil Bissoondath only one kind of difference remains fundamental, and that is the right of the individual to be different from whoever wants to forcefully include him/her in a collective. His is a claim for free will and against determinism. If difference is something that the individual activates or not, there may well be sameness and not difference that the individual prefers to stress in his positioning towards an ethnicity. Identification and affiliation in Neil Bissoondath's texts spring from a perceived sameness, a common ground. With respect to 'there' (as well as 'here') Bissoondath writes in favour of the difference between those who want to belong to a community and those who do not want to belong. Once belonging is understood as affiliation, community difference is no longer charged as an essentialist sine qua non for postcolonial activism. If difference is relegated to the individual and private sphere, the claim to difference made by collectives and communities in the public realm loses its moral legitimation together with its usefulness as a heuristic concept. If one follows Neil Bissoondath, then postcolonial activism is prejudiced in (perhaps deliberately) overlooking that community difference is in truth an ideology while individualism is truly an ethics. If difference is understood to be operating within a single ethnicity, too, it is no longer politically incorrect to pinpoint the sameness of members of different ethnicities. In other words, if intragroup differences are vehemently denied, to categorically rule out inter-group sameness becomes a non sequitur.

It is important to recognize that Bissoondath writes against postcolonial reductionism but not against postcolonialism as such. For him both individualism and postcolonialism are not mutually exclusive, as a school of postcolonial criticism argues that stresses the importance of community over the individual. For Bissoondath paying closer attention to the individual would make possible a modified postcolonialism that does not stop at exploring the calamities of colonialism in order to construct a postcolonial identity.[23] On a par with such a self-critical stance is an artistic vision which allows for shifting affiliations and the full scope of relationships between human beings who refuse to be primarily defined/determined as members of communities: "I insist on that always, that my characters are individuals unto themselves. They are not representative of any group, any race, any culture, any more than any of us is."[24] Writing against the nexus between postcolonialism and community does not mean that Bissoondath fails to take into account postcolonial phenomena. If the term postcolonialism is understood as a problematic rather than a term of radical empowerment, Bissoondath's work can, in fact, be called quintessentially postcolonial. The same hypothesis shall guide us when we now turn to a discussion of Rohinton Mistry and his works.

Transcending Difference
Rohinton Mistry

Rohinton Mistry[1] was born in Bombay on 3 July 1952 to Behram Mistry, employed in an advertising agency, and homemaker Freni, born Jhaveri. Mistry was raised in Bombay, India's most cosmopolitan city, where he attended the Villa Theresa Primary School and St. Xavier High School. Mistry, who at one point in his life had been thinking of taking up professions as diverse as a veterinarian and musician, eventually decided to study Economics and Mathematics at St Xavier's College, University of Bombay, where, in 1975, he completed a B.Sc. The same year he married Freny Elavia, a teacher. Likewise in 1975, one month after the Indian Emergency was declared, Mistry decided to emigrate. Since England was in the midst of race riots and America was not particularly attractive because of its military intervention in Vietnam, Mistry opted for Canada. He followed Freny to Toronto, where she had relatives. Rohinton Mistry became a clerk at the Canadian Imperial Bank of Commerce, Toronto. In 1978 he decided to enrol at the University of Toronto where he began to study Literature and Philosophy part time and received a BA in 1984. In 1983, one year after he had begun to write regularly, he won the Hart House Literary Contest with the story "One Sunday." On the jury was Mavis Gallant, at that time writer-in-residence at the University of Toronto. She recognized Mistry's talent and encouraged him to continue writing. In the following year another story of his, "Auspicious Occasion," received the Hart House Prize once again. In 1985 a grant enabled Mistry to give up his job at the bank and to commit himself to writing full time. The same year he won the *Canadian Fiction Magazine's* Annual Contributor's Award. In 1986/87 he spent a year in Long Beach, California, where Freny taught at a high school. In 1987 *Tales from Firozsha Baag* (1987) appeared, a collection of stories that was short-listed for the Governor General's Award for best fiction in 1988. Rohinton Mistry's reputation as a talented writer was confirmed with *Such a Long Journey* (1991), which was short-listed for the prestigious Booker Prize (1991), was awarded the Governor General's Award for best fiction (1991) as well as the Trillium Award and both the Commonwealth Writers Prize (1992) and the Smith Books/*Books in Canada* award for first novel (1992). In 1998, *Such a Long Journey* was also turned into a major film. Rohinton Mistry's next novel, the bestseller *A Fine Balance* (1995), was even more successful. It won the 1995 Giller Prize, the Royal Society of Literature's Winifred Holtby Memorial Prize, the 1996 *Los Angeles Times* Book Award for Fiction and the 1996 Commonwealth Writers Prize. It was given an award by the Danish Literacy Council and was short-listed for both the IMPAC Dublin Literary Award and the 1996 Booker Prize. In 2002 *Family Matters*, Mistry's most recent novel, was published.

A. 'Here': Towards a Hybrid Identity. *Tales From Firozsha Baag* (1987)

The majority of Rohinton Mistry's pieces in his first major work of fiction, the collection of short stories *Tales From Firozsha Baag* (1987),[1] are set in India, more precisely in a block of flats ('baag') in Bombay. The inhabitants of Firozsha Baag are mostly Parsis, a fact that has not escaped critical attention. Thus while praising Mistry's stories for their universalism, critics also emphasize that they are resonate with Parsi culture,[2] and that in their cultural specificity Mistry's tales "challenge and resist the totalization of the dominant culture within India."[3] As a matter of fact, the setting of *Tales From Firozsha Baag* inverts the situation of the Parsi community in contemporary India. While the Parsis constitute a tiny minority in demographic decline within the multicultural mosaic of the South Asian's subcontinent, the community for once constitutes the majority in the microcosm of Mistry's fictional Firozsha Baag.[4]

Three out of the collection's eleven stories are concerned with the emigration/immigration experience of members of the Parsi community who have previously lived in Bombay's Firozsha Baag. In a process of negotiating the implications of adaptation/assimilation to the radically new environment of Canada, the question whether difference is a useful strategy or an obsolete and counterproductive way of dealing with the Canadian multicultural reality becomes a pressing one. The three stories discussed in this chapter, "Lend Me Your Light," "Squatter" and "Swimming Lessons," reflect distinct and complex attitudes towards cultural difference.[5]

"Squatter": Difference as Encumbrance or Resource?

"Squatter" features the Parsi Sarosh who decides to emigrate and leaves Bombay for Toronto. The narrative focuses on the implications of migration, outlining the ways in which immigration can fail but also suggesting strategies by which it might succeed. While the usefulness of ethnic difference, i.e. the persistence of old conventions, is interrogated by Sarosh in Canada, the frame of the story remains within an Indian setting as well as within a non-Western tradition that in its reliance on storytelling and orality emphasizes difference as a tool for cultural survival. It will be argued that "Squatter" confirms rather than undermines conventional assumptions of postcolonialism with respect to cultural difference. It does not so much detail the negative sides of retaining cultural difference but foregrounds the positive effects of a politics of difference explicitly (Nariman) as well as ex negativo (Sarosh).

Sarosh, who alters his name to Sid once he arrives in Toronto, cannot use a toilet in the conventional (Western) way.[6] Being unable to sit on a toilet seat, Sarosh can only squat like an Indian once he feels the urge to relieve himself: "Morning after morning, he had no choice but to climb up and simulate the squat of our Indian latrines. If he sat down, no amount of exertion could produce success."[7] For an adequate understanding of "Squatter" it is crucial to "consider the social and cultural ramifications of [...] [Sarosh's] inability."[8] In Mistry's treatment of the immigration experience in "Squatter," toilet habits become metonymic of Otherness.[9] The implied Western reader of "Squatter" learns that there is no single way of attending to one's bodily functions. While defecating is natural and universal, the ways to defecate are cultural as well as culturally specific. Squatting becomes the sign of a different culture, a culture, moreover, in which sitting (rather than squatting) becomes the marked case, i.e. the unusual way of defecating.[10] It could be argued that in "Squatter," by way of a postcolonial counterdiscursive move, the exception becomes the norm and the cultural periphery the new centre. Mistry questions Western assumptions by making strange what the Western reader takes for granted. Thus what has been denigrated and devalued as eccentric/ex-centric is invested with new dignity in the context of an appreciation of Otherness.

Or so it would seem. For although Mistry's literary techniques resemble postcolonial strategies, it is essential to realize that if one takes as a starting point for an interpretation Sarosh's subject position, then "Squatter" departs from postcolonialism in an important aspect. In marked opposition to the strategic value postcolonial critics accord to metonymical inscriptions of Otherness for the portrayal of other cultures, difference is not celebrated by Sarosh as liberating but conceived as impediment instead. This is reflected in the persistence of old toilet habits as well as in Sarosh's failure to change his name to Sid. In "Squatter," names seem representative of different cultures in much the same way as toilet habits do. Sarosh's desire to cease to be Sarosh and to become Sid signifies a desire to become Canadian and thus a desire to erase the traces of his cultural difference. A similar case can be made with respect to toilet habits: For Sarosh a failure to defecate Western style is equivalent to a failed immigration process. A new name and the wish to defecate like a Canadian express Sarosh's yearning to die a symbolic death as an Indian as well as a wish to be reborn as a Canadian.[11]

In Sarosh's/Sid's eyes, the processes of altering one's name and one's toilet habits are not equally easily accomplished. Changing the former is regarded to be easier than using a toilet Western style. The protagonist of "Squatter" projects defecating as a cultural practice more essential than naming. Sarosh/Sid identifies toilet habits with one's core identity, while names correlate to more peripheral aspects of identity. Thus defecating and naming correspond to a view of identity that consists of an inside and an outside image of the self. Eventually, however, "Squatter" deconstructs both names and toilet habits as valid indicators of identity. Part of Sarosh's/Sid's problem is that he overestimates the effects of renaming, while simultaneously underestimating its dangers. By renaming himself, Sarosh assumes he has made progress in his assimilation to Canada. The new name indicates the will to a new identity, and thus to a self-image that is stable and fixed. However, while there is no clue that the name Sid is rejected in Canada, the new name Sarosh has given himself in a new land does not stick in the old. Nariman, the storyteller of "Squatter" refuses to acknowledge Sarosh's new identity and continues to call him Sarosh: "This Sarosh began calling himself Sid after living in Toronto for a few months, but in our story he will be Sarosh and nothing but Sarosh, for that is his proper Parsi name" (153). Nariman, who is connected with a different time and place, does not accept his protagonist's new name, thereby rendering questionable the change of names/identities from Sarosh to Sid, i.e. from Indian to (Sarosh's limited notion of what it means to be) Canadian in the first place. Renaming as well as altering one's toilet habits thus correspond to a construction of a new identity that is not truly lived, and thus will not be stable. Whereas the failure to defecate like a Westerner prevents a successful assimilation in the eyes of the protagonist, renaming proves especially deceptive. Misunderstood as a label rather than as a truthful reflection of one's identity, renaming suggests an easy transition to another culture when in fact no substantial change has taken place. Sarosh's fate demonstrates that Mistry's metonymical mode of narration is farcical. The story sees one superficial cultural practice, i.e. renaming, as compensation for another superficial cultural practice, i.e. defecating.

Implicitly, Sarosh/Sid wants to shed his old identity because he regards a change of identity as a prerequisite for getting ahead in Canada. As the double entity Sarosh/Sid makes evident, the shedding of his identity is unsuccessful, the result of which is alienation and isolation. Culturally, he is alienated from the old without being able to adapt to the new. This is underlined once again by toilet habits: "There had been a time when it was perfectly natural to squat. Now it seemed a grotesquely aberrant thing to do" (162). The constant failure to use a toilet seat in an authentic Western way results in feelings of shame and guilt: "Wherever he went he was reminded of the ignominy of his way. If he could not be westernized in all respects, he was nothing but a failure" (162).

Guilt and shame, which will also be of relevance in "Lend Me Your Light," indicate that for Sarosh/Sid, cultural difference is not a resource but an encumbrance: "He remained dependent on the old way, and this unalterable fact, strengthened afresh every morning of his life in the new country, suffocated him" (154).

It is important to stress that Sarosh's/Sid's view is not that of the story as a whole. "Squatter" does not rule out the possibility of a more positive perspective on difference but plays off the fate of its protagonist against the perspective of the story's narrator. Overlapping with the perspective of the story, Nariman's narration overrides Sarosh's view and, in diametrical opposition to the story's protagonist, advocates difference not as encumbrance but as resource. When Nariman interprets Sarosh's/Sid's endeavours as the wish to adapt (154), he is in fact mistaken. Sarosh does not want to become adapted, he wants to become assimilated,[12] hence the wish to become Sid. Assimilation, however, is at odds with the theoretical formulations of Canadian multiculturalism that envisage unity in diversity and allow the immigrant to redefine himself on the basis of what he already is. In other words, multiculturalism does not demand that Sarosh erases his old identity; in order to become Canadian, assimilation is no prerequisite. On the contrary, Sarosh/Sid could have preserved his cultural difference and would have fully qualified as Canadian. Sarosh/Sid overlooks that in a nation built by and consisting of immigrants, difference constitutes the essence of national identity. By staying the way he was, Sarosh would already have been as 'Canadian' as one could possibly become.

We learn more about Canada and multiculturalism through the story's narrator. As a matter of fact, Nariman's angle on the multicultural society of Canadian is satirical; it is Swiftian in its grotesqueness.[13] Sarosh learns through his Immigrant Aid Society that his dilemma could be resolved operationally. As Dr No-Ilaaz explains:

> A small device, Crappus Non Interruptus, or CNI as we call it, is implanted in the bowel. The device is controlled by an external handheld transmitter similar to the ones used for automatic garage door-openers—you may have seen them in hardware stores. [. . .] You can encode the handheld transmitter with a personal ten-digit code. Then all you do is position yourself on the toilet seat and activate your transmitter. Just like a garage door, your bowel will open without pushing or grunting. (160)

In employing metaphorical speech in order to illustrate the process of becoming Canadian, Nariman (as well as Mistry) questions a purely mechanistic view of identity formation. The Canadian Dr No-Ilaaz, who, significantly, has not felt the necessity to change his name on arriving in Canada, does not recommend the operation because he knows that the CNI will not turn the Parsi/Indian Sarosh into a Canadian Sid overnight. Defecating Western style signifies an understanding of Canadian identity no less questionable than a mere change of names. Although the CNI can help Sarosh modify his toilet habits, it does not make him less different. The irreversible implantation of the CNI will make him more Canadian only on the surface, while definitely making him less Indian at heart. As Dr No-Ilaaz puts it: "You will be permanently different from your family and friends because of this basic internal modification. In fact, in this country or that, it will set you apart from your fellow countrymen" (161).

For Sarosh difference does not become a tool for constructing an identity. Identity is not predicated by difference because the very character of difference is misunderstood by the protagonist of Mistry's story. For even without having the CNI implanted, difference for Sarosh/Sid translates as alienation wherever he migrates to. "Squatter" describes a circular trajectory that eventually makes Sarosh/Sid emigrate/immigrate again, this time from Toronto to Bombay. At the end of the story, Sarosh, who has called himself Sid in Canada, wants to be Sarosh again in India. But, as the narrator points out, a return is impossible: "The old pattern was never found by Sarosh; he searched in vain" (167). Although Sarosh has not become a Sid, he nevertheless is no longer the man he used to be, which means that he has unlearned to be an Indian Sarosh. Emigration/Immigration have led Sarosh/Sid nowhere and made him a casualty of "a problematic relationship between interlocking cultural landscapes."[14] Instead of offering a new perspective, migration has only brought about displacement, uprooting and "cultural dislocation."[15] Forsaking India with the hope of finding a new home, Sarosh/Sid has favoured assimilation over adaptation. This is a mistake he pays for dearly by becoming permanently Other, unable to turn any environment into home.[16] Instead of having access to the best of both worlds, he no longer fully belongs to either of them. That Sarosh/Sid always remains alienated wherever he settles down is underscored once again by his toilet habits. Only when he has boarded the flight home is he able to defecate while sitting on a toilet seat. In other words, only on the plane, i.e. neither in Canada nor in India, does he succeed in doing what he has tried to accomplish in vain for a period of ten years. The solution to his problem is located in a space that is neither 'here' nor 'there.' Thus eventually the dilemma of the in-between is only resolved in the in-between, i.e. for Sarosh/Sid not resolved at all.

Sarosh/Sid can be regarded as a tragic hero, which is underlined by the intertextual reference that the story ends with (168). Like Shakespeare's Othello, Sarosh/Sid is unable to position himself in relation to a new environment.[17] While Othello cannot internalize the values of Venice, Sarosh/Sid fails to cope with what he assumes to be the cultural conventions of the Canadian diaspora. By alluding to the requirements of classical tragedy, i.e. tragic flaw and dilemma, Mistry implicitly also suggests that Sarosh/Sid is to blame for his failure to make it in Canada as well as in India. It is neither Canada nor India that fail Sarosh/Sid but he himself that feels a failure on account of a distorted image of what both countries expect of him.

"Squatter," although coming across as a report, displays allegorical features. Nariman, who is not only the narrator but also the author of Sarosh's story, tells "the sad but instructive chronicle of his [i.e. Sarosh's] recent life" (153) for a didactic purpose. The central insight he wants to convey to Kersi, Viraf and Jehangir, i.e. those youths of Firozsha Baag most eager to emigrate, does not pertain to the impossibility of finding happiness abroad.[18] It concerns cultural difference, as the predicament of the immigrant that cannot be denied because it is written on the body. Any attempt at trying to erase this difference will result in disorientation and uprooting. Nariman invents a Sarosh/Sid in order to caution those leaving their homeland against trying to lose sight of who they really are. The reason why for Sarosh/Sid "life in the land of milk and honey was just a pain in the posterior" (168) is that he has attempted to erase his identity as a Parsi: "Sarosh seems to want to forget his ethnic past, to efface his origins, and to lose his sense of identity by immersing himself in the Western hegemonic culture."[19] Metaphorically conveyed, mistaking adaptation for assimilation has proved fatal because Sarosh/Sid, in the course of immersing himself in Canadian culture, has drowned in his wish for sameness. The attempt to be like others in Canada prevents Sarosh/Sid from perceiving that which distinguishes him from others. The desire to be identical to others erodes his identity as the unity of his self-sameness. A passion for (a mistaken because homogeneous conception of Canadian) identity overrides the fact that his identity is inevitably tied up with an awareness of difference. Nariman's interpretation of cultural retention differs from Sarosh's/Sid's in an important aspect. He regards cultural difference as resource rather than as an encumbrance, as liberating rather than restrictive. As will be explored in more detail below, not all of Mistry's other stories treat the Canadian immigrant experience in this way.

"Lend Me Your Light": Hybridity Without Double Vision

Like "Squatter," "Lend Me Your Light" is concerned with alienation. The Parsis Jamshed, Percy and his brother Kersi are close friends until Kersi and Jamshed immigrate to North America. While Jamshed goes to the US, Kersi immigrates to Canada. Life in India, America, or Canada puts into question the characters' attitude towards cultural difference as a marker of identity that can either be rejected, or accepted, or result in confusion as to how to lead one's life in a diaspora situation. While "Squatter" tells the story of a character who attempts to erase his Indian identity in order to assimilate, "Lend Me Your Light" details a broader spectrum of ways to act in a new land. More precisely, "Lend Me Your Light" explores a continuum of three ways of coping with difference. In the words of Ajay Heble:

> Jamshed, who, scornful of his native India, leaves for the Promised Land of America, and Percy, who adamantly stays in India to help villagers in their fight against exploitation, the story finds its focus in Kersi, the narrator, who comes to represent the struggle between the two extreme positions.[20]

That Jamshed assimilates to America easily is not surprising once it is taken into account that he is already alienated from India while living there.[21] For Jamshed India is a backwards country ridden by corruption and crime and unable to change for the better. It is his conviction that the problems of India are tied up with the country's so-called "*ghati* mentality":

> In the particular version of reality we inherited, *ghatis* were always flooding places, they never just went there. *Ghatis* were flooding the banks, desecrating the sanctity of institutions, and taking up all the coveted jobs. *Ghatis* were even flooding the colleges and universities, a thing unheard of. Wherever you turned, the bloody *ghatis* were flooding the place. (176)

When Jamshed talks about ghatis, i.e. about the members of a lower caste, the chaos associated with them hints at his paranoid fear of an ensuing class struggle. The water imagery, so aptly ironized by Kersi above, suggests that the upper-class Jamshed associates the social Other with a lumpenproletariat intent on depriving him of his riches. In much the same way as the individual is drowned in the mass, those who are well off are threatened by lower castes/the working class. In that light, it is possible to argue that Jamshed accommodates to America so smoothly because the difference that he is afraid of is caste/class rather than race or culture. While caste/class are unmarked within US multiculturalism, it is money that enables him to assimilate to a capitalist America.

While Jamshed as an adult continues to be preoccupied with 'ghati mentalities', both Kersi and Percy, on growing up, cease to take part in his complaints. The different development of the three of them with respect to their views on caste is telling in its irony. While Jamshed constantly accuses India of its backwardness, the story reveals that he has not matured as a person and thereby insinuates that it is not India that is outside of time, progress etc. but he himself.[22] While Kersi sees through the snobbery of Jamshed's rhetoric in retrospect but fails to act, it is Percy who commits himself to challenging social injustice within India. Percy, as a character that remains behind and does not emigrate, implicitly testifies to the fact that India is not eternally depraved and corrupt but that things in India can be changed. Fighting the rural system of money lending, Percy Boyce is not only the most courageous character in the story but also the one who practices the solidarity towards his fellow human beings indicated in the story's epitaph by Tagore: " . . . your lights are all lit—then where do you go with your lamp? My house is all dark and lonesome—lend me your light" (173). Both Jamshed and Percy want to erase differences in their lives but they configure them differently. While for the capitalist Jamshed it is America that overrides ethnic as well as caste/class difference, the Marxist Percy works towards ameliorating the social gulfs within India and thus actively fights social and class difference. Put differently, for Jamshed money and capitalism constitutes sameness, for Percy (as well as for Tagore) humanity is the central bond between individuals.

The clash between Jamshed's cynicism and Percy's idealism is reflected in the conflict of values within Kersi.[23] The protagonist and narrator of "Lend Me Your Light" experiences emigration and diaspora as sources of guilt, which become manifest in two ways.[24] Comparing his situation to that of his brother, he reflects with a bad conscience: "There you were, my brother, waging battles against corruption and evil, while I was watching sitcoms on my rented Granada TV" (184). Kersi's migration has resulted in alienation from his brother, whose activism contrasts favourably with Kersi's paralysis. Apart from a bad conscience due to his passivity, Kersi also experiences a feeling of guilt towards the culture he has left behind. A consequence of his guilt may be that the attempts by way of which Kersi tries to affiliate with the new country merely mimic his behaviour in the old. Thus the Zoroastrian Society of Ontario that Kersi joins also draws on the same scapegoat and conversational dummy so cherished by Jamshed, i.e. the ghati caste and its mentality (182–3). His effort to recover the culture he has left behind proves to be unsatisfactory. We observe Kersi in the middle of a difficult process of adaptation. Part of the difficulty lies in Kersi himself who lacks the distance to India in order to come to terms with what he has left behind. The consequence is that he "inhabits the ambivalent space between cultures."[25] He is in-between cultures, a situation he does not experience as liberating but as crippling: "Kersi sees his hybridized identity as the site of a struggle between opposing sets of cultural values."[26] Implicitly, he is in need of a Nariman Hansotia ordering his life for him and turning the muddle of migration and diaspora into a coherent story.

That the diaspora does not offer Kersi a new vision but constitutes a serious handicap is also underlined by the story's intertextual reference to Greek mythology. Before leaving for Toronto, Kersi, suffering from conjunctivitis, likens himself to the blind seer Tiresias: "I, Tiresias, blind and throbbing between two lives, the one in Bombay and the one to come in Toronto" (180). The future tense with which Canada is associated allows the conclusion that Kersi does still hope for a hybrid identity that would enable him to selectively draw on the best of several worlds. Towards the end of the story, however, the tone of his discourse has become more pessimistic and notably bleaker. Eventually, Kersi characterises himself in the following way: "I Tiresias, throbbing between two lives, humbled by the ambiguities and dichotomies confronting me" (192). The story's intertextuality reflects Kersi's failure to adapt and to cope with a fundamental conflict of values in the Canadian diaspora. While the first of the two references to Greek mythology framing "Lend Me Your Light" still speaks of hope, the latter quotation merely registers that hopes have been thwarted.[27]

So far criticism has overlooked that Mistry does not quote Greek mythology directly. In "Lend Me Your Light" the inscription of intertexts is mediated and thus acquires additional complexity. It is notworthy that Rohinton Mistry alludes to Greek mythology by taking recourse to TS Eliot[28] who in the third section of *The Waste Land* has Tiresias speak the following words:

> I, Tiresias, though blind, throbbing between two lives,
> Old man with wrinkled female breasts, can see
> At the violet hour, the evening hour that strives
> Homeward, and brings the sailor home from sea, [. . .][29]

Quoting Eliot, Mistry renders Kersi's comparison to the ancient seer as inadequate. Kersi is no second Tiresias because his blindness does not result in a new kind of vision that would enable him to predict the future.[30] Although Kersi Boyce may lead two lives, the result is not a double vision but schizophrenia, failure to adapt and, in fact, blindness. As a man temporarily displaying characteristics of both sexes as well as moving between the world and the underworld, Eliot's Tiresias is a man of the in-between who has received the gift of prophecy as compensation for the blindness he has been struck with. In fact, his hybridity is so valuable for the gods that they endow him with the ability to see into the future. Kersi on the other hand, merely suffers from his hybridity in the mundane, postreligious sphere of the diaspora. He cannot make out the sailor coming home (i.e. Ulysses) whom Tiresias in Eliot's poem speaks of, for he himself is on an Odyssee, i.e. sentenced to wander in search of a home. Kersi's failure to perceive the sailor, so to speak, is a failure to evaluate his situation in Canada as someone who is essentially homeless.[31]

In the context of the story's intertextuality, the symbolism of "Lend me Your Light" also acquires an additional layer of meaning. For the light imagery of "Lend Me Your Light" does not only allude to Jamshed's moral darkness juxtaposed to Percy's qualities as light-bringer; "Lend Me Your Light" also employs light imagery to underline its concern with vision and seeing. Thus the request for light signalled by the title is not only a demand for solidarity and humanism but also a desire and a will to truth. While the homeland in "Lend Me Your Light" grants Percy the satisfaction of finding meaning in life by helping others with a "non-usurious lending of light,"[32] the diaspora does not allow the migrant Kersi the 'in-sight' needed to come to terms with his hybrid existence: No "lucidity of thought" (186), no "clearness with which [. . .] [to] look at things" (186), "the epiphany would have to wait for another time" (192). How Kersi eventually arrives at an epiphany that sheds light on how an acceptable Canadian identity might be envisaged, is detailed by Mistry in "Swimming Lessons," the final story of his collection.

"Swimming Lessons": Difference and Distance

At the centre of "Swimming Lessons," the most complex text in *Tales From Firozsha Baag*,[33] is Kersi Boyce again. Initially, his position in the new world is characterized by his affiliation with the old. Living in Toronto, Bombay is nevertheless constantly on Kersi's mind. This dichotomy informs the structure of the story as one alternating between 'here' and 'there.'[34] However, in the course of the story, Kersi undergoes a transformation from an immigrant obsessed with the past and the culture left behind to someone who makes a conscious effort to come to terms with the social reality of Canada.[35] Shedding older notions of culture, identity and difference, he becomes able to give up the distance he has hitherto maintained towards Canadian society.

Not unlike Neil Bissoondath, Rohinton Mistry explores multiculturalism by drawing on the image of the house as microcosm reflecting the situation of Canadian society at large. "Swimming Lessons" is set in a block of flats in Toronto that resembles Bombay's Firozsha Baag, and both buildings are inhabited by a variety of ethnicities. In Bombay, Muslims and Goans live among Parsis,[36] in Toronto Scottish, Slavic and Indian/Parsi immigrants live together. However, their coexistence, albeit peaceful, is not free from friction. What is striking about the block of flats in Toronto (in contrast to Firozsha Baag) is that Kersi does not know anyone of his neighours by his/her name. The people living side by side with him are merely "the old man" (229), "the old man's son" (243), "the Portuguese woman," or "PW" (230), "Berthe's husband" (237), "two women" (232), one of them identified by her Scottish accent (242). Not only does Kersi refer to people by way of their language,[37] he also refers to them by way of their function, e.g. PW as the disseminator of information, "the communicator for the apartment building" (230), or their outward appearance. Thus the woman that he fancies during one of his swimming lessons is merely "the pink one-piece suit" (238). Kersi Boyce does not acknowledge the individuality of the persons around him; he merely refers to them metonymically. However, taking recourse to metonymy and synekdoche is indicative of an amount of anonymity within his life that is worrying. Not only does it make a point about the lack of solidarity among immigrants in Toronto, which can also be observed in Vassanji's *No New Land*, it also reveals Kersi's problematic attitude towards his host country. As McElwain points out:

> His multicultural neighbours symbolize Canada's multiculturalism, and his distance from them symbolizes his distance from his adopted country. [. . .] His failure to get to know his neighbours reflects his failure to get to know Canada.[38]

That Kersi's image of Canada is reductive is also corroborated by the following passage in which he imagines

> a gorgeous woman in the class for non-swimmers, at whose sight I will be instantly aroused, and she, spying the shape of my desire, will look me straight in the eye with her intentions; she will come home with me, to taste the pleasures of my delectable Asian brown body whose strangeness has intrigued her and unleashed uncontrollable surges of passion inside her throughout the duration of the swimming lesson. (235–6)

Kersi's sexual fantasy is interesting for two reasons. First of all, sexuality here and elsewhere in the story is not connected to love or desire but is related to deception. Illusion and disillusionment both result from varying degrees of distance that the protagonist Kersi maintains towards the objects of his fantasy.[39] The greater the distance, the more probable it generally is that the object of his desire spawns another fantasy in his mind. The farther away and the more removed Kersi feels, the more sexist do his sexual fantasies become. Reducing distance, on the other hand, brings about disillusionment and thus a more realist stance towards people and society. With respect to social relations, "Swimming Lessons" could be said to move from more to less distance, for at the end of the story Kersi will have learned that "you can't see things clearly until you get close to them."[40]

Secondly, the real perversity of Kersi's fantasy quoted above is not so much his sexism but the fact that he imagines himself as the exotic and sexually potent Asian. He downplays his cultural difference as a Parsi while simultaneously foregrounding the stereotypical image of the Easterner in the eyes of the West.[41] The identity Kersi projects, relies on a racialist understanding of Otherness that discards the complexity of the individual. As such, Kersi's self-image reflects an inferiority complex that is Fanonian in its dimensions. His sexuality displays traits of neurosis because his self-image is distorted because he has been victimized as Other.[42] While Kersi himself does not reflect on the implications of his racialist self-image, the story juxtaposes his fantasy with an instance of blatant racism. The allegedly liberal and tolerant Canada draws on stereotypes in its understanding of difference, when Kersi is discriminated against by three youths: "Paki, Paki, smell like curry. The third says to the first two: pretty soon all the water's going to taste of curry" (238). As a matter of fact, the racism of the boys only complements Kersi's racialist self-image. The question is whether Mistry sees both instances of an inadequate understanding of identity as linked in any way. There is evidence that he does.

For "Swimming Lessons" as a story detailing the confusion of the immigrant by repeatedly referring to a confusion of cause and effect,[43] the implication is that there is a connection between Canada's racism and Kersi's racialism. His self-image is distorted because Canada does not allow for difference beyond stereotypes. Although Kersi is to be blamed for the inordinate distance he maintains towards the inhabitants of his house and, by extension, to Canada in general, he also suffers from a multiculturalism that displays shortcomings. So far, so *No New Land*. Kersi's fate in the new world is characterized by a complex dialectic that does not defy causality as such but resists any kind of monocausal nexus. Kersi does not adapt because he maintains his distance, and he maintains his distance because he is discriminated against *and* because he wants to be different. That he does not want to adapt is not only revealed by the anonymity that characterises his life world. It becomes apparent, too, during one of his swimming lessons:

> This instructor is an irresponsible person. Or he does not value the lives of non-white immigrants. I remember the three teenagers. Maybe the swimming-pool is the hangout of some racist group, bent on eliminating all non-white swimmers, to keep their waters pure and their white sisters unogled. (239)

While Kersi has been discriminated against by the racism of the three boys, his instructor clearly does not have racism in mind when he relies on moderate pressure in trying to teach him to swim. Symbolically, Kersi's fear to adapt to Canada figures as fear of water. However, in an act of overcompensation the instructor is blamed by Kersi for his own failure to adapt to Canada. Kersi's inability to cope with difference is displaced onto Ron and the inability to cope with difference he is unjustly accused of. Racism is invoked because Kersi is unable yet to think beyond a notion of difference that is not racialist/racist.

Learning how to swim translates as learning how to cope in new surroundings. "Swimming is a metaphor for assimilating in the story, and both his fear of water and his dwindling efforts in his lessons symbolize his unwillingness and inability to commit to Canada."[44] Water testifies to the complexity of the emigrant/immigrant experience by symbolizing death and rebirth.[45] The emphasis is on movement,[46] the difficulties experienced in learning to swim metaphorically allude to the difficulties of getting ahead in an environment that is as alien to the nonswimmer as the element of water is to the element of earth. While swimming and water are charged with symbolic significance in Mistry's tale, the representation of his failure to swim is symbolical, too. Kersi has not become Canadian because he has failed to position himself with respect to those surrounding him in a multicultural Toronto. Metaphorically speaking, he has not learned how to swim.[47]

At the same time, Kersi's failure to adapt results from "ties to the past too strong to enable him to connect with the present."[48] He is obsessed with the past and is preoccupied with remembering and comparing. As a matter of fact, his remembrances of his time in Firozsha Baag abound: The 'old man' reminds Kersi of his grandfather (230), Rustomji of "An Auspicious Occasion" (230) and Jaakaylee of "The Ghost of Firozsha Baag" (230). In a self-conscious meditation on writing and imagery, Kersi remebers Nariman Hansotia of "Squatter" (234) and compares PW to Najamai of "One Sunday" (236). The obsession with 'there' consumes too much of Kersi's time in order to enable him to concern himself with 'here' in a serious fashion.

Two examples may serve to show that the distance towards the new is merely the other side of a past that haunts the protagonist. First of all, Kersi's distance towards the new becomes evident when he is unable to identify trees other than maples (241), thus testifying to a rather theoretical knowledge about Canada that seems to be learned by heart for an interview with the Canadian immigration authorities. Kersi's notion of Canadian identity is not only purely academic but also superficial as well as clichéd. Knowledge about his host country remains within the realm of the symbolic, the explanatory value of which is low. Secondly, Kersi's affiliation with the old becomes obvious when in the course of a commotion in the court of his block of flats he involuntarily associates the old country: "Maybe the old man is not well, it's an emergency. But I quickly scrap that thought—this isn't Bombay, an ambulance would have arrived" (242). Bombay is still so much of a reality that it surfaces time and again in the mind of Kersi when things in the outside world call for an explanation. As McElwain suggest: "Geographical separation intensifies memories; it does not lead to emotional separation,"[49] something which is also underscored by the form of Mistry's story.

The form of "Swimming Lessons" mirrors Kersi's continuing relationship to India. The structure of the story as one alternating between Toronto and Bombay is significant for an interpretation of "Swimming Lessons." While in Toronto, Kersi remembers Bombay, his parents in Bombay worry about him in Toronto because they fear that he will become alienated from his cultural roots (236). On the one hand, Kersi's parents wait for his letters and read what he writes about Toronto. Eventually, they receive stories instead of letters, a medium that conveys Kersi's experience in Canada in less superficial terms and testifies that he has not forgotten India at all. His ties to his homeland are arguably too strong, and difference seems an impediment in his process of adaptation to Canada. On the other hand, we never observe Kersi read what his parents write. Thus the communication with his parents is not only delayed and indirect, it also appears one-sided and asymmetrical. This means that the ties to India, although still intact, are no longer characterized by an active engagement with the country of his origins. It is only memories that connect him to the past. Kersi, who has not adapted to Canada yet, is not fully part of India anymore either. He is in-between cultures, i.e. he does not fully belong to either the new or the old world.

"Swimming Lessons" is Mistry's most complex narrative in an aesthetically traditional oeuvre. In particular, the complexity of the story consists in its playing off postmodern thought. "Swimming Lessons" becomes an autobiographical story when one day Kersi's parents are sent a collection of short stories that turns out to be *Tales From Firozsha Baag* (241). Thus in a self-conscious move the distinction between writer and narrator is lifted and Kersi is identified with Rohinton Mistry.[50] Kersi like Mistry attempts to deal with the past by remembering it. While the reader is in the same position as Kersi's parents and needs to make sense about his immigrant experience by reading about it,[51] both Kersi and Mistry come to terms with the past by writing about it.

Generally speaking, writing is an important activity in "Swimming Lessons." Partaking of postmodernist discourse also in other respects, "Swimming Lessons" displays characteristics of metafiction, i.e. a fiction that self-reflexively makes the conditions of its production and reception part of the act of narration.[52] Thus Kersi's parents constantly engage in poetological speculations about remembering and artistic distance. In this context they also mimic an argument often voiced by critics of Canadian immigrant literature: Canada is indispensable in laying to rest the past and is needed as a space removed that enables the writer to work through his experiences in a colonial/postcolonial land.[53] Observe, for example, Kersi's father lecturing on literary theory:

> Father explained it takes a writer about ten years time after an experience before he is able to use it in his writing, it takes that long to be absorbed internally and understood, thought out and thought about, over and over again, he haunts it and it haunts him if it is valuable enough, till the writer is comfortable with it to be able to use it as he wants; but this is only one theory I read somewhere, it may or may not be true. That means, said Mother, that his childhood in Bombay and our home here is the most valuable thing in his life just now, because he is able to remember it all to write about it, and you were so bitterly saying he is forgetting where he came from; and that may be true, said Father, but that is not

> what the theory means, according to the theory he is writing of these things because they are far enough in the past for him to deal with it objectively, he is able to achieve what critics call artistic distance, without emotions interfering. (246)

Writing is of special relevance for a discussion of difference in "Swimming Lessons," too. The distance that is so problematic for Kersi because it allegedly impedes his adaptation to Canada proves useful in one important respect: It benefits the production of fiction/literature.[54] According to Kersi's father it is crucial for Kersi as a writer not to lose his cultural difference because this difference will produce the aesthetically different:

> The last story [i.e. "Swimming Lessons"] they liked the best of all because it had the most in it about Canada, and now they felt they knew at least a little bit, even if it was a very little bit, about his day-to-day life in his apartment; and Father said if he continues to write about such things he will become popular because I am sure they are interested there in reading about life through the eyes of an immigrant, it provides a different viewpoint; the only danger is if he changes and becomes so much like them that he will write like one of them and lose the important difference. (248)

While Kersi's father argues that aesthetic difference will be valued as artistic originality and thus sell, Kersi's story also testifies that cultural difference outside the realm of literature is psychologically as well as sociologically troublesome. Although the form of "Swimming Lessons" with its fragments alternately set in India and Canada might be read as a valuable reflection of Kersi's difference,[55] the story's oscillation between 'there' and 'here,' i.e. its dichotomous imagination, could also be read as mirroring the protagonist's uprooting and disorientation.[56] The irony of "Swimming Lessons" would then be that art and life beg to differ about the usefulness of cultural difference and social distance.

Difference, understood as unwillingness to engage with society, is a shortcoming on the protagonist's part that is not successfully grappled with until the very end of the story. Maintaining "the important difference," as Kersi's father demands, is not an alternative categorically ruled out by the story; it is the way difference is lived that is at the centre of "Swimming Lessons" and that the story criticizes in its protagonist. The end of Mistry's story sees the conflict between (difference/distance in) art and (difference/distance in) life about to be resolved. As the cycle of seasons in the (symbolic) time scheme of "Swimming Lessons" indicates, the winter of discontent gives way to a spring that indicates spiritual regeneration. That some form of regeneration, or rebirth, as the water imagery of the story insinuates, has been accomplished is signalled by Kersi Boyce's new attempt at learning to swim as well as by the fact that he asks his fellow inhabitants for their names and makes an effort at identifying more trees than maples (248–9).

"Swimming Lessons" implies that Kersi's altered attitude towards Canada results from his having worked through his past artistically. While art and life have different views of cultural difference, both are connected. Life needs art to become liveable. The artistic exploration of the self is a prerequisite to Kersi's introspection signalled by his bathtub baptism: "The world outside the water I have seen a lot of, it is now time to see what is inside" (249). In accord with Mistry's extended water metaphor, being able to see underwater signals a willingness to engage with Canada and a new vision of its multicultural society. At the end of the story, Kersi Boyce sees life in "dual perspective."[57] Henceforth he will make a new effort at overcoming solipsism and inwardness in life and exchange a superficial and half-hearted attitude towards multiculturalism for genuine cultural interaction. Ethnic difference does no longer figure as distance and passivity, the emphasis is not on relinquishing but on "integrating his ethnic difference into the sameness of a Western cultural mainstream."[58] Kersi can become a full-fledged Canadian once he "unsettles the terms of sameness and difference, insisting on his full citizenship even while he explodes the idea of national belonging."[59]

By virtue of the fact that the story is strategically positioned at the end of *Tales From Firozsha Baag*, all the other stories may be read as preliminary attempts of Mistry searching for a new self-image in a new land. Writing a cycle culminating in the autobiographical "Swimming Lessons," it is Rohinton Mistry himself who makes an emphatic claim for a balanced attitude towards identity construction in the (Canadian) diaspora. In its authoritativeness "Swimming Lessons" therefore overrides the pessimism of "Squatter" and "Lend Me Your Light." Displacement may be challenged by complementing cultural difference and indigenous tradition by a general openness to new cultural influences. The openness towards the new that "Swimming Lessons" is resonant with at the end can also be identified in Mistry's narratives set 'there': *Such a Long Journey* and *A Fine Balance.*

B. 'There' I: Cultural Difference and the Struggle for Meaning. *Such a Long Journey* (1991)

Rohinton Mistry's oeuvre partakes of two discourses. On the one hand, his narratives can only be adequately understood if their local and historical specificity is taken into consideration. On the other hand, Mistry supplements the anchoring of his narratives in Indian contexts by allusions to humanism/universalism as a discourse of sameness. In what follows, I will first detail the relevance of cultural difference in Mistry's novel before I go on to illustrate how difference is supplemented by references to a humanist tradition of thought.

Similar to Neil Bissoondath, Mistry's works are concerned with difference as community difference. The community Mistry deals with in greater detail in *Such a Long Journey* is his own, the Parsi community. It will become apparent that the postcolonial implications of *Such a Long Journey* are closely connected to the responsibility Mistry takes on as representative and mouthpiece of the Parsi community. In order to realize how the postcolonial condition affects the community's identity, the central aspects of Parsi identity have to be clarified. Apart from religion, the major factor shaping the collective identity of the Parsi community is its historical awareness. This is also acknowledged by the critic Arun Mukherjee who argues that "to do full justice to *Such a Long Journey*, it is important to know the history of the Parsi community."[1]

Context: A Brief History of the Parsis in India

The history of the Parsis is rooted in the pre-Islamic history of Persia. In the wake of the Arab conquest of Iran, Zoroastrianism "became steadily marginalized, and oppression and persecution of its followers became ever more acute."[2] Seeking freedom of worship, a small group of Zoroastrians decided to emigrate.[3] In 936 A.D. the Parsis, named after the Persian province of Pars (or Fars),[4] settled near Gujarat in northwest India. Not unlike the Pilgrim fathers' journey from a hostile England towards what they hoped would become a New Jerusalem, the Parsi migration from Pars to Gujarat has been subject to mythologising.[5] Within the collective memory of the community the settlement in India is very much remembered as a reaction to the oppresion experienced under the Persian Muslim rulers.[6] The most widely circulated story about the community, however, concerns their arrival in Sanjan and the ensuing negotiations with the local Hindu rajah Jadhav Rana.[7] The Parsis were granted the right to settle on the coast of Gujarat provided they would not be disruptive to society and be willing to acculturate. The local rajah expected them to explain their religion to him, to henceforth adopt Gujarati as their native tongue, to dress according to local customs, to dispense with weapons altogether and to practice their faith only after nightfall so as to avoid giving offence to the local Hindu majority.[8] As the Parsis complied with the rajah's conditions, they were allowed to settle in Sanjan and since that time have proved loyal to their respective rulers.[9]

The trajectory of the Parsis since early modern times is impressive. Starting out as a rural community consisting predominantly of farmers, weavers and carpenters, the Parsis quickly became wealthy merchants and industrialists.[10] As a matter of fact, their rise as a community is closely connected to the British penetration of India: Parsi knowledge of trade and country became a crucial instrument in the British development of the Indian market. The community made a name for itself by serving the colonizers as cultural translators. The British (as well as other European powers)

> preferred to transact their business with the Indian hinterland through Parsee agents and 'brokers,' who, on the one hand, had at their disposal the necessary knowledge of land and language, but whose minority role in Indian society, on the other hand, gave them the necessary flexibility in commerce with foreigners.[11]

When the British shifted their centre of trade from Surat to Bombay, the Parsis, as shipbuilders and industrious merchants, were encouraged to settle there.[12] They played an important part in the development of Bombay whose dockyard they built and owned for a long time.[13] As a consequence of their entrepreneurial success,[14] the Parsis became India's most urbanized and most prosperous community. With their assistance, Bombay developed into the centre of Indian economy and industry and became the focal point of Parsi life and culture.[15]

It has been noted that the Parsis were a colonial elite. Paralleling the case of the Sikhs, who proved indispensable in overthrowing the mutiny of 1857, the British took a liking to the small community of the Parsis[16] whose identification with Western ideas corresponded to the 'Brown Sahib' that Lord Macaulay longed for in his infamous 'Minute on Indian Education' of 1835.[17] Macaulay was obsessed with the thought of training "natives who were 'Indian in blood and colour' to become 'English in taste, in opinions, in morals, and in intellect.' These people would constitute a class who would protect British interests and help them rule a vast and potentially unruly land."[18] By way of their loyalty and their weltanschauung, the Parsis qualified as Macaulay's ideal mimic men. Only through affiliations with the British were the Parsis able to rise in the colonial hierarchy, and the community was eager to acculturate indeed. No other community in India had closer contacts to the British than the Parsis.[19] They adopted the idiom of colonial discourse and supported Britain's imperial wars. Parsi cooperation with the British presupposed "a familiarization with European norms and attitudes."[20] Identification with the British and their lifestyle led to an extraordinary degree of Westernization among the Parsis. They developed a taste for Western music and became fanatic Cricket players.[21] Furthermore, they took to eating with knife and fork[22] and frequently even regarded English as their mother tongue.[23] Parsi anglophilia also led to the foundation of clubs modelled on the Victorian gentleman's favourite place of recreation.[24] Members of the community began to dress in a distinctly Western way and surrounded themselves with Western furniture.[25] They valued privacy and encouraged women's liberation.[26] Moreover, the Parsis felt a close affinity to the British because they were committed to a monotheistic faith.[27] In order to count as 'English in taste, in opinions, in morals, and in intellect,' the Parsi elite status also hinged on issues of education, or rather Western education, which became available to the Parsis in the 1820s[28] and has remained a central asset of the community in postcolonial times, too.[29]

While the role the community had played under the British was disproportionate to their number,[30] the Parsis were marginalized in postcolonial times. The community lost its privileged position in the emergent Indian nation state. They had not been happy with the end of colonial rule and had not actively supported 'Quit India,' i.e. the Home Rule movement.[31] Their "loyalty and commitment to colonial ideals were not particularly adaptive in postcolonial India."[32] Many members of the community felt that an acceptable positioning within Indian society would become increasingly difficult and decided to leave India for the international diaspora.[33] For those who stayed on, there remained the possibility of affiliating themselves with the young nation. 'Parsis had been in India a thousand years, they count as Indians,' one argument ran. On the other hand, there were also those who suffered from the Indian postcolonial reality and took refuge in a glorification of the Parsi achievements of the past[34] as well as to an uncritical nostalgia of everything British. This process of "cultural inversion"[35] becomes evident in Dinshawji's complaint about the change of street names in *Such a Long Journey*, which will be discussed in the following.

Inscribing Difference I: Postcolonial Indian Language Politics

In comparison to MG Vassanji and Neil Bissoondath, Rohinton Mistry is a writer for whom India is important as a subject matter. India, or, more specifically, Bombay, is a resource that he draws on in every piece of fiction he has published to date. Bombay as the place where he was born is not only a city that he knows intimately; Bombay, as indicated above, is also the city that is home to the Parsi community, and it is safe to suggest that Bombay becomes to Mistry what Dublin was to Joyce and Jefferson to Faulkner.

The Bombay of *Such a Long Journey* is shaken by the rise of the Shiv Sena, a local party with considerable influence in Maharashtra. Founded in 1966, the party started out as a small faction advocating the reservation of jobs in the lower ranks of white-collar workers. The name of the party translates as 'Army of Shiva,' a name drawing attention to its radical religious motivation. The Shiv Sena is a right-wing Hindu organization that openly advocates racist goals and agitates against South Indian immigrants, mostly from Tamil Nadu, who are blamed for the scarcity of jobs in Bombay. As Bharucha points out, "the Sena raised the bogey of 'the other' the religious other, the Muslim, the linguistic other, especially Tamil speakers, and the regional other, those who came from other parts of India."[36]

Mistry shows that Indian national identity construction relies on a strategy of Othering that threatens to victimize the Parsis. The Shiv Sena in *Such a Long Journey* is resented by the characters as a very real threat to a distinct Parsi identity. Dinshawji, the protagonist's confidant, fears that the Shiv Sena "won't stop till they have complete Maratha Raj" with their "Maratha for the Maharashtrians nonsense."[37] Remembering how followers of the Shiv Sena abused members of the Parsi community as "Parsi crow-eaters" (39), thereby mocking the community's burial rites, Dinshawji fears that the Parsis might become "second-class citizens" (39) in the near future.

Of central importance to the Shiv Sena's agitation are issues of language and language planning. The party advocates a translation of English road names into Marathi and overlooks the effects that such a step has on the former colonial elite of the Parsis. Responding to Gustad's remark "What's in a name" (74), Dinshawji argues:

> "Names are so important. I grew up on Lamington Road. But it has disappeared, in its place is Dadasaheb Bhadkhamkar Marg. My school was on Carnac Road. Now suddenly it's on Lokmanya Tilak Marg. I live at Sleater Road. Soon that will also disappear. My whole life I have come to work at Flora Fountain. And one fine day the name changes. So what happens to the life I have lived? Was I living the wrong life, with all the wrong names? Will I get a second chance to live it all again with these new? Tell me what happens to my life. Rubbed out, just like that? Tell me!" (74)

In order to construct a postcolonial Indian identity, the British street names so important to Dinshawji have been altered by the Indian administration in what amounts to a reckoning with British colonial rule in India. Having identified with British culture and values, the formerly formally colonized Parsis lament the departure of the colonizers. Thus Dinshawji, raised and socialized within an anglophile tradition, severely attacks the Shiv Sena's reappropriation of street names and takes issue with its psychological consequences. The change of names does not only lead to problems of spatial orientation but also refers to the troublesome implications that the building of the Indian nation-state has for a distinct Parsi identity. For inasmuch as the names of the streets and places change, the place of the community in contemporary India is on the agenda; to the same extent that the old names of places vanish, the Parsis feel displaced. Thus Dinshawji, according to David Williams, "experiences the rewriting of the map of his neighbourhood as an interruption in his self-presence."[38]

Both the Shiv Sena and the Parsis realize that the struggle for language is important because it is tied up with issues of identity. If Dinshawji discusses language to express his worries for the future of the Parsi community, Gustad Noble, the novel's protagonist, reflects on the community's precarious status, too:

> What kind of life was Sohrab going to look forward to? No future for minorities, with all these fascist Shiv Sena politics and Marathi language nonsense. It was going to be like the black people in America—twice as good as the white man to get half as much. (55)

This passage does not so much betray the Parsi community's "little fears and anxieties,"[39] as a critic has it, but details the scope of Gustad's foreboding. If the Shiv Sena manages to achieve its goals and puts its plans into practice, Sohrab's future in Bombay will become insecure indeed. A closer look reveals that Sohrab's situation is characterized by a dilemma and that his position might become dangerous if he remains in Bombay. Therefore, given the openly racist attitude of the party, Gustad seems to imply that the only way out for Sohrab is emigration. However, pointing out the condition of Others who have to be "twice as good as the white man to get half as much" (55), migration and diaspora are rejected as viable opportunities for a 'good life.'

Inscribing Difference II: Parsi History

Such a Long Journey partakes of a relativist frame of reference also by virtue of its metahistorical exploration of late twentieth century Indian history. 1971, the year in which the novel is set, saw India's Prime Minister Indira Gandhi in political trouble. Ved Prakash Malhotra, then chief cashier of India's State Bank, claimed to have had a phone call from Indira Gandhi instructing him to pay 6 million rupees (approximately 33 thousand pounds) for the Bangladeshi freedom movement to a courier who would identify himself as 'Bangladesh ka Babu' (i.e. 'gentleman from Bangladesh'). The man turned out to be Rustom Sohrab Nagarwala, a Parsi and former Army captain, who had worked for Indian Intelligence. The cashier complied but went to the police later on. Nagarwala was caught shortly afterwards and later claimed to have mimicked Indira's voice. After a hasty trial of three days, he was sentenced to four year's imprisonment and died in jail in 1972 under mysterious circumstances.

Mistry's debut sheds a different light on the so-called Nagarwala affair, and that in a particular way. Instead of reproducing mainstream history, *Such a Long Journey* presents what Brian McHale has called "secret history."[40] Suggesting a reading from the margin, Mistry's secret history finds Indira Gandhi guilty of corruption and murder. In the novel, Jimmy Bilimoria, alias

Major Uncle, is the fictional rendering of Sohrab Nagarwala. The text thus narrates the events of 1971 from the perspective of a member of the Parsi community. That *Such a Long Journey* inscribes alternative knowledge, or the historical 'truth' of events, from the point of view of a minority community is of significance for the postcolonial agenda of Mistry's first novel. Rohinton Mistry "attempts to make sense of actual historical events by narrativizing them, by extending them beyond the curtain of silence in which the official discourses have tried to enshroud them."[41] His emplotment strategy picks up orally transmitted stories about the Nagarwala affair which have been excluded from the official historiographical representation of events. On the one hand, Mistry's inscription of oral sources makes a claim for the value of indigenous cultural practices. The preservation of the community's cultural memory, on the other hand, allows the Parsis a point of identification because it works as a counterdiscursive strategy challenging the hegemonic discourse of postcolonial Hindu historiography. By laying bare the exclusions of the construction of postcolonial Indian national identity, Mistry makes a stand against the Hindu majority's affirmation of essential difference.[42] This politics of inclusion/exclusion is of central importance for Mistry. His fiction partly relies on a strategy of underscoring Parsi specificity that collides with the self-image of the postcolonial Indian nation as Hinduist. Thus Mistry writes against one kind of difference (i.e. a Hindu one) in the name of another (i.e. a Parsi one). While the Parsi community is threatened by the exclusionist politics of Hindu nationalism, writing against the mainstream seems to be an option for a minority faced with extinction and marginalization.

Although language and history play an important part for the construction of the community's self-image, the novel also pays close attention to another pillar of Parsi identity that deserves mention in this context: religion. It will be seen how the inscription of Zoroastrian assets inform Mistry's debut novel and make a point about the importance of cultural difference. Before we can establish this point, however, some information is needed on what it means to be a Zoroastrian.

Inscribing Difference III: Zoroastrianism

The Parsis have been described as an "ethno-religious minority,"[43] an assessment which testifies to the fact that within Zoroastrianism religion and ethnicity as markers of difference intermingle and eventually become indistinguishable. As "Mistry's discourse does revolve around the detailing of Parsi identity,"[44] the relevance of the Zoroastrian faith deserves mention not only as a major influence on many world religions[45] but also as a shaping factor for the characters of *Such a Long Journey.*

It is repeatedly emphasized that Zoroastrianism is a matter of birth, not of affiliation. It is not acquired by way of socialization but considered an integral part of one's genetic heritage.[46] Among the adherents of the Zoroastrian religion, the teachings of Zoroaster occupy an exceptional position. Zoroaster is the author of the five Gathas ('chants') which are an integral part of Zoroastrianism's sacred scriptures, the Avesta. In the Gathas, Zoroaster proclaimed a sole, omnipotent, and eternal God by the name of Ahura Mazda ('Wise Lord'). According to Zoroaster, Ahura Mazda or Ormazd, as he is later called, created the world and will preside over a final judgement on doomsday. He represents the Good Principle and rules over the Spenta Mainyu ('good spirits'). Ahura Mazda and the Spenta Mainyu are opposed by the Angra Mainyu ('evil spirits').[47]

The Zoroastrian world view is binarist. It distinguishes between the present world and eternity as well as between heaven and hell and the spiritual and the material world.[48] Life according to Zoroastrian doctrine presents itself as a clash between the principles of good and evil that is acted out in this world.[49] Binarist thinking also influences the angle Zorastrianism has on man. The Gathas distinguish between two kinds of people, those following the God of order ('asha') and those following the principle of disorder, wickedness or the lie ('druj').[50] Everyone is called upon to position himself in relation to this dichotomy. The human individual "participates in a battle between good and evil in which his or her own freely chosen actions determine the battle's outcome. It is usually accepted that God will ultimately win the war, but only through human initiative."[51] Recommended human initiative, i.e. support of the principle of 'asha,' consists, first of all, in a commitment to purity. This has led some critics voice the view that "in some sense Zoroastrianism is no more than a ritualistic commentary upon pollution and purity."[52] Others argue that being a Zoroastrian means to challenge and fight actively the demons polluting this world.[53] Whatever opinion one shares, for a Zoroastrian dead matter, e.g. corpses, or any substance leaving the body, e.g. breath, spit, excrement, sperm and blood are contaminated.[54] The elements, especially water, earth and fire, are divine emanations, and have to be kept pure from defilement. The so-called Towers of Silence were erected in order to grant the purity of these elements. On top of these buildings the Parsis have their deceased eaten by vultures.[55]

The individual's contribution to the fight between good and evil eventually also entails a moral choice. 'Asha' implies truth, honesty, loyalty, courage and charity.[56] Following the principle of 'asha' is an ethical commitment. Man is to care for himself and his fellow human beings as creations of God.[57] The obligation for every Zoroastrian to abide by ethically acceptable behaviour is summed up by the formula 'manashni, gavashni, kunashni,' i.e. 'good thoughts, good words, good deeds.'[58] The emphasis on ethics also means that for a believing Zoroastrian deeds will always speak louder than words: "Man cannot help the world and himself to salvation through sacrifices or magic prayers, through rites of atonement, but only through correct behaviour."[59] In other words, for the Parsis, "whose reputation for honesty and propriety is a byword,"[60] truthfulness and charity are more important than regularly going to a fire temple to worship. This explains why the role of the clergy within Zoroastrianism is on the whole negligible.[61] Priests and theologians are seldom required as mediators between God and man.[62] With the exception of burial, marriage and initiation rites, the majority of rituals to be performed can be celebrated at home. The most important ritual in Zoroastrianism is the 'kusti,' a prayer in the course of which the threads of a praying belt ('kusti') are tied and untied in a special order.[63]

The Zoroastrian faith in *Such a Long Journey* becomes a chief example of Mistry's grounding in a postcolonial frame of reference. The postcolonial agenda of *Such a Long Journey* relies on religion in the context of a process of community construction. Mistry does not comment on the problematic aspects of Zoroastrianism in *Such a Long Journey* (as he does, for example, in *Family Matters*). Telling a story previously untold in (Canadian) literature, his narration is motivated by enriching his readers' collective memory. Because the Parsi community is on the verge of extinction, the Zoroastrian faith is in danger, too. This means that with respect to Zoroastrianism memory work and representation rather than critique and deconstruction are of central relevance. The ethnographic thrust of the novel is closely connected to the writing of the Other, and religion becomes relevant in this context as an instance of the text's inscription of cultural difference. That religion in *Such a Long Journey* is important not only in ethnographic but also in sociological terms will be explored in greater detail below.

Transcending Difference I: Initiation, Alienation, and the Loss of Meaning

A superficial reading of *Such a Long Journey* seems to corroborate Bharucha's and Mukherjee's point that the novel portrays a male world. It almost exclusively focuses on its (male) protagonist Gustad Noble,[64] and the representation of its female characters is accurately described as one-dimensional indeed.[65] However, while such an assessment is doubtless true, it is also misleading, for Mistry is not concerned with (cultural or gender) difference solely but also interested in what transcends it. Following Barbara Leckie, I want to argue that "Mistry promotes a universal paradigm with respect to moral ideas"[66] in his first (as well as in his second and third) novel. While some critics explicitly reject the archetypal and universal focus at stake in Mistry's first novel, others overlook it.[67] However, it seems safe to suggest that Gustad represents more than the male gender or the Parsi community.[68] He is an Everyman who stands for mankind as a whole; Gustad does not represent a man but represents man as such.[69] The novel does not primarily advocate a gender agenda; it rather is an experiment probing and exploring fundamental human experiences, i.e. death or the fragility of social relationships. At the centre of the novel is a man, "in whose life and suffering a large rhythm of universal pattern is carved out,"[70] which can be specified as the struggle for meaning that informs much of Mistry's fiction.

In order to understand why the protagonist of Mistry's novel is forced to generate meaning, it is necessary to grasp that meaning in Gustad's life is fragile and fleeting. As many critics have pointed out, one of the central themes of Mistry's first novel is loss.[71] Loss in *Such a Long Journey* must be understood in a broad sense of the word. The novel explores implications of loss on a literal as well as on a metaphorical level. The scope of loss probed in *Such a Long Journey* encompasses the loss of material possessions as well as the loss of people by death or estrangement. Gustad Noble is faced with his family's impoverishment in the course of his father's bankruptcy; however, he also has to cope with the deaths of his friends Jimmy, Dinshawji and Tehmul. Moreover, loss for Gustad also entails a feeling of alienation of friends and dissatisfaction with the present. The semantics of loss imply a dispossession against the subject's will, the result of which can be poverty, isolation, confusion, disillusionment and disenchantment. In what follows, I will attempt to detail the causes and effects of loss making its impact on the protagonist of *Such a Long Journey*.

In *Such a Long Journey*, the experience of loss in the present is closely connected to traumatic experiences in the past. Two examples may serve to show that the past is of special relevance to Gustad: his father's bankruptcy and a childhood experience at Matheran involving a broken bowl. Gustad associates sensual qualities with the memory of his father's bankruptcy. Not only does it have "the sound of a deadly virus" [emphasis added] (101), it also feels "cold as a chisel" (6). The destructive character of this event is not merely conveyed by sound and touch, however. The chisel as a tool instrumental in tearing down buildings also deserves mention in this context. Yet the bringing down of a building should not be interpreted literally in this context: What temporarily succumbs to the "clutches of bankruptcy" (6) is Gustad's plan of attending university, something which would enhance his career prospects considerably. Metaphorically speaking, what seems to be torn down by the 'cold chisel' is the architecture of Gustad's dreams. The bankruptcy is a 'disrupting' incident indeed.[72] It (momentarily) thwarts Gustad's hopes for a promising future and radically changes the course of his life. Instead of being able to focus on his degree in relative material security, Gustad is forced to earn money in order to finance his studies. The bankruptcy sees Gustad's family at the receiving end of fate's whims.

Such a Long Journey illustrates how the vagaries of life can invert positions of control. This is corroborated by the notion of 'clutching' that the text refers to. The verb 'to clutch' denotates not only a holding tight; it also plays off connotations of power, control and influence over things and persons. However, whether the bankruptcy in *Such a Long Journey* is anthropomorphized ("the clutches of bankruptcy," 6; "How swiftly moved the finger of poverty, soiling and contaminating," 8) or the agent of the bankruptcy dehumanized ("the clutches of the vulturous bankruptcy bailiff," 22) does not make a fundamental difference. Of relevance is that the bankruptcy event is endowed with subhuman attributes (the bailiff's 'voracity') and superhuman power (swiftness and tightness/strength). It is imagined as a blow of fate too powerful to take measures against.

Apart from the bankruptcy, the broken bowl of Matheran points to a second instance in which a source of meaning in Gustad's life becomes questionable. Gustad remembers how at the end of a childhood holiday at Matheran an edible pudding bowl is broken and eaten by the manager of the hotel. This, at first sight, trivial incident resurfaces frequently in Gustad's remembrances:

> And then, the bowl was broken and eaten. There was something so final and terrible about the act. [. . .] And when the bookstore was bankrupt and the bailiff arrived, I remembered the broken bowl. [. . .] The men continuing their task, dismantling Pappa's life, breaking it up into little pieces [. . .]. And I remembering the dinner-table in Matheran, the crunching down of the broken bowl—such a terrible, final act. (242–3)

The breaking of the bowl (as well as the bankruptcy) signifies a boy's first encounter with life's complexity. Gustad's insight indicates an initiation into adulthood, and it is not a pleasant experience. The intrusion of the reality principle into an ideal childhood world leads to disenchantment, and it is the broken bowl that from this point onwards becomes a reminder of life's contingency and fragility for Mistry's protagonist.

The breaking of the bowl is indicative of the workings of destructive forces on humans, and breaking becomes a leitmotif in Mistry's text. It is, for example, not merely his father's business that is reduced to "the shambles of what had once been the finest bookstore in the country" (101); due to the shock, Gustad's father "falls [sic] to pieces" (101), too, and displays a "broken manner" (101). A breakdown of the material foundations of existence induces a backlash on individual constructions of meaning. The breakdown of the conditions and routines of everyday life has far-reaching consequences for the subject, as human resources are sapped. An indicator for the ramifications of this fundamental drain of meaning is provided by one of Gustad's flashbacks at an early stage of the novel:

> Sleep was no longer a happy thing for him then, but a time when all anxieties intensified, and anger grew—a strange, unfocused anger—and helplessness; and he would wake up exhausted to curse the day that was dawning. (8)

It is noteworthy that Gustad is not able to conceptualize his emotions exactly. His anger appears "strange" and "unfocused," the consequence of which is a feeling of "helplessness." Something similar can be observed in the account of his memories of Matheran: "There was something so terrible and final about the act" (243). Vagueness of diction as well as Gustad's helplessness to reflect on his emotional state is symptomatic of a precarious subject position. This deplorable state is brought about by the breakdown of systems that have made life meaningful. The collapse of his childhood world and the breakdown of the social system of his family have introduced confusion and meaninglessness to Gustad's life.

Such a Long Journey is a narrative about the importance of memory. Matheran becomes a 'site of memory'[73] for Gustad, i.e a place where an individual or a collective history is subject to discontinuity and fragmentation. In the context of the bankruptcy, attention should be paid to one aspect of the structure of memory in particular, i.e. the aspect of association. When Gustad visits Jimmy in Delhi, he recalls his father's bankruptcy. When he remembers his father's bankruptcy, he remembers that he remembered the broken bowl of Matheran. The working of his memory formally resembles a Chinese Box or the poststructuralist notion of a deferral of meaning brought about by a potentially infinite chain of referents. The issue at stake is not primarily a structural one though. It is not so much the working of memory that is examined by the text but the parallels and differences of the contents of the respective memories. The reader is asked to compare the two layers of the remembered past. Gustad draws analogies between the two events in such a way that the memory of a childhood experience at Matheran can be said to provide a foil for the experience of the bankruptcy. The experience of the bankruptcy, in turn, comes to haunt Gustad when he visits Jimmy in New Delhi and meets a certain Mr Kashyap who "had metal cleats on his heels, and his steps rang out on the stone floor" (266). He reminds him of the bankruptcy bailiff: "The cleats on [. . .] [his] shoes [were] clattering brazenly on the stone floor" (243). The effect of his remembrance is "a feeling of profound loss and desolation, of emptiness" (266). Matheran, the bankruptcy and the visit to Delhi have something in common in that they have not been overcome by Gustad. They have to be understood as traumatic experiences insofar as both develop a dynamic of their own that lingers and remains active in the protagonist's mind. They all are unpleasant incidents haunting the past and present idylls of Gustad's life with the threat of disintegration. The bankruptcy and Matheran represent poverty and disenchantment for Gustad Noble and, as such, are responsible for the loss of "the innocence of a happy childhood."[74] For David Williams they constitute the "'original' loss in Gustad's life,"[75] the consequences of which can also be felt in the realm of social interaction.

Transcending Difference II: Betrayal, Death, and the Loss of Meaning

Gustad's friends do not belong to the socio-cultural majority of Bombay. None of his social relations are Muslim or Hindu; most of his friends belong to the Parsi community, the only exception being Malcolm Saldanha. Like Jaakaylee in Mistry's story "The Ghost from Firozsha Baag," Malcolm is a Catholic from Goa, (like Bombay) another former Portuguese colony. He and his family helped Gustad after his father's bankruptcy, but in the course of time the two of them have drifted apart. When Gustad and Malcolm meet again after a long time, Gustad seems to find hope in their renewed friendship. However, multiple ironies undermine his expectations, for Malcolm turns out to be in charge of tearing down the compound wall so important to Gustad and the privacy he cherishes. Ironically enough, the alleged good and trusted friend Malcolm is instrumental in bringing down the wall which grants the Nobles a refuge of privacy in the midst of Bombay's noise and turmoil. As a consequence, Gustad's and Malcolm's long spatial separation seems doomed to be replaced by a far deeper alienation only shortly after their reunion several decades later. However, while Malcolm may be in charge of the tearing down of the wall, he is eventually not responsible for the implementation of the road-widening scheme in a legal sense. As Malcolm Saldanha only carries out the order of an anonymous municipal bureaucracy, it could be argued that he is as much a victim of the unpredictabilities and vagaries of life as Gustad. Unable to keep separate the occupational and the private spheres characterizing social life, Gustad blames Malcolm for destroying their friendship. The effects are dramatic in that Gustad apparently loses faith that an erosion of meaning, due to fast and seemingly aleatory change, can efficiently be opposed by the social system of friendship. It seems to him that the individual is thrown back onto himself, and that he has to cope with loss and loneliness alone.

Being thrown back onto himself also seems to be what Gustad's friendship with Jimmy Bilimoria can be reduced to. Although we meet him only briefly, Jimmy is virtually omnipresent in Gustad's and Ghulam's memories and anecdotes; his physical absence does not preclude his narrative presence. The character of Jimmy Bilimoria is closely connected to Gustad's yearning for a better past:

> Jimmy Bilimoria had been more than just a neighbour. At the very least,

> he had been like a loving brother. Almost one of the family. A second father to his children. Gustad had even considered appointing him as their guardian in his will, should something untimely happen to himself and Dilnavaz. A year after the disappearance, he still could not think of Jimmy without the old hurt returning. (14)

Mistry especially stresses the personal implications of his version of the Nagarwala affair. Thus when Gustad is drawn into the political scandal surrounding Bilimoria the emphasis is at least as much on feelings of betrayal as it is on the marginalization of the Parsi community and the stories of Indian history they circulate. Gustad's friendship to Bilimoria, who "killed trust, love, respect, everything," (178) is strained because solidarity appears unreliable. Gustad feels

> that some vital part of him had been crushed to nothingness. Years of friendship swam before his eyes and filled the piece of paper; it taunted him, mocked him, turned him into a gigantic canvas of lies and deceit. What kind of world is this, and what kind of men, who can behave in such a fashion? [. . .] Jimmy Bilimoria had trapped him, robbed him of volition. If I could let the rotten world go by, spend the rest of life in this chair. (141)

The indifference and latent paralysis manifest in the passage signal a personal crisis. Gustad experiences an erosion of faith that Alberto Manguel has described as the "treachery of the spirit."[76] In Gustad's opinion, Jimmy has violated a universal code of behaviour that confronts Gustad with a decay of values. These values, epitomized by the eponymously named Noble, are solidarity, faith, loyalty and justice. The fact that Gustad's neighbours, the municipality of Bombay and the government of India do not seem to share these values is bad enough; worse, however, and almost unbearable for Gustad, is that Jimmy, who almost counts as a member of the Noble family, causes an erosion of meaning by allegedly subscribing to lies and deceit. Betrayal thus hurts Gustad the more because it originates from a hitherto privileged site of meaning and solace, i.e. the family.[77]

Whereas the friendship between Gustad and Malcolm has been eroded by alienation, Gustad's friendships to Dinshawji and Tehmul are eventually ended by death. Responsible for a loss of meaning in this context is not the failure of friendship but death, i.e. something Manguel calls the "treachery of the flesh."[78] Death is ontologically as well as archetypically chaotic, for, as Gustad realizes, it cannot ultimately be warded off: "Hearses can be impeded by cars and barricades, he thought. But death. Death gets through every time. Death can choose to be prompt or fashionably late" (243). Speaking with EM Forster,

Dinshawji as well as Tehmul can be described as flat characters. They represent ideas rather than complex psychological dispositions, and might be read allegorically. Put bluntly, Dinshawji's death comes to signify the end of comic relief, whereas the death of the childlike, retarded Tehmul in *Such a Long Journey* can be understood as the death of innocence. In the course of the novel, Dinshawji risks his job for Gustad by opening and closing a bank account with illegal money, while Tehmul provides meaning as a surrogate son to Gustad after Sohrab has moved out. Their death is not only a shock but a lasting impoverishment of Gustad's life.

Equally important for an understanding of the erosion of meaning in Gustad's life as the implications of his friendships is the alienation from his eldest son Sohrab. Sohrab's decision not to study Engineering at the Indian Institute of Technology (IIT) but to stay in Bombay and complete a BA in Literature instead is taken as a personal offence by Gustad. His reaction towards his son's plans is reflected by an intertextual reference to *King Lear*, a play which Sohrab had staged as a child. Mistry alludes to the play in order to echo the pervasive theme of a problematic relationship between a father and his child,[79] and it is nothing short of ironic that Gustad Noble, who apparently has a high esteem of the arts, interprets Sohrab's decision as "filial disrespect and ingratitude" (122). He is disappointed that the plans for his son's career will not be realized:

> How many years have I watched over Sohrab and waited. And now I wish I was back at the beginning, without knowledge of the end. At the beginning, at least there was hope. Now there is nothing. Nothing but sorrow. (55)

Due to Sohrab's waywardness, Gustad's expectations as to the security, regeneration and recognition to be experienced within the social system 'family' are momentarily thwarted.[80] Sohrab's deviation from Gustad's expectations seems to make life meaningless: "How to make him realize what he was doing to his father, who had made the success of his son's life the purpose of his own? Sohrab had snatched away that purpose, like a crutch from a cripple" (55). However, the appropriation of the vocabulary 'crutch' is particularly interesting in this context because Gustad's choice of words reveals that he is angry at his son for egoistic reasons. Metaphorically speaking, Gustad's injury becomes more pronounced once he is robbed of his 'crutch'. He does not primarily want the best for Sohrab by sending him to IIT; rather Gustad wants Sohrab to attend IIT because he has dreamt of such a career himself. Therefore, Gustad Noble betrays questionable motives when he reasons: "All I wanted was for him to have a chance at a good career. The chance wrenched away from me" (178). Gustad Noble does not unselfishly complain that

Sohrab is deprived of a unique chance in life; he rather feels betrayed because he himself is deprived of a source of meaning.

Transcending Difference III: Making Meaning, or: Faith and Solidarity

While the previous two sections have attempted an analysis of the implications of a loss of meaning in the life of the protagonist of *Such a Long Journey*, the strategies by way of which new meaning is constructed also deserve a closer look in the context of those aspects of the text that transcend a postcolonial concern with cultural difference. In the final analysis Mistry's first novel demands to be read as a text valuing idealism over pragmatism, humanism over materialism, and altruism over egoism. Two factors become especially indicative of Mistry's program, religious faith as well as togetherness and solidarity exerted between human beings.

In *Such a Long Journey* religion is not only relevant as an aspect of the text's grounding in Parsi culture. In the course of the novel, Mistry's analysis of Zoroastrianism broadens to include other faiths in what could be called a functionalist reading of religion. Religion as a metaphysical concept is a system which potentially concerns every aspect of reality.[81] It entails, for instance, a rejection of arbitrariness as the governing principle of life, and offers a solution to the problems of giving meaning which arise with pain and death.[82] As such, it may remedy the erosion of meaning in life. A religious faith offers a possibility of finding meaning by transcending man's contingency as well as the confusions and vagaries of life in the infinity, constancy, wisdom and detachment of a spiritual being. According to the influential Freudian psychologist Viktor Frankl, religion becomes an important psychohygienic and psychotherapeutic instrument that offers man security and an anchoring in transcendence and the absolute.[83] Religion in *Such a Long Journey* is significant as a means of generating meaning in a world that is felt to be deprived of it. Such a reading becomes the more plausible because the proximity of Zoroastrianism to other kinds of religious faith is explicitly emphasized throughout the text. While Zoroastrianism may be "able to give its adherents purposeful and satisfying lives,"[84] the pavement artist, himself an important figure, as will be seen shortly, suggests that the potential of giving meaning is not restricted to the Zoroastrian religion but that all forms of faith have the power of giving meaning:

> You see, I don't like to weaken anyone's faith. Miracle, magic, mechanical trick, coincidence—does it matter what it is, as long as it helps? Why analyse the strength of the imagination, the power of suggestion, power of auto-suggestion, the potency of psychological pressures? (289)

In principle, a private mythology is deemed as potentially powerful a strategy of constructing meaning as the rituals and ethics of Zoroastrianism, or any other kind of faith. A specifically postcolonial stress on religion as marker of cultural difference is thereby complemented by a functionalist reading of a religious faith as instrumental in making life meaningful.

While friendship may be temporarily invested with unreliability by Gustad, togetherness and solidarity are powerful ways of making meaning within the novel for which there is no adequate compensation. In *Such a Long Journey* harmonious relationships to other people are a source of happiness.[85] Togetherness as a form of transcendence guarantees meaning and enables Gustad to draw meaning from a form of human solidarity removed from economic competition and political insecurity. [86] Friendship is a private sphere of meaning opposed to a public realm entailing the threat of an erosion of meaning. It is crucial to understand that much of Gustad's worries spring from the fact that both spheres intermingle. The boundary between what warrants trust, i.e. the private sphere, and the public, which is felt to be the locus of treachery, blur, thereby making impossible a distinction between what is reliable and what is unreliable for the protagonist of the novel. This holds true for Malcolm as well as Jimmy and Tehmul. Once this nexus is fully grasped by Gustad, he matures as a personality by learning from his friends who eventually represent ideals transcending a world characterized by particularities. Dinshawji's irony and humour, Malcolm's altruism and Jimmy's sense of justice are values which Gustad can identify with, and which he adopts. This becomes evident when at the end of the novel Gustad

> slipped one arm under Tehmul's shoulders and the other under his knees. With a single mighty effort he rose to his feet, cradling the still-warm body. The bandaged head lolled limply over his forearm, and he crooked his elbow to support it properly. [. . .] He began walking down the compound, away from them all [. . .]. They looked in silence now, too ashamed to follow. (335)

Gustad carries Tehmul, the tragic victim of the march, in a way similar to how he himself was carried by Jimmy after his traffic accident. This is not merely indicative of the ethical impetus inherent in Zoroastrianism; it also is a fanal for solidarity and friendship as values that count. By offering unconditional support and solidarity to Tehmul, Gustad does for his friend what Jimmy Bilimoria did for him. Far from merely being Gustad's double, Tehmul Lungraa is transfigured as a Christlike figure and Gustad becomes as a "Parsi Pietà."[87] His grief for Tehmul's death is more than the grief for a friend; it also makes a general claim for moral and respectful behaviour in life. Arguably, it is Gustad's moral code, rather than Mrs Kutpitia's magic, that makes possible the unexpected reunion of his family. "Sohrab gazed after his father with fear and admiration" (335) and learns to respect his father anew through his father's respect for others. Through Gustad's grief for Tehmul, "his almost foster son,"[88] Sohrab, the Prodigal Son, returns home and makes possible a regeneration of the family as a source of togetherness and thus of meaning.

Boundary Negotiations I: Compound Wall, Blackout Paper, and Exclusion

Such a Long Journey is concerned with discourses of sameness and difference not only on a literal but also on a metaphorical level. Boundary negotiations structure the novel in two ways, i.e. with respect to the problem of making meaning and as regards the issue of cultural difference and identity politics. In the remainder of this chapter, I will discuss the implications of exclusion for both issues.

In order to prevent Khodadad Building from becoming a potential target for the enemy's air strikes, the windows of Gustad's flat are covered with blackout paper. Grotesquely enough, the blackout paper is not removed for years, although the danger has long ceased to be imminent: "Gustad had put it up nine years ago, the year of the war with China" (9). For his wife Dilnavaz, the blackout paper becomes a "target of [. . .] frustration" (12), as it collects dirt, and, more importantly, reduces the amount of daylight in the flat to a considerable extent (11). For Gustad, however, the paper is a mechanism of defence holding chaos, i.e. an erosion of meaning, at bay. The everyday reality of 1971, together with the psychological reality of his traumas, is unpleasant and threatening for the protagonist of Mistry's first novel. Both have the power to unsettle the microcosm of his world. Their potential to erode meaning in Gustad's life is conveyed symbolically by the image of light, which represents the reality principle which Gustad attempts to withdraw from.[89] His fear of light is complemented by an obsession with darkness: "It was pitch dark but he did not switch on the light, for the darkness made everything seem clear and well-ordered" (6). Darkness discloses the escapist character of Gustad's private idyll, and there can be no doubt that this idyll, characterized by the exclusion from the political reality of the war of 1971 and the exclusion of painful events of the past, is a construction. For Gustad's memory exclusively concentrates on the better times before his father's bankruptcy: "Once again, the furniture from his childhood gathered comfortingly about him. The pieces stood like parentheses around his entire life, the sentinels of his sanity" (6). As becomes evident, Gustad's introspection depends on a careful selection.[90]

The blackout paper is not the only boundary erected and defended in *Such a Long Journey* in order to exclude an allegedly hostile environment. The compound wall of Khodadad Building becomes another line of defence, as it were, this time against the road widening scheme of which Gustad is so afraid.

As an enclave of peace and respite, the compound provides the Nobles and their neighbours with a refuge from the noise and turmoil of Bombay. Not only is it an islandlike space where the retarded and innocent Tehmul can live a protected life, the compound also is a space where Gustad can derive meaning from practising his religion in comfortable seclusion:

> With the increase in traffic and population, the black stone wall became more important than ever. It was the sole provider of privacy, especially for Jimmy and Gustad when they did their kustis at dawn. Over six feet high, the wall ran the length of the compound, sheltering them from non-Parsi eyes while they prayed with the glow spreading in the east. (82)

The compound is also place fraught with reminiscences, for it is here that Gustad used to do his kusti prayers together with Jimmy Bilimoria. The fall of the wall destroys a source of refuge and meaning for the future because it destroys the memory of the past: "For the briefest of moments he felt the impending loss cut deeply, through memory and time; the collapse of the wall would wreck the past and the future" (329). A reduced awareness of time and place, i.e. the loss of spatial and temporal deixis, signifies a severe threat to the resources of meaning in Gustad's life.

The inside of what could be called Gustad Noble's paradise is in danger of succumbing to the forces outside. Etymologically, the word paradise, which is Persian for 'garden,'[91] is derived from the Avestan word 'pairidaeza,' translating as enclosure.[92] In much the same way as an enclosure depends on a boundary, Gustad's 'paradise,' i.e. the enclosure of the compound, depends on a border, too. In the course of the novel, the boundary of the compound wall is affected by two factors. First of all, it is threatened (and eventually torn down) by the municipality in the course of the road-widening scheme, and, secondly, the value of the wall for Gustad is reduced considerably by "urinators and defecators" (183). Not only is the wall soiled, mosquitoes and flies are also attracted by the stench and haunt Gustad's paradise. The wall as dividing line no longer guarantees absolute protection but offers merely relative shelter from the environment, i.e. the world outside. When Gustad decides to fortify his defences by having the pavement artist paint the wall with Indian deities, he appropriates art to turn a profane wall into a sacred place of worship. His plan of protecting his garden by semanticising its boundary as a place of pilgrimage turns urinators into worshippers:

> What an amazing contrast to the wall of old, he thought. Hard now to even imagine the horrid shit-and-piss hell it was. Dada Ormuzd, You are wonderful. Instead of flies and mosquitoes buzzing, a thousand colours dancing in sunlight. Instead of the stink, this glorious fragrance of para-

> dise. Heaven on earth. [. . .] What a miraculous transformation. God is really in His heaven, and all is right with Khodadad Building. (286)

Gustad's idea confronts the passersby with their own religions. For the pavement artist the wall as a whole presents religious unity in diversity, thereby becoming not only a sign of artistic but also of religious syncretism. The artist himself says, "But I always like to mix them [i.e. different deities] up, include a variety in my drawings. Makes me feel I am doing something to promote tolerance and understanding in the world" (182). Given the character of the paintings, abusing the wall becomes a taboo for most passersby, whose respect for religious matters outweighs their disrespect of private property. Gustad Noble has managed to ward off an erosion of meaning for a while by endowing the wall with spiritual content for others. It is questionable whether the murals are "the embodiment of Gustad's own belief, springing from a sort of humanistic theism, that all religions are equal."[93] Rather they are a pragmatic means to a pragmatic end. Gustad fights the loss of meaning in his life by turning it into a source of meaning for others. This, and not the promotion of "religious tolerance,"[94] seems to be the function of the paintings on the wall.

While the wall provides Gustad's prayers with a refuge from an allegedly secular India,[95] it relevance transcends the private. Khodadad Building, like Firozsha Baag in Mistry's collection of stories, can be read as a microcosm of the Parsi community in India.[96] The wall guarantees the Parsis a privileged space apart, a space, moreover, that many members of the community in the novel deem essential to the practice of their culture, religion being a case in point. Criticism of Mistry's first novel has emphasized on the other hand that the protection of the wall has less of a positive effect on Gustad and the Parsis. It is said to minimize the contact with Indian reality, something which is regarded as problematic. Within such a reading, the usefulness of the wall becomes rather ambivalent and figures as a "protecting/ imprisoning wall."[97] If the wall is instrumental in preserving "the Parsi in his self-sameness and hierarchical privilege, and to protect him from the threat of difference, of Otherness itself,"[98] this is in itself not necessarily an advantage. For in the eyes of the self-centred Parsi community the outside world becomes an Other who is excluded rather than actively engaged with. The wall takes on the quality of a boundary reducing the complexity of life to binary oppositions, i.e. inside/us vs. Outside/them. Psychologically, turning a blind eye to the unpleasant reality of a postcolonial India, which has done away with the community's privileges, is an instance of repression. Sociologically, the reliance on difference advocated by the tiny, endogamous Parsi community barters short-time security for (long-term) sterility.[99] Wall and blackout paper signify not merely protection; both can be seen as boundaries which eventually prevent an active engagement with Indian reality. In this context, the pluralism of religions advocated by the wall can indeed be read as a means to a rather egotistical end. In a way, religious tolerance is overridden by the desire that Parsism might continue to rule supreme.

Boundary Negotiations II: Journey and Inclusion

The last section has outlined how difference in *Such a Long Journey* is constructed through mechanisms of exclusion. Inclusion as a remedy for the politics of identity as well as the problem of making meaning is chiefly argued along metaphorical lines, too. *Such a Long Journey* alludes to the ancient tradition of life as a journey. The relationship between life and journey can be characterized by two aspects: Journey and life can both be understood as, first of all, entailing a linear movement towards a destination. The notion of life as journey, secondly, implies continuous change. Both the notion of the journey as process and of journey as change can be made fruitful for the novel's preoccupation with the problem of making meaning on the one hand and the problem of cultural identity on the other.

(i) Questioning whether life is endowed with a telos, and deploring that there is no hope and only sorrow in life, Gustad Noble echoes "The Journey of the Magi,"[100] as one Mistry's central intertexts. The lyrical I of TS Eliot's poem vividly as well as wearily remembers the duration of the journey, when he ponders on the amount of energy mustered "for a journey, and such a long journey"[101] at that. The poem is concerned with the experience of weariness and suffering on the traveller,[102] who becomes representative of man on the journey of life. Behind this universalist as well as existentialist notion operating in Mistry's (as well as Eliot's) text is the thought that life does not reward the endeavours of the living, i.e. the thought that "this was all folly."[103] The Magus's doubts are repeated almost literally by Gustad who wonders: "Would this long journey be worth it? Was any journey ever worth the trouble?" (259). Gustad causally links the success of the journey to the achievement of an outward aim. Put differently, Gustad makes the point that life is not deemed worth living without a purpose.

Mistry's novel and Eliot's poem allude to the mediaeval tradition of the quest. Usually, the superficial objective of a quest is to find an object or a person, or accomplish a certain feat, like Frodo who is in search of the ring, Marlow who is in search of Kurtz, Ahab who is in search of the whale, or Perceval who is in search of the grail. The quest in *Such a Long Journey* seems to be of a lesser dimension. Gustad at an early point in the novel imagines his son's career as a quest, the purpose of which is a university degree. He envisions the IIT as "the home of the Holy Grail" (66). Eventually, however, it is Gustad, not Sohrab, who embarks on a quest in Mistry first novel. Positioning Mistry and Eliot within a quest tradition implies that the motif of the journey is employed with a particular emphasis. For the (Arthurian) quest is only superficially concerned with the achievement of an external goal. It is not the achievement of a superficial aim that is important, it is the way the traveller acts and behaves during the journey that determines the overall success of the quest. Thus a quest is always also a mystical journey, in the course of which the traveller comes into his own.[104] One could argue that it is the subject and not the object that is the ultimate objective of any quest.

Both Mistry and Eliot reflect the idea of the quest as a mystical experience. For the Magi in Eliot's poem, the journey is more than a physical journey; its implications are deeply spiritual.[105] As a result of travelling, the lyrical I changes and does not feel comfortable among his fellow believers and indeed among the living anymore: He is "no longer at ease."[106] Eliot's poem negotiates questions of birth, death and rebirth within a Christian frame of reference.[107] Critics also agree that Gustad Noble, the "tragic hero"[108] of *Such a Long Journey*, is on a "metaphysical quest."[109] Extrapolating from these assessments, *Such a Long Journey* can be read as a novel about the struggle of its protagonist eager to realize his idea of a meaningful life. On a symbolical level, *Such a Long Journey* therefore not only alludes to the notion of life as journey (i.e. the tradition of *The Odyssey*) but also to the tradition of life as struggle (i.e. the tradition of *The Iliad*). Fusing these strands of different literary traditions, Gustad can then be seen as life's "embattled traveller."[110]

His struggle, however, despite childhood fantasies in which he imagines himself as a "Parsi Saint George, cleaving dragons with his trusty kusti," (5) is not conceptualized as an archaic, heroic fight in order to fight evil forces and win the favour of royalties. Rather, Gustad's struggle takes on the quality of a search for meaning in human existence, figuring as faithfulness, reliability and constancy. Gustad has to learn that these values are difficult to realize permanently, as too many factors turn out to be incalculable and uncontrollable for the subject in the context of secularization, fragmentation and ontological chaos. However, realizing that permanence is, like the goal of any quest, eventually "unattainable,"[111] does not mean that the attempt to construct meaning is not worthwhile as such. Gustad eventually proves worthy of his quest (and the quest proves worthwhile for him): His relationship to Jimmy and Tehmul is a test case in which he matures as a personality and becomes a morally responsible individual.[112]

(ii) Inherent in the idea of life as a journey is also a negotiation with altered circumstances. The relevance of this point for resisting an erosion of meaning is illustrated by the pavement artist. Futility and change face him in "the vicissitudes and vagaries of street life [which] randomly dispossessed him of his crayoned creation" (212). The pavement artist has to experience that "impermanence is the one significant certainty governing his work" (212). He embodies the insight that loss and dispossession are central to life, and that the only constant in life is its inconstancy. Opting for a nomadic existence, he

> learned to disdain the overlong sojourn and the procrastinated departure, for they were the progenitors of complacent routine, to be shunned at all costs. The journey—chanced, unplanned, solitary—was the thing to relish. (184)

The pavement artist realizes that life's vagaries cannot be opposed effectively by permanence. Discarding material possessions, the artist relies on the attitude of a traveller on the journey of life. This enables him to fight the chaotic side of life by adapting to its basic features, i.e. "mutation and metamorphosis."[113] It also offers him an insight into the nature of culture, which becomes manifest in the syncretistic character of his murals.

An attitude which is protective of place, such as the one displayed by Gustad until the very end of the novel, has a negative influence on the artist. He renounces his usual way of life and for a short time exchanges travelling for settling down: "The wall and the neighbourhood were reawakening in him the usual sources of human sorrow: a yearning for permanence, for roots, for something he could call his own, something immutable" (184). The pavement artist's wish for 'something immutable' signifies a longing for material possessions, such as, for instance, a permanent place of abode. This tendency becomes manifest in the artist's altered style of painting. Instead of working with crayons, he now begins to paint in oil: "From now on, no more crayons. All pictures in oil and enamel only. Completely permanent. Nothing will spoil them" (212). Gustad's and the artist's wish for permanence is revealed to be an illusion with respect to making meaning but also with respect to the nature of culture. The compound is eventually diminished, and the wall with the artist's oil paintings is ironically brought down at the end of the novel. *Such a Long Journey* identifies the longing for permanence, epitomized by the blackout paper and the wall, as a source of cultural sterility and human sorrow.[114]

Conclusion: Inclusion over Exclusion

Erecting boundaries is a problematic way of fighting an erosion of identity as well as constructing an identity. At the end of the novel, the process of learning that Gustad has undergone makes him dispense with blackout paper, and the wrecking of the wall proves a blessing in disguise. Both instances suggest that *Such a Long Journey* eventually questions the validity of categorical exclusion as a means to construct a self-image as well as to generate meaning. Both issues, i.e. the novel's identity politics and the problem of making meaning are affected by the insight that boundaries are inadequate as enclosures and should be reconfigured as thresholds. On the one hand, Mistry proposes inclusion, i.e. cultural exchange, as a more acceptable way of constructing a new understanding of the self in postcolonial times. In this respect, *Such a Long Journey* corresponds to what has been arrived at programmatically in "Swimming Lessons," Mistry's key story 'here.' At the same time, Rohinton Mistry suggests that making meaning is a project that is best achieved by stoicism and tolerance, in short, by a general openness of which the motif of journeying becomes emblematic. As another of the novel's epithets argues, "where the/old tracks are lost, new country is revealed with its wonders." Relying on metaphorical as well as literal understandings of both journey and country, these lines from Tagore's *Gitanjali* express an undiminished hope for finding new sources of meaning in the face of chaos, while at the same time reflecting a positive attitude towards cultural exchange and the possibility of coming up with a new cultural identity.

C. 'There' II: Cultural Difference and the Struggle for Meaning. *A Fine Balance* (1995)

A Fine Balance, like *Such a Long Journey*, is concerned with life worlds deprived of meaning. In two ways can *A Fine Balance* be said to present a departure from the agenda of Mistry's debut novel. First of all, Mistry's second novel is narrated in a more traditional way. If *Such a Long Journey* displays elements of magic realism, *A Fine Balance* is a traditional realist novel. Secondly, the scope of Mistry's second novel is broader. While his debut is in the main concerned with the Parsis of Bombay, *A Fine Balance* transcends the narrow confines of the Parsi community and features Parsis, Hindus, Muslims as well as Sikhs. Finally, while *A Fine Balance* underlines the central importance of tolerance and solidarity, thereby echoing *Such a Long Journey*, Mistry's second novel enacts transculturalism and intercultural understanding as ways of constructing an identity and as remedies against a reality that is felt to be deprived of meaning.

In the subsequent sections, I will proceed in a way similar to the analysis proposed in the previous chapter. First those instances of the text which can be read as inscriptions of Otherness within a postcolonial frame of reference will be pointed out. Afterwards, I will argue that *A Fine Balance* cannot be understood by recourse to cultural difference solely.

Inscribing Difference I: Postcolonial Indian History

A Fine Balance falls into Lukács's paradigm of the historical novel.[1] Historical events of the recent past are presented from the points of view of characters of average standing in life.[2] *A Fine Balance* is not merely a family saga but narrates key events of twentieth century Indian history from the perspective of the Parsi as well as the Hindu Chamaar community. This means that *A Fine Balance*, like *Such a Long Journey*, presents history from the margin.[3] Mistry offers versions of historical events inflected by the community membership of its protagonists. Two events are crucial in this context: India's Independence (1947) and the time of the Indian Emergency (1975–77), during which most of Mistry's novel is set.[4]

India becomes independent on 15 August 1947.[5] While the majority of Indians initially welcome the departure of the British, the colonizers leave behind a political and military vacuum with serious consequences. Especially ethnic or religious minorities that have prospered during the time of the Raj, such as the Parsis or the Sikhs, complain that the British have left (too early). As portrayed in *A Fine Balance*, they fail to cope with the conditions of modernity (e.g. acceleration, industrialization, etc.) and postcoloniality and compensate by daily meeting for tea time and yearning for times past. Sikhs, usually retired soldiers, and Parsis celebrate the British rule as a time "when life proceeded in an orderly fashion, without daily being threatened by chaos."[6] Nostalgia for bygone times constitutes an attempt at ordering a confusing reality:

> Consolation, as always, was found in muddled criticism of the colonizers who, lacking the stomach for proper conclusions, had departed in a hurry, though the post-mortem was tempered by nostalgia for the old days. (209)

In the aftermath of 1947, India is split into two separate nation states, following Jinnah's claim that India has always already consisted of "two nations," i.e. Hindus and Muslims.[7] Whereas the newly formed Pakistan is to provide the Muslim community with a home, the Indian nation-state is dominated by the Hindus. However, a conflict ensues between India and Pakistan over areas on the border, and *A Fine Balance* sheds light on several of its aspects. As a farmer living in the north of the country, Maneck's father Farokh Kohlah, for example, finds himself "trapped by history" (205) when he has to give up a large part of his estate and becomes a poor man with only a small shop left: "A foreigner [i.e. Mountbatten] drew a magic line on a map and called it the new border; it became a river of blood" (205). Farokh complains about the arbitrariness of Mountbatten's decision,[8] which leaves him struggling against an anonymous bureaucracy in his fight for his lost land. At the same time, Farokh Kohlah fights for more than material advantages, he also struggles for the preservation of nature as the most important source of meaning in his life. His struggle to preserve an idyllic nature as a source of meaning also is a fight against the ramifications of chaos brought about by the Partition.

Mountbatten's borderline does not only provoke the loss of land of those living on the border; it also leads to violence and aggression "when communal slaughter at the brand-new border ignited riots everywhere, and sporting a fez in a Hindu neighbourhood was as fatal as possessing a foreskin in a Muslim one" (87). In Bengal, and especially in the Punjab, the massacres between Hindus and Muslims reach the dimension of a civil war (122). In *A Fine Balance*, Narayan and Ishvar experience the warfare during their apprenticeship. The new home they have found with the Muslim Ashraf Chacha is in danger of being destroyed by intercommunal strife (129–30). The precariousness of their situation becomes manifest in the discourse of racism circulating everywhere: "Better to drive out the Mussulman menace before we are burned alive in out huts. For centuries they have invaded us, destroyed our temples, stolen our wealth" (123).

While Farokh struggles with the consequence of the loss of his land, and the Hindus are faced with racism and violence, Dina experiences history differently. Her family's comfortable material position allows for a withdrawal from the public sphere so that Dina is not confronted with the effects of Independence and Partition directly. However, significantly, the public events have private consequences for her. Sentenced to remain within the domestic sphere, Dina is forced to face her brother's tyranny. Independence/Partition becomes responsible for an erosion of meaning in the life of the fourteen-year-old because she is forced to remain indoors and to face her brother's despotic regime: "But a few days later riots started in the city, in the wake of Partition and the British departure, and Dina was stuck at home with Nusswan" (25). Drawing attention to the fact that the public and the private are inevitably intertwined in *A Fine Balance*, Mistry appropriates hair as a leitmotif.[9] Dina cannot remove the plaits which she so detests and which her brother requires her to wear after she has got herself a new (shorter) haicut. The length of Dina's hair symbolizes the amount of freedom she is entitled to; the longer the hair, the less freedom she is allowed to enjoy. After the violence and aggression ends, Dina's ordeal is miraculously lifted, and Nusswan explicitly testifies to the link between the public and the private sphere explicitly when he says: "'The curfew is over, and your punishment is over. We can throw away your plaits now,' he said, adding generously, 'You know, short hair does suit you'" (25).

Even more important for an understanding of Mistry's novel than 1947 is the time of the Indian Emergency. The events surrounding the Indian Emergency of 1975–77 are closely linked to Nehru's daughter, Indira Gandhi.[10] The Emergency has preoccupied many Indian artists of recent times, and the fact that Rushdie, Mistry and others revisit the trauma of the Emergency testifies to "the strong socio-historical awareness of the continent's novelists."[11] In 1975, a national court finds Indira Gandhi guilty of having manipulated the election of 1971.[12] She is to give up her mandate in Parliament, which would have also meant to step down as Prime Minister.

However, Indira declined to resign and declared a state of internal emergency, in the course of which she retroactively changed the law according to which she had been sentenced for election malpractice. Fundamental rights were suspended, the press was censored, and strikes were forbidden. The forthcoming General Election was postponed, and dissidents were incarcerated. As part of an attempt to counter the growth of the population, a mass sterilization scheme was launched, which, officially, was designed to keep a balance between the growth of the population and the economic growth of the country. While Mrs Gandhi apparently feared that the Indian economy was outpaced by a population explosion, it was the poor of North India who suffered from violent sterilization against their will in particular.[13] The Emergency meets with undivided criticism and, for the first time, the opposition in Parliament speaks with one voice.[14] The intellectuals are unanimously of the opinion that the country is "decaying from the top downwards," (561) as Vasantrao Valmik has it in *A Fine Balance.*

In *A Fine Balance*, "the Emergency intrudes obtrusively into the lives of all [...] characters leading to their eventual loss and destruction."[15] Thus Om and Ishvar lose Ashraf who is beaten to death in the course of a police action, and Maneck loses Avinash, a student leader, who disappears and is tortured to death because of his critical attitude towards India's official policy. Moreover, with Ashraf dead, Nawaz denunciated and Dina being too protective of her independence at first to offer them shelter, Om and Ishvar are eventually down and out in Bombay. Due to the government's beautification programme, the two of them are not allowed to sleep on the pavement, and their hut in a jhopadpatti (i.e. a slum) is destroyed in the course of the cynical vision of a more beautiful Bombay. In this light, the government's parole "THE NATION IS ON THE MOVE" (302) acquires an ironic quality: For the tailors, 'moving' does not signal a spiritual departure or an Enlightenment metanarrative of progress; in the context of the novel 'moving' comes to signify mass-scale homelessness.

The Emergency curtails any kind of individual freedom: "What kind of life, what kind of country is this, where we cannot come and go as we please" (541). It develops a dynamic of its own which cannot be impeded. Ashraf, for instance, calls it an "evil cloud" (521), thereby referring to its demonic power and chaotic impact on the common man. According to Om, poor people like himself and his uncle are "less than animals" (540) to the government. They are, however, also looked down upon by the rich who affiliate themselves with the government.[16] A case in point is Nusswan Shroff who defends the beautification scheme:

> Counting them [i.e. the homeless] as unemployment statistics year after year gets us nowhere, just makes the numbers look bad. What kind of

lives do they have anyway? They sit in the gutter and look like corpses. Death would be a mercy. (373)

Nusswan's assessment that the Emergency is inspired by "a true spirit of renaissance" (371) is of course cynical, for the values associated with the Renaissance are diametrically opposed to those characteristic of India under the Emergency. Instead of supporting the cause of humanism, liberalism and the arts, mid-Seventies India, as it is depicted in the novel, displays corruption, stark social injustices and anarchy: "With the Emergency, everything is upside-down. Black can be made white, day turned into night" (299). According to a minor character "silly things like evidence are not necessary anymore. Nowadays we have nice things like the Emergency" (570). The effect of the Emergency is not only a loss of faith in the government but also an erosion of meaning which dooms the search for a 'good life.' As a man in a sterilization camp reasons: "When the ones in power have lost their reason, there is no hope" (535). When Indira Gandhi, the very person in power, eventually delivers a speech about the country "being threatened from inside" (5), she is unaware of the fact that for the majority of the population she herself is responsible for the threat she so urgently cautions against.

We have seen that Mistry employs irony to draw attention to the absurdities of politics and to underline the effects of politics on the underprivileged. As the next section sets out to show, Mistry is not only a fervent critic of India's policy in the latter half of the twentieth century, he is also suspicious of a fundamental dimension of Indian culture.

Inscribing Difference II: Caste

The Hindus Omprakash and Ishvar Darji occupy prominent positions in *A Fine Balance* insofar as both are crucial in illustrating the novel's central concern of how to make life liveable under unfavourable conditions and adverse circumstances. Apart from the fatal impact of political forces during the Emergency, one aspect is of particular importance in this context: "India's cruellest social constraint,"[17] caste.

Any discussion of the effects of caste on Ishvar and Om must necessarily include their family background. The Hindu family saga of *A Fine Balance* originates with Dukhi Mochi, Ishvar's father and Omprakash's grandfather. Dukhi Mochi belongs to the Chamaar caste of tanners and leather workers. This is significant, for, as VS Naipaul points out, "the worker in leather is among the lowest of the low, the most tainted of the tainted."[18] Together with the other chamaars in the village, Dukhi lives on the carcasses of dead animals, the hides of which he receives in order to produce sandals and harnesses. His social status is that of an untouchable. As such, he does not formally belong to any of the four main castes of Hindu society, i.e. Brahmins (priests), Kshatriyas (warriors), Vaishyas (traders and peasants) and Shudras (craftsmen and servants).[19] Untouchability is a stigma; other castes avoid contact with Dukhi because he is deemed impure.[20]

Hinduism explains caste by recourse to the concept of karma, which can be understood as a natural law that determines the quality of a person's rebirth on the basis of his deeds in his/her present incarnation.[21] In general, one can say that to conform to caste rules increases the chances of a better reincarnation, while a failure to accept one's role, in short opposition and resistance will be punished in the life to come.[22] A future incarnation will only bring about a rise to another stratum if the individual conforms to his present caste status. Thus the social status quo is not to be questioned; paradoxically, it better be affirmed if the individual wants to improve his standing in life. A reincarnation as a Brahmin, for instance, is taken as a sign that one has acted in accordance with his duties as a representative of his respective caste. The fact that caste postpones social mobility to a future incarnation has far-reaching consequences for a society in general. Social stratification is not based on merit, thus precluding a dynamic development of society: "Class is a system of rewards. Caste imprisons a man in his function."[23] Moreover, caste is such a powerful instrument for structuring a society not only because it is resistant to change but also because it provides psychological relief for those that are better off. For social differences and hierarchies are not man's doing but the effect of a mechanistic outlook on the way the world goes that spares those at the receiving end a bad conscience.[24]

It is crucial to realize that Mistry's portrayal of Hindu culture is not an impartial ethnographic account of Indian society but a deeply pessimistic analysis of what it means to live in India and not to be fortunate enough to belong to the right circles. He suggests that stark injustices are inherent in the practice of caste, and it is the inhumanity of untouchability that is severely criticized as a contributing to an erosion of meaning in the lives of Dukhi, Narayan, Ishvar and Om. An example for the cruelty and arbitrariness that characterises their treatment by their betters is illustrated by the following quote:

> For walking on the upper-caste side of the street, Sita was stoned, though not to death—the stones had ceased at first blood. Gambhir was less fortunate; he had molten lead poured into his ears because he ventured within hearing range of the temple while prayers were in progress. Dayaram, reneging on an agreement to plough a landlord's field, had been forced to eat the landlord's excrement in the village square. Dhiraj tried to negotiate in advance with Pandit Ghanshyam the wages for chopping wood, instead of settling for the few sticks he could expect at the end of

> the day; the Pandit got upset, accused Dhiraj of poisoning his cows, and had him hanged. (108–9)

After his sons Ishvar and Narayan have been beaten up for entering the village school, Dukhi appeals to Pandit Lalluram because he has faith in the Brahmin priest of whom it is said that "even an untouchable could receive justice at his hands" (112). However, Dukhi has to realize that justice is a concept which he as an untouchable does not have a claim to. Being outside of society, Dukhi is also considered outside the scope of justice. Mistry's portrayal satirises Pandit Lalluram as an unmannered, gluttonous reactionary who is not interested in justice for all:

> Relying on this legendary reputation for justice, Dukhi sat at Pandit Lalluram's feet and told him about the beating of Ishvar and Narayan. The learned man was resting in an armchair, having just finished his dinner, and belched loudly several times during his visitor's narration. Dukhi paused politely at each eructation, while Pandit Lalluram murmured 'Hai Ram' in thanks for an alimentary tract blessed with such energetic powers of digestion. (112)

The injustice done to Ishvar and Narayan and their futile appeal to justice deprive Dukhi of meaning and satisfaction with the life he leads as an untouchable. Because the system disregards his hope of transcending himself in his children, Dukhi, for the first time in his life, questions his identification with the order of caste. He revolts, and eventually transgresses the restrictions of caste, a reaction that becomes manifest in the decision to remove his sons from the immediate impact of discrimination.

Like Maneck, Narayan, Ishvar and Om are displaced. Maneck's father forces his son to move to Bombay for a better education, Ishvar and Narayan migrate to the city where they are apprenticed as tailors. In contrast to Ishvar, who remains in the city, his brother Narayan returns to the village after his apprenticeship, and turns into a radical political activist. While his father opposed occupational restrictions based on caste, Narayan fights for the constitutionally guaranteed political participation of untouchables in the election process.[25] Although his father warns him that he will risk his life, Narayan complains about a life not worth living. He testifies to an erosion of meaning when he laments that "life without dignity is worthless" (144). By taking on the fight against the corruption and the nepotism of the parliamentary elections, Narayan takes on the fight against an existence deprived of dignity. Narayan's failure and his tragic death in the course of a futile attempt to fight the caste system and its political practice are foreshadowed in an early passage:

> By and by she [Radha, Narayan's wife] brought a lamp to the porch. Within seconds it attracted a cluster of midges. Then a brown moth arrived to keep its assignation with the light. Dukhi watched it try to beat its fragile wings through the lamp glass. (143)

The moth's futile attempt to reach the light is symbolic of Narayan's endeavour to break with traditional caste regulations. Narayan disregards the invisible boundaries of caste in a way resembling the moth that does not realize that there is a boundary between itself and the light.[26]

For Ishvar, Narayan's death and the subsequent extinction of his family means that, like Nusswan for Dina, he is now responsible for his next of kin. Ishvar takes on the role of father for his nephew Omprakash. When Om is subsequently castrated by Thakur Dharamsi, in the meantime risen in the hierarchy of the Congress Party,[27] Ishvar has, in fact, failed as a replacement father because the family line cannot be perpetuated anymore: "I have let down your dead father! Our family name will die without children, it's the end of everything—everything is lost!" (535) Because Ishvar fails to fulfill his culturally preordained function, his life is also drained of meaning.

A Fine Balance demonstrates three things with respect to caste: First of all, the novel explores the effects of untouchability on individuals. For Dukhi and his children it is responsible for despair and an erosion of meaning in their lives, which is only delayed and not successfully countered by a transgression of caste restrictions. *A Fine Balance* explores the injustices of caste and probes the implications of defying it. While Narayan opts for political resistance, Om and Ishvar suffer from escape and exile. Secondly, *A Fine Balance* makes clear that while loyalty and trust in the sociocultural system of religion are undermined, Hinduism is not necessarily affected by this. Although caste has lost its potential to structure life in a way that guarentees meaning, Hinduism remains a major point of reference for some of the novel's characters, Ishvar being a case in point. Thirdly, the gruesome practice of caste as a cultural system is more prevalent in a rural context than in an urban one. Although the constitution of 1949 defines the Indian nation as "secular," untouchability has not been practically abolished country-wide. Already Mahatma Gandhi in the thirties and forties fails to convey the message that "untouchability poisons Hinduism as a drop of arsenic poisons milk" (107). In his wake, the Congress Party has been too weak to implement the nondiscrimination of untouchables nationwide. As one travels far enough from the metropolis, the notion of untouchability still remains a reality, and *A Fine Balance* illustrates the fact that the farther away from the centre of power one travels, the weaker the influence of that centre becomes.

Inscribing Difference III: Displacement and Diaspora

As the previous section has demonstrated, *A Fine Balance* is concerned with characters on the move. While it is really all "four main characters of this novel [who] suffer from a sense of rootlessness,"[28] Maneck occupies a special position in the text in that the effects of migration are made most explicit in his story. Maneck Kohlah experiences two instances of displacement. Like Om and Ishvar, he is forced to migrate to Bombay, and thereby moves from a rural to an urban region. In accordance with his community's capitalist ethos, Maneck afterwards leaves Bombay for Dubai. While the reasons are pecuniary, the "Petroleum Diaspora"[29] is not viewed favourably by Maneck as a country offering a lucrative job. Describing Dubai to a Sikh taxi driver[30] in the Epilogue, Maneck characterizes it by drawing attention "lots of big hotels. And hundreds of shops selling gold jewellery and stereos and TV's" (585). It is striking that instead of imagining the dollar paradise of Dubai as a place guaranteeing a comfortable income and thus material security, Maneck emphasizes the superficiality of the place. Money and glamour in a "clean and gleaming Dubai" (592) are revealed as a shallow facade depleted of substance and meaning so that despite a generous salary, Maneck feels "trapped" and "exiled" (584).

Maneck's situation in Dubai can be understood almost exclusively by referring to his homelessness. The vocabularies of 'trap' and 'exile' indicate that Dubai is regarded at worst as a punishment and at best as a place to be stuck in. In marked contrast to his year spent in Bombay, Maneck does not mention any friendships able to lend meaning to his life. In fact, after eight years he does not even know the country of his adoption in any detail: "He searched his mind and realized he did not know the place, didn't want to. The people, their customs, the language—it was all as alien to him now as it had been when he had landed eight years ago" (585). Dubai is a place that Maneck has not identified with, and which, consequently, has not transformed into a home for him. Dubai merely contributes to a confusion of Maneck's sense of identity by prolonging his displacement: "His uprooting never seemed to end" (585). Unlike Om and Ishvar, Maneck lacks the ability to adapt to his environment, a shortcoming which results in his eventual suicide.

Maneck's time in Dubai can be read allegorically as man's (futile) struggle to find meaning in life. His occupation is significant in this context. Maneck has received a diploma in 'Refrigeration and Air-conditioning.' "Supervising the refrigeration of the hot desert air" (581), however, is more than a description of his job; it also represents the endeavour to invest life with meaning. Maneck's overall pessimism is conveyed metaphorically by the refrigeration of hot desert air, a task which does not offer a perspective of prevailing over the loss of meaning in his life. His lot suggests that in the end an erosion of meaning cannot ultimately be done away with but will always make its impact on man.

Implicitly, Maneck imagines himself as a modern Sisyphus concerned with a chore which cannot be completed. This is the quasimythological background for his view of human existence as life "in the unrefrigerated world. Where everything ended badly" (504).

Maneck's pessimistic view is further elaborated on by taking recourse to physics. He describes life as ultimately hopeless, and repeatedly argues that "everything ends badly. It's the law of the universe" (466). In order to draw attention to the isomorphism of his fate and the allegedly fatal course of the world, Maneck alludes to the second law of thermodynamics, which predicts that a system will always attempt to reach the state in which it is most stable. The most stable state, however, is by definition the state characterized by the lowest level of energy, which, in turn, is the coolest state of a system, as warmth/energy will inevitably pass from the warmer to the cooler state until equilibrium is reached. According to this theory, the world will return to a state of cosmogonic chaos in which life becomes impossible.[31] Maneck alludes to this scientific theory in order to illustrate his pessimist/fatalist view of the meaninglessness of existence. Life is drained of meaning as it is emptied of an acceptable teleology. Any telos lending meaning to life is replaced by the inevitable, mechanical causality of physical laws leading to chaos.

Maneck Kohlah frequently remembers the mountains and his family while he is in Dubai: "Not one day had passed during his long exile that he did not think about his home and his parents" (584). Memory, however, is far from being a solace. Already at an earlier stage, Maneck feels he is made to "bend under the familiar weight of despair" (317) inherent in his remembrances. He even goes so far as to equate memory and meaninglessness: "No more remembering, no more suffering" (337). The remembering only conceals that Maneck is, in fact, out of touch with his native country. He does not know anything about the "tragedies and farces" (581) of India in his absence. This expression is indicative of the fact that Maneck Kohlah's image of India has become blurred. 'Tragedies' and 'farces' seem to suggest the serious and important as well as the petty and trivial events of private and public Indian history between 1976 and 1984. The important point to stress, however, is that Maneck characterizes India in terms of a stage play, thereby suggesting that it has become unreal to him in his absence. Life in India is reduced to a spectacle watched from a distance. It is neither a lived nor a livable reality. While the ties to his country of origin are inevitably severed, the country of his adoption does not provide him with ersatz ties. Emigration has brought about isolation. Isolation, however, must be regarded as the quintessentially diasporic experience.

Maneck's diaspora experience challenges the arguments of postcolonial theorists who celebrate homelessness and displacement as sources of creativity.[32] As indicated in Chapter Two, recent postcolonial critiques attempt to reclaim the concept of diaspora as a promising because potentially liberating state of mind. In particular, it is argued that the concept of diaspora is relevant to "anti-essentialist accounts of identity-formation."[33] Paul Gilroy, for example, writing from a postmodern and postnational position, has the following to say about the idea of diaspora as a vista of opportunities:

> Diaspora can be used to instantiate a different model, closer to those we find in 'chaos' theory, in which shifting 'strange attractors' (Hawkins 1995) are the only points of fragile stability amidst social turbulences and cultural flux. The importance of these nodal points is misunderstood if they are identified as overly fixed local phenomena. They allow us to perceive identity in motion—circulating across the web or network that they constitute. Where the word diaspora becomes a concept, they can mark out new understandings of self, sameness and solidarity.[34]

Paul Gilroy conceptualizes the idea of diaspora by taking recourse to the idea of self-organization. He draws an analogy to modern scientific discourse in order to argue that there is order hidden within chaos. However, this certainly does not hold true for Maneck. Identity for him is not a free-floating postmodern signifier selectively affiliating with his environment. Maneck's subjectivity, in fact, reflects a traditional, essentialist notion of identity, which precludes the possibility of celebrating his displacement. His identity remains tied up with the idea of home as a concrete place, and his story renders the notion of diaspora as a psychological entity problematic. The Parsi protagonist of Mistry's latest novel suffers from the conditions of the diaspora; his biography is no celebration of the migrant condition. Displacement is not valued as a chance or as freedom from constraints; from the point of view of systems theory, migration is conceptualized as the loss of social systems which have endowed an individual's life with meaning and psychosocial stability.[35] Anthony Giddens, for example, arguing from a related point of view, places the quality of displacement as a "disembedding"[36] to the foreground. With reference to Om, Ishvar confirms that "it's not good to go far from your native village. Then you forget who you are" (108). Trying to explain why Maneck refused to recognize the tailors in the Epilogue, Ishvar suggests that it is because "he went so far away. When you go so far away, you change. Distance is a difficult thing" (614). Ishvar maintains that "places can change people, you know. For better or worse" (157). Similarly, Maneck's mother testifies knows that "distance [. . .] [is] a dangerous thing" (223). Maneck spends more than half of his life away from a place he could call home. At the age of eleven, he changes the village for a secondary school in town. Between seventeen and eighteen he attends college in Bombay. After receiving a university certificate, he leaves Bombay for Dubai in 1976. When Maneck commits suicide in 1984, he is twenty-seven years old. Rather than being "homesick" [emphasis added],[37] Maneck is homeless. For being homesick would logically presuppose a home that one could return to. Maneck, however, has lost his home and with it his roots. His life can be described as disembedded indeed.

A Fine Balance parallels *Such a Long Journey* in that the loss of meaning experienced by the characters is central to an understanding of the text. While Mistry inscribes ethnic difference into his novel and demonstrates how history, caste and the diaspora can have fatal consequences to people, the erosion of meaning as the overriding theme of his fiction can be located elsewhere, too. More precisely, it surfaces in situations which can be understood without taking recourse to cultural difference, and it is such instances that will be examined in greater detail in the following.

Transcending Difference I: Alienation, Betrayal, and the Loss of Meaning

In this section, I will concern myself with Maneck again and argue that it is not only displacement that leads to Maneck's problematic "In-der-Welt-Sein" (Heidegger). Maneck Kohlah's life is emptied of meaning to the degree by which his social relationships are affected by death or estrangement. Such an argument can help to explain why Maneck's suicide is not cryptic but simply a reflection of his dissatisfaction with human existence and, as such, logically follows from his bleak outlook on life.[38] Of prime importance in this context is Maneck's problematic relationship to his father.

Farokh Kohlah owns a shop in the mountains of North India. Maneck, his son, attends the local school and helps his father in the evenings. He identifies with the rural area and his father's job and wants to continue his father's business after his retirement. Initially, his wish is not met with impediments, for Farokh agrees that "nowhere else can Maneck have better expectations for his future" (210). Maneck's life in the mountains is described by Mistry in terms of an Arcadian idyll.[39] Innocent love (to Suraiya), unspoilt nature, the regular pattern of life, and a harmony between the generations characterize the cosmos of Maneck's childhood: "His days were rich and full—school in the morning and afternoon, the General Store after that, followed by a walk with his father, late in the evening" (210). The pastoral world of his childhood is a perfect world. Within this realm, meaning does not have to be constituted by a conscious effort because it is already there. The bliss experienced during his childhood becomes an important point of reference for Maneck throughout the novel; the more so because, metaphorically speaking, Maneck is discarded from the Garden Eden of the Himalayas. Although Farokh Kohlah only wants the best for his son, i.e. a better education than the village school can offer, his decision to send him to a boarding school is a catastrophe for Maneck, as the following quote illustrates:

> The boarding school they selected was eight hours away by bus. Maneck detested the decision. The thought of leaving the hill-station—his entire universe—brought him to a state of panic. "I like my school here," he pleaded. "And how will I work in the shop in the evening if you send me away?" (211)

Maneck feels an "ache of betrayal" (211) when he learns of his father's plans for him. He feels cheated by a father assumed to be reliable and loving. His father's breach of faith, as well as the loss of satisfaction hitherto gained from working in the shop, contributes to the collapse of the ordered universe of his childhood. As a consequence, Maneck is faced with "despair," "rejection and loneliness" (213), all of which result in an alienation from his family.[40]

That the alienation from his father leads to a fatal erosion of meaning in Maneck's life becomes particularly obvious in the Epilogue of the novel. Here Maneck accuses his mother of having exiled him: "You sent me away, you and Daddy. And then I couldn't come back. You lost me, and I lost—everything" (591). Bearing in mind the importance of place for an individual's identity, the loss of a familiar environment affects Maneck fatally. Metaphorically, the loss of home/identity is conveyed by the notion of the slippage of a house. On returning to the mountains in 1984, Maneck feels as if his parents' house, whose foundations are tethered to the rock of a mountain by steel cables, has shifted (595). A house traditionally symbolizes a secluded area which endows human life with a centre and offers shelter and security.[41] Maneck's discourse refers to the house as an image for man[42] when he reflects that "everything was losing its moorings, slipping away, becoming irrecoverable" (595). The threat here is that of an existential "Unbehaustheit,"[43] i.e. being without a house, which, on a symbolical level, indicates an identity crisis.[44] Maneck's self has lost touch with his surroundings, something which becomes evident when in an epiphany at the end of the novel he relates the loss of meaning in his life to the misery characterising his father's life by referring to a 'slippage': "Now he felt the despair his father had felt as the familiar world slipped from around him" (595).

Maneck does not realize that he is not the only one whose world is deprived of meaning. Ironically, Farokh's world is abruptly changed, too, by the intrusion of multinational companies.[45] The ensuing competition with foreign products destroys his soft drink business; eventually, Kohlah's cola cannot prevail over the Coca-Cola marketing strategy. Moreover, the growing industrialization leads to the "ecological denudation of the Himalayas"[46] and destroys the pastoral nature of the hillsides. As a consequence, Farokh, too, is faced with a loss of meaning: "Returning home through the gloom, he decided there was no meaning in going for walks from now on. If meaning there was, it was too new and terrifying for him to explore" (219). Farokh is confirmed in his belief that there is no future for his son in the mountains, either: "'The slow coach gets left behind,' he answered. 'And I don't want the same thing to happen to Maneck'" (221). Consequently, he does not want his son to return to the village after secondary school but is determined to send Maneck even further away. While Farokh is afraid that Maneck could become a 'slow coach,' Maneck eventually ends his life by throwing himself in front of a train, thereby testifying that Farokh has tragically misjudged his son and his needs.. It is ironic that whereas the erosion of meaning in Farokh's life has an 'objective correlative' in the modern condition of rural India in the early seventies, the chaos characterising Maneck's life is the result of a misunderstanding of his father's good intentions for him. In other words, a loss of meaning for Maneck is chiefly based on his assumption that Farokh Kohlah "cares more about his stray dogs than his own son" (280).[47]

Transcending Difference II: Dependence, Death, and the Loss of Meaning

A Fine Balance, like *Such a Long Journey*, suggests that a loss of meaning at the time of the action is closely related to experiences in the characters' past. Dina is a case in point. She loses two beloved people, her father, when she is still a child, and her husband, when she is a young woman of twenty-four years of age. These traumatizing experiences determine the disposition of her character as an adult. Both instances underscore that the loss of meaning as the central issue in *A Fine Balance* must not be sought in events of cultural specificity solely but also demands to be accounted for in terms of archetypal experiences.

Dina Shroff feels a strong affinity to her father, a philanthrope whose "fervour to ease suffering" (15) eventually leads to his death in the course of a medical campaign into the interior of the country. Instead of trying "to seize the deadly sickles or, at the very least, to blunt them" (15), Dr Shroff dies of a cobra's bite, and while his grieving widow grows listless and apathetic (17), Dina "misses [sic] her father dreadfully" (17). After his death, Nusswan presides over the household, whose personality represents the antithesis to his father's character. Whereas Dr Shroff's actions are motivated by idealism and altruism, Nusswan has internalized a businessman's pragmatism[48] together with an obsession for power and control. His behaviour as replacement father is hard to stomach for his sister. Not only is she forced to neglect school because she is burdened with the entire household work, her brother also restricts her personal freedom because he is convinced that his sister needs a strong hand. His pedagogic ideal, however, is grounded in a mistaken notion of his father's character: "He had always perceived his father to be a strict disciplinarian; he had stood in awe of him, had even been a little frightened of him. If he was to fill his father's shoes, he would have to induce the same fear in others" (20).

Nusswan's personality is too weak to tolerate a teenager's harmless deviation from an adult's norm: "Dina's defiance, her stubbornness, was driving him crazy" (20). Arguably, a stronger and more mature character than Nusswan would have met his younger sister's provocative behaviour with indulgence. Nusswan, however, discloses the shortcomings of his own personality by establishing an authoritarian family regime based on surveillance ("The little devils needed monitoring," 21) and corporal punishment (23). Nusswan's attempts to conform to the role of a pater familias do not only prove disruptive to the family but also severely affect his sister's peace of mind. If he turns into a despot in order to compensate for the shortcomings of his character, Dina is at the receiving end of his whims. As a consequence, meaning for Dina becomes scarce in an autocratic system characterized by restriction and tyranny.

A consequence of the misery suffered under her brother's guardianship is that Dina becomes obsessed with the idea of personal freedom. Already in the Prologue of *A Fine Balance* it becomes evident that she holds independence in high esteem. Talking about her tailoring business, which eventually allows her to quit seeing her brother for money, she says: "No need now to visit her brother and beg for next month's rent. She took a deep breath. Once again, her fragile independence was preserved" (11). For Dina, there is a close connection between one's material conditions and the question of meaning in a person's life: Having to rely on Nusswan's money means losing her freedom; giving in to her brother's rule equals giving up her independence. Therefore, Dina's small tailoring business is not least of all an attempt to escape the sphere of her brother's influence.[49] One could also say: Dina relies on male career patterns of entrepreneurship in order to leave behind a male sphere that prevents her from coming into her own as a modern woman.

With Om and Ishvar working in her flat, the struggle for independence eventually becomes a struggle for control. Dina decides to maintain her distance in order not to lose control: "I have nothing against them, but they are tailors—my employees. A distance has to be maintained" (293). She locks them in when she leaves the house, thereby relying on strict boundary maintenance. Her decision is motivated by the fear of losing both control and independence at the same time. Dina is anxious to lose her intermediary position in the process of manufacturing and selling dresses: "The tailors will put me out of business if I don't lock them in" (285). She assumes that control guarantees economic success which, in turn, is to guarantee independence from Nusswan. Following Mrs Gupta's advice, Dina's relationship to the tailors is (at first) characterized by a strict form of control, which she feels she has to exert in order to be economically successful. It could be argued that Dina draws on the model of her brother's rule precisely in order not to have to suffer from her brother's rule again.

Dina Shroff's fear of dependence is only one aspect of the impending erosion of meaning in her life. The second major factor threatening her subject position is death and loneliness. Both her fear of dependence and of loneliness are anchored in a second traumatic experience, the loss of her husband Rustom. Rustom's death haunts Dina's mind, and it seem that it cannot be compensated. His demise confronts Dina with isolation and loneliness, concomitant with which is an erosion of meaning in her life. Isolation, loneliness, and loss (of meaning) are conceptualized in terms of a void: "When the human weight did not materialize, she awakened to emptiness, relearning the loss in the darkness before sunrise" (47). Emptiness has to be understood both on a literal and a metaphorical level. It signifies a space unoccupied by a person as well as a hollowing out of a belief into a meaningful life and an ordered cosmos. The fear of an erosion of meaning is thus imagined as fear of a 'horror vacui'.

It should not be omitted that Dina Shroff is exposed to two conflicting impulses, i.e. her fear of isolation and her misgivings about dependence. While both impulses pose a threat to the source of meaning in her life, fighting one necessarily favours the other. By fighting isolation, i.e. by investing into social contacts, Dina has to make a commitment which will affect her independenc. Fighting dependence, i.e. maintaining absolute personal independence, on the other hand, might very well thwart any hope of finding soulmates. Exerting control over her employees means that she has to keep up a distance, which will preclude a friendship from developing. In the long run, however, Dina cannot have it both ways. Only one source of chaos can be fought, only one kind of order can be institutionalized. In the course of the novel, Mistry emphasizes human company as the overriding necessity. Dina longs for a social life because the effects of isolation and loneliness threaten her with disintegration. When Dina accepts Maneck as a lodger, and Om and Ishvar spend the day in the flat sewing, the implications of loneliness are reflected explicitly. She reacts with jealousy to the gradually developing friendship between Maneck and Om because she herself is "longing for company" (277). The evenings become the time when "the emptiness of her own life appeared starkest" (193). She feels lonely when Om and Ishvar have left the flat: "Soon the evening gloom would materialize, infect the fibre-filled air, drape itself over her bed, depress her from now till morning" (274).

Transcending Difference III: Making Meaning, or: Text(ure)s

If hitherto only sources of a loss of meaning have been explored, Mistry's vision in *A Fine Balance* is by no means bleak. There are several instances where he points out possibilities of countering a loss of meaning in life and a chief example is Dina Shroff, who sews a quilt that becomes an extended metaphor for the way in which the erosion of meaning in life may be fought.

As the following paragraphs will illustrate, quilting becomes not only emblematic of connecting and remembering but also advocates story/storytelling as a means of identity construction.

A patchwork quilt is a piece of cloth combining various patches of cloth of distinct texture and colour. As a matter of fact, weaving quilts is a widespread activity in many parts of the world. It was introduced into the United States, for example, in the early years of colonization because of the scarcity of cloth. Apart from an economic motive, quilt weaving is also a form of representation with often subversive political content.[50] Moreover, as a form of representation it is frequently tied up with questions of identity, more precisely, female identity. Quilting is traditionally associated with women. It is not surprising that it is Dina Shroff, the female protagonist of *A Fine Balance*, who engages in quilting.

Structurally, the quilt can be identified as an important leitmotif in the novel. The vests which the tailors sew for Dukhi and Roopa (120–1), for example, allude to a patchwork as well as the huts in the slums which Ishvar and Om move to in Bombay (161, 379). However, more important than its function as a leitmotif is the symbolic quality of the quilt. The structure of the quilt becomes an image of human existence, or, more precisely, it becomes a projection of the 'good life.' Thus Om "would cut out all the bad parts. Snip out the scary nights and stitch together the good parts, to make time bearable. Then I could wear it like a coat, always live happily" (310). Although Om longs for a life characterized by abundance and bliss, life always also entails the opposite. He has to learn that life is essentially ambiguous: "'Some things are very complicated to separate with scissors. [. . .] Good and bad are joined like that.' He laced his fingers tight together" (311).

The image of the quilt is not only a metaphor of life; its structure also suggests a way of coping with an erosion of meaning in life. It is no coincidence that Rohinton Mistry has three of his four protagonists engage in tailoring. The three survivors in *A Fine Balance*, Dina, Om and Ishvar, produce textiles. Etymologically, the word textile is derived from the Latin word 'textum' which means fabric or texture. The root of the word 'textile' is cognate with the source of the lexeme 'text.' As such, a text as well as a piece of cloth is something which is woven. The quilt in *A Fine Balance* not only alludes to a garment as fabric, it also points to the structure of stories and storytelling and thus acquires a metafictional quality:

> She [Dina] realized that although Mr Valmik depicted life as a sequence of accidents, there was nothing accidental about his expert narration. His sentences poured out like perfect seams, holding the garment of his story together without calling attention to the stitches. Was he aware of ordering the events for her? [. . .] The lawyer's tale reminded her of her

> languishing patchwork quilt. [. . .] And Mr Valmik had his own fragments to fashion his oral quilt. (565)

As Dina Shroff realizes, there are striking parallels between the activities of tailoring and the telling of a story. Both reflect a construction which could also be understood as a weaving: "A story factory, that's what it [i.e. Bombay] is, a spinning mill" (383). The process of construction/weaving is characterized by principles of cohesion and coherence. In order to produce a quilt or a text the principles of linearity and cohesion have to be observed. One patch is connected to another as one sentence follows another. Cohesion can bring about coherence, or as Ishvar has it: "It all seems meaningless bits and rags till you piece it together" (403). To produce a coherent whole, both the maker of a quilt and the writer of a text (or the teller of a story) also engage in a process of selection: "What to select, what to leave out—and which goes next to which" (273). Both the making of a quilt and the telling of a story impose a structure.

The quilt can be regarded as an image which epitomises the construction of identity via storytelling. It becomes what sociologists term a representation, namely "the signifying practices and symbolic systems through which meanings are produced and which position us as subjects. Representations produce meanings through which we can make sense of our experience and of who we are."[51] Dina's quilt can be interpreted as illustrating the process of identity construction. More precisely, one might read the patchwork quilt as an image of a patchwork identity.[52] In much the same way as the quilt homogenises the heterogeneous, the process of identity construction is understood as a "Passungsarbeit"[53] between different and sometimes contradictory aspects of an individual subjectivity. The most apt way of constructing a coherent identity, and thus of enabling a meaningful existence, are stories and narratives.[54] The insight that meaning can be constituted by taking recourse to narrative/narrating is reflected explicitly in the novel: "Perhaps the very act of telling created a natural design. Perhaps it was a knack that humans had, for cleaning up their untidy existences—a hidden survival weapon, like antibodies in the bloodstream" (565). Narratives as psychohygienic means are important for at least three characters in *A Fine Balance*, for Dina Shroff, Ishvar Darji and Vasantrao Valmik. On remembering her time with the tailors, Dina at the end of Mistry's second novel

> covered herself with the quilt and took to recounting the abundance of events in the tightly knit family of patches, the fragments that she had fashioned with needle, thread and affection. If she stumbled along the way, the quilt nudged her forward. The streetlight through the open window was just bright enough to identify the motley of its making. Her bedtime story. (573)

Dina feels an urge to remember the past because it can explain who she is. The quilt reflects her effort to combine the different phases of her life in a unifying narrative.[55] Her patchwork quilt allows her to regard her own allegedly chaotic life as ordered and thus functions as a way of making meaning.[56]

Vasantrao Valmik, whose name echoes that of Valmiki, the storyteller of the *Ramayana*, also emphasizes the importance of storytelling for individual identities. Like Dina, he argues against forgetfulness. It can lead to a loss of meaning in life, as one might lose the awareness of who one really is. The story of one's life is a crucial aspect of one's core identity. It is, as Valmik explains to Maneck, "extremely important because it helps to remind yourself of who you are. Then you can go forward, without fear of losing yourself in this ever-changing world" (604). Ishvar argues an analogous case. He wants "to teach Om his history, remind him of his own community" (401). Valmik's and Ishvar's emphasis on storytelling is informed by an awareness of the story's power to become "a register and repository of our experiences."[57] Story is both a form of remembering and a subversive stance. By narrating the stories of the individual, official history is challenged. The multiple stories of a nation may supplement as well as contradict the great narratives of official history. Vasantrao resembles the postcolonial writer who, endowed "with a commonwealth of language" (230) narrates the stories of those previously marginalized. It is the narration of stories that guarantees a presence, or, as Robert Kroetsch points out in an interview with Margaret Laurence, "in a sense we haven't got an identity until somebody tells our story. The fiction makes us real."[58]

Valmik is particularly concerned with the aspect of communicating one's (life) story to others. His insight that "to share the story redeems everything" (604) theorises what Ishvar and Dina practice (384). Valmik realizes that identity is a negotiation between self-image and the image others have of oneself.[59] Furthermore, Valmik also testifies to the power of verbal art as a means of transcendence. Whereas Dina can "forget the troubles of this world" (30) and feel "the ecstasy of completion" (30) by listening to classical music, Vasantrao Valmik emphasizes the potential of words to function as a source of hope. According to one critic, Valmik advocates the benefit of story and storytelling as "a worry-defeating, life-embracing vehicle that confirms confidence and instills hope by holding out not only the possibility of survival but also a quasi-creative reward of telling a wise, enduring story to oneself and others."[60] At the end of the novel, Valmik is in charge of Bal Baba's mail-order service where he creates "fiction after fiction, which will become more real in the recipients' lives than all their sad realities" (604). His eloquence and rhetoric thus have a beneficial effect on others. His writings are not art for art's sake but attempt to be of relevance to an audience. As such, they offer solace to those for whom life with its "sad reality" has become meaningless. They oppose a loss of meaning brought about by social marginalization or personal loss by offering entertainment as well as transcendence in togetherness.[61]

Transcending Difference IV: Human Solidarity and Intercultural Understanding

Apart from remembering and storytelling, Rohinton Mistry also advocates the "integrative power"[62] of human solidarity and intercultural understanding as instrumental in constructing meaning and as values overriding particularities, cultural and otherwise. A superficial glance at his novel reveals that many of Mistry's characters, even the dubious ones like Rajaram and Beggarmaster, display solidarity towards their fellow human beings. In a slum in Bombay, Rajaram, for example, spends his last money on food for the children of his neighbour who is an alcoholic (181). In the epilogue, Maneck offers two Hindus to drink as they look "starved [. . .] for ordinary kindness" (8). Shirin Aunty and her husband offer their help and affection to the widow Dina: "She felt their love pour over her like something palpable" (53). Finally, Dina Shroff forgives Ibrahim, the former rent collector who used to harass her and gives him money (557).

For the four protagonists of Mistry's second novel solidarity and togetherness are primarily exerted within the realm of friendship. Friendship has the power of endowing human existence with a means of transcendence. Ishvar, for instance, "watched contentedly, smiling with happiness. In spite of everything, life was good, he thought. How could he complain when Om and he were blessed with the friendship of people like Ashraf Chacha, and Dinabai, and Maneck" (529). On the surface, friendship provides the four of them with a substitute for the family they all have lost (369). Friendship transposes the familiar principle of connecting onto the level of human relations. The developing friendship between Dina, Maneck, Om and Ishvar is interpreted in analogy to the structure of the quilt: "'And what happened is, our lives have been joined together.' 'Like these patches,' said Om" (491). Harmony and mutual understanding experienced by Dina in her relationship to Maneck and the tailors find expression in clothes as an extended metaphor. Thus their friendship takes on the quality of a "well-cut dress" (388), where "the four of them [are] fitting together without having to tug or pull to make the edges meet. The seams were straight and neat" (388). With their friendship the tailors are "wrapping her in the mantle of kindness and generosity" (388).

The reservation initially displayed towards the tailors by Dina is a repercussion of her experience with her brother. Ironically enough, a former colonial's treatment of two formerly fellow colonials is informed by colonial discourse. For the Parsi Dina at first regards the Hindu tailors Om and Ishvar as liars (276), lazy (288), undisciplined and irresponsible (272), chronically late for work (270), as alcoholics (272), dirty (302) and promiscuous (305). Control over the tailors does not only seem reasonable in order to be economically efficient and, eventually, independent; deeply ingrained into Dina's personality is also the fear of the Other. When Dina reminds Maneck that "there is a difference, and you cannot pretend there isn't—their communities, their background" (293), she advocates a segregation between the representatives of the two communities on the grounds of ethnic difference. The decision to take them is a sign of her "affection breaking barriers."[63] The relationship between Om, Ishvar, Maneck and Dina is characterized by a gradually developing mutual trust providing Dina with a new source of meaning. She asks whether she could

> describe for Zenobia the extent to which Maneck and Om had become inseparable, and how Ishvar regarded both boys like his own sons? That the four of them cooked together and ate together, shared the cleaning and washing and shopping and laughing and worrying? That they cared about her, and gave her more respect than she had received from some of her own relatives? That she had, during these last few months, known what was a family? (550)

Proof for the mutual trust between Dina and her lodgers can be found in the amount of sharing between the four of them in Mistry's novel. Sharing as a new paradigm of social interaction transcends ethnic barriers and allows reading *A Fine Balance* as a novel that advocates intercultural understanding. The "universally applicable elements of the apartment community"[64] question the relevance of cultural difference as a determining influence on social relationships. Difference is revealed to be a matter of construction and not an essentialist category. That Other is who is perceived to be Other is undermined by one of Dukhi's friends who is of the opinion that "the Muslims have behaved more like our brothers than the bastard Brahmins and Thakurs" (123). Cultural differences cease to matter in the apartment community which is not only a substitute for a family but a family in its own right.[65]

The four of them eventually grow together because everyone is willing to learn from the other, who thereby ceases to be an Other. Ishvar and Dina, for example, try out different ways of brushing their teeth: "Ishvar offered her a bit of charcoal powder to try, and she squeezed half an inch of Kolynos on his finger" (386). Maneck benefits from Om's knowledge about chappals, i.e. sandals which turn out to be footwear more adequate for the climate of Bombay (283, 474). At the same time, Om also learns from Maneck:

> Slowly but surely, Om had reinvented himself in Maneck's image, from hairstyle to sparse moustache to clothes. Most recently, he had made

> flared trousers for himself, borrowing Maneck's to trace the pattern. He even smelled like Maneck, thanks to Cinthol Soap and Lakmé Talcum Powder. (474)

In the microcosm of Dina's flat all prior hierarchies and ethnic prejudices have ceased to be of relevance. This is also demonstrated by the semiotics of food. As sociologists point out, food offers a system of signs which allows people to project who they are.[66] Food, in other words, is an important marker of identity. Not only does the food shared in *A Fine Balance* between Dina, Ishvar, Om and Maneck promote the intercultural exchange between the protagonists; more fundamentally, it also is a social event which brings people together regardless of their ethnicity: "Eating together lies at the heart of social relations; at meals we create family and friendships by sharing food, tastes, values, and ourselves."[67]

The four protagonists of *A Fine Balance* have four things in common with respect to food. They, first of all, share manners. Dina realizes that the tailors are not used to using cutlery. As a consequence, she uses her fingers, thereby underlining their equal status (396). Secondly, Dina shares her beloved china with the tailors (388–9). This event, itself anticipated by an analogous episode between Maneck and his father (212–3), underlines the new status between Dina and the tailors. By sharing the cups which have hitherto been reserved for her, she does away with a privilege of hers and inaugurates a new equality between herself and her lodgers. Thirdly, the four of them take turns cooking and share food. Eventually, they cook together, an indicator for the newly established harmony. Cooking and dinner exemplify the sense of community felt by the four of them. The meal is an instance of what Wierlacher calls a 'Solidarmahlzeit', i.e. a meal that expresses the solidarity of its participants and thus allows for a transcendence of cares and worries.[68] The sharing of food in *A Fine Balance* allows for transcendence in togetherness, which has the power of fighting the lack of meaning in the character's lives. For Dina, for example, her flat no longer reminds her of Rustom's presence and her own loneliness and isolation: "What a change she thought—from the saddest, dingiest room in the flat, the kitchen was transformed into a bright place of mirth and energy" (400). Fourthly and finally, Dina and her lodgers share the same smell:

> In the WC, the tailors' urine smell that used to flutter like a flag in the air, and in Dina's nose, grew unnoticeable. Strange, she thought, how one gets accustomed to things. Then it struck her: the scent was unobtrusive now because it was the same for everyone. They were all eating the same food, drinking the same water. Sailing under one flag. (399)

The consumption and digestion of the same food becomes indicative of an altered relationship between Dina and her lodgers. Obviously, Dina has undergone a transformative process from difference to sameness. In the passage quoted above this is corroborated by the symbolic overtones of the word flag which is used twice. However, whereas it merely signals the fleetingness of a sensual impression in the first instance, the second occurrence of flag is richer in allusions. In the latter case, flag evokes a set of metaphors surrounding sailing. In accordance with traditional symbolism, which interpretes a ship as an image of man on the journey of life, the microcosm of Dina's flat is a striking parallel to the notion of a ship as a secluded cosmos of its own. The common flag becomes symbolic of the mutual identification of Dina and her lodgers, who have established a "Sinngemeinschaft,"[69] i.e. a community that constitutes meaning for the time of its interaction. Food and its consumption illustrate an altered status of the members of the flat community.[70] The newly developing friendship between the four of them becomes instrumental in countering a loss of meaning by solidarity and sharing, which, in this case, is also an instance of intercultural hermeneutics.

Transcending Difference V: Balance and Tragic Joy

As seen above, *A Fine Balance* enacts the loss as well as the process of meaning in various ways. But in addition to that, Mistry elaborates on his theme on a philosophical level as well as on a intertextual level. The relevance is once again not so much on cultural difference but on universals.

Suggesting a remedy against the loss of meaning in life, Vasantrao Valmik, "the novel's philosopher,"[71] points out that "sometimes you have to use your failures as stepping-stones to success. You have to maintain a fine balance between hope and despair" (231). Achieving a balance requires an attitude of acceptance: "Some things cannot be changed, you just have to accept them" (82–3). Balance as acceptance is a stance that can accommodate death and loneliness as well as change and loss. In fact, "loss is part and parcel of that necessary calamity called life" (565). However, in the context of the novel balance means more than a patient suffering of what destiny has in store. Balance presupposes an effort, i.e. a drawing on sources of hope in order to juxtapose them to sources of despair. In that sense, balance structurally resembles the concept of 'journey' in *Such a Long Journey*. The principle of balance values inclusion over exclusion, which is precisely Valmik's point when he demands: "You cannot draw lines and compartments, and refuse to budge beyond them" (231). Far from amounting to fatalism, balance, like the notion of 'journey', is an attitude that takes chaos into account. In other words, because a loss of meaning cannot be contained, it has to be integrated.

A Fine Balance insinuates that Dina, Om, and Ishvar survive because they act according to Valmik's advice that "there is always hope—hope to balance our despair. Or we would be lost" (563).[72] As illustrated in the previous section, Dina, Om and Ishvar can cope with the calamities of human existence because they are able to muster personal resources and juxtapose them against the chaos characterising their lives.[73] Unlike Dina, Om and Ishvar, Maneck cannot compensate his nihilistic outlook on life by sources of hope. Put differently, Maneck fails to counter successfully the bad by connecting it to the good in his life, or as Peter Morey has it: "Maneck's own failure to sustain the connections becomes the book's final tragedy."[74] Connecting the good and the bad in a process resembling that of quilt weaving would provide Maneck with a more balanced view; however, having failed to achieve an equilibrium between good and bad, Maneck succumbs to despair and commits suicide.[75] He is unable to live according to the philosophical truth that *A Fine Balance* advocates and which Iris Murdoch describes in the following way: "Live close to the painful reality and try to relate it to what is good."[76]

The implications of the concept of balance are also reflected on an intertextual level. In the course of the novel, Vasantrao Valmik makes references to the poetry of William Butler Yeats. In the context of *A Fine Balance*, "Easter 1916," "The Second Coming" and "Lapis Lazuli" are of particular relevance. In order to understand how Valmik alludes to Yeats in order to corroborate his claim for balance, this section will conclude with an extended digression.

In many of his poems, WB Yeats is concerned with issues of history and political struggle. Yeats developed a private concept of history which he outlined in the programmatic *A Vision*. His theory of history hinges on the idea of the gyres and their movement, i.e. two interlocking cones which spin in opposite directions and which, according to Yeats, symbolize the movement of history.[77] As Smith lucidly explains:

> Every moment in time moves through these opposing spirals. Any one moment thus contains two antithetical, interpenetrating movements, for one cone is widening as the other, whirling in the opposite direction, narrows. These spiralling motions are the gyres. The times of maximum historical turbulence are those where the gyres reverse their motions. These great historical reversals occur every cycle of two thousand years [. . .] at those moments where the previously expanding cone begins to contract and the previously contracting cone to expand.[78]

History for Yeats proceeds in an antithetical way. One cycle of history gives way to another; the era of the Greeks, for example, is eventually superseded by Christendom. Around the year 2000, Yeats expected the end of the era dominated by Christianity and the advent of something new and, in fact, diametrically opposed. In "The Second Coming," composed during World War I, Yeats describes the impending new era in greater detail. Superficially, the poem is concerned with the end of a civilization. Anarchy, arbitrariness and atheism prevail at the historical moment when a reversal of the movement of the cones is taking place. The "widening gyre"[79] is a reference to the impending antithetical period of history. This moment of history is concomitant with political chaos as a state in which "things fall apart."[80]

Valmik uses Yeats's "The Second Coming" as a mythological foil for India's fate during the Emergency. The diagnosis of contemporary Indian history and politics that Valmik comes up with is full of "stories of misery, caste violence, government callousness, official arrogance, police brutality" (229). While his assessment seems hopeless, it is crucial to realize that Valmik quotes the poem in order to counter Dina's claim that "everything ends badly" (566) and to suggest less fatalistic ways of coming to terms with an erosion of meaning in life. As a matter of fact, Yeats's poem does not merely elaborate on the vision of world downfall; it also offers an apocalyptic vision, which is by definition ambivalent in that fear is coupled with the expectation of the new and hope for regeneration. Although the poem flouts the expectation of the return of a Christian God by offering its antithesis in a surrealist image of a sphinxlike monster, it is evident for Yeats that history is not at an absolute end. Although the vision outlined in "The Second Coming" is frightening, man is not to despair, for "at the end there is nothing for it but to accept the great scheme and to remain true to that delight in life which has been the guiding principle almost from the first."[81] Yeats as well as Valmik emphasizes the importance of 'delight in life' as a potential source of meaning. What is called for is an acceptance of events, a "dispassionate quality which [. . .] [sees] beyond the immediate devastation."[82]

What critics have called a "dispassionate quality" figures as tragic joy or tragic gaiety within Yeat's philosophy. While references to this concept can be found in the 1919 collection *The Wild Swans at Coole* (e.g. "Upon a Dying Lady" or "An Irish Airman foresees his Death"), it is more prominent in the works of the later Yeats. In *New Poems* (1938), Yeats outlines the notion of tragic joy paradigmatically in poems like "Lapis Lazuli." By way of alluding to Yeats's "Lapis Lazuli," Valmik puts forward an argument that identifies tragic joy as an attitude of balance which enables the individual to cope with the miserable state that the world is perceived to be in.[83]

"Lapis Lazuli" was written in July 1936 under the impression of political turmoil.[84] In the year of the poem's composition Hitler moved his troops into the Rhineland, Mussolini silenced the Ethiopian resistance with poison gas and the outbreak of the Spanish Civil War provided the Legion Condor with a testing ground for the impending world war. Yeats's poem responds to this historical situation by offering a scenario informed by the threat of destruction, anarchy and metaphysical uncertainty. During a time of war and destruction "hysterical women" are "sick of the palette and fiddle-bow,/Of poets that are always gay."[85] In the poem there is a contrast between different reactions to the external threat. The gaiety of the artist is pitted against the overreaction of others, and the poem sets out to argue the case of tragic gaiety.

"Lapis Lazuli" advocates tragic gaiety as a means of transcending the calamities of life. Tragic joy or tragic gaiety is an oxymoron[86] rather than a paradox, as it does not attempt to unify the (seemingly) contradictory. As will be seen, the distinctness of levels is crucial. Tragedy and joy refer to quite distinct concepts and thus do not contradict each other. First of all, tragedy primarily refers to a form of verbal art. Tragedy signifies a spectacle concerned with the calamities of life and their effects on characters. Tragedy is not an emotional state but describes a situation. Thus one can find oneself in a situation which is tragic, but one does not feel the tragic implications of that situation. Joy, on the other hand, draws attention to an affective reaction towards a situation. Taken together, tragic joy or tragic gaiety describes an euphorious response towards a tragic situation. Tragic joy is an attitude of rejoicing in the face of a tabula rasa situation. As "delight in an apocalyptic view of things"[87] it can become a means of transcending hopelessness and thus constitutes a form of balance in Valmik's sense of the term.

The concept of tragic joy has been identified with the sublime.[88] Immanuel Kant, for example, distinguishes between 'Verstand,' 'Vernunft' and the faculty of the 'Einbildungskraft,' i.e. the imagination.[89] Whereas the beautiful correlates 'Einbildungskraft' and 'Verstand', the sublime balances 'Einbildungskraft' and 'Vernunft.' The sublime presents itself as a mixed feeling of threat and pleasure.[90] These two responses come to bear on man's experience of nature, which is what Kant is primarily concerned with in his analysis. For the sake of analysis, the sublime can be broken up into two stages.[91] First, the individuum is overwhelmed by nature. The massif of a mountain, the height of a tree or the vastness of the ocean, for example, make excessive demands on the faculty of the human imagination which is deemed finite. Man's capacity to process sensual impressions is overloaded. In contrast to the beautiful, man cannot conceptualize his impressions anymore by breaking them up into parts. As a consequence, man's subject position becomes precarious. In a second step, the subject realizes that the vastness of nature is small, and thus negligible, in comparison to the infinity of his faculty of reason, i.e. his 'Verstand.' Man is therefore safe from the threat of nature because he can prevail over nature due to his faculty of reason. As the threat thus proves less real, it can be transformed into pleasure. The relationship between threat and pleasure, which constitute the sublime, is not conceived of by Kant as a linear process. It is, in fact, a dialectical relationship which happens quickly within the mind of the respective subject.

A comparison between tragic joy and the sublime is elucidating. On the one hand, Kant's and Yeats's ideas of the sublime and of tragic joy refer to forms of transcendence. Transcendence in both cases can be conceived as a dialectics negotiating two seemingly contradictory impulses.[92] Tragedy and joy as well as threat and pleasure are categories not easy to reconcile. Eventually, both tragic joy and the sublime remain essentially ambivalent responses to a spectacle of overwhelming nature but also, and this is important for a discussion of Mistry, to historical forces threatening the subject.[93] Closely connected to this is a second point of convergence. The dualisms of rejoicing and despairing (tragic joy) as well as of pleasure and fear (the sublime) refer to two distinct stances adopted by the subject: Involvement and distance. As man is cast into a tragic situation or experiences fear of, for example, thunder and lightning, he is involuntarily involved in situations posing a threat. Joy and the operations of reason, however, both imply distance. Thus transcendence is accomplished by a deliberate distancing of the subject from the circumstances he has become involved in.

There are, however, differences between Yeats's and Kant's concepts that make claims as to their identical nature questionable. The major difference lies in different conceptualizations of distance as the key to transcendence. For Kant, reason transforms fear into pleasure, for Yeats, the transforming potential lies on another level. Yeats's insight that man is not only implicated but also eventually removed from worldly chaos is not the outcome of man's inherent faculty of reason but the conclusion drawn from his concept of history. With respect to history, the sublime can be subversive of as well as complicit with power. Tragic joy, on the other hand, is quietist and fatalist. Thus for Yeats hope in the face of historical calamities, such as, for example, the Indian Emergency of 1975, lies in the fact that destruction will be followed by reconstruction: "All things fall and are built again,/ And those that build them are gay."[94] Informed by history's regenerative potential and the idea of an eternal recurrence,[95] tragic joy suggests displaying serenity in the face of anarchy and terror. In that it pits hope against despair, it constitutes a form of balance. Displaying joy in face of tragic situation results in an attitude of detachment, i.e. an attitude of "what matter?"[96] that is aptly described by Yeats in "The Gyres": "Hector is dead and there's a light in Troy;/ We that look on but laugh in tragic joy."[97] As Smith explains: "The only attitude to take towards all this tumult is to 'laugh in tragic joy,' accept and rejoice in whatever is coming, and stand above it."[98]

By Way of Conclusion: Family Matters *(2002)*

The works of Rohinton Mistry are preoccupied with the problem of making meaning in a world in which meaning has become scarce. The function of cultural difference is complex in this context. In *Such a Long Journey*, Mistry is interested in inscribing Parsi culture into his text in order to familiarize his readers with a culture that is on the verge of extinction. While such an ethnographical project is certainly less prominent in *A Fine Balance*, whose broader scope shifts the focus away from a single community to a variety of communities within multicultural India, the sociological interest in how people construct meaning in world otherwise impossible to bear remains constant throughout all of Mistry's narratives. While in *Such a Long Journey* aspects of cultural difference such as language, history and religion may be said to contribute to an understanding of Parsi identity, in Mistry's later publications cultural difference is often viewed more critically, i.e. as a source of an erosion of meaning, rather than as remedy against it. Despite a sometimes scathing indictment of Indian culture and communities, the kind of identity that Mistry writes in favour of is a hybrid one stressing cultural exchange and intercultural understanding. Mistry's most recent novel *Family Matters* is no exception in this context.

The plot of *Family Matters* is simple. Yezad and Roxana, a young couple, and their two sons Murad and Jehangir live together in a small flat. The routine of family life is radically changed by the arrival of Roxana's father Nariman Vakeel, whom his stepchildren Coomy and Jal try to dispose of once his health deteriorates. Roxana decides to nurse her father, an act of pity and solidarity reminiscent of Dina Shroff decision in *A Fine Balance* to take in the down-and-out tailors Ishvar and Om. If solidarity in *A Fine Balance* leads to quasi familial bonds, in *Family Matters* family demands that the bonds of blood become manifest in concrete acts of solidarity.

In accordance with Mistry's tendency "to emphasize what is universal in human experience,"[99] *Family Matters* can be read as a novel partaking of a universalist discourse concerned with the loss of as well as the subsequent struggle for meaning. Yezad is affected by the loss/death of his friends in much the same way as Gustad who loses Jimmy and Dinshawji in *Such a Long Journey*, or Ishvar and Om who lose Ashraf in *A Fine Balance*. In order to have the money ready that is needed to care for Roxana's father, Yezad indirectly attempts to blackmail his boss Vikram Kapur by having friends act as gangsters. As an indirect consequence of his plan, his friend and employer dies. Likewise Dinshawji in *Such a Long Journey* dies in the course of Gustad's efforts to help his friend Jimmy Bilimoria by laundering dirty money.

While "the narrative hub within [. . .] [*A Fine Balance*'s] urban fabric is a domestic space,"[100] *Family Matters* is almost completely set within four walls, too. More precisely, *Family Matters* has as its setting two flats, Yezad's and Roxana's as well as Coomy's and Jal's. While Coomy and Jal cast their father out, Yezad regards the old and disabled man as an invader and thus as an unwelcome presence, too. Roxana's husband is reluctant to dispense with the hermetic quality of his flat although Nariman, due to the scarcity of space in the flat, makes it necessary for family routines to be reorganised. Thus in much the same way as Dina Shroff in *A Fine Balance* is forced to give up her egoism and solipsism once the tailors move in, Yezad is called on to display flexibility and kindness in order to accommodate his father-in-law.

By virtue of its setting, *Family Matters* continues the discussion of boundaries begun in *Tales From Firozsha Baag, Such a Long Journey* and *A Fine Balance.* At stake in Mistry's most recent novel is the interrogation of how many boundaries are useful in order to reduce the erosion of meaning and how many barriers are detrimental because they prevent the most effective means against a loss of meaning in life, i.e. human interaction and understanding. The same question is implicitly posed with respect to the issue of cultural identity. It seems safe to suggest that the usefulness of boundaries in reducing an erosion of meaning in life and in constructing/maintaining a self-image is disputed throughout the text.

Due to the "muddle life had become" (189), i.e. because of the calamities that have befallen Yezad outside the cocoon of his flat,[101] the protagonist of *Family Matters*, like Gustad Noble in *Such a Long Journey*, prefers exclusion over inclusion. In both texts, such an attitude is revealed to be problematic. However, while Gustad in Mistry's debut novel changes from intolerance to forgiveness and understanding and thereby implicitly comes to privilege inclusion over exclusion, *Family Matters* ends on a more pessimistic key. Mistry's most recent work inverts the pattern of growth exemplified by Gustad Noble's in *Such a Long Journey*. In *Family Matters* the initially secular, liberal and tolerant Yezad becomes a religious fundamentalist. While at the beginning of the plot his wife encourages him in vain to pray and participate in the Zoroastrian rituals, Yezad in the course of the novel, due to the loss of meaning in his life, completely identifies with a religion he was already alienated from.

The once secular Yezad relies on religion for the construction of an identity. His stress on religion as marker of difference is informed by a notion of impenetrable boundaries and rigid borders. Like other members of the Parsi community (portrayed in *Such a Long Journey*, for example), Yezad fails to perceive the necessity of openness and inclusion as fertile ways of coping with the postcolonial condition. Like the members of his community, Yezad does not realize that a stress on essentialism, which opts for purity over hybridity, will inevitably result in paralysis and sterility. As in *Such a Long Journey* and *A Fine Balance*, boundaries play an important role in *Family Matters* in that they instrumentalize difference in order to construct a particular identity. In *Such a Long Journey* Gustad Noble's exclusionist way of fighting an erosion of meaning by way of compound wall and blackout paper becomes metonymic of the Parsi community's troublesome seclusion. The community's self-centredness, i.e. its obsession with difference, signifies stasis and solipsism rather than splendid isolation. Similarly, in *Family Matters* Mistry does not merely interpret the Parsi community's fear of incest biologistically, he also foregrounds incest as a form of degeneration both spiritually and culturally.

Family matters in a particular way in *Family Matters*. It is not merely a Parsi family that Mistry is ultimately interested in but the family of man. By way of intertextual reference to Shakespeare's *King Lear*, the cast-out Nariman becomes a test case for the humanity and solidarity of others. The plot of the novel can be understood as detailing the ramifications of Yezad's family's attempt to accommodate the "unaccommodated man" (*King Lear*), exiled by his ungrateful children. It is a test that every member of Yeazd's family passes except the head of the family himself. So far, so *Such a Long Journey*. Yezad's religious zeal is revealed to be a compensation for his faltering belief in compassion, solidarity and sharing. This is a shortcoming that the author of *Family Matters* takes issue with. Yezad is criticized for losing his faith in humanism and for replacing it by a reliance on essential difference as a dubious approach at making meaning. While Vikram Kapur emphasizes the ideal of "the community rediscovering human bonds" (222),[102] Yezad's development from secular to fiercely religious is not simply a psychohygienic strategy; his fanatism is also a psychotic overreaction informed by communal bigotry and problematic in its treatment of others.

Particularly with respect to the previous point, Yezad contrasts unfavourably with his employer Vikram Kapur. Vikram provides Husain, the traumatized victim of intercommunal violence, with a job in his shop. In spite of having suffered himself from Muslim violence in the course of the 1947 partition of India, the Hindu Vikram practices forgiveness and solidarity to his fellow human beings. By accepting Husain as an employee, he actively fights bigotry, narrow-mindedness and intolerance between the Hindu and the Muslim community and becomes representative of a humanist utopia. It is people like Vikram that make multiculturalism within India work, and it is Vikram that Mistry empathises with when he, like Dina and her lodgers in *A Fine Balance*, emphasizes the importance of sharing: "You see how we two are sitting here, sharing? That's how people have lived in Bombay. That's why Bombay has survived floods, disease, plague, water shortage, bursting drains and sewers, all the population pressures" (154). Vikram Kapur underscores a philosophy that is implicit in Mistry's other works, too. Discussing the powerfulness of stories and storytelling as ways to construct meaning in a meaningless world, he subscribes to universalism: "In fact, no matter where you go in the world, there is only one important story: of youth, and loss, and yearning for redemption. So we tell the same story, over and over. Just the details are different" (221).

Humanism in *Family Matters* does not only figure as solidarity but is also strongly associated with literature and men of letters. Vilas Rane, for example, arguably Mistry's mouthpiece, a scribe and minor character reminiscent of the proofreader Vasantrao Valmik in *A Fine Balance*, stresses the necessity to maintain and foster communication between family members by reading and writing letters (133ff.). For him family matters are matters of interaction enacted within letters. Thus Vilas is "writing and reading the ongoing drama of family matters, the endless tragedy and comedy" (136). In a fictional universe that despite its specific setting and culturally distinct grounding also talks about the conditio humana, Mistry relies on figures that function as spiritual guides. These guides may be a role model in the way they act (cf. Vikram). They lead in that they 'read,' for in the same way as Vasantrao in *A Fine Balance* 'reads' the nation[103] and what makes it fall apart, Vilas in *Family Matters* 'reads' the world and learns what holds it together.

Associated with humanist concerns is also Nariman Vakeel, professor of English literature and like Mr Biswas, Nurdin Lalani, or Sita in search of a house. But in contrast to Mr Biswas or Mr Lalani, the house is not a metaphor for an identity crisis. Nariman needs shelter, i.e. the pity and solidarity of his family. Now during old age he needs the help he gave to others in the past. It is important to realize, however, that Nariman's character is not only juxtaposed to that of Yezad, his tolerance and openmindedness also contrast favourably with that of his parents. Expecting Nariman to terminate his relationship to the Goan girl he loves, Nariman's parents, in a presumptuous gesture of alleged authority, decide over his life on the basis of the Parsi community and its endogamous marriage policy. In a move resembling the works of Neil Bissoondath such a practice is depicted as a highly problematic aspect of indigenous culture. The collective interferes with the individual's freedom of choice and becomes directly responsible for Nariman's unhappiness, Lucy's madness and her eventual death by suicide. By thwarting his marriage to Lucy, Nariman's parents vehemently opt against an inclusion of Otherness. Placing undue importance on cultural purity, an intercultural union with a dark-skinned Goan is out of the question for the members of the Parsi community, who pride themselves on their 'Englishness' and regard the family as a closed social system. Implicitly, *Family Matters* distinguishes between two kinds of families. The ideal family for Mistry is not a matter of birth but of caring, solidarity and humanity. Thus family ceases to be Yezad's essence and becomes a construction defined on the basis of empathy and altruism. In that Mistry's most recent work of fiction strongly resembles the way family is imagined in his masterpiece, *A Fine Balance*. It also resembles Bissoodath's *The Worlds Within Her* in its treatment of family as it becomes manifest and how it should ideally be.

Family in *Family Matters* matters in another way that is also familiar from *Such a Long Journey*: It can be a residual of meaning in a chaotic world. However, depending on the individual character, the family matters of *Family Matters* are as much a blessing (in disguise) as a curse. Nariman's function is that of a catalyst producing different reactions and yielding quite different results. His presence helps the members of Yezad's family come to a deeper understanding of themselves. Sharing and opening up enriches the lives of Roxana and her children. For Yezad, however, family matters become an encumbrance—not only with respect to his father-in-law but also with respect to his son. That he is unable to modify his boundary policy from one that favours borders to one that acknowledges thresholds becomes evident when taking into account his reaction towards Murad's new girl friend. By forbidding Murad to see a girl that is no Parsi, Yezad acts like Nariman's parents did before him.

A source of hope in an otherwise bleak novel is that history probably will not repeat itself. Murad may resemble Nariman, but he no longer feels obliged to obey his parents. In the context of the novel, the waywardness of Murad, as a representative of the young generation, represents a chance for the endangered Parsi community. While *Family Matters* resembles *Such a Long Journey* and *A Fine Balance* in their belief in human solidarity and compassion, in Murad *Family Matters* also emphasizes what *Tales From Firozsha Baag* demands, *Such a Long Journey* theorises and *A Fine Balance* enacts: Intercultural understanding and hybridity.

Conclusion

Identity and Difference:
The Works of MG Vassanji, Neil Bissoondath, and Rohinton Mistry

(i) I have tried to elaborate on a reading paradigm for Canadian multicultural fiction that takes as its starting point the general observation that the immigrant imagination is dichotomous. Drawing on the concepts of 'here' and 'there,' established by Frye and Atwood and developed by Birbalsingh, Dabydeen and others, I have maintained that the double focus on Canada as setting and subject matter on the one hand, and the respective writer's country of origin on the other should not lead to an exclusion of writers such as MG Vassanji, Neil Bissoondath, and Rohinton Mistry from the canon of Canadian literature. These writers can be regarded as Canadian writers not only because they live in Canada, are naturalized citizens or identify with the Canadian polity but because their work presents postnational arguments that enrich our understanding of the plurality of Canadian identities. I have argued in particular that if a canonization of the works of immigrant writers is unproblematical with respect to 'here,' it would be a non sequitur to exclude from the canon their writings set 'there.' This is because for each writer the works set 'there' and the work set 'here' present a similar construction of identity. Once it is understood that 'here' and 'there' are really variations on the same theme, it follows that 'here' and 'there' must be read together and demand equal attention from the literary critic interested in Canadian (multicultural) fiction.

MG Vassanji in *No New Land* presents integration as a two-way process. On the one hand, he demands that Canada challenges the racism that runs through its society. On the other hand, the immigrant is called upon to make an effort at identifying with the country of his adoption. *The Book of Secrets* underscores a claim for hybridity, too, albeit on a narratologically more sophisticated, self-conscious manner. While difference becomes manifest on an epistemological as well as an ontological level, Vassanji eventually writes in favour of a bridging of differences in the context of an intercultural hermeneutics.

In contrast to Vassanji, Neil Bissoondath's works present an argument which holds that the community and the group, both of which are crucial to some forms of postcolonialism as well multiculturalism, are impediments to the individual trying to find his/her position in a new land. Bissoondath is mainly interested in a specifically personal kind of identity and sets some of his narratives in a Caribbean 'there' only to level a polemic diatribe against place and tradition. For him these are essentialist categories which are not negligible but harmful for individual identity constructions, postcolonial and otherwise.

Rohinton Mistry's understanding of identity can be located in-between Vassanji and Bissoondath. Set 'here,' "Swimming Lessons," the key story in his first major publication, eloquently speaks of the need to open up to a foreign environment in a way reminiscent of Vassanji's *No New Land*. The explicit demand for hybridity can be felt in *Such a Long Journey*, *A Fine Balance* and *Family Matters*, too. However, it is crucial to perceive that apart from cultural exchange, Mistry also writes in favour of an exchange between human beings that focuses not only on cultural difference but also draws on transcultural sameness. Through Mistry's texts, in other words, runs the more or less explicit belief in a humanism that overrides the particularities of cultural difference. While it may seem paradox that both a relativist as well as a universalist frame of reference can actually co-occur, the apparent contradiction can be reconciled once Mistry's obsession with the sociological problem of making meaning is given the critical attention it merits.

(ii) As identity presupposes a difference against which to outline itself, functionalizations of difference of necessity occupy a central position within my argument. Once it is understood that identities are constructed, it becomes evident that difference also is a category that allows for and indeed demands a positioning and hence is a construction, too. Thus a concern with difference does not necessarily imply that a writer inscribes difference uncritically. For Vassanji, Bissoondath, and Mistry, as postcolonial/multicultural writers, difference is a problematic that triggers individual responses rather than a sine qua non whose affirmation is de rigeur for the immigrant writer. As Deepika Bahri confirms, multicultural and postcolonial fiction may well treat difference differently:

> The opposite of reading only in terms of difference is not necessarily reading in terms of homogenization; good reading should always be about noting the particular—problems arise only when difference is produced as a totalizing framework. The quest for "sameness," in fact, might offer surprisingly rich yields.[1]

For MG Vassanji difference translates as cultural difference, which is implicitly valued in his fiction as an integral part of a pluralist view of life. Cultural difference in *The Book of Secrets*, for example, is buttressed by postmodernist thought which shares an interest with postcolonialism in giving voice to those previously marginalized. But the Other, in this case Mariamu, resists articulation so that ontological difference is underscored by epistemological difference. Vassanji makes a point about cultural difference as well as about the problems involved in coming to terms with Otherness from a perceptual and conceptual vantage point. To that purpose he utilizes one discourse of difference (i.e. postmodernism) in order to stabilize another (i.e. postcolonialism). While it is true that Vassanji eventually argues for the necessity of bridging differences, no matter how preliminary and subjective such an attempt might be, there can be no doubt that he stresses the importance of difference as fundamental to multiculturalism and postcolonialism.

If Vassanji employs discourses of difference in order to convince the reader of the importance of cultural difference, albeit in a hybrid rather than an essentialist form, the novels of Neil Bissoondath pit two ideas of difference against each other in order to deconstruct a particular form of cultural difference. In his work, cultural difference figures as group or collective difference in particular. Neil Bissoondath is critical of such an understanding of difference because it ultimately questions the freedom of the individual. Difference for him is valid only inasmuch as it allows the individual to be different from whoever wants to claim him/her. Neil Bissoondath deconstructs cultural difference in the name of a much more important difference, i.e. that of the individual. Among other things, this also means that he dismantles one kind of essentialism only to install another.

Whereas Vassanji affirms difference as ethical and Bissoondath deconstructs difference as immoral, Rohinton Mistry seems divided between the uses and abuses of a politics of difference. If Vassanji writes postcolonial difference by way of postmodern difference and orchestrates two discourses of difference, and if Bissoondath deconstructs postcolonial (collective) difference by way of liberalism as a discourse of (individual) difference and essentialist sameness, Mistry inscribes a postcolonial discourse of difference and a universalist discourse of sameness in a dialogical manner. While *Such a Long Journey* displays familiar postcolonial positions in its endeavour to employ historiography and metahistory to a counterdiscursive aim, the novel at the same time draws on humanist/universalist thought in order to interrogate the importance accorded to cultural difference by postcolonial counter-discourse.

From Diasporic Fiction to Canadian Literature

The few critical sources on Vassanji, Bissoondath, and Mistry usually subsume these writers under the label of the South Asian diaspora.[2] According to William Safran, the concept of diaspora, while having lost its historical reference to the Jews and their exile, necessarily involves a common experience of displacement, a myth of the homeland, a feeling of alienation and isolation in the respective country of adoption and, finally, the wish to return to the country of origin that is regarded as the true home.[3] If we accept Safran's claims, then Vassanji, Bissoondath, and Mistry are not only not part of a South Asian diaspora but are not even writers of diasporic fiction at all.[4] While the three of them share the experience of international dispersal, they do not look nostalgically towards their homeland. Moreover, there is no single homeland for all three of them and certainly no wish on their part to return to their respective country of origin. This opens up the question how to classify Vassanji, Bissoondath, and Mistry as writers of fiction. If some critics continue to use 'South Asian Canadian' as an umbrella term, it seems useful instead to simply conceptualize Vassanji, Bissoondath, and Mistry as writers of Canadian literature. By way of a reading of difference and identity 'here' and 'there' it is possible to find points of convergence between Vassanji, Bissoondath, and Mistry that allow, perhaps demand, to read them as Canadian writers.

Forty years ago, John Porter wrote that the typical Canadian has two loyalities, one to Canada and one to one's country of origins. Porter drew two conclusions.[5] For one thing, he implied that every Canadian was an immigrant. Secondly, while the double loyalty of the prototypical Canadian may have been beneficial in the past in allowing for a self-image that contrasted neatly with Canada's southern neighbour, the Canadian's split loyalities were debased as conservative in contrast to assimilation as the allegedly more progressive, American alternative. Whereas the first conclusion arguably remains valid today, the second has become hopelessly obsolete. Given the fact that today countries such as America learn from Canada in how to live peacefully together in a multicultural society, the Canadian angle on the issue has proved the more fruitful one. The works of MG Vassanji, Neil Bissoondath, and Rohinton Mistry are not only Canadian literature in that they reflect Porter's double loyalty, which I have conceptualized as the dichotomy of 'here' and 'there,' but also in that they represent a wide range of identity constructions that are made possible by Canada and the pluralism of its multicultural society. If one takes the promise of multiculturalism seriously, and this is what I suggest we must do despite all of its shortcomings as a policy, then the works of Vassanji, Bissoondath, and Mistry provide us with insights into the lives of other Canadians (rather than Other Canadians). In their writing they offer case studies of postnational Canadian identities and the ways in which they may be constructed.

Notes

Introduction

1. Anthony Giddens, *Entfesselte Welt: Wie die Globalisierung unser Leben verändert*, transl. Frank Jakubzik (1999; Frankfurt/Main: Edition Suhrkamp, 2001) 28n.

2. The difference between both here is that in the case of the former, Western mainstream culture is said to have had an increasing impact on non-Western cultures, whereas in the latter multiculturalism describes the non-Western world arriving in North America and Europe.

3. for example, Arif Dirlik, a committed Marxist, who understands the effects that globalization has had on culture in exclusively materialist terms: "Corresponding to economic fragmentation [. . .] is cultural fragmentation, or, to put it in its positive guise, multiculturalism." Arif Dirlik, "The Postcolonial Aura: Third World Criticism in the Age of Global Capitalism," *Contemporary Postcolonial Theory: A Reader*, ed. Padmini Mongia (London: Arnold, 1996) 310.

4. Craig Tapping who argues that immigrant writing is concerned not only with a "recollection of the homeland, [but also with] [. . .] the active response to this 'new' world." Craig Tapping, "South Asia/North America: New Dwellings and the Past," *Reworlding: The Literature of the Indian Diaspora*, ed. Emmanuel S Nelson (Westport, CT: Greenwood, 1992) 35.

5. Linda Hutcheon, who has argued that "the cultural richness that immigration has brought to this country has changed forever our concept of what constitutes 'Canadian literature.'" Linda Hutcheon, "Introduction," *Other Solitudes: Canadian Multicultural Fictions*, eds. Linda Hutcheon and Marion Richmond (Toronto: OUP, 1990) 6.

6. Frank Davey, *Post-National Arguments: The Politics of the Anglophone-Canadian Novel since 1967* (Toronto: University of Toronto Press, 1993) 15, 17.

7. Davey, *Post-National Arguments*, 7. Almost twenty years earlier, Davey similarly maintained that: "All the writers discussed are of either Canadian birth or residence. Among expatriate and immigrant writers I have excluded those whose work has been overwhelmingly about other-than-Canadian experience. [. . .] I have seen little point here in continuing the Canadian habit of indiscriminately claiming all writers of some Canadian residence as our own." Frank Davey, *From There to Here* (Erin, ON: Press Porcepic, 1974) 10. While Davey in *Post-National Arguments* concedes that writers like Mistry and Vassanji can be of considerable importance to a specific community and that their neglect of Canadian subject matter may be read politically, the overall effect is the same: neither now nor then does he grant writers who write about a country other than Canada an analysis in his publications on Canadian literature.

8. Davey, *Post-National Arguments*, 7.

9. Davey, *Post-National Arguments*, 23.

10. Ironically enough, by denying immigrant authors the status of Canadian literature on the basis of the content of their work, Frank Davey at the same time practises the very kind of criticism that he takes issue with in an earlier, influential essay of his: "Thematic critics in Canada have been interested in what literary works 'say,' especially what they 'say' about Canada and Canadians. They have largely overlooked what literary works 'mean'—for the attempt to establish meaning

would take them outside thematic criticism." Frank Davey, "Surviving the Paraphase," *Surviving the Paraphrase: Eleven Essays on Canadian Literature* (Winnipeg: Turnstone, 1986) 3. Davey takes issue here with the kind of literary criticism practised by Frye, Atwood and others on the grounds that it runs counter to his understanding of art as primarily foregrounding language's poetic function. Cf. Konrad Groß, "Zum Problem der kanadischen Identität," *Kanada: Eine interdisziplinäre Einführung*, eds. Hans Braun and Wolfgang Klooß (Trier: WVT, 1994) 194.

11. Arun Prabha Mukherjee, "Writing from a Hard Place: The African Fiction of MG Vassanji," *Oppositional Aesthetics: Readings from a Hyphenated Space* (Toronto: TSAR, 1994) 169.

12. Ranu Samantrai, "States of Belonging: Pluralism, Migrancy, Literature," *Essays in Canadian Writing* 57 (1995): 47. For a similar argument cf. Natalia Aponiuk, "'Ethnic Literature,' 'Minority Writing,' 'Literature in Other Languages,' 'Hyphenated-Canadian Literature'—Will It Ever Be Canadian?" *Canadian Ethnic Studies* 28.1 (1996): 2.

13. Ajay Heble, "'A Foreign Presence in the Stall': Towards a Poetics of Hybridity in Rohinton Mistry's Migration Stories," *Canadian Literature* 137 (1993): 60.

14. Ella Shohat warns us that "as a descriptive catch-all term, 'hybridity' per se fails to discriminate between the diverse modalities of hybridity." Ella Shohat, "Notes on the Post-Colonial," *Contemporary Postcolonial Theory: A Reader*, ed. Padmini Mongia (London: Arnold, 1996) 331.

15. Rosemary Sullivan, "The Multicultural Divide: Where's the Mosaic? It's Time to Open the Doors of the CanLit Club," *This Magazine* 22 (1988): 26. In an interview with Aja Norgaard, Neil Bissoondath pursues the same vein. He says: "I like the term Canadian writer because it means so much. [. . .] I think once being called a Canadian writer meant that you wrote about growing up on the prairies, but Canadian writing now has moved well beyond that into all kinds of spheres. Because of that variety I accept the label." Aja Norgaard, "Up-and-Coming," interview with Neil Bissoondath, *Aurora Online*, 5 March 2002 <htttp:// aurora.icaap.org/archive/ bissoondath.html>. Cf. also Penny van Toorn, "Building on Common Ground. An Interview with Neil Bissoondath," *Canadian Literature* 147 (1995): 132.

16. Sullivan, 26.

17. See also Birbalsingh who, in the course of his discussion of the South Asian diaspora in Canada, refers to "the phenomenon of 'here' and 'there.'" Frank Birbalsingh, *Novels and the Nation: Essays in Canadian Literature* (Toronto: TSAR, 1995) 157. Concerned with Caribbean Canadian writing, Cyril Dabydeen also proposes a reading that operates with "the *here*, temperate Canada, where the Caribbean spirit asserts itself in the desire to forge a wholesome and meaningful existence" and "the *there*, the place where one came from." Cyril Dabydeen, ed., *A Shapely Fire: Changing the Literary Landscape* (Oakville, ON: Mosaic, 1987) 20. Linda Hutcheon, too, confirms that "doubleness [. . .] is the essence of the immigrant experience." Hutcheon, "Introduction," 9. For the pioneering study stressing the psychological implications of this doubleness cf. Eli Mandel, "Ethnic Voice in Canadian Writing," *Another Time* (Erin, ON: Press Porcepic, 1977) 92.

18. Alois Hahn, "Soziologie des Fremden," *Erfahrungen des Fremden: Vorträge im Sommersemester 1992*, ed. Ruprechts-Karls-Universität Heidelberg (Heidelberg: Heidelberger Verlagsanstalt, 1992) 23.

19. Northrop Frye, for whom Canadian sensibility "is less perplexed by the question 'Who am I?' than by some such riddle as 'Where is here?'" Northrop Frye, afterword, *Literary History of Canada: Canadian Literature in English*, ed. Carl F Klinck (1965; Toronto: University of Toronto Press, 1973) 826. Although Frye takes great care to draw a line between the exploration of space and the construction of a specifically Canadian identity, his argument seems flawed from a postcolonial point of view. Frye, like Margaret Atwood, homogenizes Canadian experience at the cost of the country's plurality of cultures. In other words, both Frye's garrison mentality and Atwood's concept of victimization fail to theorize the experience of Canada's first nations and immigrant writers. Cf. Margaret Atwood, *Survival: A Thematic Guide to Canadian Literature* (Toronto: Anansi, 1972).

20. "No longer does the Canadian author raise the question 'Where is here?' The immigrant writer finds Canada an exceptionally conductive [sic] milieu for asking 'What is there?' [. . .] As

Canadian literature easily mediates between the First and Third worlds, offering immigrant writers a secure home for their peregrinations, Northrop Frye might well ask, 'Where is here?', but with a different and perhaps ironic tone. For the contemporary Canadian writer, here is now an indefinable area, encompassing Canada and the world, an area with no centre and therefore no periphery, with neither the possibility nor the need of definition. The earlier obsession with the question 'Where is here?' has faded into distant memory, a question no longer necessary, valid, or even appropriate. And 'What is there?' is the question so many of our writers are now raising." David Staines, "The State of Contemporary Canadian Literature," *Canada and the Nordic Countries in Times of Reorientation: Literature and Criticism*, ed. Jørn Carlsen (Aarhus: The Nordic Association for Canadian Studies, 1998) 28.

Difference and Identity in Multicultural and Postcolonial Discourse

A. Multiculturalism in Canada

1. Wolfgang Klooß, "Vom Bikulturalismus zum kanadischen Multikulturalismus: Historische Grundlagen und gesellschaftliche Implikationen eines politischen Programms," *Gulliver* 22 (1987): 28.

2. Klooß, "Vom Bikulturalismus zum kanadischen Multikulturalismus," 28.

3. For more information about the concept of empty space cf. Chris Tiffin and Alan Lawson, "Introduction: The Textuality of Empire," *De-Scribing Empire: Post-Colonialism and Textuality*, eds. Chris Tiffin and Alan Lawson (London: Routledge, 1994) 5. While legally convenient, an empty space could become psychologically problematic if it was 'too' empty. The vast geographical extension of Canada and the frequently inhospitable character of its nature could easily render the legal fiction of terra nullius into a scene of 'colonial gothic' in which the individual was lost and threatened. In his/her attempt at survival he/she inevitably relied on the solidarity of others or drew on strategies of representing the land in an attempt at coming to terms with its immeasurable and uncanny dimensions. The former lies at the heart of Frye's garrison mentality; the latter is reflected in the Canadian obsession with charts and mapping. For more information on mapping see Aritha van Herk, "Mapping as Metaphor," *Zeitschrift für Kanada-Studien* 1 (1982): 75.

4. Manitoba and Alberta, for example, have welcomed immigrants for as long as one hundred years and longer to settle the prairies. These immigrants, who helped Canada to become the world's biggest producer of wheat, were chosen with care. At first, mostly Germans, Polish, and Ukrainians were selected because they were thought to cope best with the climate. Moreover, it was believed that they would most easily match the ideal of Anglo-conformity. Since the 1960s another wave of immigration has set in, in the course of which mostly South Asians came to Canada. For more information on Canada's multicultural regionalism see Leo Driedger, *Multi-Ethnic Canada. Identities and Inequalities* (Toronto: OUP, 1996) 75–98.

5. Elke Winter, "National Unity versus Multiculturalism? Rethinking the Logic of Inclusion in Germany and Canada," *International Journal of Canadian Studies/Revue internationale d'études canadiennes* 24 (2001): 177.

6. for example, Smaro Kamboureli, "Multiculturalism," *Encyclopedia of Post-Colonial Literatures in English*, vol.2, eds. Eugene Benson and LW Conolly (London: Routledge, 1994) 1053. See also Groß, 203.

7. Himani Bannerji, "On the Dark Side of the Nation: Politics of Multiculturalism and the State of 'Canada,'" *Literary Pluralities*, ed. Christl Verduyn (Peterborough, ON: Broadview, 1998) 131.

8. As set down in the Multiculturalism Act of 1988, Canada commits itself to cultural difference within four different areas of multicultural policy. These four issues pertain to (i) race relations and cross-cultural understanding, (ii) heritage cultures and languages, (iii) community support and participation, (iv) cross-governmental commitment. Also in 1988, the Department of Multiculturalism and Citizenship was created which was to promote an understanding of

multiculturalism throughout the country. Cf. Litvack, 126.

9. Winter, 177.

10. "Multiculturalism does not ask that we choose between our ethnicity and a national identity but that the one is a 'key content' of the other." Myrna Kostash, "Imagination, Representation and Culture," *Literary Pluralities*, ed. Christl Verduyn (Peterborough, ON: Broadview, 1998) 95.

11. In that Canadian multiculturalism was designed to distract attention not only from the issue of Franco-Canada but also from the status of the First Nations, multiculturalism cannot be understood as "a sign of the collective historical guilt (or even hypocrisy) resulting from Canada's earlier immigration policies." Cf. Litvack, 131.

12. Bannerji, 130.

13. also Klooß, "Vom Bikulturalismus zum kanadischen Multikulturalismus," 31.

14. Smaro Kamboureli, ed., *Making a Difference: Canadian Multicultural Literature* (Toronto: OUP, 1996) and Linda Hutcheon and Marion Richmond, eds., *Other Solitudes: Canadian Multicultural Fictions* (Toronto: OUP, 1990).

15. Charles Taylor, "The Politics of Recognition," *Multiculturalism and "The Politics of Recognition,"* ed. Amy Gutman (Princeton: Princeton, 1992) 32.

16. Neil Bissoondath, *Selling Illusions: The Cult of Multiculturalism in Canada* (Toronto: OUP, 1994) 82. See also Bissoondath, 88. For a critique of Bissoondath see Graham Huggan, *The Postcolonial Exotic: Marketing the Margins* (London: Routledge, 2001) 139–41.

17. Taylor, 25.

18. Bissoondath, 95.

19. Hutcheon, "Introduction," 13.

20. Lance W Roberts and Rodney A Clifton, "Multiculturalism in Canada: A Sociological Perspective," *Race and Ethnic Relations in Canada*, ed. Peter S Li (Toronto: OUP, 1990) 123.

21. Roberts and Clifton, 125.

22. Roberts and Clifton, 135. See also Augie Fleras and Jean Elliott, *Multiculturalism in Canada: The Challenge of Diversity* (Scarborough, ON: Nelson Canada, 1992) 50–1.

23. Roberts and Clifton, 134.

24. Bissoondath, 71.

25. Bissoondath, 71. Bissoondath articulates a fear which in America has been recently voiced by Huntington's notorious argument about an impending clash of civilizations. According to Huntington, multiculturalism as a policy is a non sequitur for a nation interested in a stable national self-image, i.e. for any nation. With reference to the US he holds that "a multicivilizational United States will not be the United States; it will be the United Nations." Samuel Huntington, *The Clash of Civilizations and the Remaking of World Order* (1996; NY: Touchstone, 1997) 306. For a critique of Huntington see Thomas Meyer, *Identitäts-Wahn: Die Politisierung des kulturellen Unterschieds* (Berlin: Aufbau Taschenbuch Verlag, 1997) 65–9.

26. Bissoondath, 115.

27. Bissoondath, 87.

28. Bissoondath, 73. A similar argument is advanced by Reginald Bibby. However, while Bibby, like Bissoondath, warns against the dangers inherent in multiculturalism, his polemic departs from Bissoondath's in its attack on individualism. For Bibby, individualism and pluralism, as multiculturalism's central asset overlap in relativism, which he regards as potentially divisive because it allegedly brings about a obfuscation of what is right and wrong. Reginald W Bibby, *Mosaic Madness: The Poverty and Potential of Life in Canada* (Toronto: Stoddart, 1990) 43–6. Bibby's neoliberal critique draws attention to the preliminary nature of formulations of Canadian national identity in terms of multiculturalism: "When a country like Canada enshrines pluralism through politics such as multiculturalism and bilingualism and the guaranteeing of individual rights, the outcome is coexistence—no more, no less. It's a good start in building a society out of diverse people. But there's a danger. If there is no subsequent vision, no national goals, no explicit sense of coexisting for some purpose, pluralism becomes an uninspiring end in itself. Rather than coexistence being the foundation that enables a diverse nation to collectively pursue the best kind

of existence possible, coexistence degenerates into a national preoccupation. Pluralism ceases to have a cause. The result: mosaic madness" (103–4). Taking issue with views that hold that multiculturalism in Canada is a given rather than a process of becoming which need constant efforts, Smaro Kamboureli in her most recent publication identifies populist opinions such as Bibby's as the symptoms of a "multicultural fatigue." Smaro Kamboureli, *Scandalous Bodies: Diasporic Literature in English Canada* (Toronto: OUP, 2000) 83.

29. Bissoondath, 132.

30. John Harles, "Multiculturalism, National Identity, and National Integration: The Canadian Case," *International Journal of Canadian Studies/Revue internationale d'études canadiennes* 17 (1998): 227.

31. Harles, 227.

32. Harles, 227, 228. For the author, liberalism is too firmly rooted within an American tradition in order to serve as a key element for constructing a national self-image.

33. Harles, 243.

34. Harles, 242.

35. This dovetails with arguments stressing that more rather than less multiculturalism is needed in order to solve the problems of contemporary Canada. Cf. Fleras and Elliott, 280.

36. Eric Breton, "Canadian Federalism, Multiculturalism and the Twenty-first Century," *International Journal of Canadian Studies/Revue internationale d'études canadiennes* 21 (2000): 158.

37. Breton, 158.

38. Breton, 160.

39. Will Kymlicka, *Multicultural Citizenship: A Liberal Theory of Minority Rights* (NY: OUP, 1996). For an evaluation of Kymlicka's theory cf. Bhikhu Parekh, *Rethinking Multiculturalism: Cultural Diversity and Political Theory* (Basingstoke: Palgrave, 2000) 99–109.

40. Kymlicka, 17.

41. Kymlicka, 10.

42. Kymlicka, 10.

43. Kymlicka, 10–11.

44. Kymlicka's theory balances rights and obligations of citizenship within multicultural Canada. While he points to instances where difference must end in the name of sameness, i.e. where a 'foreign' culture is to submit to the culture and values of the Canadian host society, he also takes great care to outline that group-differentiated rights are important and do not necessarily run counter to a liberal approach. While Kymlicka's approach recognizes limits to tolerance through what he calls 'internal restrictions,' multiculturalism should also grant ethnic groups 'external protection.' Cf. Kymlicka, 35. For more on multiculturalism and the debate concerning rights see Taylor, 60–1.

45. Kymlicka, 27.

46. Kymlicka, 30–3.

47. Kymlicka, 181.

48. Kymlicka, 191.

49. Richard Sigurdson, "First Nations, First Peoples and Citizenship in Canada," *International Journal of Canadian Studies/Revue internationale d'études canadiennes* 14 (1996): 57.

50. Sigurdson, 58.

51. Sigurdson, 59.

52. Sigurdson, 74.

53. Litvack, 121.

54. Robert Kroetsch, "Introduction: Ethnicity and Canadian Literature," *Canadian Ethnic Studies* 14.1 (1982): v.

55. Yoko Fujimoto, "Multiculturalism and Ethnic Writing in English Canada: A New Development in the National Literary Discourse," *Nationalism vs. Internationalism: (Inter)national Dimensions of Literatures in English*, eds. Wolfgang Zach and Ken L Goodwin

(Tübingen: Stauffenburg-Verlag, 1996) 326.

56. What Fujimoto fails to theorize is that there is not only a causal link between 'here' and 'there' but also a connection as to the treatment of difference and identity. In that sense, 'there' does not simply presuppose 'here,' 'there' can also be said to reenact 'here' with respect to an author's specific identity politics.

57. Tamara Palmer Seiler confirms that until recently "the literature produced in Canada by immigrants [. . .] whose backgrounds were neither British or French has [. . .] been marginalized, that is, not viewed as being "Canadian" literature in the same sense as the work produced by Canada's 'two founding nations.'" Tamara Palmer Seiler, "Multi-Vocality and National Literature: Towards a Post-Colonial and Multicultural Aesthetic," *Literary Pluralities*, ed. Christl Verduyn (Peterborough, ON: Broadview, 1998) 53.

58. Janice Kulyk Keefer, "'The Sacredness of Bridges': Writing Immigrant Experience," *Literary Pluralities*, ed. Christl Verduyn (Peterborough, ON: Broadview, 1998) 103–4.

59. The Canada Council was founded in 1957 as a result of the findings of the Massey Commission (1949–51), which was concerned with investigating the foreign influence on Canadian culture. Cf. Litvack, 123.

60. Michael S Batts, "Multiculturalism and Canadian Literature," *Us/Them: Translation, Transcription and Identity in Post-Colonial Literary Cultures*, ed. Gordon Collier (Amsterdam: Rodopi, 1992) 44.

61. At the same time, it is worth noting that the pluralism inherent in this concept is not of necessity divisive. While among the issues covered in multicultural writing are often explorations of the writer's respective home cultures, this does not necessarily reduce the commitment these writers are willing to make to Canada. As Litvack has rightfully pointed out: "Despite the sometimes 'other-wordly' nature of their experience, these writers also consider themselves 'Canadian.'" Litvack, 127. Put differently, only because the immigrant writer does not write about Canada, he still can, and often will, feel part of the Canadian polity.

62. While these values are often associated with the postmodern turn in the humanities, Sypnovich reminds us that the tolerance towards difference so central to multiculturalism is as much a postmodern as an Enlightenment asset. see Christine Sypnowich, "Some Disquiet about 'Difference,'" *Multicultural Experiences, Multicultural Theories*, eds. Mary F Rogers and George Ritzer (NY: McGraw-Hill, 1996) 279. Fujimoto goes even further in arguing that inasmuch as Canadian multiculturalism can be said to implicitly regard itself as the new norm that is superior to European and US-American models, "it signifies a strong belief in human universality that transcends difference." Fujimoto, 326.

63. Fleras and Elliott, 58. Also Hutcheon, "Introduction," 5. Padolsky, too, opts for a pluralist vision of Canadian literature and especially argues that minority writing offers insights into the dynamics of culture and power. Cf. Enoch Padolsky, "Ethnicity and Race: Canadian Minority Writing at a Crossroads," *Literary Pluralities*, ed. Christl Verduyn (Peterborough, ON: Broadview P, 1998) 25. See also Enoch Padolsky, "Cultural Diversity and Canadian Literature: A Pluralistic Approach to Majority and Minority Writing in Canada," *International Journal of Canadian Studies/Revue internationale d'études canadiennes* 3 (1991): 114.

64. Enoch Padolsky, "Canadian Minority Writing and Acculturation Options," *Canadian Review of Comparative Literature/ Revue Canadienne de Littérature Comparée* (1989): 602.

65. Batts, 42f. See also Bannerji, 143–4. For a different opinion cf. Francesco Loriggio, "The Question of the Corpus: Ethnicity and Canadian Literature," *Future Indicative: Literary Theory and Canadian Literature*, ed. John Moss (Ottawa: U of Ottawa P, 1987) 55.

66. Michael Thorpe, "Opposition, Multicultural Apartheid or Connection?" *The Toronto South Asian Review* 9.1 (1990): 6.

67. Thus Bharati Mukherjee left Canada for the US because America's assimilationist policy, in her opinion, presented an alternative to Canada's racist inscription of Otherness in the context of multiculturalism. Cf. Bharati Mukherjee, *Darkness* (Markham, ON: Penguin, 1985) 2–3.

68. Marlene Nourbese Philip, "Why Multiculturalism Can't End Racism," *Frontiers: Essays and*

Writings on Racism and Culture (Stratford, ON: The Mercury Press, 1992) 185. For Philip multiculturalism is not only inadequate but in fact complicit with the racist assumptions of Canadian society in that it fails to implement an effective policy of antiracism. For a related argument cf. Bannerji who also criticizes Canada's multicultural policy for its ideological blinkers: "Thus at the same time moment that difference is ideologically evoked it is also neutralized, as though the issue of difference were the same as that of diversity of cultures and identities, rather than those of racism and colonial ethnocentrism—as though our different cultures were on a par or could negotiate with the two dominant ones!" Bannerji, 126.

69. Fred Wah, "A Poetics of Ethnicity," *Faking It: Poetics and Hybridity. Critical Writings 1984–1999* (Edmonton: NeWest Press, 2000) 58.

70. Wah, "Ethnicity," 59.

71. Fred Wah, "Half-Bred Poetics," 72–3.

B. Postcolonial Theory

1. Shohat, 322. For Marxist critics, of course, the 'third world' continues to be a point of reference. See Fredric Jameson, "Third-World Literature in the Era of Multinational Capitalism," *Social Text* 15 (1986): 69. See also Dirlik, 294. For a critique of Jameson cf. Aijaz Ahmad, "Jameson's Rhetoric of Otherness and the 'National Allegory,'" *Social Text* 17 (1987): 4, 9.

2. Eberhard Kreuzer, "Theoretische Grundlagen postkolonialer Literaturkritik," *Literaturwissenschaftliche Theorien, Modelle und Methoden: Eine Einführung*, eds. Ansgar Nünning and Monika Fludernik (Trier: WVT, 1998) 200.

3. "We use the term post-colonial [. . .] to cover all the cultures affected by the imperial process from the moment of colonization to the present day." Bill Ashcroft, Gareth Griffiths and Helen Tiffin, *The Empire Writes Back: Theory and Practice in Post-Colonial Literatures* (London: Routledge, 1989) 2. Cf. Boehmer for whom "*postcolonial* [sic] literature is that which critically scrutinizes the colonial relationship." Elleke Boehmer, *Colonial and Postcolonial Literature: Migrant Metaphors* (Oxford: OUP, 1995) 3. Cf. also Ania Loomba, *Colonialism/Postcolonialism* (London: Routledge, 1998) 12.

4. The study of colonial discourse was pioneered by the Foucault disciple Edward Said, whose 1978 publication *Orientalism* still is a seminal work. See Robert Young, "Colonialism and the Desiring-Machine," *Liminal Postmodernisms: The Postmodern, the (Post-)Colonial, and the (Post-)Feminist*, eds. Theo D'haen and Hans Bertens (Amsterdam: Rodopi, 1994) 11. Underlining *Orientalism*'s importance for a discipline and beyond, Gayatri Spivak enthusiastically claims: "The study of colonial discourse, directly released by work such as Said's, has [. . .] blossomed into a garden where the marginal can speak and be spoken, even spoken for." Gayatri Spivak, "Poststructuralism, Marginality, Postcoloniality and Value," *Contemporary Postcolonial Theory: A Reader*, ed. Padmini Mongia (London: Arnold, 1996) 200.

5. Leela Gandhi, *Postcolonial Theory: A Critical Introduction* (NY: Columbia, 1998) 16.

6. Kwame Anthony Appiah, "'Is the Post- in Postmodernism the Post- in Postcolonial?'" *Contemporary Postcolonial Theory: A Reader*, ed. Padmini Mongia (London: Arnold, 1996) 63.

7. Abdul R JanMohamed, "The Economy of Manichean Allegory: The Function of Racial Difference in Colonialist Literature," *Critical Inquiry* 12 (1985): 63.

8. Alan Lawson and Chris Tiffin, "Conclusion: Reading Difference," *De-Scribing Empire: Post-Colonialism and Textuality*, eds. Chris Tiffin and Alan Lawson (London: Routledge, 1994) 230.

9. For more on the development of postcolonial literatures from an anticolonial, nationalist to a more skeptical phase cf. Revathi Krishnaswamy, "Mythologies of Migrancy: Postcolonialism, Postmodernism and the Politics of (Dis)location," *ARIEL* 26:1 (1995): 125–6.

10. Bill Ashcroft, Gareths Griffiths and Helen Tiffin, *Key Concepts in Post-Colonial Studies* (London: Routledge, 1998) 78.

11. Ashcroft et al, *Key Concepts*, 79.

12. Gayatri Spivak, "Criticism, Feminism and the Institution," interview with Elizabeth Gross,

Thesis Eleven 10/11 (1984/85): 184. For an early argument that cautions us against the dangers of essentialism as one of the pitfalls of a national postcolonial culture cf. Frantz Fanon, *The Wretched of the Earth* (1961; Harmondsworth: Penguin, 1990) 170, 180–1.

13. Ashcroft et al, *Key Concepts*, 80.

14. Ashcroft et al, *Key Concepts*, 80.

15. Ashcroft et al, *Key Concepts*, 81.

16. Stuart Hall, *Rassismus und kulturelle Identität*, transl. and ed. Ulrich Mehlem (Hamburg: Argument-Verlag, 1994) 22.

17. Stephen Slemon, "The Scramble for Post-Colonialism," *De-Scribing Empire: Post-Colonialism and Textuality*, eds. Chris Tiffin and Alan Lawson (London: Routledge, 1994) 15. In a slightly different context, Peter Hulme speaks of postcolonialism as a "*process* [sic] of disengagement from the whole colonial syndrome, *which takes many forms* [emphasis MG]." Peter Hulme, "Including America," *ARIEL* 26.1 (1995): 120.

18. Stuart Hall, "Cultural Identity and Diaspora," *Contemporary Postcolonial Theory: A Reader*, ed. Padmini Mongia (London: Arnold, 1996) 113.

19. Michel Foucault, *Die Ordnung des Diskurses*, transl. Walter Seitter (1972; Frankfurt/Main: Fischer, 1991) 11.

20. Gandhi, 71.

21. JanMohamed, 62, also Gandhi, 32.

22. Wolfgang Klooß, "Die englischsprachige Literatur," *Kanada: Eine interdisziplinäre Einführung*, eds. Hans Braun and Wolfgang Klooß (Trier: WVT, 1994) 175.

23. Boehmer, 16.

24. Loomba, 105. Race became an unstable category not only with respect to a Christian discourse of sameness but was also moulded to stabilize a concern with class difference. Thus the lower classes were imagined in terms of other races. Cf. Loomba, 124.

25. Loomba, 164.

26. Jenny Sharpe, *Allegories of Empire: The Figure of Woman in the Colonial Text* (Minneapolis: U of Minnesota P, 1993) 67.

27. Loomba, 159.

28. Martina Michel, "Postcolonial Literatures: Use or Abuse of the Latest Post-Word," *Gulliver* 33 (1993): 17.

29. For the merit of poststructuralism in helping to establish postcolonial studies in the West cf. Gandhi, 25.

30. With respect to the reception of postcolonial literature, Ashcroft et al astutely suggest that postcolonialism should side with poststructuralism/postmodernism because postcolonial literatures have too long been read according to the principles of the New Criticism, itself a largely Western reading strategy. Far from implying that a poststructuralist/postmodern approach to literature abandons the referential function of these texts, Ashcroft et al hold that a poststructural/postmodern textual practice can heighten the awareness of contexts indispensable to an adequate understanding of these texts. Ashcroft et al, *Empire*, 160–5.

31. JanMohamed, 62.

32. Laurenz Volkmann, "Universal Truths or Ethnic Particularities? On Tensions Inherent in the Reception of Post-Colonial and Minority Literature," *Intercultural Encounters: Studies in English Literatures*, eds. Heinz Antor and Kevin L Cope (Heidelberg: Winter, 1999) 134. See also Arun Mukherjee, "The Vocabulary of the 'Universal': The Cultural Imperialism of the Universalist Criteria of Western Literary Criticism," *Oppositional Aesthetics*, 17 and, especially, Arun Mukherjee, "Universals," *Postcolonialism: My Living* (Toronto: TSAR, 1998) 201.

33. Gandhi, 29–30.

34. Ashcroft et al, *Empire*, 162.

35. Tiffin, 171.

36. For a critique that stresses that poststructuralism/postmodernism are in themselves homogenizing critical practices cf. Mukherjee, "Whose Post-colonialism," 1,4 and Helen Tiffin,

"Post-Colonialism, Post-Modernism and the Rehabilitation of Post-Colonial History," *Journal of Commonwealth Literature* 23.1 (1988): 171.

37. Hutcheon, "'Circling the Downspout,'" 150. In its reliance on a political agenda, postcolonialism is closer to feminism than to poststructuralism/postmodernism. Cf. Gandhi, 44. However, whether postcolonialism depends on a political agenda to such a degree once it comes to identity politics remains doubtful. As I have contended and intend to show in the following chapters, a wider understanding of postcolonialism can be useful for theorizing identity constructions.

38. Gayatri Spivak, "Can the Subaltern Speak?" *Colonial Discourse and Post-Colonial Theory: A Reader*, eds. Patrick Williams and Laura Chrisman (NY: Harvester Wheatsheaf, 1993) 103.

39. Claudia Kotte, "Post-Colonialism or Neo-Imperialism?" *Zeitschrift für Anglistik und Amerikanistik* 43.3 (1995): 263.

40. For more on Marxism and difference in this context see Sypnowich, 280.

41. Aijaz Ahmad, "The Politics of Literary Postcoloniality," *Contemporary Postcolonial Theory: A Reader*, ed. Padmini Mongia (London: Arnold, 1996) 276. Likewise, Arif Dirlik suggests that postcolonialism is merely a label for a scholarly interest in phenomena that are by no means new. Cf. Dirlik, 295.

42. Dirlik, 276.

43. However, while Marxism can remind us of the material underpinnings of colonialism as well as of the self-centredness and complacency of many postcolonial critics who have arrived in the West, it refuses to acknowledge the importance of colonialism as a textual venture. If Marxism is out to change the world, it pays not enough attention to the ideological underpinnings of colonialism. And it is here that poststructuralism/postmodernism can be useful.

44. Liselotte Glage, "Strategien der Differenz: Was oder wie ist der postkoloniale Roman?" *Zeitschrift für Anglistik und Amerikanistik* 43.3 (1995): 81.

45. Said's *Orientalism* was frequently taken issue with because it was said to inscribe the very difference postcolonialism intends to deconstruct. In particular, it was questioned whether there was really no alternative to Orientalism as a discourse and whether Orientalism was not in itself changing and mutable rather than stable and monolithic see Dennis Porter, "*Orientalism* and its Problems," *Colonial Discourse and Post-Colonial Theory: A Reader*, eds. Patrick Williams and Laura Chrisman (NY: Harvester Wheatsheaf, 1993) 151–2. Said himself seems to have acknowledged many points of critique. One of his recent publications takes into account that imperialism and culture are often intertwined in complex formations that render the monolithic nature of colonial discourse, as described in *Orientalism*, diverse and open to multiple interventions. Edward W. Said, *Culture and Imperialism* (London: Chatto & Windus, 1993) xix.

46. Robert Young, *Colonial Desire: Hybridity in Theory, Culture and Race* (London: Routledge, 1995) 10.

47. I have borrowed the concept of horizon from Bill Ashcroft who also is interested in nonessentialist identity formation. Stressing that postcolonialism is a project of transforming, horizon becomes a metaphor that refers to the multiple perspectives of overcoming binary differences. A horizon is not only a potentially infinite but also an infinitely resourceful vista of possibilities. Bill Ashcroft, *Postcolonial Transformation* (London: Routledge, 2001) 186.

48. Hall, "Cultural Identity and Diaspora," 119–20. See also Shohat, 329 and Paul Gilroy, *The Black Atlantic: Modernity and Double Consciousness* (Cambridge, MA: Harvard, 1993) 16. For a counter argument cf. Krishnaswamy who warns us that "'diaspora' and 'exile' are being emptied of their histories of pain and suffering and are being deployed promiscuously to designate a wide array of cross-cultural phenomena" (128). The effect is a "de-linking of distress from dislocation and the attendant idea of belonging everywhere by belonging nowhere" (137). See also Gandhi, 131.

49. Monika Fludernik, "The Constitution of Hybridity: Postcolonial Interventions," *Hybridity and Postcolonialism: Twentieth-Century Indian Literature* (Tübingen: Stauffenburg, 1998) 19.

50. Gandhi, 79. See also Paul Goetsch, "Funktionen von Hybridität in der postkolonialen Theorie," *Literatur in Wissenschaft und Unterricht* 30 (1997): 138.

51. Loomba, 173.

52. Homi K Bhabha, *The Location of Culture* (London: Routledge, 1994) 33. See also Young, 27. For a critique, cf. Chow who writes: "What Bhabha's word 'hybridity' revives, in the masquerade of deconstruction, anti-imperialism, and 'difficult' theory, is an old functionalist notion of what a dominant culture permits in the interest of maintaining its own equilibrium." Rey Chow, "Where Have All the Natives Gone?" *Contemporary Postcolonial Theory: A Reader*, ed. Padmini Mongia (London: Arnold, 1996) 128.

53. It should not be overlooked that recent critical interventions do not unanimously hail Bhabha's writings. There are at least three problems with his theory. For one thing, his idea that resistance is always possible because it is a side-effect of colonial discourse is problematic in that it overlooks material conditions. Moreover, it implicitly rejects the validity of societies whose resistance relies on struggle and fight. Cf. Loomba, 178. Secondly, how viable Bhabha's alternative identity formations really are for the majority of formerly colonized subjects remains doubtful. For not only does he almost exclusively focus on the figure of the migrant, itself not representative of formerly colonized societies and their way of challenging colonialism; Bhabha also has in mind the specifically intellectual migrant, thereby excluding the situation of the lower classes. Cf. Ahmad, 286. Bhabha privileges the intellectual migrant who lives in a so-called 'third space.' In-between cultures his prototypical exile is free to engage in a form of intercultural hermeneutics. Cf. Goetsch, "Hybridität," 143–5. It seems tempting at this point to accuse Bhabha of theorizing his own community membership as a Parsi as well as his own biography as a postcolonial critic who has made it in Western academe.

Supplementing Difference: MG Vassanji

1. For the following account cf. "Moyez G Vassanji," *Contemporary Authors: A Bio-Bibliographical Guide to Current Writers in Fiction, General Nonfiction, Poetry, Journalism, Drama, Motion Pictures, Television, and Other Fields*, vol. 136.

A. 'Here': The Promise of Hybridity. *No New Land* (1991)

1. Vassanji's Shamsis are modelled after the Khoja Ismailis. The reason Vassanji invents a community lies in the greater amount of artistic freedom such a choice allows for. Cf. Rhodes, "MG Vassanji: An Interview," 116. For more on the Ismailis of East Africa cf. Peter G Forster, Michael Hitchcock and Francis F Lyimo, *Race and Ethnicity in East Africa* (Houndsmill: Macmillan Press, 2000) 76–93.

2. Amin Malak, "Ambivalent Affiliations and the Postcolonial Condition: The Fiction of MG Vassanji," *World Literature Today* 67.2 (1993): 277.

3. MG Vassanji, *No New Land* (1991; Toronto: McClelland & Stewart, 1997) 23–4. All references are to this edition.

4. Chelva Kanaganayakam, "Don Mills and Dar es Salaam," review of *No New Land*, by MG Vassanji, *Floating the Borders: New Contexts in Canadian Criticism*, ed. Nurjehan Aziz (Toronto: TSAR, 1999) 200.

5. John Clement Ball, "Taboos: MG Vassanji," *The Power to Bend Spoons: Interviews with Canadian Novelists*, ed. Beverley Daurio (Toronto: The Mercury Press, 1998) 205.

6. Vassanji in an interview with Sushila Nasta. Sushila Nasta, "Interview: Moyez Vassanji," *Wasafiri* 13 (1991): 21.

7. Kanaganayakam, "Don Mills and Dar es Salaam," 201.

8. Bissoondath, *Selling Illusions*, 110.

9. The term 'vertical mosaic' is borrowed from John Porter who in a dated but still useful study takes issue with the myth of Canadian classlessness and egalitarianism. He argues that ethnicity and race have impeded social mobility in Canada, as a consequence of which immigrants are also marginalized in terms of social class. John Porter, *The Vertical Mosaic: An Analysis of Social Class*

and Power in Canada (Toronto: University of Toronto Press, 1965) 70.

10. For Muslims, Ismail founded the Ka'ba in Mekka.

11. Nurdin's incident was to be the subject of the short story Vassanji intended to write initially before he decided to compose a longer prose narrative. Cf. Rhodes, "MG Vassanji: An Interview," 114. Thus at the core of the novel is the nexus between cultural and sexual difference.

12. Edward Said: "The Oriental was linked thus to elements in Western society (delinquents, the insane, women, the poor) having in common an identity best described as alien." Edward W Said, *Orientalism: Western Conceptions of the Orient* (1978; London: Penguin, 1995) 207.

13. Konrad Dilger, "Tendenzen der Rechtsentwicklung," *Der Islam in der Gegenwart*, eds. Werner Ende and Guido Steinbach, 4th ed. (München: CH Beck, 1996) 204–8, 832.

14. Frantz Fanon, *Black Skin, White Masks*, transl. Charles Lam Markham (1952; London: Pluto Press, 1986) 63.

15. Kanaganayakam, "'Broadening the Substrata,'" 24.

16. Vassanji himself points out that "the CN Tower represents the city. It also represents concrete, and it sends out signals. It somehow represented the mystery and the possibilities of the city, a mystery that one could not understand. [. . .] Plus, as a symbol of commercialism. It is like the daily ritual of going to a temple, worshipping, and coming back." Kanaganayakam, "'Broadening the Substrata,'" 32.

17. Kanaganayakam has first drawn attention to the importance of Fitzgerald's novel as an intertext for Vassanji's novel, without however elaborating on how exactly Vassanji's version echoes or departs from *The Great Gatsby*. Kanaganayakam, "Don Mills and Dar es Salaam," 201. Cf. also Kanaganayakam, "'Broadening the Substrata,'" 31.

18. F Scott Fitzgerald, *The Great Gatsby* (1925; Ware: Wordsworth Classics, 1993) 163.

19. Bissoondath, *Selling Illusions*, 110.

20. Malak, "Ambivalent Affiliations," 280.

21. For a different reading that holds that the text ends on a bleak note cf. Nancy Burke, "Mixing Memory and Desire: MJ [sic] Vassanji and the South Asian Novel in Canada," *Writing Canadians: The Literary Construction of Ethnic Identities*, eds. Martin Küster and Wolfram R Keller (Marburg: Universitätsbibliothek Marburg, 2002) 102–3.

22. Vassanji talking about his novel: "And there are two other younger characters who more or less have escaped the past because they are younger and they have been educated in the West or in the western style." Nasta, "Interview: Moyez Vassanji," 21. Cf. also Ball, "Taboos," 206. See also Burke, 103.

23. Bissoondath, 111.

24. "They will acquire friends of various backgrounds who share their experience, some of them will intermarry, and most if not all will blend into the mainstream of the society around them, itself already irrevocably changed. They will, in a word, integrate." Bissoondath, 111.

25. Although Vassanji maintains that the price they pay is lower than the one paid by the adult characters fully socialized within the values of the old country and with an abundance of memories. Cf. Ball, "Taboos," 206.

26. Bissoondath, 111.

27. Bissoondath, 111.

28. Strategic racism is a term inspired by Spivak's concept of strategic essentialism.

29. Neil Bissoondath: "It is unjust, to individuals and to the communities from which they emerged, to require it [i.e. immigration] to be about stasis. To do so is to legitimize marginalization; it is to turn ethnic communities into museums of exoticism." Bissoondath, 111.

30. Victor J Ramraj, "Diasporas and Multiculturalism," *New National and Post-Colonial Literatures: An Introduction*, ed. Bruce King (Oxford: Clarendon Press, 1996) 228.

B. 'There': Transforming Difference. *The Book of Secrets* (1994)

1. See also John Clement Ball, "Locating MG Vassanji's *The Book of Secrets*: Postmodern,

Poscolonial, or Other-wise?" *Floating the Borders: New Contexts in Canadian Criticism*, ed. Nurjehan Aziz (Toronto: TSAR, 1999) 90.

2. MG Vassanji, *The Book of Secrets* (1994; Toronto: McClelland & Stewart, 1997) 28–9. All references are to this edition.

3. For the relationship between literature and historiography see also Dominick LaCapra, *History, Politics, and the Novel* (Ithaca: Cornell UP, 1987) 7–9 and Michel de Certeau, *Das Schreiben der Geschichte*, transl. Sylvia M Schomburg-Scherff (Frankfurt/Main: Campus Verlag, 1991) 53. Hayden White argues that "the very distinction between real and imaginary events, basic to modern discussions of both history and fiction, presupposes a notion of reality in which 'the true' is identified with 'the real' only insofar as it can be shown to possess the character of narrativity." Hayden White, "The Value of Narrativity in the Representation of Reality," *Critical Inquiry* 7 (1980): 10. See also Hayden White, *Metahistory: The Historical Imagination in Nineteenth-Century Europe* (Baltimore: Johns Hopkins UP, 1973) and Hayden White, *The Content of the Form: Narrative Discourse and Historical Representation* (Baltimore: Johns Hopkins UP, 1987). While White discusses specimens of non-narrative as well as narrative historical accounts, Michel de Certeau stresses that history, like a narrative, is always produced, i.e. man-made, and not self-evident. Every acceptable historical narration for him must be self-reflexive. Cf. de Certeau, 62. See also Horst Steinmetz, *Literatur und Geschichte: 4 Versuche* (München: Iudicium, 1988) 32–3. Dominick LaCapra underlines that it is not only historiography that owes to fiction but that fiction can also borrow from history. Dominick LaCapra, "Geistesgeschichte und Interpretation," *Geschichte Denken: Neubestimmung und Perspektiven moderner europäischer Geistesgeschichte*, transl. Hans Günter Holl (Frankfurt/Main: Fischer, 1988) 71. For an overview of postmodern historiographic theories, see Christian Simon, *Historiographie: Eine Einführung* (Stuttgart: Ulmer, 1996) 278ff.

4. For the following cf. Moritz Baßler, "Einleitung," *New Historicism: Literaturgeschichte als Poetik der Kultur*, ed. Moritz Baßler (Frankfurt/Main: Fischer, 1996) 7–29.

5. For an overview of the various concepts of intertextuality see Manfred Pfister, "Intertextualität," *Moderne Literatur in Grundbegriffen*, eds. Dieter Borchmeyer and Viktor m egac (Frankfurt/Main: Athenäum, 1987) 197–200. See also Manfred Pfister, "Konzepte der Intertextualität," *Intertextualität: Formen, Funktionen, anglistische Fallstudien*, eds. Manfred Pfister and Ulrich Broich (Tübingen: Niemeyer, 1985) 1–30.

6. Shane Rhodes, "Frontier Fiction: Reading Books in MG Vassanji's *The Book of Secrets*," *ARIEL* 29.1 (1998): 187.

7. For on overview of mise-en-abîme in postmodern fiction cf. Brian McHale, *Postmodernist Fiction* (London: Methuen, 1987) 124.

8. Derrida: "This was the moment when language invaded the universal problematic, the moment when, in the absence of a center or origin, everything became discourse—provided we can agree on this word—that is to say, a system in which the central signified, the original or transcendental signified, is never absolutely present outside a system of differences. The absence of the transcendetal signified extends the domain and the play of signification infinitely." Jacques Derrida, "Structure, Sign and Play in the Discourse of the Human Sciences," *Modern Criticism and Theory: A Reader*, ed. David Lodge, 10th ed. (1988; London: Longman, 1997) 110.

9. Wolfgang Iser, *Der Akt des Lesens: Theorie ästhetischer Wirkung*, 3rd ed. (1976; München: Wilhelm Fink, 1990) 267ff.

10. It should however not be assumed that Vassanji plays off elements of detective fiction in order to bridge popular and high-brow culture. See Leslie Fiedler, "Überquert die Grenze, Schließt den Graben! Über die Postmoderne," *Wege aus der Moderne: Schlüsseltexte der Postmoderne-Diskussion*, ed. and transl. Wolfgang Welsch, 2nd ed. (Berlin: Akademie Verlag, 1994) 57–74.

11. For Roland Barthes secrets are characteristic of literature in general: "Obviously it is in the interest of every narrative to delay the solution to the enigma it poses, since that solution will toll its death-knell as a narrative." Roland Barthes, "Textual Analysis: Poe's 'Valdemar,'" *Modern Criticism and Theory: A Reader*, ed. David Lodge, 10th ed. (London: Longman, 1997) 193.

12. I have in mind in particular the fiction of Thomas Pynchon, John Barth, or Donald Barthelme.

13. Arnold Gehlen, "Über kulturelle Kristallization," *Wege aus der Moderne: Schlüsseltexte der Postmoderne-Diskussion*, ed. Wolfgang Welsch, 2nd ed. (Berlin: Akademie-Verlag, 1994) 133–44.

14. On orientational metaphors cf. George Lakoff and Mark Johnson, *Metaphors We Live By* (1980; Chicago: Chicago UP, 1994) 14.

15. Raymond Federman, *Surfiction: Der Weg der Literatur. Hamburger Poetik-Lektionen*, transl. Peter Torberg (1991; Frankfurt/Main: Edition Suhrkamp, 1992).

16. For Rhodes, books in *The Book of Secrets* become the "simulacra of larger national and colonial scuffles." Rhodes, "Frontier Fiction," 187.

17. On the importance of the book for the colonial enterprise and for the postcolonial challenging of colonialism cf. Paul Goetsch, "Die Macht des Buches in kolonialer und postkolonialer Literatur," *Fiktion und Geschichte in der anglo-amerikanischen Literatur*, eds. Rüdiger Ahrens and Fritz-Wilhelm Neumann (Heidelberg: Winter, 1998) 515.

18. For a different reading cf. Rhodes, "Frontier Fiction," 184.

19. Tirop Peter Simatei, *The Novel and the Politics of Nation Building in East Africa* (Bayreuth: Bayreuth African Studies 55, 2001) 82.

20. Linda Hutcheon, *The Politics of Postmodernism* (London: Routledge, 1989) 142.

21. also Shane Rhodes: "We cannot say for instance that Fernandes' narrative is simply a reverse discourse, in the Foucauldian sense, and an inversion of some slave/master hierarchy. This would necessarily ignore not only Fernandes's particular appropriation but the special relationship that Indians in East Africa have had with the British colonizers as being both ruled subjects but also an important part of the colonizing structure itself." Rhodes, "Frontier Fiction," 182. Pius story defies categorization as counterdiscursive for another reason, too. His identification with Corbin may in part be due to Corbin's moderate administration in the context of the British system of Indirect Rule, an important part of the colonising structure Rhodes refers to. For an account of the objectives of Indirect Rule and its architect Lord Lugard cf. Wolfgang Klooß, *Die englische Kulturpolitik und die Tragik des Kulturkonflikts in den Afrikaromanen von Joyce Cary* (Frankfurt/Main: Peter Lang, 1976) 74–97.

22. Vassanji's novel here lends itself to a Bachtinian analysis. According to Bakhtin the novel presents us with a multitude of voices which are orchestrated in a dialogical relation to each other. Ideological formations are countered by the subversive force of voices not totally under the artist's control. This is precisely what happens to Pius when trying to write a history that is really a piece of fiction. He fails to (re)construct an ideological, because monolithic, history of Tanzania because the voices he includes refuse to be subordinated under the logic of his history/story. Michail Bachtin, *Die Ästhetik des Wortes*, ed. Rainer Grübel, transl. Rainer Grübel and Sabine Reese (Frankfurt/Main: Edition Suhrkamp, 1979) 165.

23. Vassanji, "The Postcolonial Writer," 64.

24. Vassanji, "The Postcolonial Writer," 63.

25. Lawrence Coupe, *Myth* (London: Routledge, 1997) 4.

26. In this sense, reading magic psychologically, as Ball does, misses the point. Ball, "Locating," 92.

27. Philip Smith, *Cultural Theory: An Introduction* (Malden: Blackwell, 2001) 198–201.

28. Simon Lewis, "Impossible Domestic Situations: Questions of Identity and Nationalism in the Novels of Abdulrazak Gurnah and MG Vassanji," *Thamyris* 6 (1999): 226.

29. In contrast to this, Ball thinks that magic cannot be read as an element which throws into question the text's postmodern implications. Ball, "Locating," 92.

30. "Realism," *The Penguin Dictionary of Literary Terms and Literary Theory*, 1991 ed.

31. As Ball points out, "the broad historical sweep of [...] [*The Book of Secrets*'] recuperative, referential project can be seen as paradigmatically postcolonial." Ball, "Locating," 96.

32. Jameson, 69.

33. For Tirop Peter Simatei and for Simon Lewis *The Book of Secrets* is of relevance only for a

community, not a nation. Simatei, 77–103 and Lewis, 217. For a different reading cf. Ball, "Locating," 99.

34. Georg Lukacs, *The Historical Novel*, transl. Hannah and Stanley Mitchell (1937; Boston: Beacon, 1963) 30–63. As far as the realist historical novel is concerned, Scott is still regarded as the authoritative source, Cf. Harold Orel, *The Historical Novel from Scott to Sabatini: Changing Attitudes toward a Literary Genre, 1814–1920* (NY: St. Martin's P, 1995) 6.

35. Franz K Stanzel, *Theorie des Erzählens*, 7th ed. (1979; Göttingen: Vandenhoeck and Ruprecht, 2001) 81–5.

36. Ball, 98. In Brian McHale's terminology, adding to history's store of knowledge in such a way is called "apocryphal history." McHale, 90.

37. For an account of the history of the Ismailis and their beliefs cf. Werner Schmucker, "Sekten und Sondergruppen," *Der Islam in der Gegenwart*, eds. Werner Ende and Udo Steinbach, 4th ed. (München: CH Beck, 1996) 667–74, JND Anderson, "The Khoja Ismailis of East Africa," *Middle Eastern Studies* 1 (1964): 21–39, and Charles Ponnuthurai Sarvan, "Ethnicity and Alienation: the African Asian and His Response to Africa," *The Journal of Commonwealth Literature* 20.1 (1985): 101–10. See also the following two web pages (both of which were accessed on 15th August 2002): <http://www.muslimindia.com/comu.htm> and <http://www-personal-umich.edu/~vika/Teach-Port /islam00/esposito/chapt2.html>.

38. The difference between Sunni and Shiia Islam lies in the different belief as to who was to follow the prophet Muhammad as spiritual leader of the umma, i.e. the community of Muslims. While the Sunnites contend that the caliph, literally for Muhammad's successor, is not directed by God in his doings, Shiites believe that the leader of the umma is guided by God directly if it is a member of Muhammad's family. As this was only the case for Ali, the majority of the Shiites regard the leaders of the umma as usurpers, which renders the Shiite view of power and government pessimistic. In contrast to the large Shiite communities in Iran and Iraq, the Ismailies believe that the seventh Imam currently lies in hiding. With his eventual reappearance, however, he will solve the contradiction between the outward and inward side of the Koran. The Ismailis, who are also called Sevener Shiites, do not believe that the Koran is unalterable in its entirety. They distinguish between "zahir," i.e. the obvious meaning of the revelation, and "batin," i.e. the mystic essence and eternal truth of the revelation which can be made evident through interpretation. While "batin" is eternal, "zahir" is mutable and temporary. Such a view is considered as heretical in the eyes of many an orthodox Muslim. Cf. "Ismailiten," *Islam-Lexikon: Geschichte—Ideen—Gestalten*, 1991 ed. See also Werner Ende, "Der schiitische Islam," *Der Islam in der Gegenwart*, eds. Werner Ende and Udo Steinbach, 4th ed. (München: CH Beck, 1996) 70–89.

39. Vassanji explains that he invented a community in order to have the aesthetic freedom to slightly change the traditions of the Khoja Ismailis when necessary. Cf. Rhodes, "Interview," 116.

40. Schmucker, 669.

41. Ball, "Locating," 99.

42. They frequently worked as railway builders and plantation workers. Cf. Charles Ponnuthurai Sarvan, "The Asians in African Literature," *The Journal of Commonwealth Literature* 11.1 (1976): 160.

43. John Iliffe, *A Modern History of Tanzania* (Cambridge: CUP, 1977) 140. Referring to Vassanji's work as a whole, Birbalsingh argues with respect to the struggle of the Shamsis: "This is Vassanji's achievement: that he objectively shows the Shamsis [. . .] to be preoccupied mainly with survival and therefore not greatly with moral niceties." Birbalsingh, 165.

44. also Lewis, 223.

45. also Ball, "Locating," 97.

46. See also Lewis, 220.

47. Fanon, *Black Skin, White Masks*, 16, 18.

48. Ball, "Locating," 90, 92.

49. Ball, "Locating," 94, 101. Simon Lewis, while acknowledging the presence of both postcolonial and postmodern discourse in *The Book of Secrets*, argues a diametrically opposed case. For

him Vassanji's novel is a postmodern rather than a postcolonial text. Lewis, 224. He calls *The Book of Secrets* "misleadingly postcolonial." Lewis, 227.

50. This is a point even more strongly argued by Tirop Peter Simatei than by John Clement Ball. Simatei, 73–101.

51. Ball calls the poststructuralist doubts of *The Book of Secrets* "de rigeur." Ball, "Locating," 94.

52. Ashcroft et al, *Key Concepts*, 80.

53. If one follows Julia Kristeva's psychoanalytical analysis then even the self is made up of Others. Julia Kristeva, *Fremde sind wir uns selbst*, transl. Xenia Rajewsky (Frankfurt/Main: Edition Suhrkamp, 1990) 12. This is a point also underscored by others. Cf. Hahn, "Soziologie des Fremden," 24.

54. Lewis, 227.

Deconstructing Difference: Neil Bissoondath

1. For the following cf. Penny van Toorn, "Neil Bissoondath," *Canadian Writers and their Works: Fiction Series*, eds. Robert Lecker, Jack David and Ellen Quigley (Toronto: ECW Press, 1996) 25–36.

A. 'Here': Multiculturalism and its Discontents. *The Innocence of Age* (1992)

1. Araminta Wordsworth, "Novel shuns Toronto's 'world-class' hype," review of *The Innocence of Age*, by Neil Bissoondath, *Financial Post* 26 Oct. 1992: S8.

2. Neil Bissoondath, *The Innocence of Age* (Toronto: Alfred A Knopf, 1992) 230. All references are to this edition.

3. This is also confirmed by Espinet in her unfavourable review of the novel. She fails to perceive, however, that the use of the family is put to a specifically deconstructive use. Ramabai Espinet, "The Old and the New," rev. of *The Innocence of Age*, by Neil Bissoondath, *Floating the Borders: New Contexts in Canadian Criticism*, ed. Nurjehan Aziz (Toronto: TSAR, 1999) 210.

4. Whereas I argue that Bissoondath, in contrast to Wharton emphasizes age over innocence, Margery Fee suggests a different intepretation. Cf. Margery Fee, "Introduction," Lecker et al, 13. Concentrating on the shortcomings of the society as depicted by Wharton, she links the title of Bissoondath's novel with the old, more innocent, and the new, rather corrupt, Toronto. However, she overlooks that rather than being a proper rewriting of Edith Wharton's classic novel of New York city life, *The Innocence of Age* is a variation on several of its themes. For one thing, Wharton, like Bissoondath, explores the interrelatedness of community and individual. Newland Archer and Madame Olenska, although interested in each other, both eventually conform to the old New York code of behaviour and social conduct. While Wharton is sympathetic to her characters' desires, Bissoondath takes issue with the norms of society and community and writes in favour of the individual more radically than Wharton, although she also raises uncomfortable questions about the old New York. Secondly, *The Age of Innocence* can be read as the story of a failed assimilation, and as such becomes a negative foil for Bissoondath. Madame Olenska, Polish immigrant into America and outsider within New York upper-class society, wants "to cast off all my old life, to become just like everybody else here" (87). She "hate[s] to be different!" (88) She desires for a place where she and Newton are "simply two human beings who love each other, who are the whole of life to each other" (238). Cf. Edith Wharton, *The Age of Innocence*, ed. Cynthia Griffin Wolff (1920; NY: Penguin, 1996). In contrast to *The Age of Innocence*, *The Innocence of Age*, while also including stories like that of Sita, does not generally rule out the possibility of switching ethnicities. A case in point is Montgomery's son.

5. Penny van Toorn, "Positioning Neil Bissoondath: Post-Colonial, Multicultural and National Formations." *New Literatures Review* 27 (1994): 87.

6. van Toorn, "Neil Bissoondath," 64–5. For Giangrande, the novel's central conflict is merely that of the "old genteel Toronto," represented by Pasco, and the "new multicultural city of cold glitz

and destitution." Carole Giangrande, "Urban Logos," rev. of *The Innocence of Age*, by Neil Bissoondath, *Books in Canada* 22.1 (1993): 43.

7. van Toorn: "By writing an ethnic novel centring on people customarily perceived as nonethnic, he implicitly 'ethnifies' the dominant cultural group. *The Innocence of Age* is, in fact, Bissoondath's most concerted attempt to date to break out of the migrant or ethnic stereotype." Penny van Toorn, "Neil Bissoondath," 64.

8. Although sometimes, "whenever he impersonates the powerful, wealthy, entrepreneurial self of his fantasies," he calls himself Nathaniel Price. Penny van Toorn, "Positioning," 88. The fear of belittlement and a consequent challenge to his self-aggrandizement is also why Daniel dislikes Mr Simmons calling him 'Dano.'

9. Bissoondath admits that he is "fearful of people over-reacting: screaming racism simply because the two people involved happen to be of difference races or different colours." While he regards racism as a problem, he argues against giving it privileged status: "We always have to worry about racism, as we do with any social problem." Moreover, while racism is troublesome, invoking it too easily has the effect of rendering harmless what truly deserves to be called racist: "I'm afraid of people overusing the word. I got tired of the screams of racism. I'm very wary of that because there are truly racist incidents—but if you cry wolf often enough, people will not pay attention anymore, and racism is such a powerful charge, it's got to be reserved for when it clearly is needed." Aruna Srivastava, interview with Neil Bissoondath, *Other Solitudes: Canadian Multicultural Fictions,* eds. Linda Hutcheon and Marion Richmond (Toronto: OUP, 1990) 315.

10. Kurt defends an old Ukrainian lady against skinheads. While Ramabai Espinet criticizes this as "the long arm of coincidence" that is "disconcertingly present" in the novel, she overlooks that what smells of narrative improbability is, in fact, a functional device. A black man is accidentally killed by one of the few emphatically nonracist characters in the book, accidentally a white man. Espinet, 208.

11. That Bissoondath has a black character make this point has irritated critics. Ramabai Espinet's claim that "Montgomery's son" [is] a Ryerson engineering student and also an unmistakable nerd" is not only predicated upon speculation but also beside the point. Espinet, 210.

12. "Dancing" was published in Bissoondath's collection of short stories *Digging up the Mountains* (1985). In 1986 it won him the McClelland and Stewart Award for Fiction at the Canadian National Magazine Awards. The CBC later decided to turn it into a full-length film for which Bissoondath himself wrote the screenplay. Andrew Garrod, "Neil Bissoondath," *Speaking for Myself: Canadian Writers in Interview*, ed. Andrew Garrod (St. John: Breakwater Books, 1986) 55.

13. Bissoondath, *Selling Illusions*, 135.

14. van Toorn, "Positioning Neil Bissoondath," 84.

15. Srivastava, 319.

16. This renders Bissoondath's texts markedly different from Vassanji's *No New Land* which also concerns itself with an unconscious form of racism.

17. van Toorn, "Positioning Neil Bissoondath," 84.

18. Neil Bissoondath, *Digging up the Mountains* (1985; NY: Viking, 1986) 208. All references are to this edition.

19. van Toorn, "Positioning Neil Bissoondath," 85.

20. van Toorn, "Positioning Neil Bissoondath," 85.

21. van Toorn, "Positioning Neil Bissoondath," 85.

B. 'There' I: An Area of Darkness. *A Casual Brutality* (1988)

1. Birbalsingh, 163. Kureishi calls this "a bad case of Naipaulitis: there is decay, corruption, sordor, filth and revolution everywhere." Cf. Hanif Kureishi, "Return to Casaquemada," rev. of *A Casual Brutality*, by Neil Bissoondath, *New Statesman and Society*, 16th September 1988: 42. As a matter of fact, *A Casual Brutality* has been frequently compared with the works of VS Naipaul. Lanchester and Morris see parallels between Bissoondath's first novel and Naipaul's *A Bend in the*

River. Cf. John Lanchester, "Foreigners," rev. of *A Casual Brutality*, by Neil Bissoondath, *London Review of Books* 5th January 1989: 22, and Mervyn Morris, "Going to Extremes and Other Tales of the New World," rev. of *A Casual Brutality*, by Neil Bissoondath, *Washington Post Book World* 22nd January 1989: 4. Keneally, on the other hand, thinks that Bissoondath's first novel is not indebted to Naipaul's work but is a piece of art in its own right. Thomas Keneally, "Home Is Where the Death Squads Are," rev. of *A Casual Brutality*, by Neil Bissoondath, *New York Times Book Review* 26th February 1989: 14. For an argument that balances Bissoondath's indebtedness to his uncle with the originality of his art see Boyd Holmes, "Dislocations," rev. of *A Casual Brutality*, by Neil Bissoondath, and *Swimming Lessons and Other Stories from Firozsha Baag*, by Rohinton Mistry, *Fiddlehead* 162 (1989): 109.

2. van Toorn, "Neil Bissoondath," 31.

3. Many critics have accused Neil Bissoondath of his treatment of (colonial) Caribbean history. Cf. Marlene Nourbese Philip, "Immoral Fiction," 190, and Hena Maes-Jelinek and Bénédicte Ledent, "The Novel Since 1970," *A History of Literature in the Caribbean*, ed. A James Arnold, vol. 2 (Amsterdam: John Benjamins Publishing Company, 2001) 167.

4. Birbalsingh, 164. In contrast to Birbalsingh, Marlene Nourbese Philip, in her review of the novel, thinks that "Bissoondath ignores the exploration of powerful themes such as exile and alienation to pander to the insatiable appetite of North America for 'Third World' violence." Marlene Nourbese Philip, "Immoral Fiction," 193. For a different opinion cf. Keneally, 14.

5. Neil Bissoondath, *A Casual Brutality* (1986; Toronto: MacMillan, 1988) 63. All references are to this edition.

6. van Toorn, "Neil Bissoondath," 59. For Patricia Harkins the garden of Raj's grandfather also "becomes a symbol of the neglect the entire island is suffering." Patricia Harkins, rev. of *A Casual Brutality*, by Neil Bissoondath, *Caribbean Writer On Line* [sic] 5 March 2002 <http:www://thecaribbeanwriter.com/volume4/v4p109.html>.

7. van Toorn, 59–60.

8. "Wald," *Wörterbuch der Symbolik*, 1991 ed.

9. Etymologically as well as semantically culture is a complex word. It can mean several things, depending on context and time of usage. Here the term culture is to denote building and agriculture in particular. The religious dimension of worship that the Latin root word 'cultura' also entails is reflected, too, albeit later and only indirectly—in the reverence cultural artefacts and efforts at cultivation deserve in the eyes of a Raj who is alienated from indigenous Caribbean nature (cf. 17). For on overview of the various definitions of culture cf. Klaus P Hansen, *Kultur und Kulturwissenschaft*, 2nd ed. (1995; München: Fink, 2000) 11–19.

10. "Wald," *Wörterbuch der Symbolik*, 1991 ed.

11. By charging the island's nature with sexual overtones, Raj's depiction becomes reminiscent of colonial discourse which often imagined the culturally alien as sexual Other. Some critics have labelled *A Casual Brutality* a racist text, and this is indeed one of the few instances of the novel where the narrator Raj acts the part of the colonizer. For Bissoondath's alleged racism cf. Marlene Nourbese Philip, "Immoral Fiction," 198. See also Penny van Toorn, "Positioning," 78–9. For a diametrically opposed reading stressing that Bissoondath's novel is anything but racist see Thorpe, "'Turned Inside Out,'" 9 and van Toorn, "Neil Bissoondath," 5.

12. While Marlene Nourbese Philip admits that "Bissoondath's treatment of landscape, though limited, is significant," she blames the novel's protagonist for the underlying assumptions informing his representation of nature: "This, of course, all of a piece with a character who has no attachment to the land of his birth, from which he is completely alienated." Marlene Nourbese Philip, "Immoral Fiction," 195. She refuses to acknowledge that such an attitude is perfectly in order for a literary character. She is more interested in what the novel leaves out than what it presents us with. In her eagerness to look for socio-historic factors she overlooks that Raj's attitude towards his native country is at the centre of the novel. Methodically, her deconstructive impetus reduces her ability to 'understand' the novel (in the hermeneutic sense of the word). *A Casual Brutality* is no national allegory but primarily a private story. Cf. also Morris, 4.

13. van Toorn, "Neil Bissoondath," 59.

14. van Toorn, "Neil Bissoondath," 58.

15. In this context it is a misunderstanding that Bissoondath "represents phenomena such as violence, displacement, cultural breakdown, sexual and economic exploitation as universal human themes and experiences," as Penny van Toorn summarizes the critical evaluation of Bissoondath's work. Penny van Toorn, "Positioning," 78. Cf. also Morris, 4. However, at least with respect to violence and *A Casual Brutality* Bissoondath is quite specific, although his specificity may not be politically correct: Violence in his first novel is closely linked to the Caribbean setting of Casaquemada. While Canada may also be racist, it certainly allows for more political and existential stability and security.

16. for example, David Richards, "Burning Down the House: Neil Bissoondath's Fiction," *Narrative Strategies in Canadian Literature: Feminism and Postcolonialism*, ed. Carol-Ann Howells (Milton Keynes: Open UP, 1991) 59.

17. Eliot himself relied on a famous pretext that interpreted hollowness in a political context, Shakespeare's *Julius Caesar*. (cf. IV.ii.23).

18. TS Eliot, "The Hollow Men," *The Norton Anthology of English Literature*, eds. MH Abrams and Stephen Greenblatt, 7th ed., vol.2 (NY: Norton & Company, 2000) 2386.

19. Michael Thorpe, "'Turned Inside Out,'" 8.

20. "After settling in the Caribbean for one hundred and fifty years, Indians may be forced to emigrate, in which case the Caribbean would have to be regarded just as a stopover for them, on their journey from India to other destinations." Birbalsingh, 162. While Birbalsingh's diagnosis as to the necessity to move is accurate, he arguably thinks too much in terms ethnic collectives. Raj merely represents himself and not his community; he is alienated from his community as well as from the notion of community and what it entails.

21. Keneally, 14.

22. Bissoondath himself points out that Casaquemada's situation has relevance for the Caribbean at large: Casaquemada is a "mixture of Guyana, Trinidad, Jamaica, Grenada." Cf. van Toorn, "Building on Common Ground," 130. Thorpe, on the other hand, suggests that Bissoondath's Casaquemada is a thinly veiled account of Trinidad in the early 1970s. Cf. Michael Thorpe, "Making Waves Against the Mainstream," 140. His argument is important in that it counters claims which denounce Bissoondath as racist and forgetful of history and context. However, while Bissoondath, according to Thorpe, does reflect contemporary Caribbean history and society in his novel, the most important context for the text is said to be autobiographical. Within such a reading Raj becomes Bissoondath's alter ego. See also van Toorn, "Neil Bissoondath," 30. Similarly, Côté emphasizes that the novel is by no means oblivious of political circumstances but too complex to be captured by partial readings. Marc Côté, "Hopes or Illusions," rev. of *A Casual Brutality*, by Neil Bissoondath, *Canadian Forum* Feb.–March 1989: 31.

23. Marlene Nourbese Philip identifies several flaws in Bissoondath's text, the most severe of which is said to be its lack of socio-historic specificity. It is this social amnesia renders the novel immoral for her. Cf. Marlene Nourbese Philip, "Immoral Fiction," 190. However, it is doubtful whether her reading does justice to the text. While it is not true that the novel fails to contextualize—apart from the fact that it veils its account of Trinidadian postcolonial policy by naming its setting Casaquemada—immorality for Philip lies in Bissoondath artistic treatment of (immoral) actions!

24. David Richards argues that *A Casual Brutality* is a postcolonial novel informed by the postmodern insight into the unreliability of representations. While *A Casual Brutality* is a realist novel for van Toorn, Richards suggests that the novel is mock-realist but eventually rejects mimesis and totality. Thus Raj looks at maps but cannot position himself spatially. Furthermore, the novel's structure suggests that the postcolonial subject cannot be located by way of (colonial) history. The novel questions realism ex negativo by enacting an epistemological crisis in its protagonist. Cf. Richards, "Burning Down the House," 56. See also van Toorn, "Neil Bissoondath," 40 and David Richards, "'A History of Interruptions': Dislocated Mimesis in the Writings of Neil Bissoondath

and Ben Okri," *From Commonwealth to Post-Colonial*, ed. Anna Rutherford (Sydney: Dangaroo Press, 1992) 74–5.

25. Malak takes this as an indicator that "the racial conflict does not totally polarize the novel's characters." Amin Malak, "Postcolonial Anguish," rev. of *A Casual Brutality*, by Neil Bissoondath, *Canadian Literature* 128 (1991): 198.

26. The arguments put forward against *A Casual Brutality* are also levelled against Neil Bissoondath personally. For an overview cf. van Toorn, "Positioning Neil Bissoondath," 78 and Maes-Jelinek and Ledent, 167.

27. While Richards also identifies individualism as one discourse of difference in *A Casual Brutality*, it is postmodernism and its epistemological critique which constitutes the second discourse of difference in the novel. Although two discourses of difference were revealed to be inscribed by Vassanji in *The Book of Secrets*, too, the function towards which they were employed was fundamentally different. For Richards in *A Casual Brutality* individualism merely correlates with the representational crisis of realism: "Thus isolated from his social role, his class and his community, the individual can neither control the representations language throws up nor embrace its history." Richards, "Burning Down the House," 59.

28. Malak, "Postcolonial Anguish," 198.

29. In an interview Bissoondath testifies to his belief in universalism: "Well yes, there are universal themes. The universality of human emotion in the end will inform all of my writing. The writer in Afghanistan whose son is killed by a Russian bullet, she feels the same pain as the mother in Latin America whose son is killed by an American bullet. That pain is the same. [. . .] And this is the universality. When you strip away all the exoticism of different societies, you come down to the same basic naked emotions." van Toorn, "Building on Common Ground," 133.

30. Malak, "Postcolonial Anguish," 198.

31. For an opposed reading see Richards, "Burning Down the House," 59.

32. While for Marc Côté it is precisely the "shifts in tone from innocence to experience" that make *A Casual Brutality* a first-class novel, Holmes takes issue with the time structure of the novel. Cf. Côté, 31 and Holmes, 111. Penny van Toorn, reviewing the criticism on Bissoondath's first novel, points out that the novel's time structure and its point of view display an affinity with the dramatic monologue. van Toorn, "Neil Bissoondath," 56. However, while the style of the novel is often lyrical and its effect ironic, a first-person narrator who narrates the action on looking back is not sufficient to justify such an assessment. While van Toorn is accurate in pinpointing the irony of Bissoondath's novel, this irony seems to be less a matter of its mode of presentation than of the detached attitude of its speaker, the latter of which is, of course, not exclusive to the dramatic monologue.

C. 'There' II: Hurt and Healing. *The Worlds Within Her* (1999)

1. In that respect, *The Worlds Within Her* displays striking similarities to Graham Swift's Booker Prize winning novel *Last Orders*, in which the motif of returning and scattering the ashes of a friend also leads to remembrances that force the protagonists to critically reevaluate their self-images. Cf. Graham Swift, *Last Orders* (London: Picador, 1996).

2. According to Linda Hutcheon, both feminism and postcolonialism are intent on tracking down agency. Hutcheon, "'Circling the Downspout of Empire,'" 150.

3. van Toorn, "Building on Common Ground," 133.

4. Benedict Anderson, *Imagined Communities: Reflections on the Origin and Spread of Nationalism* (1983; London: Verso, 1991).

5. For a critique of the myth of the 'homeland' cf. Salman Rushdie, "Imaginary Homelands," *Imaginary Homelands: Essays and Criticism 1981–1991* (London: Granta, 1991) 19.

6. For more on postmodern epistemologies cf. Richard Tarnas, *Idee und Leidenschaft: Die Wege des westlichen Denkens*, transl. Eckhard E Sohns (1991; Frankfurt/Main: Zweitausendeins, 1997) 500.

7. Ngugi wa Thiong'o, *Decolonising the Mind: The Politics of Language in African Literature* (London: James Curry, 1994). Although the concept has specific reference to an (East-)African context, the term has become a catch-all phrase of postcolonial criticism.

8. It is crucial to notice that Bissoondath's feminism, contrary to Hutcheon's observation, is not interested in who did what to whom. Shakti's and Yasmin's accounts are autobiographical accounts whose confessional overtones resist essentialist agendas.

9. "Shakti," *Lexikon der Indischen Mythology: Mythen, Sagen und Legenden von A–Z*, eds. and transl. Michael Görden and Hans Christian Meiser (Wien: Seehamer Verlag, 1997).

10. For an overview of the psychologically and normative definitions of culture, see Alfred L Kroeber and Clyde Kluckhohn, *Culture: A Critical Review of Concepts and Definitions* (New York: Vintage, 1963) 101–2, 105–8. Kroeber and Kluckhohn state that a psychological definition that sees culture merely as a problem-solving device is inadequate because it is unable to theorise that culture itself might become a problem (cf. 110). This is precisely what happens to Bissoondath's protagonists.

11. Celia Sankar, "Neil Bissoondath: Hungering For An Imperfect Homeland," interview with Neil Bissoondath, *Sunday Guardian* 25 Feb. 2001, 5 March 2002 <http://www. nalis. gov.tt// Biography/NeilBissoondath.htm>.

12. Shakti's also refers to an intertextual foil for her migrant existence, namely *The Wizard of Oz*: "Dorothys live in places called Kansas, and they get swept up by things called twisters. They are tossed hither and yon [. . .] Now Dorothys—Dorothys have their lives turned upside down these twisters. They find themselves in situations that make no sense in your world. They meet, and must accept, tin men and cowardly lions. They encounter beings both good and evil, and sometimes they triumph, sometimes not. And sometimes, when the twister has returned them to their world, they have no idea which way things have gone" (8).

13. Mary Louise Pratt, *Imperial Eyes: Travel Writing and Transculturalism* (London: Routledge, 1992) 4.

14. "A *testimonio* is a novel or novella-length narrative told in the first person by a narrator who is also the actual protagonist or witness of the events she or he recounts. The unit of narration is usually a life or a significant life episode, such as the experience of being a prisoner. Since in many cases the narrator is someone who is either functionally illiterate, or, if literate, not a professional writer or intellectual, the production of a testimonio generally involves the recording, transcription and editing of an oral account by an interlocutor who is a journalist, writer or social activist." Ashcroft et al, *Key Concepts*, 230.

15. An example for this is the overdetermined and contradictory picture we get of Myra in Shakti's and Penny's accounts (cf. 91–94).

16. Therefore, strictly speaking, Jin David Kim is wrong in arguing that "under the guise of merely interring her mother Shakti's ashes, the three-day haj is the return of a culturally-starved daughter of Trinidad, a journey of rediscovering her roots." As Bissoondath confirms in the same publication, it is not so much a matter of yearning for a homeland than coming to a realization that home is elsewhere. Jin David Kim, "The Worlds Within Neil," interview with Neil Bissoondath, *Varsity Staff* 24 July 2001, 5 March 2002 <http://www.varsity. utoronto.ca/archives /119/oct29/review/the.html>.

17. It can hardly be overemphasized that for Bissoondath this is a call for a balanced stance and not a neocolonial position that preaches humanism only to practice racism.

18. As such, Bissoondath's novels also work towards demystifying the deceptive attraction of communitarianism, which falsely accuses individualism of atomism and blames it for the erosion of the ties that hold society together. Implicitly, rejecting an equation of individualism with asocial egoism, Bissoondath clarifies oppositions by pitting individualism against collectivism/communitarianism and not against altruism.

19. Structurally, Bissoondath's position resembles that of Victorian writers such as Elizabeth Gaskell or Charles Dickens. Concerned with social class as a category of difference, Gaskell and Dickens in their industrial novels also side with the individual and not with the collective. Cf.

Herbert Sussman, "Industrial," *A Companion to Victorian Literature and Culture*, ed. Herbert F Tucker (Malden, MA: Blackwell, 1999) 250. In *Hard Times*, for example, Dickens's working-class protagonist refuses to join a trade union. The reason he is sympathetically presented is precisely because he values individual difference over collective difference and acts accordingly. While in *Hard Times* individual difference is linked to a (Christian) humanism, the collective is associated with violent aggression and revolution

20. van Toorn, "Building on Common Ground," 132.

21. This is a point confirmed by Frank Davey when he writes: "The concept of cultural appropriation has strong political appeal, being founded on analogies of theft and invoking the exploitation of the weak by the strong. However, it has weak epistemological grounds. Cultures are not essences to be stolen (or even, for that matter, essences to be 'preserved' by multiculturalism legislation), but complexes of activity continually constructed in language and action." Frank Davey, "The Literary Politics of Canadian Multiculturalism," *Multiculturalism in North America and Europe: Social Practices, Literary Visions*, eds. Hans Braun and Wolfgang Klooß (Trier: WVT, 1995) 109.

22. "Those who would keep voices apart in literature are the ones who want to bring them together by getting rid of apartheid." van Toorn, "Building on Common Ground," 133.

23. Srivastava, 315.

24. van Toorn, "Building on Common Ground," 134.

Transcending Difference: Rohinton Mistry

1. For the following account cf. Martin Genetsch, "Rohinton Mistry," *Dictionary of Literary Biography: 21st Century Canadian Writers*, ed. Christian Riegel [forthcoming].

A. 'Here': Towards a Hybrid Identity. *Tales from Firozsha Baag* (1987)

1. As the stories are thematically interlinked, some critics treat *Tales From Firozsha Baag* as a novel. Cf. Robert Ross, "Seeking and Maintaining Balance: Rohinton Mistry's Fiction," *World Literature Today* 73.2 (1999): 240. However, Ross not only overlooks that the short story cycle is a genre in its own right but also that it becomes functional for Mistry. It helps him study "a community caught in a cycle of restrictive traditions, economic needs, racial and religious tensions, as well as inner psychological conflicts." Amin Malak, "The Short Stories of Bharati Mukherjee and Rohinton Mistry," *Short Fiction in the New Literatures in English: Proceedings of the Nice Conference of the European Association for Commonwealth Literature and Language Studies*, ed. Jacqueline Bardolph (Nice: Faculté des Lettres & Sciences Humaines de Nice, 1988) 190.

2. The (Canadian-) Indian critic Uma Parameswaran argues: "The themes—of boyhood initiations, of everyday frustrations and of nostalgia—are universal but the details are essentially Indian, indeed essentially Parsi." Uma Parameswaran, "Landmark," rev. of *Tales From Firozsha Baag*, by Rohinton Mistry, *Floating the Borders: New Contexts in Canadian Criticism*, ed. Nurjehan Aziz (Toronto: TSAR, 1999) 184.

3. Nilufer Bharucha, "'When Old Tracks Are Lost': Rohinton Mistry's Fiction as Diasporic Discourse," *Journal of Commonwealth Literature* 30.2 (1995): 59.

4. The baag functions as a microcosm in much the same way as Khodadad Building does in *Such a Long Journey* and the flats do in *A Fine Balance* and *Family Matters*.

5. Despite all their eloquence the stories of Rohinton Mistry certainly do not "speak so eloquently for themselves," as Robert L Ross suggests, but are in need of explanation. Ross, 241.

6. Amin Malak who concludes that "Sarosh [. . .] is transformed into Sid on arrival in Toronto" overlooks the story's central concern, for "Squatter" is really about Sarosh's inability to transform. The change of names, which he himself rather than his friends opts for, reflects his desire to become Canadian but does not make a point about whether his rebirth is successful. As a matter of fact, it is not. Although Sarosh becomes Sid in Canada, his assimilation eventually fails. Amin

Malak, "Insider/Outsider Views on Belonging," 192. See also Amin Malak, "Images of India," rev. of *Tales From Firozsha Baag*, by Rohinton Mistry, *Canadian Literature* 119 (1988): 101.

7. Rohinton Mistry, *Swimming Lessons and Other Stories from Firozsha Baag* (1987; NY: Vintage, 1997) 153. All references are to this edition.

8. Ajay Heble, "'A Foreign Presence in the Stall': Towards a Poetics of Cultural Hybridity in Rohinton Mistry's Migration Stories," *Canadian Literature* 137 (1993): 52. Malak speaks of Sarosh's/Sid's "symbolic inability to perform his normal bodily functions." Malak, "Images of India," 101. See also Malak, "Insider/Outsider Views on Belonging," 193.

9. For a discussion of metonymy as a central strategy of postcolonial literatures cf. Ashcroft et al, *Empire*, 53. Although Ashcroft et al are mainly concerned with linguistic metonymy and argue that untranslated words inscribe cultural difference, their argument is nevertheless illuminating in our context. Despite the fact that the title of the story may carry a word that the common English reader is familiar with, it is the concept rather than the vocabulary that is foreign to the Western reader. A squatter in Mistry's story is no (illegal) settler or protester but a person engaging in a specific cultural practice the average reader is arguably unfamiliar with, i.e. defecating Indian style. Relying on homonyms, Mistry deliberately confuses the reader and defies a too narrow view of the semantics of the English language in a different cultural context.

10. Interestingly enough, as his toilet habits indicate, Sarosh's ethnicity is broadly Indian rather than specifically Parsi.

11. Rebirth is also the central preoccupation of "Swimming Lessons," which will be discussed below.

12. Ajay Heble writes that "his [Sarosh's/Sid's] goal is clearly assimilation." Heble, 54. While Sarosh/Sid has assimilation in mind, Nariman speaks of adaptation.

13. Mistry's narrative treatment has attracted some attention. Malak argues that in "Squatter" "humour prevails." Malak, "Images of India," 102. Tapping reads "Squatter" as a story employing scatology for reasons of pleasure solely. Tapping, who also points out Mistry's closeness to Swift, remarks that "the scatological visions of Jonathan Swift were never such unabashed fun." Craig Tapping, "South Asia/North America: New Dwellings and the Past," *Reworlding: The Literature of the Indian Diaspora*, ed. Emmanuel S Nelson (Westport, CT: Greenwood P, 1992) 45. Both readings do not go far enough. "Squatter," as an allegory of emigration/immigration, makes use of bodily functions in order to make a case for cultural difference, which precludes understanding Mistry's story as one that indulges in breaking taboos merely for the sake of breaking them .

14. Heble, 52.

15. Heble, 52.

16. Malak is inaccurate in claiming that it is merely the "dizzying world of Toronto" that irritates Sarosh/Sid. Malak, "Images of India," 102. For India has ceased to provide orientation, too.

17. Malak, "Images of India," 102. As a matter of fact, *Othello* surfaces time and again in Mistry oeuvre, *Such a Long Journey* and *Family Matters* being cases in point. A possible reason for the attractiveness of the Shakespearean intertext might be its universal applicability, as Vikram Kapur in *Family Matters* argues: "Shakespeare is like Bombay. In them both, you can find whatever you need—they contain the universe." Rohinton Mistry, *Family Matters* (London: Faber and Faber, 2002) 295.

18. This is the moral of the story-within-the-story especially designed to warn his listeners in the frame story from taking emigration too lightly. Nariman's verdict on Canadian multiculturalism and American melting pot is scathing. However, such a reading does not exhaust the complexity of "Squatter," for Nariman conveys a point that is of relevance not only to those of his listeners eager to leave India. The success stories of Vera and Dolly, preclude reading "Squatter" as a warning against going abroad in general. It is the way that life abroad is led that is important and that is the real concern of Mistry's story.

19. Heble, 54.

20. Heble, 57.

21. For Heble, Jamshed is a "proponent of assimilation theory. As an immigrant in the United

States, he has willingly renounced his ethnic heritage and taken on the values of Americans. As far as he is concerned, he has become *one of them*." Heble, 57.

22. For Heble, Jamshed's continued use of the Indian word ghati signals his continuing affiliation with India, and thus his reliance on what he pretends to hate. Following Ashcroft et al, Heble reads Jamshed's discourse as metonymically employing terms that inscribe ethnic difference. Heble, 59. She does not make explicit, however, that in Jamshed's case signalling Otherness is ironic because it is the opposite of what Jamshed intends to project.

23. Malak, "Insider/Outsider Views on Belonging," 194, or Malak, "Images of India," 102.

24. On the central importance in "Lend Me Your Light" cf. Bharucha, "'When Old Tracks Are Lost,'" 60.

25. Heble, 57.

26. Heble, 58.

27. Many critics have called "Lend Me Your Light" "unmistakably tragic" for this reason. Heble, 57. Cf. also Malak, "Insider/Outsider Views on Belonging," 194, or Malak, "Images of India," 102.

28. Malak, "Insider/Outsider Views on Belonging," 194, or Bharucha, "'When Old Tracks Are Lost,'" 60.

29. TS Eliot, *The Waste Land and Other Poems*, ed. Frank Kermode (Harmondsworth: Penguin, 1998) 62–3.

30. Alternatively, it could be argued that Kersi/Tiresias has lost the gift of prophecy. For the Tiresias that Kersi likens himself to is a debased Tiresias that, in accord with Eliot's vision in *The Waste Land*, is wasted and exhausted (cf. 'wrinkled [. . .] breasts'), old and merely a shadow of his former self. Possibly, Kersi compares himself to the dead Tiresias, who lives as a shadow in Hades and can only predict the future under special circumstances. Cf. "Tiresias," *Lexikon der antiken Mythen und Gestalten*, 1993 ed.

31. Leckie disagrees that Kersi's blindness does not enable him to see. For her seeing is tied up with memory: "Emigration, and the postcolonial experience itself, may give rise to certain forms of blindness (autobiographical or not), but it is out of this blindness that memory, rewriting, and refiguring the trope of blindness itself emerge." Barbara Leckie, *Rohinton Mistry and His Works* (Toronto: ECW Press, 1996) 4.

32. Malak, "Insider/Outsider Views on Belonging," 194, or Malak, "Images of India," 102. Leckie reminds that light in Mistry's story also puns on the protagonist's need to lighten his heavy moral load. Cf. Leckie, 31.

33. An indicator that signals the central importance of "Swimming Lessons" within Mistry's collection is that in 1989 an American publishing house decided to publish *Tales From Firozsha Baag* as *Swimming Lessons and Other Stories from Firozsha Baag*.

34. In this context, Bharucha's claim that "Swimming Lessons" is "set fully in Canada" is a gross distortion of the plot. Bharucha, "'When Old Tracks Are Lost,'" 61.

35. Thus "Swimming Lessons" is concerned with a theme similar to that of "Squatter," except that at the end of "Swimming Lessons" there remains hope that the immigrant may succeed in settling down in Canada.

36. Mistry's employs the microcosm of the baag in order to make two points. On the one hand, he inverts the social reality of the Parsis with a postcolonial agenda in mind, creating a world in which the tiny and demographically dwindling community of the Parsis constitute the majority and the dominant group. Secondly, he also details the problematic aspects of the baag as "ghetto-like Parsi world" with a "siege-mentality" or an "insular world" whose close network ties often prevent an active engagement with the larger social reality. Bharucha, "'When Old Tracks Are Lost,'" 59.

37. Kersi about Berthe: "It's exciting to listen to her, her words fall like rocks and boulders, and one can never tell where or how the next few will drop" (237).

38. Gregory McElwain, "Paddling Away From the Past: Alienation and Assimilation in Rohinton Mistry's 'Swimming Lessons,'" *Kobe College Studies* 41.2 (1994): 18. McElwain's article is the most comprehensive study of Mistry's story that is available so far.

39. the following passage in which two women are observed by Kersi from a relatively great distance: "Two women are sunbathing on the stretch of patchy lawn at the periphery of the parking lot. I can see them clearly from my kitchen. They're wearing bikinis and I'd love to take a closer look. But I have no binoculars. Nor do I have a car to saunter out to and pretend to look under the hood. They're both luscious and gleaming. From time to time they smear lotion over their skin, on the bellies, on the inside of the thighs, on the shoulders. Then one of them gets the other to undo the strings of her top and spread some there. She lies on her stomach with the straps undone. I wait. I pray that the heat and haze make her forget, when it's time to turn over, that the straps are undone" (232).

40. McElwain, 19.

41. For a comprehensive study of the West's image of the East cf. Said, *Orientalism*, 38–9.

42. McElwain mistakes Kersi's fantasy for a serious aspect of his "Indian heritage." He overlooks the neurotic aspects of Kersi's sexuality when he suggests that "the phrases the narrator uses to refer to himself—he's a 'non-white immigrant' with an 'Asian brown body'—indicate that his Indian heritage is a crucial part of his identity." McElwain, 18.

43. the following quote: "Mummy used to take good care of Grandpa, too, till things became complicated and he was moved to the Parsi General Hospital. Parkinsonism and osteoporosis laid him low. The doctor explained that Grandpa's hip did not break because he fell, but he fell because the hip, gradually growing brittle, snapped on that fatal day. That's what osteoporosis does, hollows out the bones and turns effect into cause. It has an unusually high incidence in the Parsi community, he said, but did not say why. Just one of those mysterious things. We are the chosen people where osteoporosis is concerned. And divorce. The Parsi community has the highest divorce rate in India. It also claims to be the most westernized community in India. Which is the result of the other? Confusion again, of cause and effect" (230).

44. McElwain, 20.

45. Craig Tapping's reading of the symbolism of "Swimming Lessons" seems reductive, He suggests that water, apart from offering Mistry an opportunity to let his protagonist engage in sexual fantasies, mainly alludes to "overwhelming tides (of migration) or waves (of immigrants)." Tapping overlooks the existential quality that water imagery in "Swimming Lessons" is charged with. Tapping, "South Asia/North America," *Reworlding*, 46.

46. Gregory McElwain has characterized the story as one of constant movement. Cf. McElwain, 17. In that respect, "Swimming Lessons" strongly resembles "Lend Me Your Light."

47. "He needs to learn to swim, so to speak, so he can stay afloat in Canada." McElwain, 17.

48. McElwain, 17.

49. McElwain, 18.

50. The ontological divide between author and narrator as an invented character seems artificial to many a postmodern writer because it is reminiscent of the conventions of realism that postmodernism regards as dubious and attempts to overcome. George Bowering, for example, argues against the realist fetish of distance between character, author and reader and proposes a self-reflexive fiction that lays bare the process of writing. Questioning traditional Aristotelian concepts of mimesis, the only ethically acceptable position offered to the reader for identification is the author who intrudes into his own work: "In the post-modern novel you do not identify with the characters. If you are to identify with anyone it is likely to be the author, who may lay his cards on the table & ask for your opinion or even help in finishing the book." George Bowering, *The Mask in Place: Essays on Fiction in North America* (Winnipeg: Turnstone, 1982) 30.

51. Kersi's parents make sense of the present by reading Kersi's stories. According a new importance to the reader as part of the aesthetic endeavour, postmodernists also challenge traditional assumptions of a unified meaning conveyed homogeneously by calling for multiple interpretations formed by different readers. This postmodern turn is reflected in "Swimming Lessons" when Kersi's mother demands that different readings be respected as equally valid: "She would read them her way and Father could read them his" (246).

52. Patricia Waugh, *Metafiction: The Theory and Practice of Self-Conscious Fiction* (London:

Methuen, 1984). See also Linda Hutcheon, *A Poetics of Postmodernism* (1988; London: Routledge, 2000) 105–24.

53. David Staines speaks of "the immigrant vision, using Canada as a point of departure." For him "Canada functions as a point of arrival, which becomes, immediately, a point of departure" Staines, "State," 25–6.

54. For McElwain Kersi's distance to Canada is the result of time spent in writing the collection of stories. He overlooks that we never observe Kersi write, yet we do observe him act in a way that does anything to prevent adaptation/assimilation. Cf. McElwain, 24–5.

55. And thus testifies to the "cheering side" of the immigrant experience that is privileged because it "draws on two cultural heritages, without being inhibited or committed to either one of them." Malak, "Insider/Outsider Views on Belonging," 189.

56. And thus testifies to "the crisis of the writer's preoccupation with belonging." Malak, "Insider/Outsider Views on Belonging," 189.

57. Bharucha, "'When Old Tracks Are Lost,'" 61.

58. Heble, 60.

59. Samantrai, 48.

B. 'There' I: Cultural Difference and the Struggle for Meaning. *Such a Long Journey* (1991)

1. Arun Prabha Mukherjee, "Narrating India: Rohinton Mistry's *Such a Long Journey*," *Oppositional Aesthetics: Readings from a Hyphenated Space* (Toronto: TSAR, 1994) 147.

2. John R Hinnells, "Parsi Zoroastrians in London," *Desh Pardesh: The South Asian Presence in Britain*, ed. Roger Ballard (London: Hurst & Company, 1994) 252.

3. However, some scholars claim that the Parsis were not hindered in the practice of their religion. According to these critics, the Parsi emigration was a reaction to the tax ('jazia') imposed upon them by the Muslim invaders. Cf. Eckehard Kulke, *The Parsees in India: A Minority as Agent of Social Change* (München: Weltforum Verlag, 1974) 25.

4. Hinnells, 251 and Kulke, 13. Stausberg maintains that the name derives from the word Persia. Cf. Michael Stausberg, "Zoroastrismus," *Die Religionen der Gegenwart Geschichte und Glauben*, ed. Peter Antes (München: Beck, 1996) 161.

5. Hinnells, 253.

6. Stausberg, 165. See also Tanya Luhrmann, *The Good Parsi: The Fate of a Colonial Elite in a Postcolonial Society* (Cambridge: Harvard, 1996) 78. Hinnells points out that the Parsis' narrativization of their fate as that of a persecuted community in search of a new home also displays distinct parallels to the self-image of the Jews. See Hinnells, 253. This is also confirmed by Luhrmann, 47. Kulke reminds us that "the Parsees were frequently called Jews by the Portugese." Kulke, 30.

7. The following is recounted in a more recent Parsi novel. Cf. Boman Desai, *The Memory of Elephants* (London: Sceptre, 1990) 24.

8. Kulke, 28–9.

9. For Kulke, loyalty towards the government, close community ties, and a cautious albeit assiduous preservation of their faith in adverse circumstances have since that time become quintessentially Parsi. Kulke, 28–9.

10. Jer Randeria, *The Parsi Mind: A Zoroastrian Asset to Culture* (New Delhi: Munshiram Manoharlal Publishers, 1993) 19. See also Luhrmann, 83.

11. Kulke, 32.

12. Kulke, 33. The British were eager to settle Bombay quickly because they expected the Portugese to reclaim the city which they had given to the British crown in 1661 as part of the dowry of Catherine of Braganza. See also Luhrmann, 86.

13. Hinnells, 253.

14. According to Kulke, the Parsis introduced to India the new type of the modern entrepre-

neur. Cf. Kulke, 128. See also Luhrmann, 90.

15. Of an estimated number of circa 100.000 members worldwide, the number of Zoroastrians/Parsis living in Bombay today amounts to 50.000. Cf. Stausberg, 161. These figures are confirmed by Dorothee Wenner in a recent newspaper feature. Cf. Dorothee Wenner, "Je weniger, desto lustiger," *Die Zeit* 23rd May 2002: 54.

16. An indicator for this is that three out of the four baronetcies conferred upon Indians prior to Independence went to Parsis. Cf. Hinnells, 259.

17. Luhrmann, 49.

18. Loomba, 85.

19. Stausberg, 167.

20. Kulke, 248.

21. Luhrmann, 42 and 119.

22. Hinnells, 258.

23. Luhrmann, 113.

24. Luhrmann, 42–3.

25. Luhrmann, 110.

26. Luhrmann, 111ff.

27. Hinnells, 258.

28. Hinnells, 253.

29. In *Such a Long Journey* Gustad's daughter Roshan attends a Catholic convent school which is supposed to provide a superior education.

30. Ross, 240.

31. Luhrmann, 124.

32. Luhrmann, 99.

33. A case in point here is Maneck Kohlah who immigrates to Dubai in *A Fine Balance.* As a matter of fact, Parsis have frequently opted for emigration in order to receive a better education at a North American university, or to find a better-paid job. As such, their motives for leaving India have been economic, and have had less to do with identity politics. Since the 1960s, many have Parsis immigrated to North America where today between 5000–7000 adherents of the Zoroastrian faith live. Approximately 6000 Zoroastrians live in England today; tiny communities can also be found in Australia, Hong Kong, Yemen and East Africa. Cf. Stausberg, 172ff.

34. for example, the building of Bombay, the founding of the Indian National Congress, Parsi philanthropy, Dadabhai Naoroji and his drain theory, or Homi K Bhabhba and his concept of hybridity.

35. Paul Wilson, "Giving Free Rein: Paul Wilson Speaks with Rohinton Mistry," *Books in Canada* March 1996: 3.

36. Bharucha, "'When Old Tracks are Lost,'" 62. For more on the Shiv Sena cf. Jayant Lele, "Saffronization of the Shiv Sena: The Political Economy of City State and Nation," *Bombay: Metaphor for Modern India*, eds. Sujata Patel and Alice Thorner (Bombay: OUP, 1996) 185–213.

37. Rohinton Mistry, *Such a Long Journey* (1991; NY: Vintage, 1992) 73. All references are to this edition.

38. Williams, 57.

39. Avadesh Kumar Singh, "The Sense of Community in the Parsi Novels." *The Literary Criterion* 32 (1996): 33.

40. McHale, 91.

41. Mukherjee, "Narrating India," 145.

42. Despite Nehru's ostentation of India's secular character, Indian national identity in post-colonial times was not conceived of in multicultural terms but was constructed along lines laid down by religious difference. India was what Pakistan was not, i.e. Hinduist.

43. Kulke, 13. See also Bharucha, "'When Old Tracks are Lost,'" 59.

44. Bharucha, "'When Old Tracks are Lost,'" 59.

45. It has made a considerable impact on Judaism and Christianity as well as on Islam. Judaism

adopted from Zoroastrianism the idea of a supreme God, the belief in the coming of a Messiah and an adherence to a strict code of behaviour entailing a spiritual dimension (e.g. purity laws). There are also parallels as far as the binary vision of Heaven and Hell and a great judgement on doomsday are concerned. Islam derived from Zoroastrianism the emphasis on regular prayer, the belief into Heaven and Hell, the end of the world and the idea of a great judgement at the end of all days. Strikingly similar are also Zoroastrianism's and Islam's rejection of images and the emphasis on charity and alms-giving. Cf. Stausberg, 161, Wenner, 54 and Mary Boyce, *Zoroastrians: Their Religious Beliefs and Practices* (London: Routledge and Kegan Paul, 1979) 77, 148.

46. Stausberg, 165. See also Hinnells, 265–6.

47. Kulke, 17.

48. Kulke, 17.

49. Kulke, 17.

50. Stausberg, 163 and RC Zaehner, *The Dawn and Twilight of Zoroastrianism.* 2nd ed. (London: Weidenfeld and Nicolson, 1975) 36–7.

51. Luhrmann, 69.

52. Luhrmann, 101.

53. Stausberg, 164.

54. Stausberg, 164. In accordance to that, orthodox Zoroastrians also avoid menstruating women. How strict the ban on them actually is can be observed in a classic Parsi novel. Cf. Bapsi Sidhwa, *The Crow Eaters* (Minneapolis: Milkweed, 1978) 65–6.

55. A case in point is Dinshawji's funeral.

56. Boyce, 8.

57. Randeria, 13.

58. Mistry, "Swimming Lessons," 236.

59. Kulke, 254.

60. Sidhwa, 24.

61. Kulke, 260. Luhrmann characterises Zoroastrianism as "a solitary religion." Luhrmann, 36.

62. Stausberg, 178.

63. For details cf. Stausberg, 180 and Luhrmann 268n.

64. Nilufer E Bharucha, "From Behind a Fine Veil: A Feminist Reading of three Parsi Novels," *Indian Literature* 39 (1996): 138.

65. Mukherjee, "Narrating India," 150. For Ekelund, Mistry's novel is flawed because it does not grant its female figures development as characters. While the male characters progress from archetypes to humanity, the women remain flat characters and thus are denied humanity implicitly. Gordon Ekelund, "Left at the Station: The Portrayal of Women in Mistry's *Such a Long Journey*," *The Toronto Review of Contemporary Writing Abroad* 14.1 (1995): 7, 9.

66. Leckie, 38. Hilary Mantel seems to agree with Leckie when she speaks about the "human decency" of Mistry's fiction. Hilary Mantel, "States of Emergency," *India: A Mosaic*, eds. Robert B Silvers and Barbara Epstein (NY: The New York Review of Books, 2000) 179. For Gordon Ekelund, *Such a Long Journey* invites us to "discover shared values and a common humanity." Ekelund, 6.

67. for example, Mukherjee, "Narrating India," 148–9.

68. Many critics, in fact, argue that the Parsi community is the true hero of *Such a Long Journey*. Cf. Avadesh Kumar Singh, "The Sense of Community in the Parsi Novels," *The Literary Criterion* 32 (1996): 30, and Mukherjee, "Narrating India," 146.

69. Alberto Manguel, afterword, *Such a Long Journey*, by Rohinton Mistry (Toronto: McClelland & Stewart, 1993) 416. Amrijit Singh suggests a middle course. Discussing Rohinton Mistry's collection of stories, he argues that Mistry "frames a slice of the human experience in all its Parsi specificity." A Singh, 211.

70. M Mani Meitei, "*Such a Long Journey* and its Critical Acclaim," *The Fiction of Rohinton Mistry: Critical Studies*, ed. Jaydipsinh Dodiya (London: Sangam, 1998) 74.

71. Adams, 124. See also Williams, 61.

72. This is a point which is also acknowledged by others. Cf., for example, Amin Malak, "The Shahrazadic Tradition: Rohinton Mistry's *Such a Long Journey* and the Art of Storytelling," *Journal of Commonwealth Literature* 29 (1993): 109. Dan Coleman departs from a humanist reading by pointing out that the disruption has to be contextualized by Gustad's community membership. According to Coleman loss and bankruptcy have to be understood in connection with the decline of the Parsi community. Dan Coleman, *Masculine Migrations: Reading the Postcolonial Male in 'New Canadian' Narratives* (Toronto: U of Toronto P, 1998) 141.

73. Aleida Assmann, "Erinnerungsorte und Gedächtnislandschaften," *Erlebnis—Gedächtnis—Sinn: Authentische und Konstruierte Erinnerung*, eds. Hanno Loewy and Bernhard Moltmann (Frankfurt/Main: Campus Verlag, 1996) 16.

74. Williams, 59.

75. Williams, 59.

76. Manguel, 417.

77. On an intertextual level, the theme of trust and betrayal is conceptualized by way of reference to Shakespeare's *Othello*. Cf. Leckie, 44. As Iago exploits Roderigo for his scheme of betrayal, so does Jimmy abuse the loyalty of his friend Gustad.

78. Manguel, 417.

79. Leckie, 44. In an excellent analysis, Dan Coleman discusses *Such a Long Journey* in psychological terms. He holds that Mistry's debut should be read against the "romance of family progress," a narrative pattern that "responds to disillusion through the construction of a family fantasy." The family fantasy is, of course, the IIT, which for Gustad becomes symbolic of the community's ability to make it to the top during a (postcolonial) time in which the Parsis no longer have the influence they used to have. As Sohrab opts for arts over science, the romance of family progress seems to fail. Coleman, 131. However, Coleman overlooks that *Such a Long Journey* does come up with a romance ending after all. Significantly, it is the son who as an arts student reinvents the family romance by effortlessly displaying the humanism that Gustad struggles to approximate to. Therefore, Mistry's first novel can still be read as a romance of family progress, provided one is willing to admit that it is the son, rather than the father, who defines its terms.

80. For more on the family and its importance for the construction of meaning cf. Jürgen Kriz, *Chaos, Angst und Ordnung: Wie wir unsere Lebenswelt gestalten*, 2nd ed. (Göttingen: Vandenhoeck & Ruprecht, 1998) 34.

81. Nikolaus Wenturis, Walter Van Hove and Volker Dreiser, *Methodologie der Sozialwissenschaften. Eine Einführung* (Tübingen: Francke, 1992) 95.

82. Hahn, *Religion*, 87. Pursuing a similar argument, Vivelo speaks of the psychological reinforcement inherent in a religious belief. Frank Robert Vivelo, *Handbuch der Kulturanthropologie: Eine grundlegende Einführung*, transl. and ed. Justin and Erika Stagl, 2nd ed. (Stuttgart: Klett-Cotta, 1995) 257.

83. Viktor E Frankl, *Der Mensch vor der Frage nach dem Sinn: Eine Auswahl aus dem Gesamtwerk* (München: Piper, 1979) 73.

84. Boyce, 12.

85. Jürgen August Alt, *Wenn Sinn knapp wird: Über das gelingende Leben in einer entzauberten Welt* (Frankfurt/Main: Campus Verlag, 1997) 129.

86. Alt, 17.

87. Williams, 69.

88. Manguel, 418.

89. Bharucha, "When Old Tracks are Lost," 63, and Bharucha, "From Behind a Fine Veil," 139.

90. Brumlik: "Ob und woran wir uns erinnern können, hängt in erster Linie davon ab, woran wir uns erinnern wollen." Micha Brumlik, "Individuelle Erinnerung—Kollektive Erinnerung," *Erlebnis—Gedächtnis—Sinn: Authentische und Konstruierte Erinnerung*, eds. Hanno Loewy and Bernhard Moltmann (Frankfurt/Main: Campus Verlag, 1996) 34.

91. Boyce, 77.

92. "Paradies," *Wörterbuch der Symbolik*, 1991 ed.

93. Lucasta Miller, "Heart Land," rev. of *Such a Long Journey*, by Rohinton Mistry, *New Statesman and Society* 22th March 1991: 46.

94. Meitei, 81.

95. Shah, 97. For Khan the wall with its advantages and disadvantages represents the complexity of India. AG Khan, *Canadian Literature and Indian Literature: New Perspectives* (New Delhi: Creative Books, 1995) 21.

96. A Singh, 210.

97. Bharucha, "When Old Tracks are Lost," 63.

98. Williams, 60. See also Leckie, 40.

99. The endogamous marriage policy of the Parsis might result in the eventual extinction of the community.

100. Pharand reminds us that Eliot is not the only intertext *Such a Long Journey* makes use of. Mistry also consciously alludes to Tagore and, most importantly, to Firdausi *Shahnameh*, the ancient Persian epic. Cf. Michel W Pharand, "The Road to Salvation: Mythological and Theological Intertextuality in Rohinton Mistry's *Such a Long Journey*," *Open Letter* 8 (1994): 109–11.

101. TS Eliot, *The Waste Land and other Poems* (London: Faber and Faber, 1990) 65.

102. Peter Ackroyd, *T.S. Eliot*, (London: Penguin, 1993) 164.

103. Eliot, 65.

104. Sandra Ness Ihle, *Malory's Grail Quest: Invention and Adaptation in Medieval Prose Romance* (Madison: The U of Wisconsin P, 1983) 69.

105. "The journey of the three wise men to the birthplace of Jesus Christ is not merely an ordinary physical journey; it is symbolic of man's spiritual quest." Anita Myles, "Thematic Concerns in *Such a Long Journey*," *The Fiction of Rohinton Mistry: Critical Studies*, ed. Jaydipsinh Dodiya (London: Sangam, 1998) 86.

106. Eliot, 66.

107. Ackroyd, 164.

108. Manguel, 416. For M Mani Meitei, Gustad is "an individual depicted as a classical tragic hero," too. Meitei, 73.

109. Leckie, 42. David Townsend agrees that "the book's ultimate concerns are deeply spiritual." Townsend, 62.

110. Manguel, 416.

111. Manguel, 416.

112. "Parzival," *Stoffe der Weltliteratur: Ein Lexikon dichtungsgeschichtlicher Längsschnitte*, 1998 ed.

113. Malak, 108.

114. Leckie, 40.

C. 'There' II: Cultural Difference and the Struggle for Meaning. *A Fine Balance* (1995)

1. For an overview cf. Hugo Aust, *Der historische Roman* (Stuttgart: Metzler, 1994) 42.

2. Lynne van Luven, Rev. of *A Fine Balance*, by Rohinton Mistry. *Quill and Quire* 61 (1995): 65.

3. AK Singh, 37.

4. Also significant in this context is the epilogue of the novel which is set during four days following Indira Gandhi's assassination on 31st October 1984. For an overview of the events cf. Inder Malhotra, *Indira Gandhi: A Personal and Political Biography* (London: Hodder & Stoughton, 1989) 22–3.

5. For an overview of the events leading to Indian Independence cf. Dietmar Rothermund, *Delhi, 15. August, 1947: Das Ende kolonialer Herrschaft* (München: dtv, 1998) 9–21.

6. Rohinton Mistry, *A Fine Balance* (1995; London: Faber and Faber, 1997) 209. All references

are to this edition.

7. Dietmar Rothermund, *Mahatma Gandhi: Eine Politische Biographie*, 2nd ed. (München: Beck, 1997) 404.

8. In fact, Mountbatten deliberately left India and Pakistan in doubt as to where the new border was to be. He hoped (in vain) that the confusion resulting from this would prevent organized massacres and reduce acts of violence to a minimum. Hermann Kulke and Dietmar Rothermund. *Geschichte Indiens: Von der Induskultur bis heute*, 2nd ed. (München: CH Beck, 1998) 386–7.

9. For example, Dina learns to cut hair (58), her friend Zenobia works as a hairstylist, and Rajaram is a hair collector as well as a barber. The Sikhs are not allowed to cut their hair or trim their beard. Shankar dies in an accident because he refuses to have his hair cut. Om keeps breaking combs (5, 160, 331), and Mrs Gupta invariably makes her appearance at the hairdresser's. During the time of the Emergency "a typo in a top-level memorandum had the Beautification Police down as the Beautician Police, and now they were tackling hair as crudely as they had tackled slums" (482).

10. For an overview cf. Malhotra, 165ff.

11. Dennis Walder, *Post-Colonial Literature in English: History, Language, Theory* (Oxford: Blackwell, 1999) 89.

12. Kulke and Rothermund, 405.

13. Kulke and Rothermund, 405.

14. Kulke and Rothermund, 406.

15. Bhatnagar, 102.

16. Many Indians applauded the Emergency in its initial phase. Cf. Malhotra, 173.

17. Ross, 243.

18. VS Naipaul, *An Area of Darkness* (1964; Basingstoke: Picador, 1995) 60.

19. Originally, caste is not a religious concept but a reflection of a division of society according to function. From 2000 BC onwards, however, the caste system has been increasingly associated with Hinduism. Cf. Hans Wolfgang Schumann, *Die großen Götter Indiens: Grundzüge von Hinduismus und Buddhismus*, 2nd ed. (München: Diederichs, 1999) 30.

20. Anthony Giddens, *Sociology* (Cambridge: Polity Press, 1991) 207.

21. Schumann, 13.

22. Schumann, 27.

23. Naipaul, 88.

24. Schumann, 31.

25. Historically, the struggle against the discrimination of the untouchables is connected to Dr Ambedkar and Mochandas Gandhi. For a survey, Rothermund, *Gandhi*, 314ff.

26. Mistry's first novel employs the moth as metaphor, too. For Alberto Manguel, it conveys the "idea of impermanence, the realization that nothing will last, that everything, human beings and societies, have in the universal computation, the life span of a moth." Manguel, 418–9. For Ramachandra, also concerned with *Such a Long Journey*, the moth signals "the predicament of frail, fragile man caught in the flux and illusion struggling to complete the endless cycle of his *karma* [sic]." Ragini Ramachandra, "Rohinton Mistry's *Such a Long Journey*: Some First Impressions," *Literary Criterion* 29 (1994): 30.

27. For the historical accuracy of Mistry's representation see Malhotra, 180–1. For a different fictional rendering of the events surrounding the sterilization scheme during the Emergency, see Salman Rushdie, *Midnight's Children* (1981; NY: Penguin, 1991) 522–3.

28. Novy Kapadia, "The Politics of Survival and Domination in *A Fine Balance*," *The Fiction of Rohinton Mistry: Critical Studies*, ed. Jadipsinh Dodiya (London: Sangam, 1998) 128. Hilary Mantel reminds us that it is "the exigencies of displacement" that bring the main characters together. Mantel, 183.

29. Bharucha, "When Old Tracks are Lost," 59.

30. The novel suggests a parallel between Maneck's and the taxi driver's homelessness. The Sikhs feel deprived of a home; their claim for a Punjabi nation state has been refuted on the

grounds that the postcolonial Indian nation state projects a secular identity. Cf. Robin Jeffrey, *What's Happening to India: Punjab, Ethnic Conflict, Mrs Gandhi's Death and the Test for Federalism* (NY: Holmes and Meier, 1986) 101ff.

31. As Valentine in Tom Stoppard's *Arcadia* has it, "it'll take a while but we're all going to end up at room temperature." Tom Stoppard, *Arcadia* (London: Faber and Faber, 1993) 78.

32. See, for example, the writings of Homi Bhabha and Paul Gilroy. See also Iain Chambers, *Migrancy, Culture, Identity* (London: Routledge, 1994) 14. For a balanced account cf. James Clifford, *Routes: Travel and Translation in the Late Twentieth Century* (Cambridge, MA: Harvard UP) 257.

33. Paul Gilroy, "Diaspora and the Detours of Identity," *Identity and Difference*, ed. Kathryn Woodward (London: Sage, 1997) 334.

34. Gilroy, "Diaspora," 334–5.

35. Petrus Han, *Soziologie der Migration* (Stuttgart: Lucius und Lucius, 2000) 182.

36. Anthony Giddens, *Beyond Left and Right: The Future of Radical Politics* (Cambridge: Polity Press, 1994) 83.

37. van Luven, 65.

38. I disagree with Mantel who finds that Maneck "has nothing to commit suicide about." Mantel, 191. Maneck fails to maintain the necessary balance in his life.

39. "Arkadien," *Motive der Weltliteratur: Ein Lexikon dichtungsgeschichtlicher Längsschnitte*, 1999 ed.

40. Vinita Dhondiyal Bhatnagar, "'And everything ends badly': A Reading of *A Fine Balance*," *The Fiction of Rohinton Mistry: Critical Studies*, ed. Jaydipsinh Dodiya (London: Sangam, 1998) 107. Cf. also Ross, 243.

41. "Haus," *Wörterbuch der Symbolik*, 1991 ed.

42. "Haus," *Knaurs Lexikon der Symbole*, 1994 ed.

43. Heiner Keupp, Thomas Abhe and Wolfgang Gmür, *Identitätskonstruktionen: Das Patchwork der Identitäten in der Spätmoderne* (Hamburg: Rowohlt, 1999) 55.

44. Keupp et al, 55.

45. Bhatnagar, 106.

46. Bhatnagar, 106.

47. Robert Ross is mistaken in claiming that Maneck's problems are "more invented, than real" at this point. Maneck's problems are not less 'real' for him, even if they may indeed be "self-imposed or a result of his overdrawn sensitivity." Ross, 243.

48. Rushdie reminds us that the name 'Shroff' translates as banker, which, not surprisingly, is the occupation Nusswan opts for. Salman Rushdie, *The Ground Beneath Her Feet* (London: Jonathan Cape, 1999) 19. See also Kulke, 51.

49. Ross, 243.

50. Bettina Aptheker, *Tapestries of Life: Women's Work, Women's Consciousness, and the Meaning of Daily Experience* (Amherst: U of Massachusetts P, 1989) 68ff.

51. Woodward, "Concepts," 14.

52. Keupp et al.

53. Keupp et al, 28.

54. Heiko Ernst, *Psychotrends: Das Ich im 21. Jahrhundert* (München: Piper, 1998) 202.

55. Hahn, *Religion*, 116. A biography is a coherent narration, i.e. a story displaying various emplotment strategies. As Alois Hahn has pointed out elsewhere, there is an important difference between a 'Lebenslauf,' i.e. one's vita or the sum of one's life as flux, and one's biography. The 'Lebenslauf' existed at all times, a biography, however, is a relatively recent way of ordering an individual life. A biography is a selection of events, and, as such, a construction. Moreover, it is a reflexive approach which thematises life by way of a deliberate looking back. It is a narration which is an act of giving meaning by going beyond the mere enumeration of events and dates (characteristic of the 'Lebenslauf'). Hahn writes in this context: "Die Biographie verhält sich gegenüber den Sinngebungsprozessen der ihr vorausliegenden 'naiven' Lebensführung reflexiv, ist

also eine Sinnbildung zweiten Grades." A biography thus amounts to more than the sum of events of an individual life. This is mirrored in the structure of the patchwork quilt: "'The whole quilt is much more important than any single square'" (490). Alois Hahn, "Sinn und Sinnlosigkeit," *Sinn, Kommunikation und soziale Differenzierung*, eds. Hans Haferkamp and Michael Schmidt (Frankfurt/Main: Suhrkamp, 1986) 158–9.

56. Aptheker 68–9 and 74.

57. Malak, 116.

58. Robert Kroetsch, "A Conversation with Margaret Laurence," *Trace: Prairie Writers on Writing*, ed. Birk Sproxton (Winnipeg: Turnstone Press, 1986) 30.

59. Meyer, 29.

60. Malak, 116.

61. The importance of storytelling and the social obligation of the writer to tell a story are reflected upon by Mistry in an early interview. Cf. Hancock, 150.

62. Pramod K Nayar, "The Text of Cruelty: Power and Violence in *A Fine Balance*." *The Fiction of Rohinton Mistry: Critical Studies*, ed. Jaydipsinh Dodiya (London: Sangam, 1998) 122–3.

63. Mantel, 184.

64. Moss argues that the eventual disruption of the apartment community overrides its importance as shelter. Laura Moss, "Can Rohinton Mistry's Realism Rescue the Novel?" *Postcolonizing the Commonwealth: Studies in Literature and Culture*, ed. Rowland Smith (Waterloo: Wilfrid Laurier UP, 2000) 163. Moss overlooks that notwithstanding the fact that at the end of the book the apartment community no longer exists, the "temporary supportive unit in the flat" (Morey, 181) has initiated a friendship between Dina, Om and Ishvar that provides them with a source of meaning beyond the end of the flat community and the end of the novel's plot. I would like to suggest that Mistry, preoccupied with ways of countering the loss of meaning in life, has envisaged a mildly positive ending. While Moss takes issue with the novel's realism, it is in fact Mistry's realism that prevents him from ending in a sentimental tableau.

65. van Luven, 65. See also Ball who argues that "over time her [i.e. Dina's] new household becomes a moderately happy and prosperous 'family.'" John Clement Ball, "Taking the Measure of India's Emergency," rev. of *A Fine Balance*, by Rohinton Mistry, *Floating the Borders: New Contexts in Canadian Criticism*, ed. Nurjehan Aziz (Toronto: TSAR, 1999) 236.

66. Woodward, "Concepts," 31.

67. Carole M Counihan, *The Anthropology of Food and Body: Gender, Meaning, and Power* (London: Routledge, 1999) 6. For a similar argument see also Alois Wierlacher, *Vom Essen in der Deutschen Literatur: Mahlzeiten in Erzähltexten von Goethe bis Grass* (Stuttgart: Kohlhammer, 1987) 41.

68. Wierlacher, 118.

69. Wierlacher, 58.

70. also Ross, 243.

71. Ross, 244.

72. In that sense it is inaccurate to argue that in *A Fine Balance* everything ends badly for the main characters. Cf. Bhatnagar, 102.

73. Ross, 243–4.

74. Peter Morey, *Fictions of India: Narrative and Power* (Edinburgh: Edinburgh UP, 2000) 177.

75. Ross, 243.

76. Murdoch, 503.

77. Daniel Albright, "Introduction," WB Yeats, *W.B. Yeats: The Poems*, ed. Daniel Albright (London: JM Dent & Sons Ltd., 1990) xxxviii.

78. Stan Smith, *W.B. Yeats: A Critical Introduction* (Basingstoke: Macmillan, 1990) 107.

79. William Butler Yeats, *Selected Poetry*, ed. Norman Jeffares, 4th ed. (London: Pan, 1976) 99.

80. Yeats, *Selected Poetry*, 99. This line also provided Chinua Achebe with the title for his debut novel. His appropriation has aroused the interest of postcolonial critics. For Ashcroft, Griffiths and Tiffin the turning of the gyres as the moment of greatest chaos is configured as a turning of

the tables in the former colonies. Within such a reading the "rough beast" of Yeats's poem signifies the former colonies who haunt the metropolis with the threat of vengeance. Cf. Ashcroft et al, *Empire*, 158.

81. SB. Bushrui and Tim Prentki, *An International Companion to the Poetry of W.B. Yeats* (Gerrards Cross: Colin Smythe, 1989) 58.

82. Bushrui and Prentki, 58.

83. *W.B. Yeats: The Poems*, 769.

84. R Jahan Ramazani, *Yeats and the Poetry of Death: Elegy, Self-Elegy and the Sublime* (New Haven: Yale UP, 1990) 89.

85. Yeats, *Selected Poetry*, 181.

86. Ramazani, *Yeats and the Poetry of Death*, 87.

87. Smith, 106.

88. R Jahan Ramazani, "Tragic Joy and the Sublime," *PMLA* 104 (1989): 163. For an overview of different concepts of transcendence cf. Thomas Weiskel, *The Romantic Sublime: Studies in the Structure and Psychology of Transcendence* (Baltimore: The Johns Hopkins UP, 1976) 3–33. See also Andrew Ashfield and Peter de Bolla, eds., *The Sublime: A Reader in British Eighteenth-Century Aesthetic Theory* (Cambridge: CUP, 1996).

89. For the following account cf. Christine Priest, ed., *Das Erhabene: Zwischen Grenzerfahrung und Größenwahn* (Weinheim: VCH, 1989) 8ff.

90. Friedrich Schiller, who closely follows Kant's ideas on the sublime, argues that the sublime is "ein gemischtes Gefühl. Es ist eine Zusammensetzung von Wehsein, das sich in seinem höchsten Grad als Schauer äußert, und von Frohsein, das sich bis zum Entzücken steigen kann." Friedrich Schiller, "Über das Erhabene," *Vom Pathetischen und Erhabenen: Ausgewählte Schriften zur Dramentheorie*, ed. Klaus L Berghahn (Stuttgart: Reclam, 1977) 87.

91. Weiskel distinguishes between three steps. Cf. Weiskel, 23–4.

92. Ramazani sees the link between tragic joy and the sublime in a "conversion of affects from defeat and terror to freedom and joy." Cf. Ramazani, "Tragic Joy," 164.

93. Rolf-Peter Janz, "Die ästhetische Bewältigung des Schreckens: Zu Schillers Theorie des Erhabenen," *Geschichte als Literatur: Formen und Grenzen der Repräsentation von Vergangenheit*, ed. Hartmut Eggert (Stuttgart: Metzler, 1990) 155–6.

94. Yeats, *Selected Poetry*, 182.

95. Ramazani, "Tragic Joy," 160.

96. Yeats, *Selected Poetry*, 180.

97. Yeats, *Selected Poetry*, 180.

98. Smith, 106.

99. Leckie, 3. Hilary Mantel also testifies to Mistry's "aspirations to universality," although she views them rather critically. Mantel, 193.

100. Ball, "Taking the Measure," 235.

101. For example, his friend and employer dies, his attempt at Matka fails and his immigration into Canada does not come to pass.

102. Strikingly enough, he associates this rediscovery with food and drink, too. Thus it is "over a cup of tea" (222) that a common ground between human beings is found.

103. Morey, 176.

Conclusion

1. Deepika Bahri, "Once More with Feeling: What Is Postcolonialism?" *ARIEL* 26.1 (1995): 75–6.

2. Chelva Kanaganayakam, "South Asian-Canadian Literature," *The Oxford Companion to Canadian Literature*, eds. Eugene Benson and William Toye (Toronto: OUP, 1997) 1084–5. See also Suwanda Sugunasiri, "The Literature of Canadians of South Asian Origins: An Overview," *Canadian Ethnic Studies* 17.1 (1985): 2.

3. William Safran, "Diasporas in Modern Societies: Myths of Homeland and Return," *Diaspora* 1 (1991): 83. For arguments that do not see the wish to return to a homeland as an essential part of diaspora consciousness cf. Ramraj, 215. See also Clifford, 249–50.

4. Arun Mukherjee takes issue with the homogenizing implications of the category South Asian Canadian writing. Cf. Mukherjee, "How Shall We Read South Asian Canadian Texts?" *Postcolonialism: My Living*, 38–9. This also admitted by Frank Birbalsingh, who nevertheless retains the label as an umbrella term. See also Frank Birbalsingh, "South Asian Canadian Novels in English," Vassanji, 58–9 and Kanaganayakam, "South Asian-Canadian Literature," 1083.

5. Porter, 71.

References

A. Primary Sources

MG Vassanji

Vassanji, MG. *No New Land*. Toronto: McClelland & Stewart, 1997.
Vassanji, MG. *The Book of Secrets*. Toronto: McClelland & Stewart, 1994.

Neil Bissoondath

Bissoondath, Neil. *Digging Up the Mountains*. NY: Viking, 1986.
Bissoondath, Neil. *A Casual Brutality*. Toronto: MacMillan, 1988.
Bissoondath, Neil. *The Innocence of Age*. Toronto: Alfred A Knopf Canada, 1992.
Bissoondath, Neil. *The Worlds Within Her*. London: Vintage, 2001.

Rohinton Mistry

Mistry, Rohinton. *Swimming Lessons and Other Stories from Firozsha Baag*. NY: Vintage, 1997.
Mistry, Rohinton. *Such a Long Journey*. NY: Vintage, 1992.
Mistry, Rohinton. *A Fine Balance*. London: Faber and Faber, 1997.
Mistry, Rohinton. *Family Matters*. London: Faber and Faber, 2002.

B. Secondary Sources

MG Vassanji

Ball, John Clement. "Taboos: MG Vassanji." *The Power to Bend Spoons: Interviews with Canadian Novelists*. Ed. Beverley Daurio. Toronto: The Mercury Press, 1998. 200–209.

Ball, John Clement. "Locating MG Vassanji's *The Book of Secrets*: Postmodern, Postcolonial, or Other-Wise?" *Floating the Borders: New Contexts in Canadian Criticism*. Ed. Nurjehan Aziz. Toronto: TSAR, 1999. 89–105.

Bissoondath, Neil. *Selling Illusions: The Cult of Multiculturalism in Canada*. Toronto: Penguin, 1994. 108–11.

Burke, Nancy. "Mixing Memory and Desire: MJ [sic] Vassanji and the South Asian Novel in Canada." *Writing Canadians: The Literary Construction of Ethnic Identities*. Eds. Martin Küster and Wolfram R Keller. Marburg: Universitätsbibliothek Marburg, 2002. 97–105.

Kanaganayakam, Chelva. "'Broadening the Substrata': An Interview with MG Vassanji." *World Literature Written in English* 31.2 (1991): 19–35.

Kanaganayakam, Chelva. "Don Mills and Dar es Salaam." Review of *No New Land*, by MG Vassanji. *Floating the Borders: New Contexts in Canadian Criticism*. Ed. Nurjehan Aziz. Toronto: TSAR, 1999. 200–3.

Lewis, Simon. "Impossible Domestic Situations: Questions of Identity and Nationalism in the Novels of Abdulrazak Gurnah and MG Vassanji." *Thamyris* 6 (1999): 215–29.

Malak, Amin. "Ambivalent Affiliations and the Postcolonial Condition: The Fiction of MG Vassanji." *World Literature Today* 67.2 (1993): 277–82.

Mukherjee, Arun Prabha. "Writing from a Hard Place: The African Fiction of MG Vassanji." *Oppositional Aesthetics: Readings from a Hyphenated Space*. Ed. Arun Prabha Mukherjee. Toronto: TSAR, 1994. 169–78.

Nasta, Susheila. "Interview: Moyez Vassanji." *Wasafiri* 13 (1991): 19–21.

Rhodes, Shane. "MG Vassanji: An Interview." *Studies in Canadian Literature* 22.2 (1997): 105–17.

Rhodes, Shane. "Frontier Fiction: Reading Books in MG Vassanji's *The Book of Secrets*." *ARIEL* 29.1 (1998): 179–94.

Simatei, Tirop Peter. *The Novel and the Politics of Nation Building in East Africa*. Bayreuth: Bayreuth African Studies 55, 2001. 73–103.

Neil Bissoondath

Birbalsingh, Frank. *Novels and the Nation: Essays in Canadian Literature*. Toronto: TSAR, 1995.

Côté, Marc. "Hopes or Illusions." Rev. of *A Casual Brutality*, by Neil Bissoondath. *The Canadian Forum* Feb.–Mar. 1989: 31–2.

Espinet, Ramabai. "The Old and the New." Rev. of *The Innocence of Age*, by Neil Bissoondath. *Floating the Borders: New Contexts in Canadian Criticism*. Ed. Nurjehan Aziz. Toronto: TSAR, 1999. 208–11.

Garrod, Andrew. "Neil Bissoondath." *Speaking for Myself: Canadian Writers in Interview*. St. John: Breakwater Books, 1986. 55–85.

Giangrande, Carole. "Urban Logos." Rev. of *The Innocence of Age*, by Neil Bissoondath. *Books in Canada* 22.1 (1993): 43–4.

Gorjup, Branco. "Trinidad." Rev. of *On the Eve of Uncertain Tomorrows*, by Neil Bissoondath. *World Literature Today* 65.2 (1991): 353–4.

Gorra, Michael. "Fiction Chronicle." *Hudson Review* 40.1 (1987): 139–40.

Harkins, Patricia. "Neil Bissoondath. *A Casual Brutality*." Rev. of *A Casual Brutality*, by Neil Bissoondath. *http://www.thecaribbeanwriter.com/volume4/v4p109.html*. Accessed 5.3.2002.

Holmes, Boyd. "Dislocations." Rev. of *A Casual Brutality*, by Neil Bissoondath. *Fiddlehead* 162 (1989): 109–12.

Hutcheon, Linda and Marion Richmond. "Neil Bissoondath." *Other Solitudes: Canadian Multicultural Fictions*. Eds. Linda Hutcheon and Marion Richmond. Toronto: OUP, 1990. 313–20.

Keneally, Thomas. "Home is Where the Death Squads Are." Rev. of *A Casual Brutality*, by Neil Bissoondath. *New York Times Book Review* 26 Feb. 1989: 14.

Kim, Jin David. "The Worlds Within Neil." Rev. of *The Worlds Within Her*, by Neil Bissoondath. *http://www.varsity.utoronto.ca/archives/119/oct29/review/the.html*. Accessed 5.3.2002.

Kureishi, Hanif. "Alistair Ramgoolam Does Well To Be Uneasy." Rev. of *Digging Up the Mountains*, by Neil Bissoondath. *New York Times Book Review*. 17 Aug. 1986: 10.

Kureishi, Hanif. "Return to Casaquemada." Rev. of *A Casual Brutality*, by Neil Bissoondath. *New Statesman and Society* 16 Sept. 1988: 42.

Lanchester, John. "Foreigners." Rev. of *A Casual Brutality*, by Neil Bissoondath. *London Review of Books* 5 Jan. 1989: 22.

Maes-Jelinek, Hena and Bénédicte Ledent. "The Novel since 1970." *A History of Literature in the Caribbean*. Ed. Albert James Arnold. Vol. 2. Amsterdam: John Benjamins Publishing Company, 2001. 149–98.

Malak, Amin. "Postcolonial Anguish." Rev. of *A Casual Brutality*, by Neil Bissoondath. *Canadian Literature* 128 (1991): 197–9.

Morris, Mervyn. "Going to Extremes and Other Tales of the New World." Rev. of *A Casual Brutality*, by Neil Bissoondath. *Washington Post Book World* 22 Jan. 1989: 4.

Mukherjee, Arun Prabha. "'Digging Up the Mountains': Bissoondath's Doomed World." Arun Prabha Mukherjee. *Oppositional Aesthetics: Readings from a Hyphenated Space*. Toronto: TSAR, 1994. 152–7.

Norgaard, Aja. "Up-and-Coming. Interview with Neil Bissoondath." *http://aurora.icaap.org/archive/bissoondath.html*. Accessed 5.3.2002.

Philip, Marlene Nourbese. "Immoral Fiction." Rev. of *A Casual Brutality*, by Neil Bissoondath. *Frontiers: Essays and Writings on Racism and Culture*. Stratford, ON: The Mercury Press, 1992. 190–200.

Richards, David. "Burning Down the House: Neil Bissoondath's Fiction." *Narrative Strategies in Canadian Literature: Feminism and Postcolonialism*. Ed. Carol-Ann Howells. Milton Keynes: Open UP, 1991. 49–60.

Richards, David. "'A History of Interruptions': Dislocated Mimesis in the Writings of Neil Bissoondath and Ben Okri." *From Commonwealth to Post -Colonial*. Ed. Anna Rutherford. Sydney: Dangaroo Press, 1992. 74–82.

Sankar, Celia. "Hungering for an Imperfect Homeland. Interview with Neil Bissoondath." *http://www.nalis.gov.tt/Biography/NeilBissoondath.htm*. Accessed 5.3.2002.

Srivastava, Aruna. "Interview with Neil Bissoondath." *Other Solitudes: Canadian Multicultural Fictions*. Eds. Linda Hutcheon and Marion Richmond. Toronto: OUP, 1990. 312–20.

Thorpe, Michael. "'Turned Inside Out': South Asian Writing in Canada." *ARIEL* 22.1 (1991): 5–24.

Thorpe, Michael. "Making Waves Against the Mainstream: Divergent Prospects for Canadian Literature." *ARIEL* 27.4 (1996): 139–54.

Tiffin, Helen. "'Continental Drift' and the Fourth Naipaul." Rev. of *Digging Up the Mountains*, by Neil Bissoondath. *CRNLE Reviews Journal* 1 (1987): 7–12.

Toorn, Penny van. "Positioning Neil Bissoondath: Post-Colonial, Multicultural and National Formations." *New Literatures Review* 27 (1994): 78–90.

Toorn, Penny van. "Building on Common Ground: An Interview with Neil Bissoondath." *Canadian Literature* 147 (1995): 127–35.

Toorn Penny van. "Neil Bissoondath." *Canadian Writers and Their Works: Fiction Series*. Eds. Robert Lecker, Jack David and Ellen Quigley. Toronto: ECW Press, 1996. 25–72.

Wordsworth, Araminta. "Novel Shuns Toronto's World Class Hype." Rev. of *The Innocence of Age*, by Neil Bissoondath. *Financial Post* 26 Oct. 1992: 8.

Rohinton Mistry

Adams, Phoebe-Lou. Rev. of *Such a Long Journey*, by Rohinton Mistry. *Atlantic Monthly* 267 (May 1991): 124.

Ball, John Clement. "Taking the Measure of India's Emergency." Rev. of *A Fine Balance*, by Rohinton Mistry. *Floating the Borders: New Contexts in Canadian Criticism*. Ed. Nurjehan Aziz. Toronto: TSAR, 1998. 234–9.

Bharucha, Nilufer E. "From Behind a Fine Veil: A Feminist Reading of three Parsi Novels." *Indian Literature* 39 (1996): 132–41.

Bharucha, Nilufer E. "'When Old Tracks are Lost': Rohinton Mistry's Fiction as Diasporic Discourse." *Journal of Canadian Literature* 30 (1995): 57–64.

Bhatnagar, Vinita Dhondiyal. "'And Everything Ends Badly': A Reading of *A Fine Balance*." *The Fiction of Rohinton Mistry: Critical Studies*. Ed. Jaydipsinh Dodiya. London: Sangam, 1998. 102–10.

Coleman, Dan. *Masculine Migrations: Reading the Postcolonial Male in 'New Canadian' Narratives*. Toronto: U of Toronto P, 1998. 131–58.

Dodiya, Jaydipsinh. "The Parsi Community in *Such a Long Journey*." *The Fiction of Rohinton Mistry: Critical Studies*. Ed. Jaydipsinh Dodiya. London: Sangam, 1998. 93–6.

Dodiya, Jaydipsinh. "*Such a Long Journey*: A Critical Study." *The Fiction of Rohinton Mistry: Critical Studies*. Ed. Jaydipsinh Dodiya. London: Sangam, 1998. 70–3.

Ekelund, Gordon. "Left at the Station: The Portrayal of Women in Mistry's *Such a Long Journey*." *The Toronto Review of Contemporary Writing Abroad* 14.1 (1995): 6–14.

Genetsch, Martin. "Rohinton Mistry." *Dictionary of Literary Biography: 21st Century Canadian Writers*. Ed. Christian Riegel [forthcoming].

Hancock, Geoff. "An Interview with Rohinton Mistry." *Canadian Fiction Magazine* 65 (1989): 143–50.

Heble, Ajay. "'A Foreign Presence in the Stall': Towards a Poetics of Cultural Hybridity in Rohinton Mistry's Migration Stories." *Canadian Literature* 137 (1993): 51–62.

Kapadia, Novy. "The Politics of Survival and Domination in *A Fine Balance*." *The Fiction of Rohinton Mistry: Critical Studies*. Ed. Jaydipsinh Dodiya. London: Sangam, 1998. 127–35.

Kelly, Jennifer. "Rohinton Mistry." *Encyclopedia of Post-Colonial Literatures in English*. 2 vols. Eds. Eugene Benson and LW Conolly. London: Routledge, 1994. 1027.

Khan, AG. "Rohinton Mistry alias Peerbhoy Paanwala." *Canadian Literature and Indian Literature: New Perspectives*. Ed. AG Khan. New Delhi: Creative Books, 1995. 15–25.

Leckie, Barbara. "Rohinton Mistry." *Canadian Writers and Their Works: Fiction Series*. Eds. Robert Lecker, Jack David and Ellen Quigley. Toronto: ECW Press, 1996. 215–68.

Luven, Lynne van. Rev. of *A Fine Balance*, by Rohinton Mistry. *Quill and Quire* 61 (1995): 65.

Malak, Amin. "Insider/Outsider Views on Belonging: The Short Stories of Bharati Mukherjee and Rohinton Mistry." *Short Fiction in the New Literatures in English: Proceedings of the Nice Conference of the European Association for Commonwealth Literature and Language Studies*. Ed. Jacqueline Bardolph. Nice: Faculté des Lettres & Sciences Humanies de Nice, 1988. 189–96.

Malak, Amin. "Images of India." Review of *Tales from Firozsha Baag*, by Rohinton Mistry. *Canadian Literature* 119 (1988): 101–3.

Malak, Amin. "The Shahrazadic Tradition: Rohinton Mistry's *Such a Long Journey* and the Art of Storytelling." *Journal of Commonwealth Literature* 29 (1993): 108–18.

Manguel, Alberto. "Afterword." *Such a Long Journey*. By Rohinton Mistry. Toronto: McClelland & Stewart, 1993. 415–9.

Mantel, Hilary. "States of Emergency." *India: A Mosaic*. Eds. Robert B Silvers and Barbara Epstein. NY: The New York Review of Books, 2000. 179–94.

McElwain, Gregory. "Paddling Away From the Past: Alienation and Assimilation in Rohinton Mistry's 'Swimming Lessons.'" *Kobe College Studies* 41:2 (1994): 15–26.

Meitei, M Mani. "*Such a Long Journey* and its Critical Acclaim." *The Fiction of Rohinton Mistry: Critical Studies*. Ed. Jaydipsinh Dodiya. London: Sangam, 1998. 73–85.

Miller, Lucasta. "Heart Land." Rev. of *Such a Long Journey*, by Rohinton Mistry. *New Statesman and Society* 22 Mar. 1991: 46.

Morey, Peter. *Fictions of India: Narrative and Power*. Edinburgh: Edinburgh UP, 2000. 161–90.

Moss, Laura. "Can Rohinton Mistry's Realism Rescue the Novel?" *Postcolonizing the Commonwealth: Studies in Literature and Culture*. Ed. Rowland Smith. Waterloo: Wilfried Laurier Press, 2000. 157–65.

Mukherjee, Arun Prabha. "Narrating India: Rohinton Mistry's *Such a Long Journey*." Arun Prabha Mukherjee. *Oppositional Aesthetics: Readings from a Hyphenated Space*. Toronto: TSAR, 1994. 144–51.

Myles, Anita. "Thematic Concerns in *Such a Long Journey*." *The Fiction of Rohinton Mistry: Critical Studies*. Ed. Jaydipsinh Dodiya. London: Sangam, 1998. 85–93.

Nayar, Pramod K. "The Text of Cruelty: Power and Violence in *A Fine Balance*." *The Fiction of Rohinton Mistry: Critical Studies*. Ed. Jaydipsinh Dodiya. London: Sangam, 1998. 119–27.

Novak, Dagmar. "Interview with Rohinton Mistry." *Other Solitudes: Canadian Multicultural Fictions*. Eds. Linda Hutcheon and Marion Richmond. Toronto: OUP, 1990. 255–62.

Parameswaran, Uma. "Landmark." Rev. of *Tales from Firozsha Baag*, by Rohinton Mistry. *Floating the Borders: New Contexts in Canadian Criticism*. Ed. Nurjehan Aziz. Toronto: TSAR, 1999. 184–7.

Pharand, Michael W. "The Road to Salvation: Mythological and Theological Intertextuality in Rohinton Mistry's *Such a Long Journey*." *Open Letter* 8 (1994): 107–16.

Ramachandra, Ragini. "Rohinton Mistry's *Such a Long Journey*: Some First Impressions." *Literary Criterion* 29 (1994): 25–34.

Ross, Robert L. "Seeking and Maintaining Balance: Rohinton Mistry's Fiction." *World Literature Today* 73 (1999): 239–44.

Samantrai, Ranu. "States of Belonging: Pluralism, Migrancy, Literature." *Essays on Canadian Writing* 57 (1995): 33–50.

Shah, Nila. "Novel as History: A Study of *Such a Long Journey* and *A Fine Balance*." *The Fiction of Rohinton Mistry: Critical Studies*. Ed. Jaydipsinh Dodiya. London: Sangam, 1998. 96–102.

Singh, Amrijit. "Rohinton Mistry." *Writers of the Indian Diaspora: A Bio-Bibliographical Critical Sourcebook*. Ed. Emmanuel S Nelson. Westport: Greenwood Press, 1993. 207–17.

Singh, Avadesh Kumar. "The Sense of Community in the Parsi Novels." *The Literary Criterion* 32 (1996): 28–38.

Tapping, Craig. "South Asia/North America: New Dwellings and the Past." *Reworlding: The Literature of the Indian Diaspora*. Ed. Emmanuel S Nelson. Westport, CT: Greenwood Press, 1992. 35–49.

Townsend, David. "Multiple Pleasures in Mistry's Journey." Rev. of *Such a Long Journey*, by Rohinton Mistry. *Quill & Quire* 57 (1991): 62.

Williams, David. "Cyberwriting and the Borders of Identity: 'What's in a Name' in Kroetsch's *The Puppeteer* and Mistry's *Such a Long Journey*?" *Canadian Literature* 149 (1996): 55–71.

Wilson, Paul. "Giving Free Rein: Paul Wilson speaks with Rohinton Mistry." *Books in Canada* (March 1996): 2–4.

C. General Sources

Multiculturalism and Canada

Aponiuk, Natalia. "'Ethnic Literature,' 'Minority Writing,' 'Literature in Other Languages,' 'Hyphenated-Canadian Literature'—Will It Ever Be 'Canadian?'" *Canadian Ethnic Studies* 28.1 (1996): 1–7.

Atwood, Margaret. *Survival: A Thematic Guide to Canadian Literature*. Toronto: Anansi, 1972.

Bannerji, Himani. "On the Dark Side of the Nation: Politics of Multiculturalism and the State of 'Canada.'" *Literary Pluralities*. Ed. Christl Verduyn. Peterborough, ON: Broadview Press, 1998. 125–51.

Batts, Michael S. "Multiculturalism and Canadian Literature." *Us/Them: Translation, Transcription and Identity in Post-Colonial Literary Cultures*. Ed. Gordon Collier. Amsterdam: Rodopi, 1992. 41–6.

Bibby, Reginald W. *Mosaic Madness: The Poverty and Potential of Life in Canada*. Toronto: Stoddart, 1990.

Birbalsingh, Frank. "South Asian Canadian Novels in English." *A Meeting of Streams: South Asian Canadian Literature*. Toronto: TSAR, 1985. 49–61.

Bissoondath, Neil. "No Place Like Home." *http://www.oneworld.org/ni/issue305/multiculturalism.html*. Accessed 5.3.2002.

Breton, Eric. "Canadian Federalism, Multiculturalism and the Twenty-first Century." *International Journal of Canadian Studies* 21 (2000): 155–77.

Dabydeen, Cyril, ed. *A Shapely Fire: Changing the Literary Landscape*. Oakville, ON: Mosaic, 1987.

Davey, Frank. *From There to Here*. Erin: Press Porcepic, 1974.

Davey, Frank. "Surviving the Paraphrase." *Surviving the Paraphrase: Eleven Essays on Canadian Literature*. Winnipeg: Turnstone P, 1986. 1–12.

Davey, Frank. *Post-National Arguments: The Politics of the Anglophone-Canadian Novel since 1967*. Toronto: U of Toronto P, 1993.

Davey, Frank. "The Literary Politics of Canadian Multiculturalism." *Multiculturalism in North America and Europe: Social Practices, Literary Visions*. Eds. Hans Braun and Wolfgang Klooß. Trier: WVT, 1995. 103–14.

Davey, Frank. "Destabilizing the Anthology." Rev. of *Making a Difference: Canadian Multicultural Literature*, by Smaro Kamboureli. *International Journal of Canadian Studies* 14 (1996): 265–70.

Driedger, Leo. *Multi-Ethnic Canada. Identities and Inequalities*. Toronto: OUP, 1996.

Elliott, Jean Leonard and Augie Fleras. *The Challenge of Diversity: Multiculturalism in Canada*. Scarborough: Nelson Canada, 1992.

Frye, Northrop. *Literary History of Canada: Canadian Literature in English*. Ed. Carl F Klinck. Toronto: U of Toronto P, 1973. 821–52.

Fujimoto, Yoko. "Multiculturalism and Ethnic Writing in English Canada: A New Development in the National Literary Discourse." *Nationalism vs. Internationalism: (Inter)national Dimensions of Literatures in English*. Eds. Wolfgang Zach and Ken L Goodwin. Tübingen: Stauffenburg, 1996. 325–33.

Groß, Konrad. "Zum Problem der kanadischen Identität." *Kanada: Eine interdiszipliäre Einführung*. Eds. Hans Braun and Wolfgang Klooß. Trier: WVT, 1994. 194–206.

Harles, John. "Multiculturalism, National Identity, and National Integration: The Canadian Case." *International Journal of Canadian Studies* 17 (1998): 217–49.

Herk, Aritha van. "Mapping as Metaphor." *Zeitschrift der Gesellschaft für Kanada-Studien* 1 (1982): 75–83.

Hutcheon, Linda. "Introduction." *Other Solitudes: Canadian Multicultural Fictions*. Eds. Linda Hutcheon and Marion Richmond. Toronto: OUP, 1990. 1–16.

Kamboureli, Smaro. "Multiculturalism." *Encyclopedia of Post-Colonial Literatures in English*. Vol 2. Eds. Eugene Benson and LW Conolly. London: Routledge, 1994. 1053–55.

Kamboureli, Smaro. *Scandalous Bodies: Diasporic Literature in English Canada*. Oxford: OUP, 2000.

Kanaganayakam, Chelva. "South Asian-Canadian Literature." *The Oxford Companion to Canadian Literature*. Eds. Eugene Benson and William Toye. Toronto: OUP, 1997. 1083–5.

Klooß, Wolfgang. "Vom Bikulturalismus zum kanadischen Multikulturalismus: Historische Grundlagen und gesellschaftliche Implikationen eines politischen Programms." *Gulliver* 22 (1987): 25–35.

Klooß, Wolfgang. "Canadian Multiculturalism: Some Recent Trends in Anglophone Writing." *Us/Them: Translation, Transcription and Identity in Post-Colonial Literary Cultures*. Ed. Gordon Collier. Amsterdam: Rodopi, 1992. 65–73.

Klooß. Wolfgang. "Die englischsprachige Literatur." *Kanada: Eine interdisziplinäre Einführung*. Eds. Hans Braun and Wolfgang Klooß. Trier: WVT, 1994. 170–93.

Kostash, Myrna. "Imagination, Representation, and Culture." *Literary Pluralities*. Ed. Christl Verduyn. Peterborough, ON: Broadview Press, 1998. 92–6.

Kroetsch, Robert, Tamara J Palmer and Beverly J Rasporich. "Introduction: Ethnicity and Canadian Literature." *Canadian Ethnic Studies* 14.1 (1982): iii–vii.

Kulyk Keefer, Janice. "'The Sacredness of Bridges': Writing Immigrant Experience." *Literary Pluralities*. Ed. Christl Verduyn. Peterborough, ON: Broadview Press, 1998. 97–110.

Kymlicka, Will. *Multicultural Citizenship: A Liberal Theory of Minority Rights*. NY: OUP, 1996.

Litvack, Leon. "Canadian Writing in English and Multiculturalism." *English Postcoloniality:*

Literatures From Around the World. Eds. Radhika Mohanran and Gita Ranjan. Westport, CT: Greenwood Press, 1996. 119–34.

Lorrigio, Francesco. "The Question of the Corpus: Ethnicity and Canadian Literature." *Future Indicative: Literary Theory and Canadian Literature*. Ed. John Moss. Ottawa: U of Ottawa P, 1987. 53–70.

Mandel, Eli. "Ethnic Voice in Canadian Writing." *Another Time*. Erin, ON: Press Porcepic, 1977. 91–102.

Mukherjee, Arun Prabha. "How Shall We Read South Asian Canadian Texts?" *Postcolonialism: My Living*. Toronto: TSAR, 1998. 24–40.

Mukherjee, Bharati. "Introduction." *Darkness*. Markham, ON: Penguin, 1985. 1–4.

Padolsky, Enoch. "Canadian Minority Writing and Acculturation Options." *Canadian Review of Comparative Literature* (1989): 600–18.

Padolsky, Enoch. "Cultural Diversity and Canadian Literature: A Pluralistic Approach to Majority and Minority Writing in Canada." *International Journal of Canadian Studies* 3 (1991): 111–28.

Padolsky, Enoch. "Ethnicity and Race: Canadian Minority Writing at a Crossroads." *Literary Pluralities*. Ed. Christl Verduyn. Peterborough, ON: Broadview Press, 1998. 19–36.

Palmer Seiler, Tamara. "Multi-Vocality and National Literature: Towards a Post-Colonial and Multicultural Aesthetic. *Literary Pluralities*. Ed. Christl Verduyn. Peterborough, ON: Broadview Press, 1998, 47–63.

Parekh, Bhikhu. Rethinking *Multiculturalism: Cultural Diversity and Political Theory*. Basingstoke: Palgrave, 2000.

Philip, Marlene Nourbese. "Why Multiculturalism Can't End Racism." *Frontiers: Essays and Writings on Racism and Culture*. Stratford, ON: The Mercury Press, 1992. 181–86.

Porter, John. *The Vertical Mosaic: An Analysis of Social Class and Power in Canada*. Toronto: U of Toronto P, 1965.

Ramraj, Victor J. "Diasporas and Multiculturalism." *New-National and Post-Colonial Literatures*. Ed. Bruce King. Oxford: Clarendon Press, 1996. 214–29.

Roberts, Lance W and Rodney A Clifton. "Multiculturalism in Canada: A Sociological Perspective." *Race and Ethnic Relations in Canada*. Ed. Peter S Li. Toronto: OUP, 1990.120–47.

Sigurdson, Richard. "First Peoples, New Peoples and Citizenship in Canada." *International Journal of Canadian Studies* 14 (1996): 53–77.

Sugunasiri, Suwanda. "The Literature of Canadians of South Asian Origins: An Overview." *Canadian Ethnic Studies* 17.1 (1985): 1–21.

Sullivan, Rosemary. "The Multicultural Divide: Where's the Mosaic? It's Time to Open the Doors of the CanLit Club." *This Magazine* 22 (1988): 25–30.

Sypnowich, Christine. "Some Disquiet about Difference." *Multicultural Experiences, Multicultural Theorizing*. Eds. Mary F Rogers and George Ritzer. NY: McGraw, 1996, 278–91.

Taylor, Charles. "The Politics of Recognition." *Multiculturalism and "The Politics of Recognition."* Ed. Amy Gutman. Princeton: Princeton UP, 1992. 25–74.

Thorpe, Michael. "Opposition, Multicultural Apartheid or Connection?" *The Toronto South Asian Review* 9.1 (1990): 1–10.

Wah, Fred. "A Poetics of Ethnicity." *Faking It: Poetics and Hybridity. Critical Writings 1984–1999*. Edmonton: Newest Press, 2000. 51–66.

Wah, Fred. "Half-Bred Poetics." *Faking It: Poetics and Hybridity. Critical Writings 1984–1999.* Edmonton: NeWest Press, 2000. 71–96.

Winter, Elke. "National Unity versus Multiculturalism? Rethinking the Logic of Inclusion in Germany and Canada." *International Journal of Canadian Studies/Revue internationale d'études canadiennes* 24 (2001): 169–93.

Postcolonial Theory

Ahmad, Aijaz. "Jameson's Rhetoric of Otherness and the 'National Allegory'" *Social Text* 17 (1987): 3–25.

Ahmad, Aijaz. "The Politics of Literary Postcoloniality." *Contemporary Postcolonial Theory: A Reader*. Ed. Padmini Mongia. London: Arnold, 1996. 276–293.

Anderson, Benedict. *Imagined Communities: Reflections of the Origin and Spread of Nationalism*. London: Verso, 1991.

Appiah, Kwame Anthony. "Is the Post- in Postmodernism the Post- in Postcolonial?" *Contemporary Postcolonial Theory: A Reader*. Ed. Padmini Mongia. London: Arnold, 1996. 55–72.

Ashcroft, Bill, Gareth Griffiths and Helen Tiffin. *The Empire Writes Back: Theory and Practice in Post-Colonial Literatures*. London: Routledge, 1989.

Ashcroft, Bill, Gareth Griffiths and Helen Tiffin. *Key Concepts in Post-Colonial Studies*. London: Routledge, 1998.

Ashcroft, Bill. *Post-Colonial Transformation*. London: Routledge, 2001.

Bahri, Deepika. "Once More with Feeling: What is Postcolonialism?" *ARIEL* 26.1 (1995): 51–83.

Bhabha, Homi K. *The Location of Culture*. London: Routledge, 1994.

Boehmer, Elleke. *Colonial & Postcolonial Literature: Migrant Metaphors*. Oxford: OUP: 1995.

Chambers, Iain. *Migrancy, Culture, Identity*. London: Routledge, 1994.

Chow, Rey. "Where Have All the Natives Gone?" *Contemporary Postcolonial Theory: A Reader*. Ed. Padmini Mongia. London: Arnold, 1996. 122–48.

Clifford, James. *Routes: Travel and Translation in the Late Twentieth Century*. Cambridge, MA: Harvard UP: 1997.

Dirlik, Arif. "The Postcolonial Aura: Third World Criticism in the Age of Global Capitalism." *Contemporary Postcolonial Literature: A Reader*. Ed. Padmini Mongia. London: Arnold, 1996. 294–321.

Fanon, Frantz. *Black Skin, White Masks*. London: Pluto Press, 1986.

Fanon, Frantz. *The Wretched of the Earth*. Harmondsworth: Penguin, 1990.

Fludernik, Monika. "The Constitution of Hybridity: Postcolonial Interventions." *Hybridity and Postcolonialism: Twentieth-Century Indian Literature*. Ed. Monika Fludernik. Tübingen: Stauffenburg, 1998. 19–53.

Ghandi, Leela. *Postcolonial Theory: A Critical Introduction*. NY: Columbia UP, 1998.

Ghosh-Schellhorn, Martina. "Post-Colonial Literature?" *Gulliver* 33.1 (1993): 37–43.

Gilroy, Paul. *The Black Atlantic: Modernity and Double Consciousness*. Cambridge, MA: Harvard UP, 1993.

Gilroy, Paul. "Diaspora and the Detours of Identity." *Identity and Difference*. Ed. Kathryn Woodward. London: Sage, 1997. 299–347.

Glage, Liselotte. "Strategien der Differenz: Was oder wie ist der postkoloniale Roman?" *Zeitschrift für Anglistik und Amerikanistik* 43.1 (1995): 77–90.

Goetsch, Paul. "Funktionen von Hybridität in der postkolonialen Theorie." *Literatur in Wissenschaft und Unterricht* 30 (1997): 135–45.

Goetsch, Paul. "Die Macht des Buches in kolonialer und postkolonialer Literatur." *Fiktion und Geschichte in der anglo-amerikanischen Literatur*. Eds. Rüdiger Ahrens and Fritz-Wilhelm Neumann. Heidelberg: Winter, 1998. 515–33.

Hall, Stuart. *Rassissmus und kulturelle Identität*. Transl. and ed. Ulrich Mehlem. Hamburg: Argument-Verlag, 1994.

Hall, Stuart. "Cultural Identity and Diaspora." *Contemporary Postcolonial Theory: A Reader*. Ed. Padmini Mongia. London: Arnold, 1996. 110–21.

Han, Petrus. *Soziologie der Migration*. Stuttgart: Lucius und Lucius, 2000.

Huggan, Graham. *The Post-Colonial Exotic: Marketing the Margins*. London: Routledge, 2001.

Hulme Peter. "Including America." *ARIEL* 26.1 (1995): 117–24.

Hutcheon, Linda. "'Circling the Downspout of Empire': Post-Colonialism and Postmodernism." *ARIEL* 20 (1989): 149–75.

Jameson, Fredric. "Third-World Literature in the Era of Multinational Capitalism." *Social Text* 15 (1986): 65–88.

JanMohamed, Abdul R. "The Economy of Manichean Allegory: The Function of Racial Difference in Colonialist Literature." *Critical Inquiry* 12 (1986): 59–87.

Kotte, Claudia. "Post-Colonialism or Neo-Imperialism?" *Zeitschrift für Amerikanistik und Anglistik* 43.4 (1995): 253–64.

Kreutzer, Eberhard. "Theoretische Grundlagen postkolonialer Literaturkritik." *Literaturwissenschaftliche Theorien, Modelle und Methoden. Eine Einführung*. Eds. Ansgar Nünning and Monika Fludernik. Trier: WVT, 1998. 199–213.

Krishnaswamy, Revathi. "Mythologies of Migrancy: Postcolonialism, Postmodernism and the Politics of (Dis-)Location." *ARIEL* 26.1 (1995): 125–46.

Loomba, Ania. *Colonialism/Postcolonialism*. London: Routledge, 1998.

Michel, Martina. "Postcolonial Literatures: Use or Abuse of the Latest Post-Word." *Gulliver* 33.1 (1993): 6–23.

Mukherjee, Arun Prabha. "Whose Post-Colonialism and Whose Postmodernism?" *World Literature Written in English* 30.2 (1990): 1–9.

Mukherjee, Arun Prabha. "The Vocabulary of the 'Universal': The Cultural Imperialism of the Universalist Criteria of Western Literary Criticism." *Oppositional Aesthetics: Readings from a Hyphenated Space*. Toronto: TSAR, 1994. 17–30.

Mukherjee, Arun Prabha. "Universals." *Postcolonialism: My Living*. Toronto: TSAR, 1998. 197–214.

Ngugi, Wa Thiongo. *Decolonising the Mind: The Politics of Language in African Literature*. Portsmouth, NH: Heinemann, 1986.

Porter, Dennis. "Orientalism and Its Problems." *Colonial Discourse and Post-Colonial Theory: A Reader*. Eds. Patrick Williams and Laura Chrisman. NY: Harvester Wheatsheaf, 1993. 150–61.

Pratt, Mary Louise. *Imperial Eyes: Travel Writing and Transculturalism*. London: Routledge, 1992.

Rushdie, Salman. "Imaginary Homelands." *Imaginary Homelands: Essays and Criticism 1981–91*. London: Granta, 1991. 9–21.

Safran, William. "Diasporas in Modern Societies: Myths of Homeland and Return." *Diaspora* 1 (1991): 83–99.

Said, Edward W. *Orientalism: Western Conceptions of the Orient*. London: Penguin, 1995.

Said, Edward W. *Culture and Imperialism*. London: Chatto & Windus, 1993.

Sharpe, Jenny. *Allegories of Empire: The Figure of Woman in the Colonial Text*. Minneapolis: U of Minnesota P, 1993.

Shohat, Ella. "Notes on the Post-Colonial." *Contemporary Postcolonial Theory: A Reader*. Ed. Padmini Mongia. London: Arnold, 1996. 322–34.

Slemon, Stephen. "The Scramble for Post-Colonialism." *De-Scribing Empire:Post-Colonialism and Textuality*. Eds. Chris Tiffin and Alan Lawson. London: Routledge, 1994. 15–32.

Spivak, Gayatri. "Poststructuralism, Marginality, Postcoloniality and Value." *Contemporary Postcolonial Theory: A Reader*. Ed. Padmini Mongia. London: Arnold, 1996. 198–222.

Spivak, Gayatri. "Criticism, Feminism and the Institution." Interview with Elizabeth Gross. *Thesis Eleven* 10/11 (1984/85): 175–87.

Spivak, Gayatri. "Can the Subaltern Speak?" *Colonial Discourse and Post-Colonial Theory: A Reader*. Eds. Patrick Williams and Laura Chrisman. NY: Harvester Wheatsheaf, 1993. 66–111.

Tiffin, Chris and Alan Lawson. "Introduction: The Textuality of Empire." *De-Scribing Empire: Post-Colonialism and Textuality*. Eds. Chris Tiffin and Alan Lawson. London: Routledge, 1994. 1–11.

Tiffin, Helen. "Post-Colonialism, Post-Modernism and the Rehabilitation of Post-Colonial History." *The Journal of Commonwealth Literature* 23.1 (1988): 169–81.

Vassanji, MG "The Postcolonial Writer: Myth Maker and Folk Historian." *A Meeting of Streams: South Asian Canadian Literature*. Ed. MG Vassanji. Toronto: TSAR, 1985. 63–8.

Volkmann, Laurenz. "Universal Truths or Ethnic Peculiarities? On Tensions Inherent in the Reception of Post-Colonial and Minority Literature." *Intercultural Encounters: Studies in English Literature. Essays presented to Rüdiger Ahrens on the Occasion of his Sixtieth Birthday*. Eds. Heinz Antor and Kevin L Cope. Heidelberg: Winter, 1999. 131–52.

Walder, Dennis. *Post-colonial Literatures in English: History, Language, Theory*. Oxford: Blackwell, 1998.

Young, Robert. "Colonialism and the Desiring-Machine." *Liminal Postmodernisms: The Postmodern, the (Post-)Colonial, and the (Post-)Feminist*. Eds. Theo D'haen and Hans Bertens. Amsterdam: Rodopi, 1994. 11–34.

Young, Robert. *Colonial Desire: Hybridity in Theory, Culture and Race*. London: Routledge, 1995.

Other Sources

Ackroyd, Peter. *T.S. Eliot*. London: Penguin, 1993.

Albright, Daniel. "Introduction." *W.B. Yeats: The Poems*. Ed. Daniel Albright. London: JM Dent & Sons Ltd., 1990. xvii–xlvii.

Alt, Jürgen August. *Wenn Sinn knapp wird: Über das gelingende Leben in einer entzauberten Welt*. Frankfurt: Campus Verlag, 1997.

Anderson, JND. "The Ismaili Khojas of East Africa." *Middle Eastern Studies* 1 (1964): 21–39.

Aptheker, Bettina. *Tapestries of Life: Women's Work, Women's Consciousness, and the Meaning of Daily Experience*. Amherst: U of Massachusetts P, 1989.

Ashfield, Andrew and Peter de Bolla, eds. *The Sublime: A Reader in British Eighteenth-Century Aesthetic Theory*. Cambridge: CUP, 1996.

Assmann, Aleida. "Erinnerungsorte und Gedächtnislandschaften." *Erlebnis—Gedächtnis—Sinn: Authentische und Konstruierte Erinnerung*. Eds. Hanno Loewy and Bernhard Moltmann. Frankfurt/Main: Campus Verlag, 1996. 13–29.Aust, Hugo. *Der historische Roman*. Stuttgart and Weimar: Metzler, 1994.

Bachtin, Michail. *Die Ästhetik des Wortes*. Ed. Rainer Grübel. Transl. Rainer Grübel and Sabine Reese. Frankfurt/Main: Edition Suhrkamp, 1979.

Barthes, Roland. "Textual Analysis: Poe's 'Valdemar.'" *Modern Literary Criticism and Theory: A Reader*. Ed. David Lodge. 10th ed. London: Longman, 1997. 172–95.

Baßler, Moritz. "Einleitung." *New Historicism: Literaturgeschichte als Poetik der Kultur*. Ed. Moritz Baßler. Frankfurt/Main: Fischer, 1996. 7–28.

Bowering, George. *The Mask in Place: Essays on Fiction in North America*. Winnipeg: Turnstone P, 1982.

Boyce, Mary. *Zoroastrians: Their Religious Beliefs and Practices*. London: Routledge & Kegan Paul, 1979.

Brumlik, Micha. "Individuelle Erinnerung - Kollektive Erinnerung: Psychosoziale Konstitutionsbedingungen des erinnernden Subjekts." *Erinnerung—Gedächtnis—Sinn: Authentische und Konstruierte Erinnerung*. Eds. Hanno Loewy and Bernhard Moltmann. Frankfurt/Main: Campus Verlag, 1996. 31–45.

Bushrui, SB and Tim Prentki. *An International Companion to the Poetry of W.B. Yeats*. Gerrards Cross: Colin Smythe, 1989.

Certeau, Michel de. *Das Schreiben der Geschichte*. Transl. Sylvia M Schomburg-Scherff. Frankfurt/Main: Campus Verlag, 1991.

Counihan, Carole M. *The Anthropology of Food and Body: Gender, Meaning, and Power*. London: Routledge, 1999.

Coupe, Lawrence. *Myth*. London: Routledge, 1997.

Derrida, Jacques. "Structure, Sign and Play in the Discourse of the Human Sciences." *Modern Criticism and Theory: A Reader*. Ed. David Lodge. 10th ed. London: Longman, 1997. 108–24.

Desai, Boman. *The Memory of Elephants.* London: Sceptre, 1990.

Dilger. Konrad. "Tendenzen der Rechtsentwicklung," *Der Islam in der Gegenwart.* Eds Werner Ende and Guido Steinbach. 4th ed. München. CH Beck, 1996. 170–97.

Eliot, TS. *The Waste Land and other Poems.* London: Faber and Faber, 1990.

Ende, Werner. "Der schiitische Islam." *Der Islam in der Gegewart.* Eds. Werner Ende and Udo Steinbach. 4th ed. München: CH Beck, 1996. 70–89.

Ernst, Heiko. *Psychotrends: Das Ich im 21. Jahrhundert.* München: Piper, 1998.

Federman, Raymond. *Surfiction: Der Weg der Literatur. Hamburger Poetik-Lektionen.* Transl. Peter Torberg. Frankfurt/Main: Suhrkamp, 1992.

Fitzgerald. F Scott. *The Great Gatsby.* Ware: Wordsworth Classics, 1993.

Fiedler, Leslie. "Überquert die Grenze, Schließt den Graben! Über die Postmoderne." *Wege aus der Moderne: Schlüsseltexte der Postmoderne-Diskussion.* Ed. Wolfgang Welsch. 2nd ed. Berlin: Akademie Verlag, 1994. 57–74.

Forster, Peter G, Michael Hitchcock and Francis F Lyimo. *Race and Ethnicity in East Africa.* Houndsmill: Macmillan Press, 2000.

Foucault, Michel. *Die Ordnung des Diskurses.* Transl. Walter Seitter. Frankfurt/Main: Fischer, 1997.

Frankl, Viktor E. *Der Mensch vor der Frage nach dem Sinn: Eine Auswahl aus dem Gesamtwerk.* München: Piper, 1979.

Gehlen, Arnold. "Über kulturelle Kristallation." *Wege aus der Moderne. Schlüsseltexte der Postmoderne-Diskussion.* Ed. Wolfgang Welsch. 2nd ed. Berlin: Akademie Verlag, 1994. 133–44.

Giddens, Anthony. *Sociology.* Cambridge: Polity Press, 1991.

Giddens, Anthony. *Beyond Left and Right: The Future of Radical Politics.* Cambridge: Polity Press, 1994.

Giddens, Anthony. *Entfesselte Welt: Wie die Globalisierung unser Leben verändert.* Transl. Frank Jakubzik. Frankfurt/Main: Edition Suhrkamp, 2001.

Hahn, Alois. *Religion und der Verlust der Sinngebung: Identitätsprobleme in der modernen Gesellschaft.* Frankfurt: Herder & Herder, 1974.

Hahn, Alois. "Sinn und Sinnlosigkeit." *Sinn, Kommunikation und soziale Differenzierung: Beiträge zu Luhmanns Theorie sozialer Systeme.* Eds. Hans Haferkamp and Michael Schmidt. Frankfurt/Main: Suhrkamp, 1986. 155–65.

Hahn, Alois. "Soziologie des Fremden." *Erfahrungen des Fremden. Vorträge im Sommersemester 1992.* Ed. Ruprechts-Karls-Universität Heidelberg. Heidelberg: Heidelberger Verlagsanstalt, 1992. 23–34.

Hansen, Klaus P. *Kultur und Kulturwissenschaft: Eine Einführung.* 2nd ed. Tübingen: Francke, 2000.

Huntington, Samuel P. *The Clash of Civilizations and the Remaking of World Order.* NY: Touchstone, 1997.

Hutcheon, Linda. "Canadian Historiographic Metafiction." *Essays on Canadian Writing* 30 (1984): 228–37.

Hutcheon, Linda. *The Poetics of Postmodernism: History, Theory, Fiction.* London: Routledge, 1988.

Hutcheon, Linda. *The Politics of Postmodernism.* London: Routledge, 1989.

Hinnells, John R. "Parsi Zoroastrians in London." *Desh Pardesh: The South Asian Presence in Britain.* Ed. Roger Ballard. London: Hurst & Company, 1994. 251–72.

Ihle, Sandra Ness. *Malory's Grail Quest: Invention and Adaptation in Medieval Prose Romance.* Madison: The U of Wisconsin P, 1983.

Iliffe, John. *A Modern History of Tanzania.* Cambridge: CUP, 1977.

Iser, Wolfgang. *Der Akt des Lesens: Theorie ästhetischer Wirkung.* 3rd ed. München: Wilhelm Fink, 1990.

Janz, Rolf-Peter. "Die ästhetische Bewältigung des Schreckens. Zu Schillers Theorie des Erhabenen." *Geschichte als Literatur: Formen und Grenzen der Repräsentation von*

Vergangenheit. Ed. Hartmut Eggert. Stuttgart: Metzler, 1990. 151–60.

Jeffrey, Robin. *What's Happening to India: Punjab, Ethnic Conflict, Mrs Gandhi's Death and the Test for Federalism*. NY: Holmes and Meier, 1986.

Keupp, Heiner, Thomas Abhe, Wolfgang Gmür. *Identitätskonstruktionen: Das Patchwork der Identitäten in der Spätmoderne*. Hamburg: Rowohlt, 1999.

Khan, AG. *Canadian Literature and Indian Literature: New Perspectives*. New Delhi: Creative Books, 1995.

Klooß, Wolfgang. *Die englische Kulturpolitik und die Tragik des Kulturkonflikts in den Afrikaromanen von Joyce Cary*. Frankfurt/Main: Peter Lang, 1976.

Kristeva, Julia. *Fremde sind wir uns selbst*. Transl. Xenia Rajewsky. Frankfurt/Main: Edition Suhrkamp, 1990.

Kriz, Jürgen. *Chaos, Angst und Ordnung: Wie wir unsere Lebenswelt gestalten*. 2nd ed. Göttingen: Vandenhoeck & Ruprecht, 1998.

Kroeber, Alfred L and Clyde Kluckhohn. *Culture: A Critical Review of Concepts and Definitions*. NY: Vintage, 1963.

Kroetsch, Robert. "An Interview with Margaret Laurence." *Trace: Prairie Writers on Writing*. Ed. Birk Sproxton. Winnipeg: Turnstone Press, 1986. 19–31.

Kulke, Eckekard. *The Parsees in India: A Minority as Agent of Social Change*. München: Weltforum Verlag, 1974.

Kulke, Hermann and Dietmar Rothermund. *Geschichte Indiens: Von der Induskultur bis heute*. 2nd ed. München: Beck, 1998.

LaCapra, Dominick. *History, Politics, and the Novel*. Ithaca: Cornell UP, 1987.

LaCapra, Dominick. "Geistesgeschichte und Interpretation." *Geschichte Denken: Neubestimmungen und Perspektiven moderner europäischer Geistesgeschichte*. Eds. Dominick LaCapra and Steven T Kaplan. Transl. Hans Günter Holl. Frankfurt/Main: Fischer, 1988. 45–86.

Lakoff, George and Mark Johnson. *Metaphors We Live By*. Chicago: U of Chicago P, 1980.

Lele, Jayant. "Saffronization of the Shiv Sena: The Political Economy of City State and Nation." *Bombay: Metaphor for Modern India*. Eds. Sujata Patel and Alice Thorner. Bombay: OUP, 1996. 185–213.

Luhrmann, Tanya. *The Good Parsi: The Fate of a Colonial Elite in a Postcolonial Society*. Cambridge: Harvard UP, 1996.

Lukacs, Georg. *The Historical Novel*. Transl. Hannah and Stanley Mitchell. Boston: Beacon, 1963.

Malhotra, Inder. *Indira Gandhi: A Personal and Political Biography*. London: Hodder & Stoughton, 1989.

McHale, Brian. *Postmodernist Fiction*. NY: Methuen, 1987.

Meyer, Thomas. *Identitäts-Wahn: Die Politisierung des kulturellen Unterschieds*. Berlin: Aufbau Taschenbuch Verlag, 1997.

Murdoch, Iris. *Metaphysics as a Guide to Morals*. London: Penguin, 1993.

Naipaul, VS. *An Area of Darkness*. Basingstoke: Picador, 1995.

Pfister, Manfred. "Konzepte der Intertextualität." *Intertextualität: Formen, Funktionen, anglistische Fallstudien*. Eds. Manfred Pfister and Ulrich Broich. Tübingen: Niemeyer, 1985. 1–30

Pfister, Manfred. "Intertextualität." *Moderne Literatur in Grundbegriffen*. Eds. Dieter Borchmeyer and Viktor m'egac. Frankfurt/Main: Athenäum, 1987. 197–200.

Priest, Christine, ed. *Das Erhabene: Zwischen Grenzerfahrung und Größenwahn*. Weinheim: VCH, 1989.

Ramazani, R Jahan. "Tragic Joy and the Sublime." *PMLA* 104 (1989): 163–77.

Ramazani, R Jahan. *Yeats and the Poetry of Death: Elegy, Self-Elegy and the Sublime*. New Haven: Yale UP, 1990.

Randeria, Jer Dara. *The Parsi Mind: A Zoroastrian Asset to Culture*. New Delhi: Munshiram

Manoharlal Publishers, 1993.

Rothermund, Dietmar. *Mahatma Gandhi: Eine Politische Biographie*. 2nd ed. München: Beck, 1997.

Rothermund, Dietmar. *Delhi, 15. August 1947: Das Ende kolonialer Herrschaft*. München: dtv, 1998.

Rushdie, Salman. *Midnight's Children*. NY: Penguin, 1991.

Rushdie, Salman. *The Ground Beneath Her Feet*. London: Jonathan Cape, 1999.

Sarvan, Charles Ponnutharai. "The Asians in African Literature." *The Journal of Commonwealth Literature* 11.1 (1976): 160–70.

Sarvan, Charles Ponnutharai. "Ethnicity and Alienation: The African Asian and His Response to Africa." *The Journal of Commonwealth Literature* 20.1 (1985): 100–10.

Schiller, Friedrich. "Über das Erhabene." Friedrich Schiller. *Vom Pathetischen und Erhabenen: Ausgewählte Schriften zur Dramentheorie*. Ed. Klaus L Berghahn. Stuttgart: Reclam, 1977. 83–101.

Schmucker, Werner. "Sekten und Sondergruppen." *Der Islam in der Gegenwart*. Eds. Werner Ende and Udo Steinbach. 4th ed. München: CH Beck, 1996. 667–74.

Schumann, Hans Wolfgang. *Die großen Götter Indiens: Grundzüge von Hinduismus und*

Shakespeare, William. *Julius Caesar*. Ed. David Daniell. Thomson: London, 1998.

Shaw, Harry E. *The Forms of Historical Fiction: Sir Walter Scott and His Successors*. Ithaca: Cornell UP, 1983.

Sidhwa, Bapsi. *The Crow Eaters*. Minneapolis: Milkweed, 1978.

Simon, Christian. *Historiographie: Eine Einführung*. Stuttgart: Ulmer, 1996.

Smith, Philip. *Cultural Theory: An Introduction*. Malden: Blackwell, 2001.

Smith, Stan. *W.B. Yeats: A Critical Introduction*. Basingstoke: Macmillan, 1990.

Staines, David. *Beyond the Provinces: Literary Canada at Century's End*. Toronto: U of Toronto Press, 1995.

Staines, David. "The State of Contemporary Canadian Literature." *Canada and the Nordic Countries in Times of Reorientation: Literature & Criticism*. Ed. Jörn Carlsen. Aarhus: The Nordic Association for Canadian Studies Text Series, 1998. 21–30.

Stausberg, Michael. "Zoroastrismus." *Die Religionen der Gegenwart: Geschichte und Glauben*. Ed. Peter Antes. München: Beck, 1996. 161–87.

Steinmetz, Horst. *Literatur und Geschichte: 4 Versuche*. München: Iudicium, 1988.

Stoppard, Tom. *Arcadia*. London: Faber and Faber, 1993.

Sussman, Herbert. "Industrial." *A Companion to Victorian Literature and Culture*. Ed. Herbert F Tucker. Malden, MA: Blackwell, 1999. 244–57.

Swift, Graham. *Last Orders*. London: Picador, 1996.

Tarnas, Richard. *Idee und Leidenschaft: Die Wege des westlichen Denkens*. Transl. Eckhard E Sohns. 7th ed. Hamburg: Rogner & Bernhard bei Zweitausendeins, 1998.

Vivelo, Frank Robert. *Handbuch der Kulturanthropologie: Eine grundlegende Einführung*. Transl. and ed. Justin and Erika Stagl. 2nd ed. Stuttgart: Klett-Cotta, 1995.

Waugh, Patricia. *Metafiction: The Theory and Practice of Self-Conscious Fiction*. London: Methuen, 1984.

Weiskel, Thomas. *The Romantic Sublime: Studies in the Structure and Psychology of Transcendence*. Baltimore: The Johns Hopkins UP, 1976.

Welsch, Wolfgang. *Unsere postmoderne Moderne*. 5th ed. Berlin: Akademie Verlag, 1997.

Wenner, Dorothee. "Je weniger, desto lustiger." *Die Zeit* 23rd May 2002: 54.

Wharton, Edith. *The Age of Innocence*. Ed. Cynthia Griffin Wolff. NY: Penguin, 1996.

White, Hayden. *Metahistory: The Historical Imagination in Ninenteenth-Century Europe*. Baltimore: Johns Hopkins UP, 1973.

White, Hayden. "The Value of Narrativity in the Representation of Reality." *Critical Inquiry* 7 (1980/81): 5–27.

White, Hayden. *The Content of the Form: Narrative Discourse and Historical Representation*.

Baltimore: Johns Hopkins UP, 1987.

Wierlacher, Alois. *Vom Essen in der Deutschen Literatur: Mahlzeiten in Erzähltexten von Goethe bis Grass*. Stuttgart: Kohlhammer, 1987.

Woodward, Kathryn. "Concepts of Identity and Difference." *Identity and Difference*. Ed. Kathryn Woodward. London: Sage, 1997. 7–63.

Yeats, William Butler. *Selected Poetry*. 4th ed. Ed. Norman Jeffares. London: Pan, 1976.

Yeats, William Butler. *W.B. Yeats: The Poems*. Ed. Daniel Albright. London: JM Dent & Sons Ltd., 1990.

Zaehner, RC. *The Dawn and Twilight of Zoroastrianism*. 2nd ed. London: Weidenfeld and Nicolson, 1975.